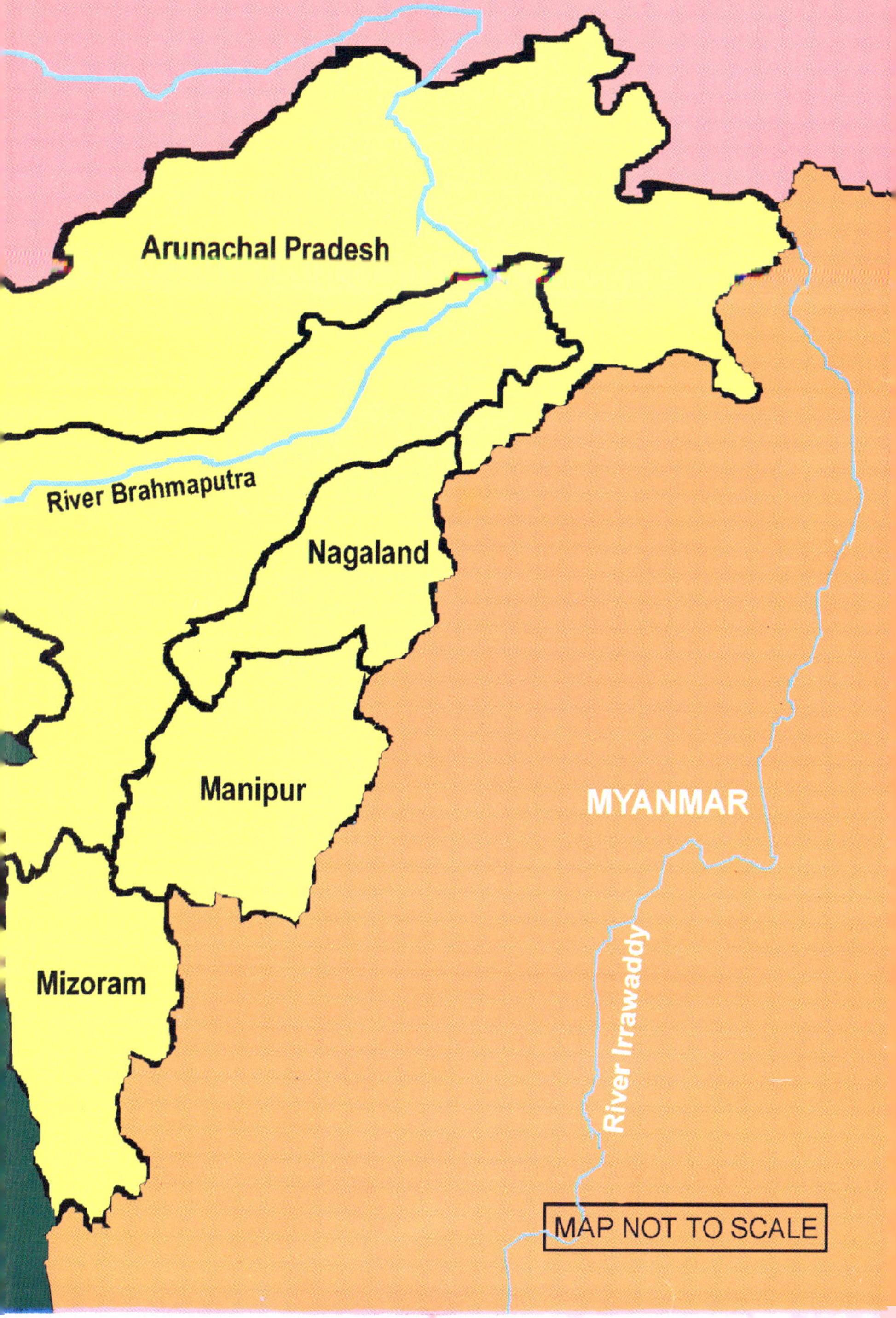
Arunachal Pradesh
River Brahmaputra
Nagaland
Manipur
MYANMAR
Mizoram
River Irrawaddy
MAP NOT TO SCALE

Lost Opportunities

50 Years of Insurgency in the
North-east and India's Response

Lost Opportunities

50 Years of Insurgency in the North-east and India's Response

Brigadier (Dr) SP Sinha, VSM (Retd)
9 Gorkha Rifles

Lancer Publishers & Distributors

ISBN 81 7062 162 3

Published in India by **Lancer Publishers & Distributors**
K - 36A (FF) Green Park Main, New Delhi-110016
lancer@lancerpublishers.com

For my parents
Smt Shyama Devi
Shri Jaimangal Singh

Contents

Foreword XV
Preface XXV
Acknowledgements XXVI1
Abbreviations XXIX
Overview XXXIII

PART 1

1. Geo-Strategic Significance of North-east India 1

Historical Background 1
Physiography 4
The Meghalaya Plateau 7
The Brahmaputra River and Valley 7
Surma or Barak Valley 8
The Imphal Valley 8
Communications 8
Mineral Resources 10
Geo-political Significance of North-east India 11
Interplay of Ethnicity along India-Myanmar Border 13
A Brief Historical Perspective of Burmese Insurgencies 15
Chittagong Hill Tract 18
Insurgent Linkages Across India-Bangladesh Border 20
Appraisal 21

2. The Ethnic and Demographic Composition 24

The Ethnic Profile 24
The Demographic Profile of Assam 27
The Role of Saadulla 28
The Aftermath of Partition 29
The Exodus of 1971 31
Situation after Emergence of Bangladesh 33
Demographic Changes in Tripura 37
Muslim Population 38

Demographic Changes in Nagaland 39
Nepali Migrants 40
The Arrival of Bengali Immigrants 41
Immigration of other Indians into Assam 41
Analysis of the Migration Pattern 42

PART 2

3. Nagaland 48

Early History 48
The Formation of Naga Club 51
The Formation of Naga National Council
Clause 9 52
The Beginning of Insurgency 55
The Army is Called Out 56
Phizo's Escape to East Pakistan 57
Sixteen Point Agreement and Formation of Nagaland
Overground Politics 57
Peace Mission and Cessation of Hostilities 59
Role of Michael Scott 60
Ministerial Talks 61
Split in the Underground 62
Capture of Mowu Angami 63
The Shillong Accord 64
Formation of National Socialist Council of Nagaland 65
The NSCN Manifesto 66
Split in the National Socialist Council of Nagaland 66
Admission to the Unrepresented Nations and
Peoples Organisation 67
Drift in Naga Movement 67
A Fresh Peace Initiative 68
Demand for Greater Nagaland 71
Appraisal 71

4. Mizoram 80

Historical Perspective 80
Physical Geography 81
The British Period 81
Period Prior to the Transfer of Power 82
Political Scenario after Independence 84

Formation of Mizo National Front 85
MNF Prepares for Revolt 86
The Beginning of Insurgency: Operation Jericho 87
The Insurgent Plan 88
Strikes by the Indian Air Force 88
The Army is Called Out 89
Grouping of Villages: Operation Accomplishment 90
Overground Politics: Mizoram becomes Union Territory 91
The Aftermath of 1971 War 92
Mizo National Army Regroups and Strikes Back 92
Peace Moves and 1976 Agreement 94
Progress of Talks under the Janata Government 95
Rift in Mizo National Front 96
Sailo's Victory in 1978 Assembly Elections 96
Resumption of Talks after Return of Indira Gandhi to Power in 1980 97
Events after the Assassination of Indira Gandhi: Memorandum of Settlement 98
Appraisal 99

5. Manipur 103

Physiography 103
Historical Backdrop 104
The Defeat of the Burmese and the Treaty of Yandeboo 106
Annexation of Manipur 106
Politicisation of Manipur Politics 109
Radicalism of Haijam Irabot 110
Events Immediately Prior to Independence 110
The Growth of Secessionist Movement and Insurgency 111
The Genesis of Insurgency 112
Spread of Insurgency 113
Formation of People's Liberation Army 113
Resurfacing of United National Liberation Front 116
Formation of Indo-Burma Revolutionary Front 116
Restructuring of People's Liberation Army 116
Upsurge in Violence and Political Instability in the 1990s 117

The Naga-Kuki Conflict 120
Political Mobilisation of Kukis 120
The Beginning of Naga-Kuki Clashes
Present Situation in Manipur 121
Appraisal 122

6. Tripura 127

Physical Features 127
Historical Background 128
Independence and Merger of Tripura with India 131
The Early Tribal Unrest and the Communist Revolt 132
Advent of Electoral Politics 135
Formation of Tripura Upjati Juba Samity 137
The Return of Sengkrak (Clenched Fist) 137
From Sengkrak to Tripura National Volunteers 138
The Formation of Amra Bengali and
Polarisation of Tribals and Non-Tribals 140
Formation of All Tripura People's Liberation
Organisation 141
The Accord 142
Post Accord Scenario 142
Appraisal 143

7. The Quest for Swadhin Asom 147

Historical Backdrop 147
Pragjyotisa and Kamrup 148
The Origin of the Name Assam 149
Early History 149
Assamese Nationalism and the Growth of the
Idea of Swadhin Asom 155
Centre-State Relations: Genesis of Assam's
Alienation 158
Assam Students Movement (1979-1985) 161
The Nellie Killings 163
The Assam Accord 164
The Rise of United Liberation Front of Asom (ULFA) 164
Operation Bajrang 166
Operation Rhino 167
Split in ULFA 168

Shift in ULFA's Ideology 169
Recrudescence of ULFA Violence 169
Illegal Migrants Detection Tribunal Act (1983) 170
The Unified Command 170
Assam Gana Parishad in Crisis 171
The Current Scenario 172
Destruction of ULFA Camps in Bhutan 173
Emergence of Islamic Fundamentalism in Assam and North-east India 175
The Bodo Insurgency 176
Appraisal 186

8. Meghalaya 195

Background 195
Areas of Discord 197
Pattern of Militancy 197
Present Scenario 198

9. Arunachal Pradesh 199

Background 199
Political Evolution 199
Rumblings of Discord 202

PART 3

10. The External Dimension 204

Background 204
The Idea of a Crown Colony 204
The Western Perception of North-east India 205
Pakistan's Support to Naga Rebels 206
China's Support to Naga Rebels 208
Pakistan's Support to Mizos 212
Situation after Emergence of Bangladesh 213
China's Support to Mizos 213
Pakistan's Support to Meitei Insurgents 214
China's Support to Meitei Insurgents 215
Pakistan's and Bangladesh Support to Insurgents of Tripura 215
Pakistani and Bangladeshi Support to ULFA 217

Sanctuaries in Myanmar and Bhutan 218
Appraisal 218

11. The Religious Dimension 221

Background 221
Christianity in Nagaland 222
Spread of Christianity in Manipur 223
Phenomenal Success in Mizoram 223
Christianity in Meghalaya 224
Arunachal: A Different Story 224
Exposure to Hinduism 225
Situation after Independence 226
The Impact of Christianity on Tribal Societies 227
Charge of Encouraging Secessionist Groups 229

12. The Role of Narcotics and Arms Trafficking 234

Kuomintang (KMT) and the American Connection 235
Linkages Between Narcotics and Arms Smuggling 236
Narcotics Trade and the North-east 236
Acetic Anhydride Seizure in India 238
Trafficking Routes in the North-east 239
Drug Abuse in the North-east 240
Arms Trafficking 241
Appraisal 242

13. The Ethnic and Linguistic Factors 245

PART 4

14. Counter-Insurgency Operations 252

Background 252
Evolution of Counter-Insurgency Strategy 255
Minimum Force 257
Isolating the Populace from Insurgents:
Grouping of Villages 258
Nature of Counter-Insurgency Operations 259
Employment of Air Power 259
Political and Diplomatic Initiatives 260
Re-organising of Infantry Battalions for

Counter-Insurgency Operations
Composition of the Assam Rifles 261
Civic Action: Winning the Hearts and Minds 262
Psychological Operations (Psy Ops) 263
Human Rights 265
Media Policy 267
Unified Command 269
Formation of North-eastern Council 270
Counter-Insurgency Operations in Nagaland 271
Counter-Insurgency Operations in Mizoram 284
Counter-Insurgency Operations in Manipur 288
Counter-Insurgency Operations in Assam 295
Appraisal 299

PART 5

15. Future Prospects 306

Illegal Immigration 306
Islamic Fundamentalism 307
Rise of Terrorism 308
The Demand for Nagalim 308
Narco-Terrorism 309
Pakistan's Alternative Proxy War 309
The Chinese Shadow 309

16. The Way Forward 312

Background 312
Reintroduction of Indian Frontier
Administrative Service 312
Economic Development 312
Special Package for the North-east 313
Border Trade 314
Curbing Illegal Immigration 315
Reorganisation of Assam 316
Control of Trafficking in Narcotics and Small Arms 317
Rebuilding the Shattered Communications with
Bangladesh 317
India-Myanmar Cooperation 318
India-Bangladesh Relations 319

Shift in Counter-Insurgency Strategy 319
Legal Framework 321
Intelligence 322

Appendix 'A' 324

Nagaland Accord (1975) 324
Supplementary Agreement of January 5, 1976 326

Appendix 'B' 327

Memorandum of Settlement with MNF 327
Preamble 327
Restoration of Normalcy 327
Legal, Administrative and other Steps 328
Other Matters 329
Sequence of Events 331

Appendix 'C' 332

Memorandum of Understanding with TNV (1988) 332

Preamble 332
Rehabilitation of Undergrounds 332
Measures to Prevent Infiltration 333
Reservation of Seats in the Tripura Legislative Assembly for Tribals 333
Restoration of Alienated Lands of Tribals 333
Redrawing of the Boundaries of Autonomous District Council Area 333
Measures for Long-term Economic Development of Tripura 334

Appendix 'D' 335

Memorandum of Settlement on Bodoland Territorial Council (BTC) 335

Select Bibliography 343

Index 351

Governor
Jammu & Kashmir

Raj Bhavan,
Srinagar 190001

FOREWORD

India is perhaps the most diverse country in the world with wide diversity of religion, language and ethnicity. Yet, there is an underlying unity in the country based on geography, history and culture. This has enabled the Indian Civilisation State to survive from the dawn of history. In fact, ours is the only surviving ancient civilisation of the world. As India is the most diverse country of the world, her North-eastern Region is the most diverse part of the country. The religious, linguistic and ethnic divides here are sharper and the bonds of history, geography and culture not so strong. The several insurgencies that have erupted in this region have to be seen against this backdrop.

Politically independent and economically affluent societies enjoying good governance do not get afflicted by insurgency. The people in such countries are naturally interested in the maintenance of *status quo*. Developing societies harbouring a feeling of neglect or discrimination, and having a large unemployed youth population, provide a breeding ground for insurgency. These conditions are to be found in ample measure in the North-east and hence the mushrooming of different insurgencies in that region.

The five requirements for an insurgency movement are, an Ideal, a Charismatic Leader, a Popular Base, a Favourable Terrain and Outside Support. These have been available to insurgency movements in varying degrees in the North-east. They fuel the secessionist agenda of the insurgents. We have had different types of secessionist movements in the country like linguistic, tribal, cultural and religious. On the whole, we have been battling against them successfully keeping our national frontiers inviolate. The linguistic secessionism in Tamil Nadu was successfully tackled through a democratic process and without resort to force. The other South Indian States did not join the anti-Hindi movement and the 1962 war generated a nationalist upsurge, throughout the country. Our economy improved due to the ushering in of the Green Revolution. All these factors helped us in tackling linguistic secessionism in Tamil Nadu. On the other hand, linguistic secessionism succeeded in Pakistan. Democratic process had been thwarted there and military committed numerous atrocities. This led to a people's movement for freedom and armed rebellion. Thus, Pakistan got dismembered. Tribal insurgencies erupted in Nagaland, Mizoram, Manipur and Tripura. In Nagaland it has been in suspended animation for the last ten years through a cease-fire but the source of conflict has not yet been resolved. The tribal insurgency in Mizoram, was resolved through a political settlement, with Laldenga, the undisputed Mizo insurgent leader, joining the Nation's political mainstream. This has been a success story and Mizoram is now the most peaceful State of the North-east. Manipur continues to boil and is today the most violent State in the North-east. The situation there is compounded by conflict between different segments of the population on the basis of ethnic differences. Insurgency in Tripura is more of a "civil war" between the tribal population and the post-1947 Bengalee immigrants, who have reduced the original population of the State to a minority. Assam is the most important State in the North-east, strategically, economically and demographically. Although tribal insurgency notably that of Bodos has taken place in that State, the insurgency there has been mainly cultural with the bulk of the population being men of the plains, seeking a separate cultural and historical identity. Religious insurgency as such has not erupted in the North-east. Large-scale conversions have taken place in that region post

Independence. This has been a continuation of the process started in the pre-Independence era. Apart from a few incidents, and inclinations of some elements on the basis of religious identity, religion as such has not been a major factor motivating insurgents. However, we have had to contend with religious insurgency in the North, first in Punjab and then in Jammu and Kashmir. We successfully managed to combat insurgency in Punjab, through firm Police action supported by the Army and the cooperation of the people. Normalcy was restored in that State. Religious secessionism in Jammu and Kashmir has been an ongoing militancy movement with a vicious mix of insurgency, terrorism and proxy war. Vigorous efforts are being made towards both conflict management and conflict resolution. There is a marked improvement in the situation but daily killings, albeit on reduced scale, and occasional incidents of high profile violence, continue.

Insurgency which is also for good reason, called People's War, is primarily a post Second World War phenomenon. No doubt there have been innumerable previous instances of irregular bands operating in mountains and forests against regular armies. Tsi Yao of the Ming race engaged Emperor Huang in a long drawn war in fourth century BC. The Old Testament describes the guerilla campaign of Macabes against the Syrian armies. Fabius Maximus adopted this tactics in Italy against Hanibal. In early nineteenth century, the Spanish guerillas wore down the army of Napoleon. In fact, the word 'guerilla' is derived from the Spanish word 'gorilo' meaning little warfare. Guerilla tactics may have often been practiced in the past, but the concept of insurgency is a modern phenomenon, requiring irregular bands to wear down regular armies through guerilla tactics and preventing them to bring to bear their superior military strength, securing a sanctuary to build conventional military power and finally delivering a coup de grace in a crushing defeat on the occupying/ruling power in a conventional battle. Mao demonstrated the successful culmination of this process in China leading to driving out the US supported Chiang-Kai-Shekh's Army from the Chinese mainland. Ho Chi Minh did the same when he ultimately inflicted a stunning defeat on the French at Dren Bien Phu in a conventional battle. Although this form of insurgency is essentially a post Second World War phenomenon, it would not be out of place to mention that this concept was perhaps pioneered, centuries earlier, by the great Shivaji. Starting with irregular bands, he wore down the armies of first Bijapur Sultan and then the Mughal Emperor in the hills of the Western Ghat. His victories against overwhelmingly superior forces demonstrated the success of the weak against the strong. What he lacked in military strength, he made up with surprise and mobility. Thus he managed a sanctuary ringed by hill forts which became virtually impregnable. His one reverse at Purandar led to his being taken a prisoner and he had to suffer the ignominy of having to appear in the Mughal court at Agra. His dramatic escape from Agra had an electrifying effect on the people of Maharashtra. He now renounced the Purandar treaty imposed on him. At the height of Mughal imperial power, he could celebrate his coronation at Raigad with priests coming from far away Varanasi, making it a landmark national event of the time. This was followed by a victorious advance at the head of a large Army, over a distance of 1000 Kms across the Deccan, from the West Coast to the East Coast.

Till the Second World War, insurgency or people's war, was hardly a problem. Fate of nations was decided mostly in conventional battles. Exceptions apart, like mobilisation of people's power as in the case of operations by Shivaji, the common man showed little concern and was generally apathetic. He did not consider it necessary to combat the enemy. This was considered 'the exclusive domain of soldiers'. No role was visualised for the people who had to resign themselves to the outcome of battles. Thus, the fate of India was repeatedly decided on a frontage of a few thousand yards at Panipat with the people resigning themselves to accepting the outcome of the battle. This was so even in Europe, even though Nation States had got established there from sixteenth/seventeenth centuries and large national armies were being raised through conscription. Thus as at Panipat, so at Waterloo the fate of Europe was decided on a frontage of about 3000 yards without any subsequent popular upheaval by the people. Moreover, in the past there was little awareness among the people. With improved communications and higher level of public consciousness, the situation got altered in the twentieth century and more so as we advanced to the present Information Age.

With the process of decolonisation starting after the Second World War, greater awareness and consciousness among the people, promotion of Communist philosophy as also nuclear balance of terror, low intensity conflicts like insurgencies have become the order of the day. A few hundred such conflicts have taken place in different parts of the world since 1945. Mobilising the people to fight an occupying/ruling power has become common. Major colonial powers like the French in Indo-China and Algeria, the Dutch in Indonesia, the British in Malaya and Kenya, the US in Vietnam and the Soviets in Afghanistan, had to pull out from those countries, withdrawing their regular Army. Currently we see the strongest military power in the world which won a spectacular victory in a conventional war in Iraq with its overwhelming military power and shock and awe tactics, mired in the quagmire of insurgency in that country.

The British devised a strategy for counter-insurgency operations in Malaya based on trying to win the hearts and minds of the people. The organisation and strategy devised by them in Malaya, became a role model for fighting insurgency. No doubt they succeeded in Malaya in dealing with "Communist terrorists" but at the end of the day, the solution of the problem was found in their withdrawing their imperial hold on that country.

In India we have been combating insurgency in our country, with certain sections of our own people, wanting to secede through armed rebellion. Our imperative need is to counter these armed uprisings using minimum force, winning the hearts and minds of the people and finding an acceptable political solution. I recall that in the fifties, a view was held in Army circles, that we should counter Naga insurgency demographically. The Naga population at that time was only 5 lakhs. There were plenty of open spaces there in which we could settle people from our mainland, particularly ex-Servicemen, to neutralise the Nagas. The Chinese tried this technique successfully in Tibet. We decided not to do so and seek a value-based democratic solution. The Inner Line was imposed restricting movement of population from the mainland to preserve Naga culture and identity. Political concession was given. A region with a population of much less than half of any major city in the country, was made a full-fledged State with all the trappings of Statehood at the expense of the Indian taxpayer. I do not propose to sit in judgment over this approach. The fact remains that despite various insurgencies we have kept our borders inviolate in North-east as in the rest of India. This was achieved despite the insurgents managing outside support in a fair measure. Initially, China and East Pakistan supported insurgencies in this region but after the 1971 war, this changed. Pakistan was now not in a position to do so and Chinese for their own reasons, generally gave up doing so. However, in the case of our other neighbours, Bhutan, Myanmar and Bangladesh, the case has been different. The former two have not been supportive of Indian militants operating from their territory but were not in a position to prevent them from raiding Indian territory. After some years, Bhutan geared itself to destroy Indian militant camps in its territory and carried out a successful operation in 2004. Today, Bhutan stands cleansed of Indian militant camps. Myanmar is not in effective control of its Northern region and Indian militants continue to have their bases in that area. However, in 2001 Myanmar Army successfully cooperated with the Indian Army in operations against Nagas in their territory. So far as Bangladesh is concerned, the position has been getting increasingly worse. Apart from unabated influx of illegal migration from that country, militant leaders and militant camps are being provided asylum in that country. It is unfortunate that no curb is put in Bangladesh to anti-India activity and of late 151 has become very active in that country.

During my tenure as Governor in Assam from 1997 to 2003, we worked on a three pronged strategy of unified command, economic development and psychological initiatives. Despite our *efforts* to have a unified command in the North-east starting with the outbreak of Naga insurgency in the fifties, it took us over forty years to set up a unified command for the first time in 1997. This helped in coordinating the operations of the Army, the Para Military and the Police and ensuring that they worked as complimentary rather than competing forces. Thus, we could inflict heavy attrition on the militants, almost breaking their back, even though during this period, militants were operating from their havens inside Bhutan, which were beyond the reach of our Forces. Some 2500 militants were killed in encounters, about 3500 surrendered, 3000 weapons were recovered and so was over one crore in cash. The second prong of the strategy of economic development was also a great success. Here we hit a jackpot. Assam was dependent upon the monsoon for agriculture and used to have only one crop a year and even that got damaged due to annual floods. Assam was a food-deficit State. The water table in the Brahmaputra Valley is very high. We installed one lakh shallow tube wells in a year enabling us to have two to three crops a year. Assam now became a food surplus State. The third prong of our strategy of psychological initiatives became the real success story of our counter-insurgency operations in the State. Apart from various civic action programmes undertaken by the Army under Operation Samaritan like free medical camps, road construction, vocational training and so on, we decided to touch the emotional chord of the people of Assam. We utilised religion, history and local sentiments for this purpose. The militant propaganda of Assamese being a separate Nation was effectively countered on the basis of historical facts. Vashishta near Guwahati was given a face lift and made into a tourist spot. Guru Vashishta of Ramayan era is supposed to have had his Ashram there. I went to Dwarka and first paid obeisance at the temple of Rukmini, the consort of Lord Krishna. Rukmini was from Sadiya District in Assam. All this was done to underscore the religious, historical and cultural unity of Assam with the rest of India. The three great heroes of Assam, Mahapurush Sankaradeva, Lachit Borphukon and Lokpriya Gopinath Bordoloi were projected as national heroes. Documentary films were prepared on them and telecast on the television. A large painting of Mahapurush Sankaradeva was put up as a backdrop of a tastefully constructed new Durbar Hall at Raj Bhavan like Gautam Buddha's statue at Ashoka Hall in Rashtrapati Bhavan. The guns used by the great Assamese military leader Lachit Borphukon were placed at the gate of Raj Bhavan and a replica of his victory pillar was put in the foyer of Raj Bhavan. Lachit had decisively defeated the nearly one lakh strong Mughal Army of Aurangzeb at Saraighat in 1670. Lachit Park was developed in Guwahati where Lachit's victory day started being celebrated with much fanfare every year. A statue of Lachit was installed at National Defence Academy in Pune and a gold medal instituted in his name for the best passing out cadet in officer like qualities in every batch. As for Lokpriya Gopinath Bordoloi, we had the Guwahati airport named after him and got Government of India to confer a posthumous award of Bharat

Ratna on him fifty years after he had died. We also had his life size bronze statue installed in the Lok Sabha at Delhi. Besides these measures with a high emotional content in Assam, as Governor, I submitted a 42 page printed special report to the President of India on illegal migration into Assam from Bangladesh. This report was serialised in every newspaper in Assam. This took the people of Assam by storm. Among the measures recommended was the repeal of the IMDT (Act) which appeared to have been designed more to facilitate illegal migration rather than prevent it. Ultimately, the Supreme Court repealed the IMDT (Act) quoting extensively from my report. The result of these initiatives was that the Governor started being referred to in the Press and among the people as "our man in Raj Bhavan" and his being called "a true son of the soil of Assam". Thus, a mind change came about among the people of Assam and this helped to bring them into the national mainstream. It is pertinent that towards the end of my tenure, 81 militants were apprehended by the Assamese people in the villages. A few of them were lynched and the remainder handed over to Security Forces. Recently, there has been a spurt in violence in Assam but there appears to be no popular support for it. This is almost like incidents of terrorist violence taking place in the rest of the country.

I have had a long association with the North-east, as a Company Commander in the fifties, as a Brigade Commander in the Sixties, as a Divisional Commander in the seventies, as the Chief of Military Intelligence also in the seventies and finally as Governor of Assam in nineties and in early years of this century. I have found that this book is a *magnum opus* on North-eastern States and insurgencies in that region. Brig SP Sinha has produced an exhaustive treatise giving in-depth and very extensive information about history, geography, demography, economy and insurgency in that region. The large bibliography and numerous quotes from various sources in the text of the book, bear testimony to his extensive and painstaking research. The strategic importance of this region has also been well brought out. I am one of those who feel that our strategic thinking has been much too West and North centric with a tendency to overlook the North-east. Our decision-makers cannot afford to ignore the North-east. This region is of vital strategic importance and its problems must be addressed suitably in our national interest. I consider this book a must for anyone studying the North-east and working on the strategy to deal with the threats that we face in that region.

Lt Gen (Retd) SK Sinha, PVSM
Governor of Jammu & Kashmir.

Raj Bhavan
Srinagar
15 June, 2006

Preface

Even after more than half a century of Independence, the Indian polity has failed to satisfy the aspirations of the people of North-east. The Nagas revolted soon after the Independence followed by Mizos and today more than fifty years later the whole of North-east is in grip of some form of insurgency or the other. There are a large number of scholars who have attempted to find the reasons for their alienation, chart the course of insurgencies and suggest ways to overcome the problem. In fact, the literature on the North-east is growing at a fast pace; on an average one or two books are published every year on some aspect of 'North-east Insurgency.'

What then is the purpose of this book? I was posted in the North-east for many years in the seventies as a young company commander in my Battalion. The Battalion took active part in counter-insurgency operations, mainly in Nagaland and Khonsa area of Arunachal Pradesh, and won many laurel, and awards and made many friends. But when you are 'jungle bashing' there is hardly any time to think about the larger picture - the genesis, the undercurrents of hopes, aspirations and frustrations of the many tribes and the consequences of your actions. It was only much later after I left the North-east, did I realise that all of us in the Battalion knew so little about the North-east. In retrospect I would have responded quite differently had I been more knowledgeable about the region's past. This book is an attempt to present the North-east in its totality. Though each state has its own personality, to analyse the many insurgencies for their genesis, aspirations of tribal groups, ideological persuasions of insurgent groups and administrative response to them, I have purposely avoided tactical aspects of counter-insurgency operations that I took part in with my Battalion.

The study of North-east has been a rich experience. The abiding impression is that of people who have zest for life, love for music, dance and rejoicing. Even though living in troubled times, people haven't lost their optimism and zest for life; boys and girls in their colourful dresses, their smiling faces and carefree demeanour, which no doubt also camouflage their frustrations, are images that at once uplift your spirits. In contrast, travelling in north India, the images are stark; faces burdened with the grind of daily life, young girls exposed to motherhood much before their time and young boys in groups moving aimlessly without hope, but mimicking the cricketing style of Sachin, which makes their hopelessness more heart rending.

The book, however, is not a personal narrative. It is written to fill a personal void but with the hope that military, police and civilian officers who serve in the North-east, may derive some benefit from it. If this book helps their understanding of the region 'a little more', it would have served its purpose.

The book is divided into five parts. Part 1 deals with the geo-strategic significance, ethnicity and demography. Part 2 reviews the state of insurgencies in the seven states of the region. The review of the major insurgencies concludes with an appraisal. Part 3 analyses the factors that fuel insurgencies and Part 4 deals with the counter-insurgency operations by the security forces and the political and administrative response by the State and Central government. Part 5 looks at the crystal ball and suggests ways to move forward.

ACKNOWLEDGEMENTS

This book is the revised and updated version of the dissertation that I wrote on Insurgencies in North-east India for my doctoral degree from the Department of Defence Studies, Deen Dayal Upadhyay Gorakhpur University, in 1998. I had served in Nagaland and Arunachal Pradesh and was fascinated by the diversity of the North-east region. During service one is so overwhelmed with routine work and operational responsibilities that there is hardly any time for deeper and focused study. After my retirement in 1994, I decided to do just that and enrolled myself as a student in the Department of Defence Studies, Gorakhpur University. I am most grateful to Dr Rajendra Prasad, Head of the Department, for his guidance and encouragement without which this dissertation would not have been possible.

I extensively used the United Service Institution of India Library and the Nehru Museum and Library, New Delhi. I am grateful to the staff of the USI library, who scoured the racks to find the references I wanted. I also used the North East Council library at Shillong - my thanks to the librarian for allowing me to use the library.

I visited many places in the North-east in April-May 1997 to get a feel of the ground realities and to see the changes that had taken place since my service years in the seventies. I am grateful to Lieutenant General SS Grewal, PVSM, AVSM, SM, VSM, the then General Officer Commanding 3 Corps, Brigadier KVM Nair, the then Deputy Inspector General Assam Rifles, Nagaland, Brigadier Gangadharan, the then Deputy Inspector General Assam Rifles, Manipur Range, Brigadier M Dutta, VSM, the then commander of a brigade in Manipur and Colonel Prakash Singh, the then Officiating Commandant 58 Gorkha Training

Centre at Shillong for the help extended to me to visit important places in the North-east.

My thanks also to Mr DK Sen the then Principal, Mount Olive College, Kohima, for his views on Naga youth and to Miss Lalramsiami, the librarian of Mizoram Campus Library of North East Hill University at Aizwal. I am indebted also to my wife, Shashi, who accompanied me on my tour to the North-east and bore the rigours of travel by different modes of transport without complaining.

I owe debt to many authors whose books I have frequently consulted and quoted; foremost amongst them are BG Verghese (North-east India Resurgent), Sanjoy Hazarika (Strangers of the Mist), Subir Bhaumik (Insurgent Crossfire), Prakash Singh (Nagaland), VIK Sareen (North-east India in Flames), Verrier Elwin (Nagaland), YD Gundevia (War and Peace in Nagaland), Nirmal Nibedon (The Ethnic Explosion), Lieutenant General VK Nayyar (The Threat Within), Lieutenant General Narhari (Security Threats to North-east India), General Shankar Roy Chowdhury (Officially at Peace), Major General DK Palit (Sentinels of the North-east: The Assam Rifles), Colonel RD Palsokar (Forever in Operations), Asoso Yunuo (The Rising Naga), P Tarapot (Insurgency Movement in NE India), Udayon Misra (Problems of a Periphery), SK Chaube (Hill Politics in NE India) and many others, who are duly acknowledged in the bibliography.

My abiding thanks to my daughter, Arti, who after doing her post graduation in Social Sciences from Tata Institute of Social Sciences, Deonar, Mumbai, opted for service in Nagaland for a year at Nagaland Gandhi Ashram at Chuchuyimlang (Mokokchung district). I had the benefit of her views on North-east and her insights helped me crystallise my own ideas. She sent me a number of books written on Naga insurgency by Naga authors, published from Mokokchung, which gave the rebel side of the story. She also typed and formatted the final draft on the computer. This book owes a lot to her.

ABBREVIATIONS

AAGSP	All Assam Gana Sangram Parishad
AAPSU	All Arunachal Pradesh Students Union
AASU	All Assam Students Union
ABSU	All Bodo Students Union
ABUSS	Asamiya Bhasha Unnati Sadhani Sabha
ADG	Army Development Group
AGP	Asom Gana Parishad
AJYCP	Asom Jatiyabadi Yuva Chatra Parishad
ALMA	Achik Liberation Matgrik Army
ANSAM	All Naga Students Association of Manipur
APHLC	All Party Hill Leaders Conference
APLA	Assam People Liberation Army
ASDC	Autonomous State Demand Committee
ATPLO	All Tripura People's Liberation Organisation
ATTF	All Tripura Tiger Force
BAC	Bodoland Autonomous Council
BdSF	Bodo Security Force
BPAC	Bodo People Action Committee
BSF	Border Security Force
BSPP	Burma Socialist Programme Party
BTC	Bodoland Territorial Council
CEC	Chief Election Commissioner

CHT	Chittagong Hill Tract
C-in-C	Commander-in-Chief
Congress (I)	Congress (Indira)
CPB	Communist Party of Burma
CPI	Communist Party of India
CRPF	Central Reserve Police Force
DGFI	Director General of Field Intelligence
DIG	Deputy Inspector General
EITU	Eastern India Tribal Unit
ENRC	Eastern Naga Revolutionary Council
FGN	Federal Government of Nagaland
GOC	General Officer Commanding
GOC-in-C	General Officer Commanding-in-Chief
GR	Gorkha Rifles
HALC	Hynniewtrep Achik Liberation Council
IAF	Indian Air Force
IB	Intelligence Bureau
IBRF	Indo-Burma Revolutionary Front
IMDT Act	Illegal Migrants Detection Tribunal Act
IPFT	Independent People's Front of Tripura
IPKF	Indian Peace Keeping Force
ISI	Inter Service Intelligence
J&K	Jammu and Kashmir
JCO	Junior Commissioned Officer
KNU	Karen National Union

KIA	Kachin Independence Army
KMT	Kuomintang
KNF	Kuki National Front
LTTE	Liberation Tigers of Tamil Eelum
MCPU	Mizo Common People's Union
MEA	Ministry of External Affairs
MNF	Mizo National Front
MHA	Ministry of Home Affairs
MNA	Mizo National Army
MNFF	Mizo National Famine Front
MoD	Ministry of Defence
NDF	National Democratic Front
NEFA	North East Frontier Agency
NGO	Non-Governmental Organisation
NHTA	Naga Hill Tuensang Area
NLD	National League of Democracy
NNC	Naga National Council
NNO	Naga National Organisation
NPC	Naga People's Convention
NSCN	National Socialist Council of Nagaland
NSCN (IM)	National Socialist Council of Nagaland (Isac-Muivah)
NSCN (K)	National Socialist Council of Nagaland (Khaplang)
OBC	Other Backward Classes
PLA	People's Liberation Army

PREPAK	People's Revolutionary Party of Kangleipok
PPV	Protected and Progressive Village
Psy Ops	Psychological Operations
PTCA	Plain Tribal Council of Assam
RAW	Research and Analysis Wing
RBA	Royal Bhutan Army
RGM	Revolutionary Government of Manipur
RGN	Revolutionary Government of Nagaland
SLORC	State Land and Order Restoration Council
TLR & LRA	Tripura Land Revenue and Land Reforms Act
TNVF	Tripura National Volunteer Force
TTADAC	Tripura Tribal Areas District Autonomous Council
TUJS	Tripura Upjati Juba Samity
UDF	United Democratic Front
ULFA	United Liberation Front of Asom
UMFO	United Mizo Freedom Organisation
UMPP	United Mizo Parliamentary Party
UNLF	United National Liberation Front
UNPO	Unrepresented Nations and People's Organisation
UPDS	United Peoples Democratic Solidarity
USI	United Service Institution
UT	Union Territory
VGC	Voluntary Group Centre

Overview

People who are ethnically different from rest of India inhabit the North-east predominantly. The tribal population, both in the hills and the plains, is of Mongoloid origin, whose culture, language and life style is quite apart from the rest of the country. Before the advent of the British, Assam which in effect constituted the major part of the North-east, was conquered by the Ahoms in the 13th century. They ruled over Assam for nearly 600 years and in the process got assimilated in the Assamese society. The British absorbed Assam in the British Empire in the 19th century after the Treaty of Yandeboo in 1826; the consolidation of British rule over the North-east was, however, a gradual process spread over time. Assam plain was annexed in 1826, the Cachar plain in 1830, Khasi Hills in 1833, Jaintia in 1835, Karbi Anglong in 1838, North Cachar in 1854, Naga Hills between 1866 and 1904, Garo Hills between 1872 and 1873 and finally Lushai Hills in 1890. The tribes of NEFA along India's border with Tibet were left undisturbed until much after the agreement on McMahon Line in 1914.

At the time of Independence, Assam incorporated almost whole of North-east except the princely states of Manipur and Tripura. The Ministry of External Affairs administered North East Frontier Agency (NEFA), which was technically under Assam, from Shillong much in the same way as the British had done before Independence until August 1, 1965 when the administration was transferred to the Ministry of Home Affairs at the Centre. Today the North-east consists of what is commonly known as 'Seven Sisters', namely, Assam, Arunachal, Manipur, Mizoram, Meghalaya, Nagaland and Tripura. Sikkim has recently been included in the North East Council. North-east less Sikkim has a total area of 2,55,083 sq km i.e. 7.76 percent of the geographical area of India. The total population of North-eastern states as per 2001 census is 3,84,95,089, which is 3.75 percent of the population of India. With the inclusion of Sikkim, the population of North-east will rise to 38.8 million i.e. 4.1 percent of India's population. (Sikkim's population as per 2001 census is 5,40,493) There are as many as 209 schedule tribes in the North-east speaking as many as 420 different dialects. It has aptly been described as "Miniature Asia" a place where the brown and yellow races meet.

The British interest in the North-east was primarily commercial; the development of tea and oil industries and exploitation of forest resources were their main concerns. To advance these interests, the British developed the road and rail communications and established administrative infrastructure in the hill areas. Their concern with the tribals was limited; as long as the hill tribes did not interfere with the British commercial interests, they were left alone to live as they liked. The extension of tea plantation during the period 1869-73 caused friction between the tea planters and Nagas, which resulted in British enacting the *Inner Line Regulation* in 1873. The regulation enacted that no outsider could go without an official pass beyond a certain line that was drawn along the foothills of the whole northern and North-eastern tribal areas; the line was by no means confined to Assam. It served twofold purpose; one, it prevented encroachment on tribal land, and the other, it protected the tea planters and their labour from raids by tribesmen. Its principal aim was not to isolate but to protect the tribes from exploitation by planters.

The words 'Backward Areas', 'Excluded Areas', and 'Partially Excluded Areas' often crop up in any discussion on development of the North-east. In pursuance of the policy of least interference in the affairs of the tribes, the British enacted the Scheduled District Act of 1874, which removed remote and backward areas from the operation of General Acts and Regulations. Later, the Government of India Act of 1919 empowered the Governor General in Council to declare any territory to be backward and deny application of any legislative act in the areas so declared. Subsequently, the term backward was omitted and the same areas were re-grouped under 'Excluded and 'Partially Excluded Areas' in keeping with the provisions of Government of India Act of 1935. Thus North East Frontier to include erstwhile Sadiya, Lakhimpur and Balipura Tracts (which became NEFA and later Arunachal), Naga Hills (present Nagaland), Lushai Hills (present Mizoram), and North Cachar Hills were grouped under excluded areas and the Garo Hills, the Mikir Hills (present Karbi Anglong) and the British portion of Khasi and Jaintia Hills less Shillong municipality became partially excluded areas. The governor himself administered the excluded areas in his discretion whereas partially excluded areas were to be special responsibility of the governor. The basic point of governance of these two groups was that the power of the provincial legislature was not extended to these areas. Nari Rustomji, one of our ablest administrators, who implemented the tribal policy in the early years after Independence was to record that throughout the British period there was deliberate and determined endeavour to restrict the administrative apparatus to rock-bottom minimum.

At the time of framing of the constitution, the Constituent Assembly had appointed a sub committee headed by Bordoloi to examine and recommend the constitutional arrangements, which would fulfil the aspirations of the tribes of the North-east and thus set at rest the fears of their unique identity being lost in the vastness of India. The recommendations were extensively debated in the Assembly, which resulted in the incorporation of the interests of the tribes in the Sixth Schedule. No law passed by the Parliament or the Assam Assembly would have effect in the tribal areas unless the district council passed it. The underlying intention was to allow the tribes to administer themselves without the least outside interference.

But as events unfolded, hopes were belied. The Nagas revolted soon after India gained Independence. Although there is a cease-fire in Nagaland since 1997, the rebellion has not been called off; the final solution is nowhere in sight and has the potential to erupt again any time in the future. Manipur was gripped by insurgency at its peak in early eighties and at the moment of writing (October 2004) Manipur is in flames and the law and order situation there is the worst among the North-eastern states. Tripura keeps regressing into ethnic violence even after the accord with the insurgent Tripura National Volunteer Force (TNV) in 1988. Many militant groups have mushroomed since then.

The Assamese are rightly concerned by the growing influx of illegal Bangladeshis, which they fear erodes their distinctive identity. As time passed, their hope that Assamese distinctive culture and language will find its rightful place lay shattered. One by one, the hill districts of Assam became separate states or union territories. Assam had shrunk beyond recognition. The diminution of Assam's size and status and the spectre of being overwhelmed by illegal immigration made the Assamese so fearful of losing their identity that it found expression in the students' movement in 1979 and then in the rise of ULFA. The 1985 Assam Accord was signed with great hope but its provisions were never implemented. In due course, another insurgency, this time spearheaded by the Bodos, was born.

Why did things go wrong? Surely, there was no lack of goodwill for the tribes among the leaders of independent India. Nehru was eager to protect the uniqueness of tribal societies and was against interfering with their way of living. And yet, some form of insurgency plagues the whole of North-east. Indians from other parts of the country who travel to North-east or reside there for work are baffled and offended when they are called *Vais* in Mizoram, *Dhakars* in Meghalaya or *Mayangs* in Manipur. These terms are used for foreigners or outsiders. Some are so sensitive as to cite this as proof of tribal ingratitude to India, which has done so much for their development. Ironically, the same Indians fail to see either the offence or surprise of a Mizo or a Naga or a Meitei who is asked in Delhi or any other north Indian city if he is a Thai or a Vietnamese. Clearly, there is a wide communication gap between the plainsmen and the Mongoloid people of the North-east; and regrettably the gap is not seen in historical perspective. After all, the hill areas of the North-east were neither part of Assam nor of any kingdom of north India before the advent of the British.

North-east is vital to India's security. 99 percent of its external boundary represents international border. Contrary to popular perception, our political leaders were aware of the strategic importance of the North-east. A committee headed by Maj Gen Himmat Sinhji was constituted soon after Independence, which *interalia* looked in to the administrative set up for Sikkim, Bhutan, NEFA and the eastern frontiers bordering Myanmar. For Naga Hills, Manipur and Lushai Hills, all of which had borders with Myanmar, the committee suggested the unification of administration under one directing head, and opening new police stations and road communications. [1] Ram Manohar Lohia had propagated that India should extend its frontiers to Brahmaputra (Tsang Po) in Tibet; it is only then that Indian troops could meet the Chinese claim on equal terms so far as physical condition and acclimatization were concerned.[2] The threat from China was clearly foreseen. BN Mullick records: "China could react in several ways; firstly by inciting, training and arming the tribal population in India's frontier region; secondly, by fostering armed revolutionary movement inside the country; thirdly, by carrying hostile propaganda against India;

fourthly, by arming and inciting countries hostile to India; and fifthly, by an outright aggression."[3]

Both Nehru and Sardar Patel had recognised the importance of the North-east. In a letter to Deshmukh, Nehru wrote: " They live near the frontier of India and some of the same tribes live on the other side of the border, like the Nagas in Burma. They occupy thus a strategic position of great importance, which has grown in many years."[4] Sardar Patel was equally concerned about the situation in the North-east and was kept informed about the happenings there by the Governor. In a letter addressed to Sardar from Shillong dated June 29, 1950, Jairamdas Daulatram warned: " But in the meantime the situation in Tripura has deteriorated and the latest secret report shows that they (communists) have set up a kind of parallel government in Khowai and they are as good as administering the country on the lines of Telengana. - - - Conditions for guerrilla action are almost ideal for our opponents in Assam and neighbouring states on account of hills and other inaccessible areas."[5] Ironically, having realistically assessed the situation in the North-east, no long-term view was taken to meet the threats to India's internal and external security. The British, on the other hand, had recognised the strategic importance of the North-east and the role it could play in containing communism. There was that Coupland Plan, which envisaged the formation of Crown Colony comprising hill areas in India and Myanmar.

1962 was a watershed in the contemporary history of North-east India. The Chinese attack resulting in the fall of Sela and Bomdila and the rout of the Indian Army left a deep wound not only on the psyche of Assamese but all Indians. But there was a silver lining to the traumatic defeat. The hostile Nagas did not attempt any hostile activity during the war. The opposition of the Naga church leaders to communism, which denied the existence of God, may explain this. The tribes of NEFA helped the Indian Army in movement of supplies and evacuation of wounded. The defeat also led to an appraisal of the security of northern borders and spurred the government to build border roads and improve communications.

Of the many rebellions, the Naga rebellion attracted worldwide attention, mainly because the Nagas had played a key role in defeating the Japanese forces in the epic Battle of Kohima in the World War II, and partly because it started so soon after India's Independence. The exposure of the Nagas to the Japanese invasion and the wind of change that was blowing over the whole of South-east Asia in the wake of the collapse of colonial powers left an indelible impression on them. There was lurking fear among the Nagas, reinforced by imaginative propaganda by the rebels, that they will loose their ethnic identity in the vastness of India. In fairness to the Government of India it went out of its way to allay their fears, but failed in the absence of a coherent long-term policy. On reflection, the Naga problem would have been resolved by now had it not been for the obduracy of Phizo.

Over the last fifty years many myths have been formed, which obscure the correct understanding of the many biases, prejudices and perceptions that have cropped up. Naga secessionist leaders seldom fail to put forward the argument that the Naga Hills was, till it was annexed by the British between 1866 and 1904, an independent entity. This claim is not based on historical facts. The Ahom policy towards Nagas was marked by a combination of conciliation and force. Having realised that the conquest of Nagas would serve no great purpose, the Ahoms were content to receive their submission and allowed them to enjoy tribal autonomy. Nonetheless, they treated the Nagas as their subjects and took taxes from them in the form of slaves, elephants, spears and hand woven cloth.[6] According to Mackenzie, the British historian, Manipur exercised some sort of authority over the southern portion of

Naga Hills. Raja Gambhir Singh of Manipur had ambitions of permanently conquering Naga Hills. In 1832-33, he marched through Naga territory and reduced many villages to submission including Kohima, at which place he stood upon a stone and had his footprint sculpted on it as a token of conquest.[7] The distortion of history, mainly by Phizo and his associates, is illustrated by this correspondence by Phizo in the *Times*, published from London: "It should perhaps be more widely known that Nagaland consists of two parts; Free Nagaland in the north [Tuensang] which the British never sought to conquer or administer and the Naga Hills Excluded Area, which from 1879 to 1947 were to a limited extent administered by the British Governor of Assam as the agent of the Crown, but the civilian and criminal administration over the people has always been under the control of the Naga Assembly and the British never interfered." JH Hutton, an authority on British administration of Naga Hills, replies: "The civil and military control of the Naga Hills was exercised by the deputy commissioner (DC) appointed by the Governor of Assam. No Naga Assembly, nor anything like one, existed before 1947, nor was there any common language spoken among the Naga tribes...except in cases of serious crime, which were dealt with under the Indian Penal Code, the Nagas were administered by the DC and his assistants according to their own (Naga) customs, which varied from tribe to tribe and even from village to village; but to write of a Naga National Assembly with which from 1879 to 1947 the British never interfered is more completely nonsense than I could have expected to read from anyone literate enough to write a letter to you, sir."[8]

Much has been written about the alleged atrocities of the army in counter-insurgency operations in Nagaland. But the humiliation and human rights abuses inflicted on security forces by the underground have been glossed over. Early in 1956, armed Nagas attacked the few police posts established by Assam State, captured the bewildered policemen, stripped them of all clothing and ordered them to march to the plains in nude. In Satakha, 72 policemen were stripped by the rebels and asked to start walking to the foothills.[9] The dissenters in the underground set-up were liquidated; many were tortured to death. In January 1956, the supporters of Phizo assassinated Sakhrie, general secretary of NNC and one of the moderate leaders in the rebel camp. It is alleged that Phizo had personally signed the order of execution *(Azha)*. He was pinned to a tree, tortured for two days before he died. Dr Inkongliba Ao, who was the chairman of Nagaland Interim Body, was killed in Mokokchung on August 22, 1961 for supporting the creation of a separate State of Nagaland. Kaito Sema, one time chief of the underground army, was shot dead in broad daylight in Kohima on August 3, 1968 after he parted with Phizo and formed a parallel underground government. An assassin killed Kevichusa, who was at one time the general secretary of NNC, in his house in Dimapur on January 4, 1996. The political assassinations *(Azha)* hardly testify to the democratic credentials of the underground. The assassinations continue even after the split in the underground movement. Dolly Mungro, general secretary of NSCN (K), was assassinated in August 1999.

In the beginning the Naga rebels received a good deal of support. But as taxes were levied and extortions of money, clothes and food were done at gun point, the villagers began resenting and put up some resistance. To secure compliance, the rebels adopted more violent measures. For example, a body of rebels attacked Pangsha village in 1955, but the villagers put up stiff resistance and drove them off with heavy casualties. The villagers of Thevopesimi were less fortunate. A part of village, which had refused to pay taxes, was attacked by a gang of 200 rebels; 48 villagers were killed, whose widows were looked after by the government.[10] The depredations of the rebels extended to the plains, where in a raid on a Cachari village, on either side of Dhansiri River, they set fire to houses rendering some 500 people homeless.[11]

There has been no lack of initiative on the part of the government to find a solution of the Naga problem. The merger of Tuensang Division of NEFA with Naga Hills in 1957, the formation of a separate state of Nagaland in 1963, the peace initiative that led to the cessation of hostilities in 1964 and ministerial level talks with the underground and the Shillong Accord of 1975, were all initiatives directed towards achieving a lasting peace. The Shillong Accord failed because a section of Naga underground, which split from Phizoites and formed NSCN, repudiated it. NSCN itself split into two factions, both of which are at loggerheads with each other.

The rebel Nagas lost a historic opportunity to arrive at a solution when during the ministerial level talks in October 1966, Indira Gandhi made a significant concession by offering complete autonomy and was prepared to consider a settlement, which would not necessarily be within the present constitutional framework, meaning thereby that the constitution could be amended to accommodate the Naga's aspirations. Dinesh Singh, the then Foreign Minister, went so far as to tell the rebel delegation that the Nagas could have complete autonomy apart from communication, defence, external affairs and currency. The Nagas rejected the offer. Looking back at the negotiating stance of the rebels, their inflexibility, arrogance, the self-created myth that the Nagas were a nation from the earliest times, their obsession of equating the so called Federal Government of Nagaland with the Government of India and unrealistic and at times naïve demands of protocol cost them decades of strife and bloodshed.[12] The tragedy of Naga intransigence was expressed in eloquent words by JH Hutton and Keith Cantalic, both former British administrators of Naga Hills and known friends of the Nagas, in a letter to the *Times*, London, dated

January 27, 1965, commending to the Nagas the status and powers conferred on the State of Nagaland in 1963, thus:

> *"In effect this means that Nagaland is completely independent in all matters except those of foreign relations and external defence. Obviously, India could go no further than this most generous offer. Nagaland lies along the natural frontier of the North-east and from the North-east she has been only recently threatened with invasion. Nor is it easy to conceive how in any other way the Naga tribes could thus have the best of the two worlds, complete self-government for themselves; as much or as little, administrative isolation from the rest of India as they wish; and the backing of India, of which their country is essentially a geographic entity after all, in the case of aggression from outside. Indeed the dissidents have gained not only all they could have hoped, but more. To refuse a settlement on such terms would be worse than a blunder, it could be a crime against their own people for it is they who will suffer most if peace be not now be achieved."*[13]

The Mizo rebellion was the result of disaffection of people caused by the total failure of the Government of Assam to provide adequate relief during the famine of 1965. The counter-insurgency did succeed in establishing the writ of the government but measures like the grouping of villages alienated the villagers further. The turning point of the Mizo insurrection came after the creation of Bangladesh: The Mizos lost their bases in CHT and the freedom of movement and the advantage of safe sanctuaries, which are crucial in running an insurgent war over a long period.

The Mizo rebels correctly read the writing on the wall and opted for peace and signed the Memorandum of Understanding with the Government of India in 1986. The main reason for the success of the Mizo Accord when other similar accords failed to end hostilities was the supremacy of Laldenga in the underground set-up. He was able to persuade his followers to lay down arms and return to civilian life. There were dissenting voices but Laldenga was a shrewd man and was able to out-manoeuvre his opponents. The other reason was that amongst the Mizos there always were two shades of opinion - one in favour of Independence and the other for a negotiated settlement. Those who favoured negotiations were called *Dumpwal*; *Dum* means black and *Pawl* meaning blue. Although in the beginning the rebels had a large following, there was an equally influential section, including church leaders, who were opposed to violence.[14]

There were some important differences between the Naga and Mizo insurgencies. At the ideological level, the main problem in the Mizo Hills was economic than political. It was the demand for Independence that triggered the rebellion in Nagaland, whereas in Mizoram it was the acute deprivation of the people that was the main cause. The Naga insurgency was jungle-based, whereas in Mizoram it was urban-oriented. The post of town commandant for Aizwal was unique to Mizo insurgency. The MNF carried out many terrorist acts in the town.[15] There was a special cell to carry out assassinations. Unlike Nagaland where the local administration was manned by and large by local people, Mizoram's total administration was in the hands of non-locals (outsiders), which explains the antipathy towards the outsiders.[16]

KPS Gill has drawn comparison between insurgencies in Nagaland, Mizoram and Punjab. Initially both Naga and Mizo insurgencies enjoyed wide support, but petered out as more and more people came in contact with people in Shillong and Delhi and saw the opportunities there and realised the narrowness of the objectives of the insurgents. In Punjab the support came from the fringe elements and never more than one or two percent of the population. In Punjab sub-nationalism did not take root because there were more Sikhs outside Punjab. The majority in Punjab saw the propagation of Khalistan as fascism. The strength of the terrorists in Punjab never exceeded 10,000 of which nearly four to five thousand were active. At the height of insurgency there were 2,500 AK rifles, mostly given by Pakistan's ISI. In the North-east by contrast, the comparable number of hostiles was not as large nor were they equipped as well as their counterparts in Punjab. Pakistan and China did give them some modern small arms in the sixties, but the Lee Enfield .303 was the basic weapon.[17] In Mizoram, the insurgents did not lack trained men, for 2nd Battalion of Assam Regiment had been disbanded a couple of years earlier for collective indiscipline while serving in Kashmir, and the bulk of who were Mizos, joined the rebel ranks. Naga and Mizo lack of numbers in insurgent ranks as compared to Khalistanis was made by favourable terrain. The external support system was also different. The Nagas had safe haven in Kachin territory and the Mizos in CHT in East Pakistan and later Bangladesh.

Religious fanaticism marks the difference between the Kashmir and North-east insurgencies. Religious fanaticism has defined the character of the militancy in Kashmir, but the insurgencies in the North-east have by and large had some sort of ideological orientation. Nagaland and Mizoram are both Christian majority states, yet religion was not the driving force of separatism, even as the separatists in Nagaland claim "Nagaland for Christ". Ethnicity was the prime mover accentuated, of course, by Christianity.

The rise of Meitei sub-nationalism, which took a violent turn in late seventies, was an expression of Manipur's sense of neglect and discrimination, largely justified, by the Centre. Manipuris were deeply hurt that despite their long and distinctive history, it was granted statehood only in 1972, a decade later than Nagaland, over part of which Manipur had exercised suzerainty in the past. Similarly, the Manipuri language was included in the Eighth Schedule of the Constitution in 1992 after a prolonged agitation.[18] When insurgency in the hills of Manipur and Naga Hills was at its peak in the sixties, the Nagas were given many concessions in order to appease them at the cost of Hindu Meiteis. As a protest many have lately renounced their *Vaishnav* faith and gone back to their original *Sanamahi* faith. In a wider sense, Meitei look upon themselves as inheritors of a glorious past and are animated by the historic memory of an empire, which extended to the Chindwin River in Myanmar; the past glory playing upon their present, when they find themselves marginalised.

Ironically, the occupation of the Kangla Fort at Imphal by the Assam Rifles since Independence was resented by Manipuris of the valley, who saw the occupation as symbol of foreign rule. The British occupied the fort in 1891, which marked the subjugation of Manipuris. The fort has been the focus of Meitei pride and a symbol of a lost empire; and the Assam Rifles, which has occupied it since Independence, had done nothing to desecrate the symbolism. In fact, they have taken as much pride in Manipur's past as Manipuri themselves and many acknowledge that the fort complex was maintained well by the Assam Rifles. In the face of persistent demand, the Prime Minister, Shri Manmohan Singh, handed over the fort to the Chief Minister of Manipur on November 20, 2004.[19]

Insurgency in Tripura has spread mainly due to the large influx of refugees initially from erstwhile East Pakistan and later illegal infiltration from Bangladesh. The refugees who poured into Tripura in the decade after Independence were mainly Hindu Bengalees who fled to escape from the communal riots. The migrants who have been illegally infiltrating after the creation of Bangladesh are predominantly Muslims. This large-scale influx of refugees and illegal immigration has dramatically changed the demographic profile of the state, resulting in the tribal population becoming a minority. The pressure on land has resulted in alienation of tribal land, which is at the root of insurgency in Tripura.

The insurgency has been aided and abetted by Bangladesh. Tripura is almost entirely surrounded by Bangladesh, the only opening to the rest of India by land being through Assam extending to 288 km, while its boundary with Bangladesh is 839 km. The geographical proximity to Bangladesh has been a boon for the insurgents of Tripura, who have found safe haven in the Chittagong Hill Tracts (CHT) of Bangladesh. The active support given by Bangladesh to Tripura insurgents to counter the support given to Chakmas of CHT by India was another important factor in the growth of insurgency. The present militancy in Tripura is not an outcome of any secessionist demand but is the result of sectarian tribal versus non-tribal hostility. In the recent years, criminal gangs have been operating in the guise of insurgent groups, whose main purpose is to make quick money and increase their influence.

The Assam situation is quite different from the other insurgencies of the North-east. Unlike the hill areas, the Assamese took an active part in the struggle for Independence from the British rule and are proud of their Indian heritage. The problem in Assam is not of integration but provides an excellent case study of how a proud people, endowed with abundant natural resources have been alienated over a period of time due to neglect and the fear of the loss of their identity due to Bengali cultural imperialism and illegal immigration from Bangladesh. Their fear found expression in the agitation launched by AASU to detect and deport illegal immigrants from Bangladesh, which began in 1978 and culminated in the Assam Accord in 1985. But the provisions of the accord remain largely unfulfilled. The rise of ULFA began on anti-foreigner plank directed against illegal immigrants, but as it so often happens in most insurgent movements, ULFA has not only abandoned its original ideology but now considers Bangladeshi immigrants as comrades in the struggle against Indian hegemony.

A number of Muslim fundamentalist organisations were formed, trained and armed in Assam in the closing decade of the last century by Pakistan's intelligence with the connivance of Bangladesh. The initial aim of these organisations was self-protection from Hindu depredations in the 1990s, particularly after the destruction of the Babri Masjid in December 1992. However since 1994, in keeping with Bangladesh philosophy of '*Lebensraum*', and egged on by Pakistan, the emphasis has shifted to building a support base for a Muslim majority areas of North-east and West Bengal to secede to Bangladesh.[20]

According to an official estimate the figure of illegal immigrants from Bangladesh has crossed the 15 million mark out of which five million have settled in Assam, where they are in a position to influence state politics in a decisive way in around 50 of the 126 assembly constituencies. When this problem is seen from a larger national perspective, the situation is alarming. Lt Gen SK Sinha, the former Governor of Assam, in his official report to the President in 1988, had drawn attention to the danger thus: "The silent and invidious aggression of Assam may result in the loss of strategically vital districts of lower Assam. The influx of these illegal migrants is turning these districts into a Muslim majority region. It will only be a matter of time when a demand for their merger with Bangladesh may be made." Assamese fear of being rendered minority in their own backyard is not recent but is rooted in pre-independence days. Mr Jinnah is reported to have made a remark to his private secretary, Shri Moin-ul-Huq Chaudhury on the eve of partition: "Wait for ten years, I will present Assam on a plate to you."[21] Similar sentiments were expressed by Zulfikar Ali Bhutto in the book titled 'The Myth of Independence': "It would be very wrong to think that Kashmir is the only dispute that divide India and Pakistan, though it is undoubtedly the most important. One at least is nearly as important as the Kashmir dispute - that of Assam and some districts of India, adjacent to East Pakistan. To these, East Pakistan has very good claim, which should not have been allowed to remain quiescent."[22] The rapid Islamisation of Bangladesh in the recent years and the unabated infiltration of Bangladeshi Muslims, which is slowly giving rise to Muslim militancy in Assam point in the direction envisaged in the past.

The Bodo insurgency is the result of Assamese chauvinism. The callous disregard of Bodo grievances by both Congress and AGP governments, alienation of tribal land and Assam's language policy all added to a situation in which the Bodos took up arms. The creation of Bodo Territorial Area in 2004 has been welcomed but it has not satisfied all sections of Bodo militants. The tribes of Meghalaya also agitated for separation, but separation from Assam and not India. The steady increase of Nepali and Bangladeshi migrants in Meghalaya has made the tribes feel uneasy and insecure and passions have been raised against the so-called foreigners in the past. Arunachal is the only state in the North-east, which has remained peaceful. But this idyllic scene may change if the resentment against the Chakma refugees is not addressed soon. In the recent past the national political parties have encouraged permissiveness and political defections, a game in which the winner can only be Naga insurgents – either NSCN (IM) or NSCN (K); both have considerable stake in sensitive Arunachal districts of Khonsa and Chaglang, which fall on the shortest route to camps in Myanmar.

The external support given to the insurgents initially by East Pakistan and China and by Bangladesh after its creation in 1971 has been a major factor in the spread of insurgency in the North-east. Although China stopped giving support to the insurgents sometime after 1978, some analysts speculate that China has continued to give occasional support clandestinely using

Pakistan's ISI as proxy. It was hoped that with the emergence of Bangladesh the support given to North-east insurgents would stop, but that hope has been belied. As events have unfolded, all insurgent groups have found safe haven in Bangladesh. The ideal guerrilla terrain across the border in CHT in Bangladesh and Myanmar's Naga Hills, which are home to ethnically similar tribes, have facilitated insurgents easy access to safe camps across the border.

The arrival of Christianity, its rapid spread in the hills of the North-east and the impact on the social, cultural and political life of the tribes is controversial. Christianity gave the tribes a distinct identity and introduced many reforms, forbade perpetual feud, head hunting and curtailed propriation of evil Gods. It pushed Nagas out of seclusion and isolation into open ideas and other civilisations of the world. It also brought education and modern medical facilities. In the process, however, it destroyed many positive elements of tribal life. A Naga intellectual has written that conversion to Christianity required abandonment of indigenous cultures and practices. The loyalty of the converts was divided towards their own groups; non-converts were regarded as sinners.[23] Another negative was the excommunication carried out against unfaithful church Nagas who used to break the Sabbath and participated in traditional dancing and singing of folk songs. The effect has been ruinous in many ways. The art of weaving suffered since generally the convert took to wearing European mill made clothes. Verrier Elwin has expressed it thus; "the activities of the Baptist mission among the Nagas have demoralised the people, destroyed tribal solidarity and forbidden the joys and feasting, decorations and romance of community life". JH Hutton, an ICS officer posted in Mokokchung, was of the same view that the 'role of the Baptist Mission among the tribals in general and Nagas in particular has been injurious and disruptive to their culture.' There is a common refrain among scholars such as JH Hutton, JD Mills, Verrier Elwin and Furer Haimendrof that 'Christianity will eclipse the distinct tribal culture.' The converts adopted western dress and a taste for everything western.[24] The criticism forced the missionaries to change the method of proselytising. In the words of Sir Robert Reid: " But methods of proselytising had become modified as the years passed, and latter day missionaries sensibly tried to preserve all that was good in old tradition."[25]

Another charge levelled against the Church is that it sowed the seeds of separatism amongst the tribes of the North-east. There is some truth in the allegation. Christianity widened the barrier, tension and conflict between the people of the hills (predominantly Christians) and plains (predominantly Hindus). In their zeal to convert the tribes, the missionaries painted Hinduism in a very negative way, which perpetuated the chasm between the Christians and Hindus.[26] After Independence "the aim of an influential part of the church was to carve out states, or areas within states in which Christians could be in majority as Christians or, at the least areas in which persons running the governments would be amenable to the influence of the church. The effort has proceeded furthest in the North-east."[27]

In the recent years, the North-east has emerged as the major transit route for narco-trade and gunrunning. An indicator of the scale of illegal narcotic trade is the high incidence of drug abuse mainly in Manipur and Mizoram; the malaise is now spreading to Assam and Arunachal.[28] The Naga-Kuki internecine feuds are a direct consequence of insurgent groups trying to control the road from Moreh, on the Indo-Myanmar border, to Imphal to facilitate illegal trade. The demand for money to finance the many insurgencies in the North-east will fuel illegal trade in narcotics in future in a big way.

How have the army, the civil servants, the insurgents, the Church and the politicians responded to the insurgencies in the North-east, particularly in Nagaland, which is regarded as the fountainhead of North-east insurgencies? The discourses that Ved Mehta had with a cross-section of Indian and Naga officers and his observations reinforce author's own perceptions formed during long military service in the North-east and subsequent travels and study, are quoted here verbatim: "I listen to the Prime Minister of the Naga Federal Government (If the Indian government doesn't recognise Nagaland to be a separate nation, we will fight... We are not the Naga hostiles, we are the Nagas. The state Government of Nagaland is a stooge of the Indian government.), to the Chief Minister of Nagaland (I say to hostiles, "Now that you have got a state, why ask for trouble? Let's have peace."), to a leader of the Naga Baptist Christian Convention, the association of all Naga churches ('We don't want any part of heathen India, Nagaland is for Christ. We are intellectually and spiritually a part of the west, not of India at all'). I also listen to an Indian military leader who is a hardliner (I was here at the time when we were asked to solve the problem of Nagaland. We had started a programme of regrouping all the people in Nagaland from three thousand villages into two hundred villages with stockades around them. We had told the people that anyone seen outside the stockades at night would be shot. .... In time, we would have made them happier by converting the regrouped villages into modern villages with schools and hospitals. For some months they might have disliked living in regrouped villages, but then they would have got used to it. But just when we were getting somewhere, our politicians stopped us. The military solution has never really had a fair trial in Nagaland) to an Indian military leader who is a softliner ('The Naga hostiles are always using military atrocities as propaganda. Some are imagined, some are real. But how do these real military atrocities come about? Once, the guerrillas not only killed some recruits but also mutilated them in order to steal their guns – the guns were chained to the recruits' bodies. The comrades of the recruits couldn't trace the murderers, so they simply razed all the villages where they thought the murderers were hiding. If their superiors had tried to stop the retaliation, they would have a mutiny. But we know now that the guerrillas can never be defeated, because the conditions in all the tribal areas are such that the guerrillas can strike and vanish and live in the jungles indefinitely. The tribal problem requires a political solution.'), to an Indian civil servant who is a pessimist ('everything here is mad and impossible. Some of these Nagas are so westernised that they think we Indians are backward. Others are more backward than any other savages in the world. If we had done certain things in Nagaland – for instance, given the Nagas statehood in the union in 1948, when they first asked for it - may be they would have accepted the idea of staying with India, or enough of them would have done so to deprive the guerrillas of means of support. Our relations with the Nagas have always been a story of our missing the bus.'), to an Indian civil servant who is an optimist ('I know that from the outside this still looks like a boiling pot. But, perhaps because we are in the middle of it, we don't feel that it is a boiling pot. A general of the Naga Federal Republic who used to march forty-five miles a day in the jungle – he married a girl who used to be my office assistant; it was love marriage, and now they lead a very bourgeois town life – recently came and asked me to help him to get a priority for a Fiat – and he is only one of many from the Naga Federal Government who are constantly asking me for cars and petrol – I think something has changed.'), and, finally to a visiting Indian politician ('Suppose we agree to give the Nagas Independence. It might not be a great loss to us. You could cut off Nagaland from India without creating any geographical anomaly. But then what are we going to do with the Lushais, who, as it happens, look like Europeans? May be we could let them make a separate nation out of the Mizo Hills; this would mean only cutting off the tail of Assam. But then how are we going to stop other tribes – other regional and linguistic groups

- from seceding? Ultimately, everything is going to depend on our ability to deal with the guerrillas in Nagaland and Mizo Hills.')."[29]

India has travelled a long way since above observations were made. It has approached the counter-insurgency operations in the North-east as exercises in nation building. Unfortunately, the military initiatives have not been exploited by timely political initiatives, resulting in loss of momentum. Paradoxically, the growth of democracy in the region has helped the insurgents.[30] The political parties at the centre in the race to capture power have, lamentably, indulged in such divisive politics, which can only be termed adventurism. "Most political parties have their dirty trick department. The technique is to first create clandestine fundamentalist armed groups with their own ethnic agenda; provide them with weapons, funds and the aim of causing serious law and order problem, which state government cannot control. Should the game plan succeed, the state government is dismissed citing constitutional breakdown, followed by the imposition of President's Rule, followed some months later by fresh elections, which can be steered to victory of the favoured party by ample funds and benign civil administration. This has resulted in the country being saddled with a number of terrorist organisations, especially in the North-east."[31] Gen VN Sharma, the former army chief, has described an incident, which illustrates this phenomenon: " In 1988 Bodos became active in North Bengal. They decided that no rail move would be allowed between North Bengal and Assam until their demand for autonomous Bodoland was met. They proceeded to ambush vehicles and trains, which disrupted and adversely affected life in Assam. An army goods train carrying ammunition supplies for troops in Assam and the Bhutan Government was ambushed and three men of military escort were killed. Two selected officers were sent to find out from the Bodo chief for the outrage on the pain of immediate army action.

The (Bodo) chief was apologetic and offered full monetary compensation of any amount demanded. He was only obeying orders of agents of the Central Government, who had instructed to carry out such action, paid crores and provided weapons and training. The aim was to destroy Assam trade through Siliguri Corridor in North Bengal to cause riots in Assam. The AGP government was dismissed in due course and came under President's rule for not being able to control lawlessness. Some weeks later the Bodos went on rampage, occupied large tracts in protected game sanctuary, felled trees and hunted wild animals. Army was asked to take control, but refused." [32]

"The constitution of tribal districts into states with the administrative and legislative trappings and other paraphernalia of larger states may have been satisfying to the tribal ego, but it also resulted in the disintegration of the core values of the tribal communities, a fundamental in their value judgements and ever widening gap between the villagers and the leadership. Soon the perks of office infected the tribal leadership who proved themselves equal to the image of dirty politicians in the rest of the country. There were few who could see the long-term implications of a primitive village-based tribal community being transformed into a parliamentary system of governance without any preparation." (Nari Rustomji: Imperilled Frontiers).

It is often argued that enough economic investment has not been made in the North-east. The charge is only partially correct. The Centre has pumped in thousands of crores of rupees year after year as central assistance to special category states. Unfortunately, over the decades a nexus between politicians, bureaucrats and contractors has developed resulting in misappropriation of developmental fund. The Centre's policy of softening up the tribal communities with funds has proved counter-productive. Niketa Haralu sums up the situation well: " Fifty years of fruitless confrontation characterised by carrot and stick by Delhi to secure compliance of the Nagas has resulted in Nagas being addicted to carrot without acquiring respect for the stick."

There are other disturbing trends that have emerged in the North-east. The dividing line between overground and underground politics is becoming increasingly blurred. Lt Gen VK Nayyar candidly brought this out in his report to the President when he was the Governor of Manipur and Nagaland. Even more worrying is the withering away of the duly elected state governments. The insurgents in Nagaland, Manipur and some parts of Assam are running parallel governments. Taxes are levied not only on villages but also on private industries. In Nagaland and Manipur government employees with the exception of armed forces pay regular taxes to one or the other insurgent group. In Assam tea gardens and other industrial houses pay taxes to ULFA, euphemistically called 'protection money.'

The North-east is at its most vulnerable point at the moment. Neighbours whose domestic politics adversely affect our North-east region surround it. Bangladesh is slowly transforming into a fundamentalist Islamic state. Slogans like '*Amra Hobo Taliban, Bangla Hobe Afghan*' (We will be Taliban, Bangladesh will be Afghanistan) are raised in the countryside. The Maoist insurgency in Nepal has equally negative fallout for North-east insurgencies. Intelligence reports suggest that the Maoists are already in touch with ULFA and other groups. Our relations with Myanmar are cordial and have improved. Practical geo-political considerations favour cooperative approach with the Military *Junta* but India's diplomacy will be put to hard test to strike a balance between the practical considerations of maintaining friendly relations with the Military *Junta* and extending support to pro-democracy groups led by Aung San Swu Kyi. The external events are more likely to influence the internal situation in the North-east in future.

Notes and References

1. BN Mullick, *My Years with Nehru: The Chinese Betrayal*, (New Delhi: Allied Publishers, 1971), p 126
2. Ibid, p130
3. Ibid, p 620
4. Letter dated January 29, 1953 addressed to Deshmukh, *Selected Works of Jawahar Lal Nehru*, vol 21, second edition, (1 January-31 March 1953, a project of Jawahar Lal Nehru Memorial Fund, p 158
5. Durga Das, ed, *Sardar Patel Correspondence 1949-50*, Vol 9, (Ahmedabad: Navjivan Trust, 1974) pp 200-202
6. Verrier Elwin, *Nagaland*, (Research Department, Shillong, 1961), p 18
7. J Johnstone, *Manipur and Naga Hills*, (New Delhi: Gyan Publishers 2002), p 41
8. Quoted by Ved Mehta, *Portrait of India*, (England: Penguin Books, 1973) p 228
9. Nirmal Nibedon, *The Night of the Guerrillas*, (New Delhi: Lancers, 1978), p 74
10. Verrier Elwin., n.6., p 59
11. Ibid, p 60
12. YD Gundevia, who headed the delegation on behalf of the Government of India, has highlighted the inflexible negotiating stance of the underground delegation during the peace talks in 1964. See YD Gundevia, *War and Peace in Nagaland*, (Dehradun: Palit and Palit,1975) Chapter viii, pp 130-145
13. Quoted in DR Mankekar, *On Slippery Slope in Nagaland*, (Bombay: Manaktala, 1967), pp 16-17
14. Nirmal Nibedon., n.9, op cit., p 100. Zairema and his colleagues expressed strong disapproval of the violence.
15. SC Dev, *The Untold Story*, (Calcutta: 106 Regent Estate, Mrs Gauri Dev, 1998), p 133. SC Dev was the Commissioner of Nagaland for seven years. In his book Dev analyses the differences between the two insurgencies in some detail.
16. Ibid
17. KPS Gill, 'The Dangers Within: Internal Security Threats' in Bharat Karnad (ed), '*Future Imperilled: India's Security in the Nineties and Beyond*, (New Delhi: Viking, 1994), pp 117-119
18. Tribals of Manipur also speak Meiteilon, the Manipuri language. About 10 lakhs in India and nearly 5 lakhs outside speak the language. On the other hand there are only 9 lakhs Sindhi who speak that language

and there is not a single village in India where Sindhi is spoken, and yet, Sindhi was included in the Eighth Schedule of the Constitution.

19. The house in which Field Marshal Slim, the legendary Commander-in-chief of the 14th Army, lived during the campaign in Burma in the World War II, is located in the Kangla Fort.

20. Lt Gen JR Mukherjee, "A Perspective on the North-east" in Shankar Basu Roy, ed, *New Approach: Our East and North-east'*, published by the editor, Hastings Garden, 5, Hastings Park Road, Kolkata, 700 027. Lt Gen Mukherjee was the Chief of Staff of Eastern Command, based at Kolkata.

21. Quoted by Bhanu Pratap Shukla, *What ails India's North-east*, (New Delhi: Suruchi Sahitya, 1980), pp 20-21. Ironically Moin-ul- Huq opted for India, joined Congress and became a minister in Assam Government.

22. Ibid, p 22

23. P Moasosang, "The Naga Search for Self-Identity" in Rathin Mitra and Barun Dasgupta, (ed.), "*A Common Perspective for NE India*', (Calcutta, 1967). Quoted "*Hill politics in NE India*", (Hyderabad: Orient Longman updated 1999 Edition,), p 43.

24. Ved Mehta describes a visit to a Naga Christian household for dinner thus: " The house is cosy. The drawing room is filled with Naga guests, all wearing western-style clothes – suits and frocks – and all very friendly. There are sofas and chairs in the room, a log fire in the fireplace, whisky in the glasses, Mozart on the gramophone, a Bible on the side table." See Ved Mehta, *Portrait of India*, (USA, Penguin, 1973), p 230

25. Sir Robert Reid, Years of Change in Bengal and Assam, (London, 1966) p 109. Quoted by Asoso Yonuo, *The Rising Nagas*, (New Delhi: Vivek Publishing, 1973), p 170

26. Ved Mehta describes a conversation he had with an influential elderly Angami gentleman in Kohima while writing his book '*Portrait of India*'. The Naga gentleman recounts how an Indian official was set upon by ordinary Nagas many times. The gentleman ends the conversation with the remark, "He (Indian official) should go. Naga and Indians can never live together.' Majority may not share the remark, but it gives an idea of the estrangement. See Ved Mehta, *Portrait of India*, (USA: Penguin Books, 1973), pp 230-232

27. Arun Shourie, *Missionaries in India*, (New Delhi, Asa Publications, 1994), p 205

28. When I (the author) travelled to Imphal in 1998 I had the opportunity to visit a privately run drug de-addiction centre, *Kripa*, which had more than 30 addicts, mostly addicted to intravenous injections of heroin. Most were HIV+ adult males in their early thirties

29. Ved Mehta, n. 26, pp 232-234. Many in the army, who have served in the North-east, share the observations by Ved Mehta.

30. Ved Marwah in Yonah Alexander, ed, *Combating Terrorism*, (New Delhi: Manas, 2003), p 315. Ved Marwah, a former police officer, was the Governor of Manipur for several years.

31. The above *modus operandi* has been described by the former Army Chief, Gen VN Sharma, in an article titled 'North-east Imbroglio' in Shankar Basu Roy (ed), *'New Approach: Our East and North-east'*, published by the editor, Hastings Garden, 5, Hastings Park Road, Kolkata.

32. Ibid, p11. Also see Gen VN Sharma's, *India's Defence Forces: Building Sinews of a Nation* (USI National Security Papers, Number Thirteen, USI of India, New Delhi, October 1994) pp 25-26. Gen VN Sharma was the GOC-in-C Eastern Command based at Kolkata prior to taking over as the Army Chief.

1

Geo-Strategic Significance of North-east India

North-east India as a geographical region is a colonial construct, the concept of North-east Frontier Region evolved during the British period for administrative reasons.[1] Prior to Independence North-east India consisted mainly of Assam and the kingdoms of Manipur and Tripura. After Independence North-east India as a distinct geographical region having its own identity, aspirations and problems took shape. The term North-east also came to be widely used in official texts and correspondence.

The early history of North-east India is very obscure. "But in the main, the region drew its earliest inhabitants from the Mongolian race in Western China, which in very ancient times threw off a series of swarms that afterwards found their way into frontier lands of India; some went along the Northern slopes of Himalayas; some to the South, down the courses of Chindwin, Irrawady, Salween and Mekong rivers, peopling Burma and adjoining countries; and some to the South-west descending the Brahmaputra to Assam. Those who found their way to the South-west probably moved along the Brahmaputra; and as each swarm was forced to yield to the pressure from behind, it either moved Westwards or turned aside into the hills of the Assam Range."[2]

Some scholars believe that Khasis and Jaintias appear to be descendants of proto-austroloids of ancient Assam. They were probably of Austic stock and were its earliest inhabitants. They are called so because they are said to have migrated from the Australian and some other islands of the Pacific Ocean. The beautiful megaliths or pillars of stones, which they created over the graves of the dead, are found in Meghalaya. They spoke Mon-Khemer language and introduced cultivation.[3]

After the Austrics, the Mongolians had migrated to Assam from the North and North-east. The larger group had migrated from China and Tibet; some had, however, entered from Myanmar. The Mongoloids are referred to as Kiratas in Aryan literature. Among the Mongolians the great Bodo tribe had established over the Brahmaputra Valley fairly early. The Bodos had extended into North and East Bengal and into North Bihar. North of Brahmaputra Valley is even today occupied by the Bodos.[4] Other branches of this great tribe are Cacharis, Meches, Garos, Rabha, Tipra, etc. The North Assam tribes of Akas, the Daflas, Abors, Miris and Mishmis, all Mongolians, appeared to have come later and established themselves to the North of the Brahmaputra plains. Other tribes of the same stock are Nagas, Kukis, Mikirs and Mizos.

Some historians speculate the time of the first Mongolian migration to have taken place long before 1000 BC. Next came Aryans. In the early Vedic literature Eastern India is referred to as Mlecha country. But the later Vedic literature in the Brahman period i.e. 6th and 7th century BC, the Aryans are believed to have migrated to the North-west of Karatoya River, which in ancient time was the Western boundary of Assam.[5] The Aryan settlement in ancient Assam is hinted in the legends of Naraka. It is generally admitted that Aryans were not very numerous in ancient Assam, which is racially the land of non-Aryans, but the Aryans established their cultural supremacy over the country. Aryanisation was, however, never complete or total: many non-Aryans lived in the hills preserving their way of life. Before the coming of the Aryans the inhabitants of Assam practiced animism, magic, ancestor worship and Sakti (fertility cult). After the advent of Aryans, Hindu religious beliefs were intermixed with the prevailing tribal cult. Before the coming of the Ahoms in the 13th century, Tantricism (worship of the Mother Goddess or Sakti) was prevalent in Assam in a debased form. Tantric rituals included the sacrifice of ducks, pigeons, goats, buffaloes and even men, to Sakti or Durga. Magic rites where drinking and dancing by naked women were striking features of Tantric worship. Assam was known to the outside world as the land of magic.[6] At such a critical stage in Assam's history, Sankaradeva (1449 AD - 1568 AD) came as deliverer. He condemned the practice of sacrificial rites and brought the message of Bhakti; the religion taught by him was known as Vaishnavism.

Reliable history of this region was first recorded in the narrative of the Chinese pilgrim Huien Tsang, who visited the country then known as Kamrupa, about 640 AD during the reign of Bhaskarvarma (594-650 AD). Bhaskarvarma was contemporary of Harsha of North India. Nothing very definite is known about rulers before or after Bhaskarvarma till the advent of Ahoms in 1228 AD. But the discovery of several inscribed copper-plates, which appear to have belonged to the period between the latter part of the 10th century and the middle of the 12th century throw more light on its history. It would seem that soon after Huien Tsang's departure the country fell into the hands of aboriginal chiefs, who were subsequently converted to Hinduism.[7]

In the beginning of the 13th century before the advent of Ahoms in Assam, the Bodo-Cacharis ruled over the Brahmaputra Valley from Cooch Behar to East Bengal extending up to Naga Hills, with its capital at Dimapur. The Ahoms, a Shan tribe whose ancient kingdom was situated in the upper portion of Irrawady Valley, invaded Assam in 1228 AD and slowly expanded their empire and ruled for nearly 600 years, longer than any other empire in India.

Manipur and Tripura existed as independent kingdoms. The Mughals never succeeded in annexing the North-east in their empire. But what the mighty Mughals could not do, the British achieved, taking advantage of palace intrigues and the decadence of the kings. Hinduism spread in the North-east in the Brahmaputra and Surma valleys and the Vaishnavite cult took roots in the Imphal Valley. The surrounding hills, however, retained their animist faith and each tribe developed according to its own genius till the advent of Christianity, which rapidly spread in the hills in the 19th century.

Physiography[8]

The administrative divisions of the North-east include the states of Assam, Arunachal, Manipur, Tripura, Meghalaya, Mizoram and Nagaland, popularly known as the Seven Sisters.[9] The total area is 2,55,083 sq km, which is 7.76 percent of the geographical area of India. 70 percent of the region is hilly and mountainous terrain and 30 percent constitute valley lands mainly of three rivers; Brahmaputra, Barak and Imphal with related wetlands. The total population of North-east states is 3,84,95,089 (2001 census), which accounts for 3.75 percent of the population of the country.

The North-east has approximately 4200 km of India's international boundary with China (Tibet), Myanmar, Bangladesh and Bhutan. It is connected with the rest of the country by the narrow strip of land, known as the Siliguri Corridor-just 20-km wide at its narrowest, which is also referred to as the Chicken's Neck. The Northern frontier of the North-east region from Sankesh River in the West to the entrance point of the Brahmaputra into Assam in the east is guarded by the Assam Himalayas. The McMahon Line separates North-east India from China (Tibet). The region is bounded by Bhutan in its North-east, autonomous region of Tibet and China in the North, Myanmar in the East and South and Bangladesh in the South.

The North-east has varied physical features. It has mountains, hills, rivers, valleys, plateaus, and riverine islands (Majuli Islands) and can thus be divided into three major groups: hills and mountains, plateaus and plains. The physiographic divisions of the region are: North-east mountain ranges, South-eastern hill ranges, Assam plateau, Assam Valley and Cachar plains.

The North-eastern mountain ranges extend from Tista River in Sikkim to Namcha Barwa (7756 m) peak in Mishmi Hills. Here the Brahmaputra (known as Tsang Po in Tibet) makes a hairpin bend and cuts across the mountains before flowing into the plains of Assam. The total length of this region is 720 km. The Namcha Barwa is the highest peak in this region.

The region has many hills named after the tribes, which occupy these hills. In the North-east the Mishmi Hills are occupied by Mishimis; further to the East on the frontiers of Arunachal is the Khamati Hills occupied by Khamatis, who are of Shan origin; Singpho Hills lying South-east of Lakhimpur district of Assam are occupied by Singphos; the Aka Hills, which lie North of Darang district of Assam between Dhansiri and Dikali rivers are named after the Akas; the Dafla Hills North of Darang and Lakhimpur districts of Assam between Ranganadi in the North-west and Bhareli River in the West are occupied by Daffla tribes; the Abor Hills between the Sion River on the West and Dibang on the North-west are occupied by Abors; the Miri Hills which lie North of Lakhimpur district of Assam and North-west of Ranganadi are inhabited by Miri tribes. A large number of Miris have settled down in the plains of Assam as well. Many of these hills have high altitudes.

The Southern hill ranges (South of Brahmaputra) include the Patkai, the Naga, the Barail Hills, the highlands of Manipur and Lushai (Mizo) Hills. With the exception of Manipur basin, the entire region is undulating. The general elevation of the ranges is 3145 m above sea level. Narrow, steep sided valleys separate the ranges from each other. The location and importance of these hills are described below.

- **Patkai Range:** It lies to the North-east of Assam. This is the range, which has influenced the history of Assam the most. More about the importance of this range is discussed subsequently.

- **The Naga Hills:** The Naga Hills is a continuation of the Patkai Range towards the South and divides India from Myanmar. The highest peak in the Naga Hills is Saramati (3826 m). To the North-west of Naga Range is Kohima Hills, the highest peak of which is Javpo (2995 m). Tizu is the only river that cuts through the Naga Range and flows North-west to join the Chindwin in Myanmar. These hills are home to various tribes. Naga Hills was constituted into a new state of Nagaland in 1963.

- **The Mizo Hills:** This is also known as Lushai Hills. These now constitute the area of Mizoram. The important features of these hills are six parallel ranges running North to South with five deep river valleys between the ranges. Several tribes that are together called by the generic term Mizo inhabit Mizo Hills.

- **The Barail Hills:** It lies in the North Cachar district of Assam running east to west and connects the Naga and Jaintia Hills. The hills are densely forested and several peaks rise to 6000 feet.

- **The Manipur Hills:** The North-western boundary of Manipur Hills runs along the frontier between India and Myanmar and the Western boundary abuts against the Cachar plains and hills. The central part is a large basin 50 km long and 30 km broad surrounded on all sides by high mountains. This appears to be the bed of an old lake, a remnant of which occupies the South-east corner of the basin and is known as the Loktak Lake, 12 km long and 8 km broad, having centripetal drainage. The Barak is the largest river in the Manipur Hills. It rises from the Javpo peak and flows South-west for 180 km.

- **The Tripura Hills:** Tripura Hills comprise long ranges alternating with valleys. This range and valley type of topography has rendered communication very difficult and the transport problem has been accentuated since the creation of Pakistan (now Bangladesh), which almost encircles it. Tripura Hills can be divided physiographically into four valleys, named after the towns of Dharamnagar, Kailashahar, Kamalpur and Khowai, and one upland named after Agartala.

The Meghalaya Plateau

The Meghalaya plateau includes Garo, Khasi and Jaintia Hills. The length of the plateau from the River Dhansiri in the North-west and Singaimari in the West is approximately 420 km and the width is 40 km. It lies between the valleys of Brahmaputra and Barak. The range of these hills combined together now constitute the territory of Meghalaya.

The Brahmaputra River and Valley

The Brahmaputra River is the chief geophysical feature of the region. The river flows out of Mansarovar, under its Tibetan name Tsang Po, and then flows North-west passing through the highlands of Tibet. At the extreme corner of North-east India, it pierces through the Himalayas and makes a right about turn to the West and passes through Assam and Bangladesh, where it meets the River Ganga. It is 2,880 km in length, of which approximately 1,600 km is in Tibet, 870 km in India and 410 km in Bangladesh. After crossing the Himalayas, the river takes the name Dihang. Downstream it is met by another river Dibang. It then enters Brahma Kunda, which is a sacred religious spot for Hindus. Emerging out of this lake it takes the name of Brahmaputra.[10] In Assam the river flows through length of 720 km, creating the Brahmaputra Valley around which the history of Assam has been built.

The valley is approximately 600 km long and 75 km wide. It extends from Sadiya in the North-east to Dhubri in the West where the river takes a turn towards the South, round the spurs of Garo Hills. The valley is heavily populated and may be divided into two parts – upper and lower Assam – each about 75 km wide. The Brahmaputra flows through the centre of this valley. The fertility of the soil attracted hordes of Muslims from the overcrowded districts of Bangladesh, even during the period when East Bengal was part of India.

Surma or Barak Valley

The other valley in Assam, which is not so well known, is the Surma or Barak Valley named after Barak River. The valley covers the district of Cachar in Assam and extends to the district of Sylhet in Bangladesh. The valley is about 185 km long and 200 km wide.[11]

The Imphal Valley

The valley is approximately 50 km long and 30 km wide, with hills on all sides. It lies about 790 m above sea level. The Meitei population of Manipur is concentrated in the valley.

Communications

The North-east was well linked to markets at home and abroad by river and rail links through Calcutta and Chittagong. But the partition of the country disrupted the existing communication links to such an extent that the region was practically cut off from the rest of the country. The only railroad connection with the heartland was the tenuous metre gauge rail link and the National Highway (NH) 31 through the Siliguri corridor. The Brahmaputra was bridged only in 1962 at Saraighat near Guwahati but the low-lying North bank remains vulnerable to floods during monsoons The Saraighat Bridge is a road cum rail bridge, 1.43 km in length.

The NH 31 is the lifeline to North-east. The neglect in building frontier roads was highlighted at the time of the Chinese invasion in 1962. It is only after that tragic event that frontier roads were developed in the North-east, particularly in Arunachal. The main artery of communication, the inland water transport, was severed by partition and continued fitfully until altogether suspended after 1965 war with Pakistan.[12]

During the World War II supplies were moved to China via Stilwell Road from Margherita to Kunming or by air across the Hump to Chunking.[13] The availability of a large number of airstrips all over North-east facilitated air communication. After Independence, non-scheduled airlines flew passenger and cargo to NEFA and elsewhere, a task since taken over by the Indian Air Force (IAF), which operates possibly the largest air maintenance operation anywhere in the world to far flung inaccessible areas.

After 1962 war with China, communications in the North-east have been improved. The Kalia Bhomara road bridge over the Brahmaputra near Tezpur (3.01km) followed in 1987 and a third railroad bridge, the Narnarayan Setu at Jogighopa (2.21km) near Goalpara was commissioned in 1996. The Jogighopa bridge will provide flood proof routing along the South bank. The conversion of rail line to broad gauge up to Guwahati was completed in 1984. The entire South bank line from Guwahati to Tinsukia and Dibrugarh was also converted to broad gauge by 1997. Another road cum rail bridge is under construction at Bogibeel, 17 km downstream of Dibrugarh, which may take eight years to complete. The construction has been inordinately delayed due to non-availability of funds. The project was initially to be funded by the World Bank but due to large investments required and non-availability of funds they backed out. The gauge conversion of Rangia-Murkong-Selek section was also linked to the Bogibeel bridge. Both projects are important for linking remote areas of Assam and Arunachal and would also help in flood control (*The Indian Express*, New Delhi, August 15, 2005 p6)

185 km long Lumding-Badarpur line, which traverses Mikir and North Cachar Hills, is still metre gauge. This rail link connects the Brahmaputra and the Barak valleys. The gauge

conversion has not yet taken place mainly because of extensive tunnelling involved, which is very costly and time consuming. The Central Government in 2005 agreed to fund projects that were not financially viable but required for socio-economic development of the region. These include Jiribam-Imphal Road, Kumarghat-Agartala rail link and Lumding-Silchar-Jiribam gauge conversion. The Ministry of Defence has agreed to fund Senchoa-Silghat gauge conversion on strategic considerations.

The air link to North-east has also been upgraded. Guwahati is being developed as an international airport. The airports at Dibrugarh, Agartala and Silchar are being upgraded. Two new airports at Lengpui in Mizoram and Tura in Meghalaya have been sanctioned.

The IAF flies civil ferry and air maintenance sorties in Arunachal, Nagaland and Sikkim and other inaccessible hill areas. In the early 1950s it was Dakotas, Caribous and Otters aircraft and MI 4 helicopters, now it is AN 32 aircraft and MI 8/17 helicopters operating to and from 179 helipads, 14 advance landing grounds, 50 dropping zones for AN 32 and 180 dropping zones for helicopters at altitudes ranging from 3,200 feet to 1,6200 feet.[14]

Mineral Resources

Assam produces 5.25 million tonnes of oil annually, which is 60 percent of India's production and 80 percent of on-shore domestic production. There are three refineries located in Assam viz. Digboi having a capacity of 0.58 million tonnes, Guwahati 0.77 million tonnes and Bongaigaon 0.46 million tonnes per annum. A new refinery is being set up at Numligarh with a capacity of 3 million tonnes of crude oil per annum. Assam has an estimated 1180 million tons of gas and oil resources. It has 25 percent of hydrocarbon potential of the country. (Source: *Mineral Year Book: Task Force Report;* Ministry of Mines, 1997).

Tea is the major agricultural product, which is exported from Assam. Out of 4,32,876 kg tea produced in the entire North-east in 1997, 4,25,430 kg was produced in Assam. Assam itself produces more than 50 percent of the total tea production in India. Tea is a major foreign exchange earner for the country. (*Source: Tea Board, Kolkata*). Regrettably, the production of tea in the North-east has declined. Assam including Cachar produced 34,1,586 kg in 2003 and 32,2,227 kg in 2004. (*Source: - J Thomas & Co*).

The North-east has a vast forest resource, which has been exploited, regrettably, to the extent of leading to ecological imbalance in many parts. Assam provides timber to many factories in Kolkata. Assam also exports timber, bamboo, cane, paper pulp and agar oil.

Geo-political Significance of North-east India

It is not only natural resources, which make North-east an area of strategic importance but also its geographical location. India regards the McMahon Line as the border between India and China (Tibet), though the Chinese claim this line to be further South. India has 4,200 km long international border with China of which 1,500 km lie in North-east India. In 1962 war, China had captured areas upto Bomdila in Kameng district and Walong in Lohit district of Arunachal Pradesh. China claims the entire Arunachal Pradesh to be part of China and does not recognise the sanctity of McMahon Line. It has recognised Sikkim as part of India only recently. The Chinese deleted Sikkim from their list of independent countries in 2003.

The partition of the country in 1947 altered the geo-strategic situation of the whole of the North-east India in a profound way. All communication channels that once passed through that region were disrupted and India's North-east was cut-off from the rest of the country; connected only by a narrow strip of land near Siliguri, the famous 'Chicken's Neck', which is a strategic passageway, just a few kilometres from Bhutan, Bangladesh, Nepal as well as the Indian state of Sikkim. The defence of this strategic corridor has been and will remain the major concern of the Indian Army. Recent reports that Bhutan might make territorial adjustments in the sensitive Chumbi Valley with China to the detriment of India have rung alarm bells in the security establishment of the country.[15] In military terms, the Chumbi salient is a dagger pointed at the Siliguri Corridor that links India with the North-east and lies in the gap between Nepal, Bhutan and Tibet to the North and Bangladesh to the South. The Western shoulder of the valley lies along India's Sikkim and the Eastern shoulder along Bhutan.

The Brahmaputra flows through the heart of India's North-east. Its history is woven round this river. Its source is in Tibet, where it is called Tsang Po River. The Chinese in fact control the upper course of the river, thus having a bargaining chip against India. Defence analysts suspect Chinese hand behind flash floods in North-east.[16]

The other geographical area, which is of great significance, is the Patkai Range. This forms the watershed between India and Myanmar and has dramatically influenced the history of North-east India. The passes through the Patkai Hills have proved to be as significant as the Khyber Pass in the North-west of India. It was through Patkai Hills that the Ahoms came into the then Kamrup and laid the foundation of a kingdom, which lasted 600 years till the arrival of the British.

The Patkai Range was surveyed in 1896 for the construction of a railway line connecting Ledo in Lakhimpur district of Assam with the Taungni station in the Mu Valley of Burma via Hukwang Valley. It was planned to blast through a 5,000 ft long tunnel through the Patkai Range for the construction of the railway line, which was never built.[17] It was again through this pass that during the World War II, the British built the famous

Ledo Road, also called the Stilwell Road connecting North-east India with Burma Road, which runs from Myanmar to China. During the World War the Stilwell Road was a strategic highway for the movement of troops and equipment.[18]

Interplay of Ethnicity along India-Myanmar Border

The borderland between India and Myanmar is of great military significance. During the British rule, the administration of the Northern and Western borders of Myanmar with India was minimal as was the case in the hills of Assam. Various ethnic groups of Myanmar, namely the Kachins, Shans, Was, Karens, Mons, Chins, and Rohingiyas rose in revolt (many are still rebellious) against the Burmese rule soon after its Independence from the British as did the Nagas, Mizos and Manipuris in India.

There are many linkages between the insurgencies on both sides of India- Myanmar border. The border between India and Myanmar has been porous for most of history. There is no major natural obstacle to movement except the hills, which do not prevent free movement of tribals. The post-colonial era saw the emergence of artificially formed nation states. For example, a large Naga population exists in Myanmar with close ethnic ties with Nagas in North-east India. The Naga ethnic group is spread extensively beyond the existing boundary of the state of Nagaland into the neighbouring states of Manipur, Assam, Arunachal Pradesh and, especially, into Myanmar's territory - Sagaing Division and the Kachin state.

Kachin state[19] in the extreme North of Myanmar is inhabited by Kachins who account for about three percent of the total Myanmar's population. They were converted to Christianity in the nineteenth century by missionaries and are ethnically closer to their neighbours to the South – the Nagas. The Nagas, caught between the Kachins in the North, the Chins to the South and the Burmans to the North-west inhabit the Patkai regions, between the Brahmaputra plains and the bed of the Chindwin River in Myanmar. They too were converted to Christianity in the nineteenth century, as were the Chins forming a Christian cordon along the Indo-Myanmar border.[20] The Chins living in Myanmar have much in common with Mizos across the border in India. They occupy the Chin Hills in Western Myanmar, along the boundary with India's Mizoram. They are of Mongoloid origin and have much in common with Kuki, Lushai and Lakhar tribes and speak related Tibeto-Burman language. Many Chins were ruled by council of elders and others by hereditary chiefs, as was the custom in the Mizo Hills. The first British expedition into Chin Hills in 1889 was soon followed by annexation, which brought to an end the raids by Chins on the Burmese plains.[21]

To the extreme South, in the foothills of the Arakan range on the Bay of Bengal, live the Rakhines or Arakanese, as the British colonialists called them, a majority of whom have been Buddhists. The Sultans of Bengal in the 15th century converted a small minority of Arakanese to Islam - the Rohingiyas, many of whom have fled to Bangladesh in recent times to escape alleged persecution by the Myanmar regime, thus souring relations between Myanmar and Bangladesh.

It was the Kachin Independence Army (KIA), which gave shelter and support to Naga and Manipuri rebels in the formative years of insurgency. Khaplang, a Burmese Naga, formed the Eastern Naga Revolutionary Council (ENRC) in 1965 and cooperated with the Naga National Council (NNC) of Nagaland. In 1963, KIA helped Kaito, then a self-styled General in the underground Naga Army, in establishing a base in the Somra tract in Myanmar.

The KIA, founded in 1961 with a strength of 8,000 to 10,000 men, have long controlled the extreme North of Myanmar as well as the Myanmar's part of Naga country, particularly the famous Stilwell Road, now densely covered by thick jungle, which makes it ideal for clandestine flows that have kept the

Kachin and Naga guerrillas well supplied, making them financially and militarily autonomous[22]. Both the factions of NSCN have received help from KIA, and in return Kachin rebels often found refuge in the Naga areas of Arunachal, which are difficult to reach. Further South, the Chins continue to support the Indian Mizos and Kukis, upholding their kinship. The UNLF of Manipur, on their part, has bases in the vicinity of Tamu and Kalemyo.

A Brief Historical Perspective of Burmese Insurgencies

In order to fully understand the significance of the interplay of factors that fuel insurgencies in India's North-east and its linkages with the rebellions and insurrections by the ethnic minorities of Myanmar, an understanding of the colonial and post independence history of Myanmar will be instructive. The British had annexed Burma in stages: the two maritime provinces of Arakan and Tenaserrin (East Burma) were annexed in 1826 as a result of the First Anglo-Burman War and so was Assam after the Treaty of Yandeboo. The whole of lower Burma fell into British hands after the Second Anglo-Burman War of 1852 and finally the Burmese Kingdom came under British rule in 1886 after the Third Anglo-Burman War. Burma was made a province of British India in 1897, and remained so till April 1, 1937 when it was separated from British India. The continuous occupation of Burma by the British till its independence in January 1948 was interrupted by the Japanese occupation from 1942-45.[23]

The British had tried to confine Burma to the territory largely inhabited by Burmans. All of lower Burma and most of upper Burma came to be called Burma Proper, which was also referred to as Parliamentary or Ministerial Burma. The region of indirect rule came to be known by various names, such as, Frontier, Excluded or Scheduled Areas. The areas occupied by Wa and Nagas in the North-west were called "Backward Areas." As in the frontier region of North-east India, the British administration in the excluded or backward areas of Burma's North, North-west and South-east was minimal. The similarity of administration of frontier areas on both sides of Indo-Burma border is, therefore, significant.

Ethnic minorities inhabit the excluded areas, measuring around 113,000 sq miles, which is about 43 percent of Myanmar's territory, one-third of its 48 million population. They are principally Shans in central and Northern Myanmar, the Kachins in the North-west, the Chins in the West, and the Karens and a subgroup Kareni in the lower reaches of Shan plateau along Salween River. Chins and Kachins held on against British pacification as late as 1894-95.

After independence in 1948, the ethnic minorities were organised into Shan, Kachin, Karen and Chin Special Division, each having a degree of autonomy. Political violence erupted in Burma in 1948 with the Communist Party of Burma (CPB) revolting and taking up arms. Soon many ethnic minorities also began armed struggle of their own but some adopted communist ideology and fought on the side of the communists. The CPB was at its most powerful in North-east Burma where it was backed by China. The rebellion by the communists and the ethnic minorities forced the Prime Minister U Nu to transfer power to a caretaker government headed by General Ne Win in 1958. U Nu returned to power after the general elections in 1960, but in a reversal of fortune General Ne Win staged a military coup and captured power. General Ne Win had promised peace but ironically renewed insurgencies became the major problem of his regime. Constantly changing alliances and military expedients have characterised the politics of Burma since then. By 1980s the insurgencies could be divided into two main groupings – those allied with CPB and those in the National Democratic Front (NDF)[24], which sought the formation of a federal Burma. In short, guns remained dominant in post independence Burma. Over 20 armed opposition groups including the CPB, the Karen National Union (KNU) and the NDF and its allies remained in control of vast regions of the country, principally in the ethnic minority states.

The pro-democracy protests that erupted in 1988 precipitated three events in short succession that dramatically rearranged Myanmar's political landscape. Firstly, the demise of Ne Win's Burma Socialist's Programme Party (BSPP) in 1988 and assumption of power by the supporters of Ne Win in the newly formed State Law and Order Restoration Council (SLORC) headed by General Saw Maung in September 1988; secondly, the collapse of CPB in 1989 which was brought about by the mutiny of its ethnic minority troops who entered into peace talks with SLORC; and thirdly, general elections of 1998 in which the National League of Democracy (NLD) led by Aung San Swu Kyi won a landslide victory.[25] Despite the victory of NLD, the military rule continued.

The State Peace and Development Council (SPDC) superseded the military government of SLORC in November 1997. Since then three-cornered struggle has marked the political scene in Myanmar - the SPDC government, the NLD led by Aung San Swu Kyi and the ethnic minorities.

After decades of conflict the situation has begun to change. A new cease-fire movement began in 1989 prompted by the sudden collapse of CPB. Unlike the previous cease-fire the present cease-fire is generally holding mainly because the SLORC allowed the insurgent groups to keep the weapons and exercise control over the territory but cooperate with the government in regional development initiative.

Ironically, at a time when almost entire population had turned against the regime, scores of former insurgents rallied behind the Military *Junta*. The KIA, which was Burma's most powerful ethnic army controlling most of Kachin State in the far North, bordering North-east India, entered into an agreement with

SLORC in 1993 and signed a formal cease-fire in 1994. The Chin National Front and Arakan Rohingya Islamic Front that are active in areas bordering Mizoram have not accepted the cease-fire. Interestingly, NSCN, both Muivah and Khaplang factions, which are active on both sides of India-Myanmar border, have not declared cease-fire with the Burmese forces.[26] The linkages between the insurgent groups operating in India's North-east and Myanmar's North and North-west have been discussed in some detail in the chapter on external dimension of insurgency.

Chittagong Hill Tract (CHT)

CHT in Bangladesh having common borders with both India and Myanmar is another tract of land, which is strategically significant for its relevance and influence on insurgencies in the North-east. It is situated in the extreme South-east of Bangladesh, bounded in the North and North-east by the Indian states of Mizoram and Tripura and in the South and South-east by Myanmar. It comprises of the districts of Rangamati, Bandarban and Khagrachhri and has a significant population of minorities who belong to Mongoloid group and live in a compact area. The minorities in CHT constitute 0.45 percent of the total population of Bangladesh.

The area formed by the hill tracts east of Bangladesh port city of Chittagong and the Indian states of Tripura and Mizoram, which Subir Bhaumik calls the 'Triangle', has vast stretches of tribal population. The tribes in this region have a long history of enjoying ethnic independence or effective autonomous existence. But by the end of 19th century, the 'Triangle' had come under British control except the kingdom of Tripura, which retained its autonomous existence by accepting British suzerainty.

The partition of the subcontinent in 1947 has shaped events in this troubled area. As CHT had a population, which was 97 percent non-Muslim, it was logically assumed that it would go to India. But the Radcliffe Award dealt the Chakmas an unjust blow by giving the CHT to Pakistan. The Chakmas raised the Indian tri colour at Rangamati on August 15, 1947 in anticipation of the award going in favour of India. As a result, on 21 August, Pakistani troops pulled the Indian flags down. The raising of Indian flags by Chakmas has remained etched in the Bengali psyche as an expression of Chakma betrayal. They remained as suspect even after the birth of Bangladesh.[27]

After independence, a large number of Muslims were rehabilitated in the sparsely populated CHT. The Pakistanis followed a policy of internal colonisation to facilitate with the help of which the special status of CHT was abolished in 1964. The problem was aggravated by the submergence of nearly 40 percent of cultivable land within the Chakma homeland due to the construction of Kaptai Dam on Karnfuli River in 1964. The displacement occurred without any compensation or rehabilitation. Thousands of Chakma refugees took shelter in the neighbouring Indian states of Tripura and Mizoram.

CHT is inhabited by thirteen Buddhist, Christian and Hindu tribes who lived in seclusion as the tract was designated excluded area by the British, much as was the case with hill areas of North-east India. The liberation of Bangladesh in 1971 did not change the situation. Zia-ur-Rehman continued the policy of internal colonisation and in fact encouraged settlement of Bengali families in the hilly tracts. Zia-ur-Rehman settled nearly 30,000 Bengali Muslim families in 1980. The internal colonisation over the years has changed the demography of the area against the Chakmas, as the two tables below will show.

Table 1:Total Population in CHT 1951-91[28]

	1951	1961	1971	1981	1991
Tribals	91%	69%	73%	59%	51%
Non-Tribals	9%	31%	27%	41%	49%

Table 2: Religious Composition in CHT 1991 Census

Muslims	44.12%
Buddhists	43.65%
Hindus	9.01%
Christians	2.28%
Others	0.94%

The change in the demographic profile of CHT has caused tension and introduced ethnic strife. An ethnic insurgency broke out under Prabattya Chattagram Jansanghati (PCJSS) and its armed wing, the Shanti Bahini. Social strife forced more Chakmas to take shelter in neighbouring Tripura as refugees. After much negotiation an agreement was finally reached in 1997 ending the insurgency. But the situation has still to normalise.

Insurgent Linkages Across India-Bangladesh Border

The governments of erstwhile East Pakistan and later Bangladesh have provided sanctuary in CHT to nearly all the insurgent groups of North-east India at sometime or the other. Inter Service Intelligence (ISI) of Pakistan in connivance with Bangladesh intelligence has been very active in this region since 90s and has given covert aid to United Liberation Front of Assam (ULFA).

After the assassination of Sheikh Mujib in 1975 and the installation of an anti-India government, a decision was taken by India to assist the Chakma rebels with arms, supplies and training. As a way of getting even with India, Bangladesh tacitly supported Bijoy Hrangkhawl's Tripura National Volunteer Force (TNVF).[29]

The linkages between ULFA, the main insurgent group of Assam, with the ISI of Pakistan and the Director General of Field Intelligence (DGFI) of Bangladesh have profound implications for the security of North-east. The ULFA-ISI nexus had, in fact, begun way back in 1990 and since then has acquired a sinister dimension; ULFA has already abdicated its original ideology which was rooted in illegal immigration from Bangladesh, now calls the same immigrants as Assamese of East Bengal origin.

Appraisal

The North-east has a long porous border with Myanmar and Bangladesh. Many of the tribes of the North-east have ethnic linkages with the tribes of Myanmar along India-Myanmar border. The similarity of administration evolved by the British in the hill areas, the rise of ethnic insurgencies on both sides of the border, the flourishing illegal narcotic trade from Golden Triangle through the North-east are factors that have combined to give rise to a situation which is ideal for insurgencies to flourish. Similarly, the CHT in Bangladesh has a population, which is ethnically closer to the hill tribes in Mizoram, Assam and Tripura. After the partition of the country in 1947, there has been massive internal migration of Muslim population from other parts of East Pakistan/ Bangladesh to CHT, which has changed its demography in their favour vis-a-vis Buddhists. On the other hand, the demography of Tripura has changed initially due to large-scale influx of Bengalis, mainly Hindus, from erstwhile East Pakistan to escape the communal riots, and later after the creation of Bangladesh, the illegal immigrants have been from both communities. Between 1951 and 1991, the number of Muslims in CHT has increased by 41.84 percent, which was above the state's average rate of increase of 34.30 percent. The concentration of a large illegal immigrant Muslim population along the Indo-Bangladesh border is an ideal condition for fomenting disaffection.

The CHT along with the hill areas of Mizoram and Tripura, aptly called the 'Triangle', is of great importance for India to fight insurgencies in the North-east. The rise of Muslim militancy in Assam in the recent years is yet another dimension which flows directly from the changing demography and geo-political milieu obtaining in this region.

Notes and References

1. Subir Bhaumik, "North-east India: The Evolution of Post Colonial Region" in Partha Chatterjee, ed., *Wages of Freedom*, (New Delhi: OUP, 1998), p301. Quoted by Binalakshmi Nepran, *South Asia's Fractured Frontiers:* Armed Conflict, Narcotics and Small Arms Proliferation in India's North-east. (New Delhi: Mittal Publication, 2002), p 70.
2. *Imperial Gazetteer of India*, (London: Oxford,, 1908), p23
3. NN Acharya, *Brief History of Assam: From earliest times to 1983*, (Guwahati: Osmos Publication, 1987) pp 10-14
4. This is borne out of the names of places and rivers. Ti or Di in Bodo language stands for water. Thus, Dikhu, Dikrong, Digaru and Dibru in Assam and Tista, Koroti, Reti, Kunti, etc. in North Bengal bear testimony to this. See Chandana Bhattacharjee, "Bodoland Movement: Issues and Lessons" in PS Dutta (ed), *North-east and the Indian State: Paradoxes of a Periphery*, (New Delhi: Vikas, 1995), p194
5. NN Acharya, n. 3, p 11
6. Ibid, pp. 60 and 105-106
7. *The Imperial Gazetteer of India*, n. 2, op cit., p24
8. The physiography of the North-east has been compiled from the Gazetteer of India and Baljit Rai, *Demographic Aggression against India*, (Chandigarh: BS Publishers, 1993), pp 55-62
9. Sikkim is the latest addition to the North-east region. But the demographic details and physical characteristics of Sikkim have not been included in this chapter.
10. RK Chatterjee, *India's Land Borders*, (New Delhi: Sterling Publishers, 1978), pp 63, 64. Also see KK Bhattacharjee, *North-east India, Political and Administrative History*, (New Delhi: Cosmo Publications, 1983), p.8.
11. Baljit Rai, *Demographic Aggression against India*, (Chandigarh: BS Publishers, 1993), p. 57.
12. BG Verghese, *India's North-east Resurgent*; (New Delhi: Konark, 1996), p. 335.
13. In 1944, as Allied forces from Assam advanced into Northern Burma, they constructed a supply road from Ledo (India), which finally connected with Burma Road. The Ledo or Stilwell Road, as it was called, was opened in 1945. Burma Road was the highway linking Lashio (Eastern Burma) with Kunming in Yunnan province (China), a distance of 1,154 km. Completed in 1939 but closed by the Japanese in April 1942 at its source at Lashio. See *Encyclopaedia Britannica, Vol 2.*,

15th edition., (Chicago: Encyclopaedia Britannica, Inc, 1987), p. 658.

14. BG Verghese; n. 12., p.35.
15. C Raja Mohan, "Bhutan King in Delhi, Focus on Chumbi Trade Corridor", *The Indian Express*, New Delhi, August 4, 2005.
16. Rediff.com quoted by Renaud Egreteau, *Wooing the Generals,* (New Delhi: Authorspress, Cetre De Sciences Humaines, 2003) p 46
17. Baljit Rai, n.11., p. 60.
18. *Encyclopaedia Britannica*, n. 13. op.cit, p. 658.
19. Seven ethnic minorities are marked by states on Burma's political map under 1974 Constitution: The Chin, Kachin, Karen, Kareni, Rokhini and Shan. Among the other larger minorities are Nagas. There are other substantial ethnic Chinese and Indian minorities throughout the country, but other than Rohingiya Muslims, they are not associated.
20. Renaud Egreteau, n. 18, op cit, p. 58.
21. *Encyclopedia Britannica*, n. 18.,, pp. 218-219.
22. Renaud Egreteau, n.16, p. 62.
23. After the World War II Burma gained independence on January 4, 1948. The name Burma was changed to Myanmar by the then ruling Military Junta in 1989. Here Burma is used for the period before 1989 and Myanmar thereafter; Burman for the major ethnic group and Burmese for the citizen of Burma/Myanmar.
24. National Democratic Alliance was formed in 1976 and consisted of fluctuating alliance of upto a dozen ethnic insurgent groups.
25. Martin Smith; "Burmese Politics after 1988" in Robert H Taylor, ed, *Burma: Political Economy under Military Rule*, (London: A Hurst Company, 2001), p.17.
26. Ibid., p. 34.
27. Sanjoy Hazarika, *Strangers of the Mist: Tales of War and Peace from India's North-east,* (New Delhi: Penguin, *1995,)* pp. 279-280.
28. BP Barua, *Ethnicity and National Integration in Bangladesh; A Study of Chittagong Hill Tracts*, (New Delhi: Har Anand, 2001), p 90
29. Sanjoy Hazarika, n. 27, pp. 280-283..

2

The Ethnic and Demographic Composition

The North-east India is made up of many tribes, cultures, languages, dialects and traditions. There are 209 scheduled tribes: Arunachal has 101, Manipur 28, Assam 23, Nagaland 20, Tripura 18, Meghalaya 14 and Mizoram 05.[1] This agglomerate has nearly 420 languages and dialects: 95 in Nagaland, 87 in Manipur, 112 in Tripura, and the balance in Assam.

The tribes of North-east have close ethnic and cultural links with tribes across the border in Myanmar, Tibet and China. Almost all the tribes barring the Khasis and Jaintias of Meghalaya belong to the Tibeto-Chinese linguistic fold and mainly to its Tibeto-Burman sub family. As these tribes came in waves at different points of time, the ethnic and cultural mosaic of the North-east has wide variations. It has 130 major tribal groups each with distinctive traits and characteristics.[2]

North-east India has stood at the crossroad of history as much as the North-west. The Muslims invaded India through the Khyber Pass but the Ahoms came to India through the Patkai Hills from Upper Burma. We in India are obsessed with the history of the Mughals and the British but know very little about the history of Ahoms whose contribution to the culture and civilisation of the North-east has been immense.

The mountain routes linking India to South-east Asia and China formed the corridor through which Mongoloid races and cultures came to the Brahmaputra Valley and the surrounding hills. It is strange that whereas Buddhism spread to Myanmar, Thailand, Cambodia, Laos and Vietnam, the tribes like Kachins, Shans, Nagas, Mizos and Chins living in the hills and mountains remained animists. One explanation could be that the hills and mountains were so inaccessible that the tribes were left to themselves. There is another little known historical fact that Bodos ruled over almost whole of North-east India at different points of time under different names. The Bodos also occupied North Bengal, parts of Bihar and even some parts of East Bengal and Tripura. Following the advent of Ahoms in the 13th century, they were pushed to remote areas and got scattered.

The Ahoms, a branch of Shan race, crossed the Patkai Range through Burma in 1236 AD under Sukapha. The Ahoms whose numbers did not exceed even thousand had left behind their womenfolk and were thus compelled to marry non-Ahoms, original settlers of the land. The Ahom rulers assimilated the Assamese language and the Hindu religion. From 13th to 16th century, the Ahoms consolidated their power and forged their relationship with the neighbouring principalities, namely Cooch Behar and Kamrup. Kamrup was contiguous to the Mughal territories, and thus became the battleground between the forces of Mughals and Ahoms. Ahom's heroic fight to prevent the Muslim penetration into Assam marked the history of Ahoms in the 17th century.[3]

Manipur and Tripura were never part of Assam. Unlike other states of the North-east, which have been carved out of Assam at different points of time, Manipur retained its independent identity and culture but little is known of its history before 1762 AD. Manipur had a history of attacks by the Burmese, who were finally defeated in the first Anglo-Burman war in 1824. Consequently, the British assumed the title of Manipur and Assam by the Treaty of Yandeboo in 1826. Broadly there are four ethnic groups in Manipur: Meitei, Pangal (Muslim), Naga and Kuki-Chin-Mizo. Meiteis occupy the Imphal Valley and were converted to Vaishnavaite Hinduism some 200 years ago. Manipuri dance and music developed on the themes of Lord Krishna and became one of the four classical dances of India. The tribes occupy the hill areas of Manipur.

The kingdom of Tripura became a part of the Mughal Empire in the 18th century and the British India in the 19th century. Tripura is inhabited by 32 communities of which 19 are tribes[4]; the Chakmas, the Chins, the Halams, the Hill Tipperahs, the Jamatias, the Kukis, the Lushais, the Maghs, the Reangs and nine other tribes. Tripuris and Reangs are the biggest tribal groups and earliest inhabitants. The tribes of Tripura are a Mongolian race and appear to be akin to Murungs of Arakan. The Tripuris belong to Bodo group of Indo-Mongoloid stock whereas the Reangs are considered to be of Kuki origin.

Bengalis of Tripura, who now form the majority, are non-Mongoloid. They follow the same social customs, family traditions and cultural pattern as was prevalent in erstwhile East Bengal. Besides Bengalis and tribals, other heterogeneous sections of the population of Tripura include Manipuris, Nepalese, Oriyas, Biharis, Marwaris and Punjabis. Punjabis are the recent settlers who came when oil exploration was undertaken by Oil and Natural Gas Commission.

The NEFA was renamed as Arunachal and given the status of a full-fledged state of the Indian Union in 1972. The state is a tract of bare, craggy hills, large tropical and alpine forests, steep rugged valleys, and cascading rivers. The Indo-Mongoloid tribes of Monpas, Sherdukpens, Mijis, Akas, Khowas, Sulungs, Apatanis, Daflas, Adis, Mishmis, Khamptis, Singphos, Wanchos, Noctes, Tangsas and many other sub tribes and sub sub tribes inhabit the land. The region is so wild that even today much of it can be traversed only on foot.

The Demographic Profile of Assam

If there is one single factor that is at the heart of the problem in Assam and the other parts of the North-eastern states, it is the changing demographic profile. In fact, the problem began much before the partition of the subcontinent. It will be worthwhile to go back into history to understand the genesis of this problem. After the Treaty of Yandeboo (1824) Assam was brought under the British rule and administered by a British agent and later made part of Bengal Presidency by the Charter Act of 1853. The Bengal Presidency, which included Bengal, Orissa and Bihar, now included Assam as well. It was soon realised that the enlarged Bengal Presidency was too unwieldy to administer and therefore Assam was detached from the Bengal Presidency in 1874, but the two Bengali dominated districts of Sylhet and Cachar remained part of Assam. The rationale of grouping the Bengali dominated districts of Sylhet and Cachar with Assam, which are geographically cut off from the Brahmaputra Valley by hills and Assam Range is hard to explain. The territorial reorganisation of Bengal Presidency in 1874 increased the Muslim population of Assam from five percent to 28.3 percent. This was the beginning of Bengali Muslim factor in the politics of Assam. Although the increase did not alter the demographic balance in the Brahmaputra Valley, it added enormously to the political clout of Muslims in Assam.[5]

The partition of Bengal in 1905 was to aggravate the situation further. Assam ceased to exist as separate political unit and was amalgamated with East Bengal to be known as the province of East Bengal and Assam. This resulted in large-scale influx of peasants from East Bengal districts to Assam. Although the partition was undone in 1912 but by that time the damage to the demographic balance of Assam had already been done. As early as in 1911, the census commissioner warned that the unchecked immigration was "likely to alter permanently the whole future of Assam and destroy, more severely than the Burmese invaders of 1821, the whole structure of Assamese culture and civilisation."

Maximum migration of Bengalese from East Bengal was from the most heavily populated district of Mymensingh. The influx of Mymensinghias increased the district population of Goalpara, which was as low as 1.4 to 2 percent, to a whopping 30 percent for 1910-11. The trend continued in the following decades and extended to other valley districts of Assam. The then census commissioner, CS Mullan had this to observe in his census report of 1931: "Where there is wasteland, thither flock the Mymensinghias. In fact, the way in which they have seized upon the vacant areas in the Assam Valley seems almost uncanny. Without fuss, without tumult, without trouble to the district revenue official, a population that must amount to over half a million has transplanted itself from Bengal to Assam Valley during the last 25 years. It looks like a marvel of administrative organisation on the part of the Government but it is nothing of the sort, the only thing I can compare it to is the mass movement of a long body of ants." He went on further and warned "in another thirty years Sibsagar district will be the only part of Assam in which an Assamese will find himself at home."

The Role of Saadulla

Sir Mohammad Saadulla formed the Muslim League ministry in Assam after the elections of 1937 for provincial legislature with the support of minor parties particularly the Europeans. During his tenure a planned effort was made to encourage migration of Bengali Muslims into Assam with a view to alter its demographic profile. In order to conceal his objective, Saadulla cleverly gave his immigration policy the veneer of contribution to the war effort to grow more food but what he was really after was to increase the Muslim population. Lord Wavell, the viceroy, was to remark: "The chief political problem is the desire of the Muslim ministers to increase the immigration into the uncultivated government lands under the slogan 'Grow more Food' but what they are really after is grow more Muslims". In a letter written in 1945, Saadulla boasted to Liaquat Ali Khan of the Muslim League, that in the four districts of Assam Valley Bengali Muslim immigrants have quadrupled the Muslim population during the last 20 years. There was clearly a bid by the Muslim League to absorb Assam in Pakistan of their conception. That is why immigrants to Assam used to raise the slogan: *"Uppar Allah, Niche Saadulla, Chalo Bhai-o-Sala, Ja kare Allah."* Meaning, with Allah above and Saadulla below, come o' brothers and brothers-in-law, let us do the bidding of Allah.

The Aftermath of Partition

There was widespread resentment amongst the people of Assam to a proposal put forward by the Cripps Mission according to which Assam was to be grouped with the Muslim majority East Bengal to form a Muslim majority State. The people's revolt against this proposal forced the British Government to drop it. It was decided that in the event of partition of Bengal on communal lines, a referendum would be held in Sylhet, to find out if it wanted to stay in Assam or opted for East Pakistan. Thus a referendum was held one month before the independence in which Sylhet had opted for Pakistan.

In the aftermath of the partition of the subcontinent, millions of Hindus from East Pakistan left their homes for an unknown destination in West Bengal, Assam and Tripura. To give adequate time for the move of families, July 26, 1949 (the day of formal adoption of the Constitution of India, but made effective from January 26, 1950) was fixed by which date Hindus from Pakistan could move to India and Muslims from India could move to Pakistan. Sardar Patel even proposed a complete exchange of Hindu and Muslim population between the countries.[6] The proposal was not adopted but in the West the unofficial exchange of population was almost total amid horrific communal riots. This was the biggest exchange of population in history. After July 26, 1949 the movement across the border should have stopped, but in the East it not only continued but also in fact increased. Communal violence in East Bengal had led to large-scale migration of Hindu population into Assam, Tripura, Manipur and West Bengal especially after the Noakhali riots in August 1947. The riots had a backlash in Bihar and many Muslims fled to East Pakistan. The influx from East Pakistan continued periodically between 1947 and 1950 due to communal clashes and Muslim League's reign of terror. During this period not only Hindu refugees poured into India but also Muslims who infiltrated mainly for economic reasons. The infiltration of Bengali Muslims, however, remained camouflaged by their intermingling with Hindu refugees. To put a stop to the illegal immigration, the Immigrants Act (Expulsion from Assam, Act of 1950) was passed mainly on the initiative of Sardar Patel. The Act provided that only those persons who were displaced because of civil disturbances in East Pakistan could come to Assam. When the immigrants, who did not fall into displaced category were deported, Pakistan claimed that Indians were being pushed across the border illegally.[7]

But before the Act could be effectively implemented large-scale communal violence broke out in East Bengal and Assam in February-March 1950. Hindus from East Pakistan fled to India and Muslims from India fled to East Pakistan. In the aftermath of 1950 communal riots, the Nehru-Liaquat Pact was signed on April 8, 1950 and ratified by the Parliament. The Pact provided that "in respect of migrants from East Bengal, West Bengal, Assam and Tripura where communal disturbances have occurred, the landed property of the migrant who returned to his respective homeland by December 31, 1950 would be restored to him. In the case of the migrant who did not return, ownership of all his movable property shall continue to vest in him and he shall have unrestricted right to dispose it of". The net result of the pact was that most of the Muslims who left for East Pakistan from the Indian side due to the outbreak of communal riots in West Bengal and Assam in February/March 1950 came back to Assam before December 31, 1950. But a very few Hindus went back to East Pakistan. On the contrary free movement between East Pakistan and Assam as promised in Nehru-Liaquat Pact resulted in fresh influx of Muslim immigrants into Assam. There was hardly any machinery to keep track of fresh Muslim immigrants, most of whom eventually settled in Assam posing themselves as Indian citizens with the help of their relatives and friends. The problem was anticipated by Sardar Patel as early as 1950, which is evident from the letter he wrote to Pandit Nehru on September 29, 1950: "I am sending herewith a copy of the report which we have received from Intelligence Bureau and which you have also seen because a copy was marked to Dharma Vira (Principal Secretary to the Prime Minister). The report that 15 to 20 percent of the incoming Muslims are new immigrants is rather disquieting... I do not know what we can do about it; but problem must be dealt with. We should either ask the Pakistan Government to stop these men from coming, or we should ask the Assam Government authorities to return them. This is the only course that suggests itself to me, but you might be able to think of some other and better method."[8]

The problem, which was anticipated by Patel so clearly more than 50 years ago, was allowed to fester because of misplaced ideas of secularism and vote bank politics. The communal riots in East Pakistan in 1960s forced fresh waves of Hindus to flee East Pakistan into Tripura, Assam and parts of West Bengal. Along with the Hindu refugees, Muslim migrants continue to move into Tripura and parts of Assam.

The Exodus of 1971

In the wake of Pakistan Army crackdown in East Pakistan in 1971, there was an exodus of refugees into Tripura, Assam and parts of West Bengal. Initially the minority Hindus, who were accused of collaborating with the Awami League, were targeted. According to Sanjay Hazarika, an early estimate of the time said that of the first seven million refugees, at least six million were Hindus.[9] But according to Marcus Franda who had lived in India for more than ten years and worked with the American University Field Staff Programme, the number of refugees was initially 6 .8 million listed in the camps and three million living with friends and relatives.[10] An External Affairs Ministry of August 1,1971 gave the figure of 6.97 million Hindus; 5,41,000 Muslims and 44,000 others.[11] By early March 1972, only 2,00,000 refugees remained in the camps and 8,17,000 continued to stay with their friends and relatives in West Bengal, Tripura, Meghalaya and Assam. The balance, nine million, had been sent back to Bangladesh within three months of its liberation.[12] For all practical purposes, the last million have continued to stay in India for good.

The demographic profile of North-eastern states, mainly Assam and Tripura, has undergone a sea change following the continuous immigration from East Pakistan and now Bangladesh. The reasons for this are mainly economic. Besides there are other contributory factors like the demand for cheap Bangladeshi labour and in some cases encouragement given to migrants to create a vote bank. It is difficult to assess accurately the exact number of Muslim and Hindu migrants, particularly the Muslims who try to hide their identity in the hope of obtaining Indian citizenship. Thus only broad estimates can be arrived at based on figures given by the Governments of India and Bangladesh from time to time and by researchers. The process of extrapolation may arrive at a reasonably fair idea of the extent of illegal immigration.

A study of migration by a Bangladeshi researcher, Sharifa Begum, which acknowledged the massive migration from Bangladesh into India, has some interesting figures. According to her 3.15 to 3.5 million people migrated to India from Bangladesh between 1951 and 1961. She placed the number of migrants from Bangladesh at 1.5 million between 1961 and 1974, the years when national censuses were held in Bangladesh. This does not take into account nearly 10 million refugees who fled East Pakistan in 1971 and from which nearly one million never returned to Bangladesh. Thus we have a figure of not less than six million migrants in twenty-three years.[13]

Situation after Emergence of Bangladesh

People infiltrating into Assam, West Bengal, Tripura, Bihar and other parts of India after liberation of Bangladesh are not refugees but are illegal migrants seeking employment and land. The magnitude of the problem has assumed serious proportions as large-scale infiltration has changed the demography of many border districts of Assam, West Bengal and Bihar. As per internal note prepared by the Ministry of Home Affairs, Government of India, in March 1992, the figures available (in 1987) with the Government of West Bengal put the number of infiltrators in the state around 4.4 million. For Assam, the note puts the figures at (in 1992) nearly two to three million. Infiltrations from Bangladesh have also seriously affected Tripura and Bihar.[14] According to TV Rajeshwar, former Governor of West Bengal and former Director of Intelligence Bureau, while the unofficial estimate of Bangladeshis living in India in 1996 was 15 million, which included about seven million in West Bengal, about five million in Assam and about two million in Bihar, the official estimate was said to be 10 million plus with corresponding reduction of figures for the respective states.[15]

In recent years the pattern of illegal immigration from Bangladesh has changed in that Muslims have been infiltrating in much larger numbers. In late 1991, Shri Jyoti Basu, the Chief Minister of West Bengal revealed in the State Assembly that in the first six months of 1991, of the 39,055 Bangladeshis intercepted while crossing the border as many as 28,000 were Muslims. The figures released by BSF from time to time confirm this trend. [16]

Lt Gen SK Sinha (Retd), Governor of Assam in his report on "Illegal Migration into Assam" dated 8th November 1998, submitted to the President, gives figures, which are revealing. According to the report, Shri Inderjeet Gupta, the then Minister of Home Affairs stated in Parliament on May 6, 1997 that there were 10 million illegal migrants residing in India. Quoting Ministry of Home Affairs sources, *'India Today'*, the weekly magazine, gave the breakdown of 11.1 million illegal immigrants in India by states; West Bengal 5.4 million, Assam 4 million, Tripura 0.8 million, Bihar 0.5 million, Maharashtra .05 million, Rajasthan .05 million and Delhi 0.3 million.[17] Again as per the Governor's report, Hiteshwar Saikia, the then Chief Minister of Assam stated in the State Assembly on April 10, 1992 that there were three million illegal migrants in Assam although later he denied saying it. Recent enumeration of electoral list in Assam by the Election Commission shows more than 30 percent increase in voters in 17 assembly constituencies and more than 20 percent in 40 constituencies between 1994-97. All India average growth for a three year period intervening the two intensive revisions in 1994 and 1997 is just seven percent, whereas the growth of Assam for the same period is 16.4 percent (quoted in the Governor's Report to the President).

The relative percentage of decadal growth of Assam and All India, shown below, are also instructive:

Table 1 : Percentage of Decadal Growth of Population

Year	Assam	All India
1901-1911	16.99	5.75
1911-1921	20.48	0.31
1921-1931	19.91	11.00
1931-1941	20.40	14.22
1941-1951	19.93	13.31
1951-1961	34.98	21.64
1961-1971	34.95	24.80
1971-1981	23.36	24.66
1981-1991	24.24	23.86
1991-2001	18.85	21.34

Notes:

There was no census in Assam in 1981. The figures for the decade 1971-91 growth rate indicated have been worked out on the basis of 1971-1991 growth rate.

The much higher percentage of growth rate in Assam from 1911-71 over All India growth rate indicates migration into Assam. The All India growth rate for 1921 should be treated as an aberration.

The reduced percentage of growth rate for Assam in 1971-1991 presents a distorted picture unless one relates it to community-wise percentage of growth in Assam as compared to All India figures. This is shown below: -

Table 2: Community-wise Percentage Growth in Assam

	Assam		All India	
Year	**Hindu**	**Muslims**	**Hindu**	**Muslims**
1951-61	33.71	38.35	20.29	26.61
1961-71	37.17	30.99	23.72	30.85
1971-91	41.89	77.42	48.38	55.04

Source: - "Population and its Growth, India (1901-2001)" Census of India, Series 1, Paper 1, Statement 2, p 34

Explanatory Notes:

The decadal growth rate of both Hindus and Muslims for the periods 1951-61 and 1961-71 was higher than their respective All India growth rate, indicating migration of both communities in Assam. However, during the period 1971-91 Hindu growth rates in Assam was much less than All India figure. Possibly this was due to large-scale population of non Assamese moving out of Assam in the wake of Assam agitation. In the case of Muslims, the Assam growth rate was much higher than the All India figure. This indicates continued large-scale Muslim illegal migration into Assam.[18] *The explanatory notes form part of the Governor's report.*

Assam's population in the last 20 years (1971-1991) had grown from 15 million to close to 23 million. The population has grown to 26,638,407 as per 2001 census. There was no census in 1981. In 1991 census the Hindus comprised 15 million or 67.13 percent of the population and Muslims 6.3 million or just over 28 percent. Trends indicate that while non-Muslim population grew at the rate of 45.39 percent over the 1971 level that of Muslims rose at 77.42 percent.[19]

Demographic Changes in Tripura

Tripura is often identified as the classic example of a state where its original inhabitants were rendered minority by influx of Bengalee migrants. It is commonly understood that the demographic change in favour of Bengalis occurred after partition of the country, when Bengalis in large numbers fled from East Bengal and took refuge in Tripura. But the immigration of Bengalis to Tripura is not of recent origin. Bengalee settlements in Tripura started in the 14th century. Tribal kings of Tripura had a '*zamindari*', Chakla Roshanabad, under the British in the adjoining Bengali districts of Tipperah, Noakhali and Sylhet. Its population was overwhelmingly Bengali. Ratna Manikya, who ruled over Tripura in the later part of 13th century, had settled about 10,000 Bengalis from various walks of life in his kingdom. In the 19th century, Bengalis were encouraged to settle in Tripura to develop plough cultivation. Their gradual immigration resulted in their becoming a sizeable minority by the beginning of the 20th century as will be evident from the table showing the percentage of tribal population to total population of Tripura: -

Table 3 : Tripura, Percentage of Tribal Population to Total Population

Year	Percentage of tribal population to total population	Year	Percentage of tribal population to total population
1874-75	63.77	1941	53.16
1881	52.19	1951	37.23
1891	51.09	1961	31.50
1901	52.89	1971	28.95
1911	48.47	1981	28.44
1921	56.37	1991	30.95
1931	52.00		

The demographic metamorphosis, however, came soon after the partition in 1947, as the table below will show.

Table 4: Decade-wise Variations in Population of Tripura

Year	Variation %	Year	Variation %
1901-1911	32.48	1951-1961	76.87
1911-1921	32.59	1961-1971	36.28
1921-1931	25.63	1971-1981	31.92
1931-1941	34.14	1981-1991	34.30
1941-1951	25.87		

Note: The abnormal increase in the decade 1951-1961 was due to influx of Bengalis from East Pakistan after partition.

In the decade 1949-1959, following the partition, 3,73,500 refugees entered Tripura from erstwhile East Pakistan. After the communal riots of 1963, Bengali immigration into the state swelled into a tide. In the year 1964-1965 itself 1,00304 people migrated to Tripura. The total number of immigrants entering into Tripura between 1947-1971 is estimated to be 6,09,998.[20]

Muslim Population

The population of Tripura is overwhelmingly Hindu. According to 1991 census, 86 percent of the population was Hindu; both Bengalis and tribals are Hindus. Contrary to popular belief the absolute number of Muslim population increased from 1,36,981 to 2,30,002 between 1951 and 1961. This rise was above normal rate of growth and can be explained only by fresh immigration from East Pakistan. True, the Muslim share to the total population declined during the same period. But a marginal decline – from slightly more than 21 percent to just above 20 percent, which was caused by immigration of Hindus in larger proportion. Thus in the first decade of partition both Hindus and Muslims immigrated to Tripura. In the next decade 1961-1971, the Muslim population decreased sharply. It was halved from 2,30,002 to 1,03,962, though population in general increased substantially. The massive decline in Muslim population can be explained by organised eviction of Muslim immigrants by Hindu refugees. After the emergence of Bangladesh in 1971, the Muslim population in Tripura is on the rise again. Between 1981 and 1991, the number increased again by 41.84 percent. This is much above the state's average rate of increase of 34.3 percent during the same period. This confirms the speculation of silent immigration of Muslim along with Hindu refugees from Bangladesh.[21]

As stated earlier the population of Tripura is overwhelmingly Hindu. The Christian population is very small. In 1951 there were only 6181 Christians in Tripura, but the number trebled between 1981 and 1991. This indicates increasing presence and success of Christian missionaries and their work. This could also imply that the propaganda about discrimination against Christians is not based on facts.[22]

Demographic Changes in Nagaland

During 1991-2001, the population growth rate of the country had declined nominally. While the states like Tripura, Mizoram and Arunachal were in conformity with this trend, the population growth rate of Nagaland registered a perceptible increase. It was normally higher in Manipur and noticeably lower in Assam. The phenomenal rise in population of Nagaland can only be explained by immigration from Bangladesh, which has been inadvertently abetted by the younger generation of Nagas who abhor jobs involving manual labour, both skilled or unskilled. Like in Assam, in Nagaland too, one can see this happening. In Dimapur itself there are nearly 70,000 Bangladeshi immigrants, doing manual labour, rickshaw pulling, construction work and so on. A similar situation exists in Kohima. Young Nagas want easy Delhi money. In Dimapur area, many Bangladesi Muslims have married Sema girls; they are named *'Semias'*, i.e. marriage between *Mias* (Bangladeshi Muslims) and Sema Nagas.[23]

Nepali Migrants

The Indo-Nepal treaty of 1950 allows free flow of each other nationals across the border. Indo-Nepal migration is unique. No documents are required, no registration is done at border check posts and by and large no questions are asked. In the 19th and 20th centuries the British encouraged Nepalese to immigrate to Darjeeling, Kalimpong, Sikkim and Assam for work mainly in road construction and tea plantations. The unrestricted immigration of Nepalese from early 19th century has already changed the ethnic profile of Sikkim, Darjeeling and Kalimpong in their favour. The census of 1951 placed the Nepalese population in Assam at 1,01,335, which increased to 3,53,673 in the census of 1971.[24] According to one estimate, in 1996, there were an estimated four million Nepalese in India. The exact population of Nepalese (of Nepal origin) in North-east India is not available. The level of immigration from Nepal into India is not considered very significant. The Nepalese immigrants have seldom faced any hostility in India. In fact they have been held in high esteem for their faithfulness, honesty and hard work. But the situation had changed after the agitation in Assam against foreigners in the 1980s. The movement against foreigners spread from Assam to other states of the North-east. In 1985, nearly 10,000 Nepalese had to flee from Meghalaya in the wake of anti foreigner agitation. At other time, violence against outsiders has similarly resulted in Nepalese having to leave Mizoram, Manipur and Assam. The imposition of Restricted Area Permit on Nepalese visiting certain areas of North-east, which came into effect in 1996, has caused resentment amongst them. Hostility has been building up against recent arrivals of Nepalese in Assam,

Meghalaya and other states of the North-east, resulting in growing disquiet in the scattered Nepalese settlements in the region.

The Arrival of Bengali Immigrants

In the beginning of 19th century, the British started extending the railways into remote North-east region to facilitate communication and access to markets. Labourers from Mymensingh, Sylhet, Rangpur and other districts of Bengal were brought to work on the railways. As the administration, trade and commerce in the North-east began to grow, the British brought a large number of educated Bengalis middle class mainly Hindus, to man the various administrative posts, which resulted in most of the white collar jobs going to the Bengalees in Assam. This was to cause tension between the Bengalees and Assamese after Independence.

Immigration of Other Indians into Assam

The British started tea cultivation in Assam in 1830 and explored oil in Digboi in 1890. As there was a shortage of local labour, tens of thousands of labourers from Bihar and Orissa, mainly from Chotanagpur region, were brought to North-east to work on oil pipeline and in the tea plantations. Although this group of migrants is quite large, they were rarely seen as a threat to Assamese culture. But in the closing decades of 20th century, Bodo militants, who have resorted to ethnic cleansing to bolster their claim to a separate Bodoland, have targeted this group.

The Marwaris from Rajasthan, also came to Assam looking for new opportunities and captured the trade and commerce, tea, jute and plywood industries. The Punjabis became dominant in government contracts and transport sectors. The Bengali Hindu cornered bulk of the white-collar jobs and services. Punjabis, Biharis and Bengalis monopolised even semi-skilled jobs, which caused great resentment amongst the Assamese and contributed to the growth of insurgency in Assam in the 1980s.

Analysis of the Migration Pattern

The phenomenon of migration into Assam is not a recent one. It really started with the advent of the British in Assam after the Treaty of Yandeboo. Initially, a large population of Bengalis, mostly Muslims from the districts of Mymensingh and Sylhet, migrated mainly to the Brahmaputra Valley, looking for land. Then came the planned shipment of labourers from Bengal and later East Bengal to lay the railway tracks in Assam. This was followed by the influx of tea garden labourers from Bihar and Orissa. The migration of Muslims from Bengal reached its peak in 1930s and 1940s, particularly from Mymensingh district of East Bengal, encouraged by Saadulla and his Muslim League ministry. The aim was to change the demography ratio of Assam in favour of Muslims with a view to lay a claim for the inclusion of Assam in East Pakistan at the time of partition.

Illegal migration from East Pakistan continued even after the Independence. A few paragraphs from the booklet 'Influx' published in 1963 by the Ministry of External Affairs, Government of India, will provide an official acknowledgement of the problem: 'The census operation in 1961 revealed the magnitude of the problem of infiltration from East Pakistan. The table below gives the statistical picture of the growth of Muslim population in Assam, West Bengal and Tripura.'[25]

Table 5: Growth of Muslim Population in Assam, West Bengal and Tripura (Figures in thousands)

State	Year		Percentage increase
	1951	1961	
Assam	1996	2765	39
West Bengal	5118	6995	38
Tripura	131	230	68

In recent years the pattern of illegal migration from Bangladesh has changed in that Muslims have been infiltrating into India in much larger numbers. Another observation made in the Ministry of Home Affairs Note of March 1992 is that more and more Muslim immigrants are settling down in the border areas. Consequently large stretches of the border in Assam, West Bengal and Bihar are becoming predominantly inhabited by Bangladeshi Muslims.

It is necessary to make a distinction between refugees and infiltrators. A large number of Hindus had to flee East Pakistan/ Bangladesh due to political and religious persecution. The flow of people into Assam and West Bengal after the liberation of Bangladesh was not of refugees but of illegal migrants, mostly Muslims seeking employment and land. The early immigrants from East Pakistan to West Bengal were predominantly Hindus. However, from early 1980s the ratio of Muslim immigrants has increased. The political class is sharply divided over the status of migrants from Bangladesh; the Congress is in favour of treating all as illegal migrants, whereas the BJP is of the view that Bangladeshi Hindu migrants should be treated as refugees. (Rajya Sabha debate, *The Indian Express*, New Delhi, August 24, 2005, p 4). There is some logic in the stand taken by the BJP. The population of Hindus has progressively declined in East Pakistan/ Bangladesh; declining from 22 percent of the population in 1951 to 18.4 percent in 1961.[26] The Hindu population, according to one estimate, must have fallen below 10 percent of the total population of Bangladesh by now. Surely, this abnormal decline must be factored in any discussion while deciding the status and fate of Bangladeshi migrants.

Lt Gen SK Sinha, in his report to the President, cited earlier, pointed out that the Muslim population in Assam went up from 24.68 percent in 1951 to 28.42 percent in 1991. As per 1991 census, four districts (Dhubri, Goalpara, Barapeta and Hailakandi) have become Muslim majority areas. Two more districts (Nowgong and Karimganj) should have become so by 1998 and another district (Morgaon) is fast approaching the situation. The Governor warned that if the influx of Bangladeshis is not checked they may swamp the Assamese people and may sever the North-east landmass from the rest of India. Similar apprehensions were expressed by Mr TV Rajeshwar, the former Governor of West Bengal and former Director of Intelligence Bureau, in a series of three articles published in *The Hindustan Times*, (Patna) dated February, 7, 8 and 9, 1996, which drew attention to the concentration of Muslim population in the districts of West Bengal bordering Bangladesh from 24 Parganas to West Dinajpur and the contiguous Kishanganj district of Bihar. This contiguous landmass with a population of 28 million has a clear Muslim majority. Mr Rajeshwar goes on to warn: "There is a distinct danger of another Muslim country, speaking Bengali predominantly, emerging in the Eastern part of India at a time when India may find itself weakened politically and militarily.[27] Rajeshwar goes on to paint a grim scenario: "Let us look at the map of East India – starting from the north 24 Parganas district, proceeding through Nadia, Murshidabad, Malda, and West Dinajpur before entering the narrow neck of land lying through Raiganj and Dakola of Islampur subdivision before passing through the Kishanganj district of East Bihar to enter Siliguri. Proceed further and take a look at the North Bengal districts of Darjeeling, Jalpaiguri and Cooch Behar before entering Assam, and its districts of Dhubri, Goalpara, Bongaigaon, Kokrajhar and Barpeta, a more sensitive region in Asia is difficult to locate..."

The influx of illegal immigration has changed the demographic profile of Assam and border districts of West Bengal and Bihar with frightful political and security consequences. The foreboding expressed by Henry Kissinger, the former Secretary of State of USA, in his book "The White House Years" published in 1979 merits attention. This is what he had to say: "The inevitable emergence of Bangladesh – which we postulated – presented India with fierce long term problems. For Bangladesh was in effect East Bengal separated only by religion from India's most fractious and most separatist state, West Bengal. They share language, tradition, culture, and, above all, a volatile national character. Whether it turned nationalist or radical, Bangladesh would over the years accentuate India's centrifugal tendencies. It might set a precedent for the creation of other Muslim States, carved this time out of India. Once it was independent, its Muslim heritage might eventually lead to a rapprochement with Pakistan."

The rise in the Bengalee population of Tripura was initiated by the kings of Tripura themselves in the 13th century and by the beginning of the 20th century they had become a sizeable minority. The metamorphosis, however, came after the partition in 1947, when refugees from the newly created East Pakistan poured into Tripura. The situation has not abated even after the creation of Bangladesh in 1971; only the pattern of immigration has changed in that Muslims have been infiltrating illegally in large numbers.

Notes and References

1. PS Dutta, ed., *North-east and the Indian States: Paradoxes of a Periphery*, (New Delhi: Vikas Publishing House, 1995), p. 3.
2. Of the 5653 communities in India, 635 are tribal. Of the latter, a little over 200 categories are found in the North-east. KS Singh, *People of India, vol (ix), 1993.*
3. S K Bhuyan, *Tungkhungia Buranji: A History of Assam*, (Calcutta: OUP, 1993), p p. xvii-xviv.
4. KS Singh, *People of India: Tripura*, Vol xvi, (Calcutta: Scagull Books, 1996), p xiii. Also Imperial Gazetteer of India, Vol xiii, New Edition, (London: , Oxford, 1908), p. 119.
5. For details of demographic profile of Assam before and after the reorganisation of Bengal Presidency see Baljit Rai, *Demographic*

Aggression against India, (Chandigarh: BS Publishers, 1993), pp 107-109..

6. Amiya Kumar Das, *Assam's Agony*, First Edition, (New Delhi: Lancers, 1982, pp. 55,56..
7. Ibid, p. 54.
8. Durga Das, ed., *Sardar Patel Correspondence*, 1949-50, Vol. 9. (Ahmedabad: Navjivan Trust,, 1974), p .220.
9. Sanjay Hazarika, *Stranger of the Mist: Tales of War and Peace from India's North-east*, (New Delhi: Penguin, 1995), pp. 27-29.
10. Ibid.
11. Ibid.
12. Ibid.
13. Ibid, pp. 30-32.
14. Internal note prepared by the Ministry of Home Affairs, Government of India, March 1992. Reproduced in Arun Shourie, *A Secular Agenda*, (India: Harper and Collins, 1998), pp. 269-293.
15. TV Rajeshwar, "Migration or Invasion", *The Hindustan Times*, Patna, February 7, 1996.
16. *Internal Note by Ministry of Home Affairs*, n. 15, p. 273.
17. *India Today*, New Delhi, August 10, 1998, quoting Ministry of Home Affairs /Intelligence Bureau sources.
18. *Governor of Assam Report on Illegal Migration into Assam* to the President vide Governor's DO Letter No. GSAG3/98 dated November 8, 1998.
19. Sanjoy Hazarika, "India's North-east: The Challenges of Regionalism and Migration", in Kousav J Azam, ed., *Ethnicity and Identity in South Asia, (*New Delhi: *South Asia* Publishers, *2001)*, p. 199.
20. SR Bhattacharjee, *Tribal Insurgency in Tripura: A study in Exploration and Causes*, (New Delhi: Inter India Publications, 1989). Also Gayatri Bhattacharya, *Refugee Rehabilitation and its Impact on Tripura's Economy*, (Guwahati: Osmos Publications, 1988).
21. Satyabarta Chakrabarty, *Identity, Autonomy, Development: A Study of Tripura Tribal Area Autonomous District Council*, (Calcutta: Ekushe, 2000).
22. Ibid.
23. NS Narhari, *Security Threats to North-east India*, (New Delhi: Manas, 2002), p. 122.
24. See Baljit Rai, *Demographic Aggression against India*, (Chandigarh: BS Publishers, 1993), p. 5.
25. Quoted by Bhanu Pratap Shukla,, *What ails India's North-east*, (New Delhi: Suruchi Sahitya, 1980), pp. 20,21.

26. See, Talukdar Maniruzzsaman, "The Future of Bangladesh", in A Jeyaratnam Wilson and Denis Dalton, *The States of South Asia: Problem of Integration,* (London: C Hurst & Co.,1982).
27. TV Rajeshwar, "Creation of New States", *The Hindustan Times*, Patna, February 7, 8 and 9, 1996.

3

NAGALAND

The origin of the word 'Naga' is shrouded in mystery. It is however clear that the appellation "Nagas" was quite foreign to Nagas themselves. It is only after the advent of the British that the word 'Naga' began to be widely used for tribes inhabiting the Naga Hills. Before that the inhabitants of these hills knew themselves by their tribe names. "To most Assamese and people in east India, it meant naked hill people, who were head hunters"[1].

It is not intended here to go into anthropological or racial origins of the Naga tribes, but briefly, they belong to Indo-Mongoloid family and migrated from west and north to their present habitat over a period of time from different directions. They do not have a common language or dialect; each tribe has its own dialect or dialects, which are unintelligible to other tribes. For the purpose of this study the term Naga includes the various tribes who have spread across the present states of Nagaland, Manipur, Arunachal Pradesh and some parts of Assam, as also across the border in parts of Myanmar.

The chronicles of Ahom Kings, Buranjis, throw some light on Naga relations with Ahoms. The first contact of the Nagas with them took place during the time of Sukapha, the founder of the Ahom kingdom in about 1228 AD. As the Ahom kingdom expanded, there were frequent clashes between the Ahoms and the Nagas, but on the whole the Ahoms kept the bordering tribes under control and extracted tributes from them. In return, the Nagas were granted revenue free lands and fishing waters on the understanding that they would desist from making any predatory raids into plains. The Ahoms never tried to conquer the Nagas and amalgamate them in their kingdom but left them to live the way they liked. The Nagas lived in comparative isolation during the 600 years rule of Ahoms over Assam. It was only after the conquest of Assam by the British in 1826 that they came in contact with the British. The first contact was established during Anglo-Burmese war when Capt Neurf Ville crossed the Patkai Hills to free 6,000 Naga slaves from Singhpos. In 1832, Capts Jenkins and Pemberton led an expedition of 700 Manipuri troops and 800 coolies across the Naga Hills and occupied Papoolongmai in the face of fierce resistance by the Angami Nagas. Nearly a decade later in 1841, Lt Briggs in conjunction with Capt Gordon led another expedition into Angami area, which resulted in demarcation of the boundary between Manipur and Naga Hills and payment of yearly tribute by the Angamis to the British. These engagements were mainly to protect the tea gardens of Assam from raids by Angamis. The contacts with the Nagas grew as the British opened up communications between Assam and Manipur through the Naga Hills. But the agreements between the British and the Nagas proved to be temporary, as no sooner the troops had left the hills, the Nagas began their marauding raids into the plains. Between 1849 and 1850 as many as ten expeditions were sent under Lt Vincent. In the tenth expedition the British captured a strong Naga fort at Khonoma and fought a bloody battle against the tribes of Kekrema, but the British troops were withdrawn in 1851.[2] This was in pursuance of the new policy of Lord Dalhousie under which it was decided to abstain from any type of intervention in the affairs of the Nagas. In his minute of February 20, 1851 Lord Dalhousie recorded: "I dissent entirely from the policy which is recommended of what is called obtaining control, that is to say, of taking possession of these hills and establishing our sovereignty over their savage inhabitants. Our possession could bring no profit to us, and would be as costly to us as it would be unproductive - - - Hereafter, we should confine ourselves to our own ground; protect it as it can and must be protected; not meddle in the feuds or fight of these savages; encourage trade with them as long as they are peaceful towards us and rigidly exclude them for all communication either to sell what they have got, or buy what they want if they should become so turbulent or troublesome."[3]

The policy of non-interference lasted for the next 15 years, which emboldened the Nagas and they made twenty-two raids in the Assam Valley in 1851 alone. The situation became so hopeless that in 1862 the Commissioner of Assam in a report to the Lt Governor wrote: "the non-interference policy is excellent in theory, but the government will probably be inclined to think that it must be abandoned."[4] The British at the instance of Cecil Beadon, Lt Governor of Bengal, adopted a policy of slow but positive control over Naga territory. In keeping with this policy, Lt Gregory established his headquarters at Samaguting in 1866 and by 1877 the British had decided on a forward policy and consequently two posts, one at Kohima and the other at Wokha, were established in 1878 to check Angami raids on Nowgong and to dominate Lotha country east of Dikhu. The Naga Hill district was formed in 1881 mainly with Angami and Lotha areas.

Beyond the administered area, the British created a zone of political control. The Ao area of Mokokchung was brought under the British administration in 1890. The expansion of administered hill district continued eastward on one pretext or the other. In 1907 AW Davis, Deputy Commissioner of Nagaland observed: "we shall have no real peace until we have absorbed the whole of hill area between this and Chindwin. This can be done gradually and economically. As it is, the huge area of uncontrolled hill country between Assam and Burma is an anomaly." The views of local officers were echoed by Sir

Archdale Earl, the Chief Commissioner, who said in 1914 that the process of expansion would have to be continued, "until the whole of the country between Assam and Burma had been taken over."[5] The expansion of administered hill district continued till 1927 when the Melomi (Meluri) and Primi (Akhegwo) were included in the Naga Hill district in 1922.[6]

The Formation of Naga Club

The first stirrings of Naga identity and politics started with the formation of Naga Club in 1918. The members of this club were mainly government servants and many Nagas who had returned from France after the World War I. When the Statutory Commission, headed by Sir John Simon, visited Kohima on January 10, 1929, representatives of the Naga Club submitted a memorandum to the commission demanding that Nagas be excluded from the scope of proposed constitutional reform and kept under direct administration of the British. They told the commission: "you are the only people who have conquered us and when you go, we should be as we were." However, in the report of the Simon Commission, the representation made by the Nagas was ignored and thus the Government of India Act 1935 came into effect from May 1, 1937, making Naga Hills Backward Tract of 1919 as Excluded Area under Assam but directly under the administration of the Governor.

The Japanese invasion of Burma during the World War II and the battles fought by the British in the hills around Kohima had brought the Nagas in contact with the outside world. Their leaders were exposed to the prevailing sentiments against British and European colonialism in Asia. But there was considerable uncertainty amongst the Naga leaders in deciding their political future. When it became clear that India would soon become a free country, the leadership of Nagas was in the hands of moderate leaders like Alibaimti and T. Sakhrie. Although there were different shades of opinion, some for independence for the Nagas, but there was no overwhelming demand or unanimity for immediate separation from India.

The Formation of Naga National Council

After the war, Sir Charles Pawsey, the District Commissioner, established an organisation called Naga Hills District Tribal Council with the main objective of bringing together all Naga tribes on one platform, to help in repairing the damages caused by the war. The council was converted into a political organisation at its Wokha Conference in February 1946, and was named NNC with T Alibaimti as its President and T Sakhrie as the General Secretary. In its early years it was the only organised political formation, which subsequently became the political wing of the underground federal government.

The idea of complete independence had not yet crystallised. Sakhrie declared in Kohima in December 1946: "The NNC stands for the unification of all the Naga tribes and their freedom. Our country is connected with India, connected in many ways. We should continue that connection. I do not mind whether future India be a Congress Government or a League Government. But as a distinct community, as I stated before, we must also develop according to our own genius and taste. We will enjoy home-rule in our country, but on broader issues be connected with India."[7] T Alibaimti, the president of NNC, expressed similar sentiments in a public meeting at Kohima thus: "You are looking beyond the ocean for help. Cutting it short, I declare to you that Great Britain will never endanger her foreign policy for the sake of you. Lastly, never forget that you have been excluded for enough time, excluded from every angle of life, who is responsible for it? I have but one word to say, our country is connected with India in many ways. We should continue that connection."[8]

As Independence came closer, NNC sent a political memorandum to Lord Mountbatten in February 1947, suggesting that India might act as guardian power for a period of ten years after which Naga people would be free to determine their political future. The NNC took the same position before the advisory committee for Assam headed by Gopinath Bordoloi. To break the impasse, discussions were held between Akbar Hydari, Governor of Assam, and Naga leaders at Kohima from 27 to 29 May 1947, which led to the Nine-Point Agreement, popularly known as Akbar Hydari Agreement. The preamble of the agreement recognised "the right of the Nagas to develop themselves according to their freely expressed wishes," but Clause 9 of the agreement which read as follows, created controversy over its interpretation:

Clause 9

"The Governor of Assam or the Agent of the Government of Indian Union will have a special responsibility for a period of ten years to ensure the due observance of this agreement; at the end of the period NNC will be asked whether they require the above agreement to be extended for a further period, or a new agreement regarding future of the Naga people arrived at."

The NNC claimed that Clause 9 of the agreement gave the Nagas right to complete independence on the expiry of ten-year period, whereas the Government of India interpreted the agreement in the light that Nagas had the freedom only to suggest revision of administrative pattern after ten years, an interpretation, which was unacceptable to the NNC.[9]

Despite the meeting with Gandhi, the NNC under pressure from Phizo declared Independence on August 14, 1947 and the next day the NNC under the presidentship of Temjenliba unanimously amended Clause 9 to read: -

"The Governor of Assam as the agent of the Government of India will have a special responsibility for a period of ten years to ensure the due observance of the Agreement

at the end of the period the Nagas will be free to decide their own future."[10]

An ultimatum was issued on November 4, 1947 to the effect that unless the Government of India implemented the Akbar Hydari Agreement, as amended by NNC within one month, the Nagas would form their own parallel government.[11] The ultimatum was however not carried out in deference to the statements issued by Gandhi. In July 1948, a delegation of Naga moderates met Bordoloi to seek a written assurance for the implementation of Akbar Hydari Agreement, which was given signed by both the Governor and the Chief Minister of Assam."[12] This assurance was sought to set at rest the apprehensions of some of the Naga leaders that the provisions of Akbar Hydari Agreement were nullified by the provision in the draft constitution. It was explained to the delegation at length that the draft constitution was in no way inconsistent with the agreement. On the contrary, it prescribed the machinery whereby the agreement might be translated into action. In the light of earlier submissions of the NNC to the Governor of Assam, it was obviously intended that at the end of ten years, the Nagas would be free to select for themselves the exact administrative set-up within the constitution. They would be free to remain in Assam or join Manipur.[13] However the last paragraph was interpreted differently by NNC, and became the genesis of all future convulsions.

When Nehru visited Assam in December 1951, a five man delegation led by Phizo met him at Silighat (Tezpur) and presented the result of the plebiscite, Nehru is reported to have replied that in the present context of affairs, both in India and abroad, it is impossible for a moment to consider such an absurd demand for independence.[14] The next meeting of Phizo with Nehru at New Delhi on March 1952 turned out to be stormy and quite unpleasant for both. When

Phizo insisted on his demand for independence for Nagas, Nehru was furious and is reported to have replied: "Even if heaven falls and India goes to pieces and blood runs the country, I will not allow the Nagas to be independent."[15] The visit of Nehru with U Nu, the Prime Minister of Myanmar, on March 30, 1953 to Kohima was another unhappy episode. The Nagas walked out of the meeting organised in their honour when they were prevented from submitting any memorandum demanding self-determination or making an address to that effect.[16]

The Beginning of Insurgency

Phizo and his followers were now on a course of confrontation with the government. The Nagas boycotted the first general elections of free India in 1952. Sakhrie opposed Phizo on this headlong confrontation with India as he felt that Nagas were ill prepared for such a clash. Sakhrie was later tortured and murdered. Phizo toured the districts extensively and exhorted the people not to pay taxes to the government, which led to clashes between his followers and the law enforcement agencies. The first violent incident occurred in June 1953 in Tuensang, then part of NEFA. The violence continued in 1954; the rebels ambushed patrols of Assam Rifles, telephone wires were cut, government buildings were set on fire and people were forced to meet the requirement of food and other expenses of the hostiles. By 1955 violence had escalated to an alarming degree and had spread from Tuensang to the neighbouring areas of Mokokchung. To stem the tide of violence, nine police posts were opened in Tuensang Frontier Area in 1953. Simultaneously the Assam Rifles began operations in Tuensang from where they spread to Mokokchung area. Both Tuensang and Mokokchung were declared disturbed areas under the newly enacted Assam Maintenance of Public Order (Autonomous District) Act-1953 and the Assam Disturbed Areas Act-1955.

The Army is Called Out

NNC formally declared the formation of Federal Government of Nagaland (FGN) in March 1956, and hoisted its flag at Phenshinyu, some 40 km from Kohima, in the Rengma area. A parliament *(Ho Ho)* of one hundred members *(Tatars)* and a president *(Kedaghe)* with 15 ministers *(Kilnosers)*, governors, magistrates and many other officials with the trappings of a full-fledged government was announced. The Naga Home Guards, which was by now 3,000 strong and armed with weapons left behind by Allies and the Japanese after the end of fighting in World War II, constituted the army of the underground.[17] The Government of India intervened by sending troops of its regular army to quell the rebellion. Maj Gen RK Kochar was appointed the General Officer Commanding Naga Hills and Tuensang in April 1956. The Army began its operations in September 1956 and by the year end 619 rifles (including muzzle loaders), eight machine guns, 17 sten guns, and some other arms and ammunition were seized or recovered.[18] But the hostiles were by now fairly well organised and had intimate knowledge of terrain and an efficient intelligence network. In a well-planned action the hostiles ambushed a road protection party of one junior commissioned officer and thirty-two other ranks of 9 Punjab on road Khonoma-Jaluke on April 1, 1957 and killed all except one who survived to tell the tale.[19] The ambush party had consisted of two to three hundred Nagas. The assembly and concealment of such a large body of hostiles demonstrated the skill of Nagas in guerrilla warfare.

The hostiles attempted seize of Kohima in June 1956 led by Kaito Sema and Tungti Chang.[20] The town was attacked from three different directions on June 10, 1956. The rebels cut off telephone lines, electricity, water supply and destroyed few bridges. The army sent reinforcements, which brought the situation under control.

Phizo's Escape to East Pakistan

With the intensification of operations by the army, Phizo thought it prudent to flee Nagaland. He escaped to Dacca, then the capital of East Pakistan, taking the North Cachar route to cross the border on December 6, 1956. He had attempted to sneak into Pakistan earlier in 1952 through Burma but was captured by the Burmese and sent back to India. He was subsequently released on compassionate grounds when his wife met with an accident while travelling in a jeep near Khonoma. Phizo was welcomed with open arms in East Pakistan. After a prolonged stay of three years in Dacca, he went to London via Zurich on a Peruvian passport with the help of Michael Scott, about whom we will hear more in the narrative. He died in exile in Britain on April 30, 1990.[21] His body was brought to India by a chartered flight and then taken to his village Khonoma where he was buried.

Sixteen Point Agreement and Formation of Nagaland

Naga Hills witnessed much violence between 1956-58. There was, however, a silver lining in the dark clouds. Many moderate Nagas who saw the futility of violence joined the Peace Committee, which was formed at the initiative of the government. The first convention of all Naga tribes, called the Naga People's Convention (NPC) was held from 22 to 26 August in Kohima on whose recommendation the Naga Hill District and Tuensang Sub Division of NEFA were amalgamated to form Naga Hill-Tuensang Area (NHTA) on December 1, 1957. This new unit was administered by the President with the Governor of Assam as his agent and through the Ministry of External Affairs. In order to create a proper atmosphere for the new administration to function, an amnesty was declared and in the hope that hostiles would respond, further grouping of villages was stopped and it was made known that degrouping of villages would take place as and when situation improved. On their part the delegates gave up the demand for independence. The second convention of NPC was held in May 1958 at Ugma where a liaison committee to contact underground leaders was formed. The historic third convention was held in October 1959 at Mokokchung and was attended by 3,000 delegates drawn from all Naga tribes. The convention inter-alia asked for the formation of a separate state to be named Nagaland within the Indian Union, which virtually over turned the plebiscite held by the supporters of Phizo in 1951. The church leaders also gave a call for peace. A delegation met Nehru in July 1960 with the proposal, which was accepted and came to be called the Sixteen Point Agreement. President Dr Radhakrishnan inaugurated the new State of Nagaland on December 1, 1960 on the basis of the above agreement, which was earlier signed by the Government of India and the Naga delegation. A crowd of 10,000 Nagas had lined up the three-mile route from the high school helipad to Raj Bhawan in Kohima to welcome the President; an expression of peoples enthusiasm on the creation of the new State of Nagaland.

Overground Politics

The Governor, Gen Srinagesh, swore in an Interim Executive Council headed by Shilu Ao on March 16, 1961. After the transitional period of three years elections to the new state assembly were held from 8 to 18 January 1964 in the Naga Hills except Tuensang. Two political parties, the Nagaland Nationalist Party and the Democratic Party participated in the elections. The former won 34 seats and the latter 12. Despite threats from the underground, to boycott the election, 74 per cent voters cast their votes.[22] A new state government was formed under the leadership of Shilu Ao, who became the first Chief Minister of Nagaland. The successful election was a resounding expression of people's mandate for peace. Unfortunately the hostiles saw this as a slap on their face and expressed their frustration by stepping up violent activities.

Peace Mission and Cessation of Hostilities

The formation of a democratically elected government had raised the hopes of Nagas for peace. With the initiative of church leaders a Peace Mission consisting of Shri Jaiprakash Narayan, Bimla Prasad Chaliha, Shri Shankar Rao Deo[23] and Rev Michael Scott was formed, which succeeded in bringing about a cease-fire with effect from September 6, 1964, applicable not only in Nagaland but also in the three sub divisions of Manipur, namely, Ukhrul, Mao, and Tamenglong. It was initially effective for a period of one month but later extended several times to enable the peace talks to continue.[24]

There were eight round of talks after the cessation of hostilities between the so-called Federal Government of Nagaland (FGN) and the Indian delegation. The Indian delegation consisted of YD Gundevia, secretary in the Ministry of External Affairs, Silu Ao, Chief Minister Nagaland, NC Santok, Deputy Secretary MEA and UN Sharma, Chief Secretary to the Government of Nagaland. The underground delegation was led by Zashie Hurie and included Issac Swu, the underground foreign secretary and Thinusillie, the self-styled Chief of the Underground Army. This was the first serious attempt to negotiate peace, which was held first at Chedema from September 1964 to January 1965 and then at Khensa from February to May 1965.

As the talks progressed, it became clear to Gundevia that the so-called FGN delegation had no authority to negotiate the essentials of the settlement. The Naga delegation was obsessed with protocol and was caught up in projecting the trappings and symbolism of being the representative of a make-believe sovereign state. There was also wide intellectual gap between the two sides.[25] The underground delegation had lived in the jungles for a decade and had lost touch with the political forces, which had been set in motion by the creation of Nagaland as a separate state. The talks were a disaster except that the cease-fire continued to hold, which meant there were no clashes.

The Peace Mission made one last attempt to break the impasse by proposing that FGN could "of their own volition decide to participate in the Union of India and mutually settle the terms and conditions for that purpose. On its part the Government of India could consider to what extent the political structure between the governments of India and Nagaland should be adapted to meet their (Nagas) demand." The Peace Mission made a prophetic observation that the "approach herein suggested is not only the fairest but also the only practical one in the given circumstances."[26] The Indian delegation welcomed the proposal but the underground scuttled it by submitting that the proposal had to be determined by a referendum.

In clear breach of the cease-fire agreement, the underground continued to coerce villages to pay taxes and forcibly recruit cadres and send them for training and procurement of arms to East Pakistan. When this was pointed out to them, they took the plea that the agreement did not prohibit movement of their cadres outside Nagaland and that the agreement prohibited smuggling of arms into Nagaland during the truce but did not prohibit receiving arms from a friendly country. As no arms had been smuggled into Nagaland, and were kept in sanctuaries in Myanmar territory, no violation had technically taken place.[27] It is a good example of how the underground has consistently twisted facts to support its line of argument.

Role of Michael Scott

Michael Scott had served in India as domestic chaplain to the Bishop of Bombay between 1935-37, and chaplain of St Bishop Cathedral in Calcutta between 1937-39. The man was a veritable champion of underdogs. In 1960, he had helped Phizo to travel from Zurich to London on an irregular passport and helped him to obtain British citizenship. During the third Baptist Convention at Wokha, in February 1964, he was nominated by the church leaders to be a member of the Peace

Mission. He was expected to represent the Naga case impartially. But all his actions were not only partisan but also hostile to the Indian Government. In April 1964, he came to Kohima with BP Chaliha who provided ten white jeeps to facilitate Scott to travel freely and meet Nagas including the underground. When he returned to Delhi from his visit to Kohima, Scott's first act was to circulate a sheaf of papers accusing the Government of India and the Indian troops of foulest atrocities. Indian troops were accused of having butchered 34,000 men, women, and children in the Sema area alone whereas in the 1961 census, the total population of Semas was around 47000. The Indians were accused of the destruction of 79,794 houses. The total population of Nagaland and Tuensang in 1951 was 2,50,000 and it would be reasonable that total houses would be around 50-60,000 @ 5 person per house.[28]

Scott's conduct at the negotiations, his public statements and the letters he drafted on behalf of the underground, were all unequivocally partisan and subjective. Dr Mankekar, the distinguished journalist, described Scott's conduct "as passionately subjective and packed with defence counsel's cynical tricks addressing a jury – a play upon emotions, suppressio veri, suggestio falsi, manipulation of facts, that straight away disqualified him for the role of a neutral arbitrator, which was bestowed on him by the two parties at the negotiations when he was appointed one of the three members of the Peace Mission."[29]

Ministerial Talks

When the ongoing talks failed to produce any result, it was submitted by the underground delegation that the talks should now be held at ministerial level. Six round of talks between the underground led by Kughato Sukhai and the Prime Minister, Smt Indira Gandhi, were held in 1966-67, which resulted in a stalemate, as the underground refused to agree to any settlement within the Constitution of India. The underground lost a historic opportunity to find a lasting solution when they refused the offer of a settlement by Mrs Gandhi not within the framework of the constitution but within the framework of the Indian Union meaning thereby that the constitution could be amended to accommodate a settlement.[30]

As the ministerial talks progressed, Jaiprakash Narayan resigned from the Peace Mission due to intransigence of the underground leaders. Michael Scott was expelled from India as his attitude had become openly partisan and hostile. The Peace Mission, which had come into existence on 5 April, 1964 ceased to exist on May 7, 1966. A six-member Commission was later formed to investigate allegations of cease-fire violations.

Split in the Underground

At this stage two important developments took place that were to profoundly affect the underground struggle for independence. The first was the split in the underground and the second, the decision to seek Chinese help. The failure of peace talks heightened the differences in the approach to peace talks and the strategy to be adopted to find a political solution. While Kughato Sukhai, a Sema and brother of Kaito, was blamed for the failure of peace talks, Kaito was unhappy with the Angami leadership for sidelining him in the underground military hierarchy. Scato Swu resigned as the president of NNC and was replaced by Mhiasiu, who was close to Phizo. Mowu Angami was appointed the chief of the underground army, and Muivah was made the general secretary of the party. Angamis replaced the hegemony of Semas.

For opposing Phizoites, Kaito was brutally murdered in broad daylight in Kohima on August 31, 1968. He was accused of having links with the Indian Army. His followers formed the Revolutionary Government of Nagaland (RGN) on November 1, 1968 with a political wing called Council of Naga People. The

RGN was led by Kughato Sukhai and self-styled General Zuehoto. The splinter group appointed Scato Swu as the Prime Minister, who had earlier resigned as the president of the FGN, and favoured peaceful solution of the Naga problem, continuance of the cease-fire and talks with the Government of India. The other development was the decision taken sometime in 1966 to send a group of Naga youths to China for training in guerrilla warfare. There were groups in the underground, which did not favour links with the Chinese. Even the church was not very comfortable with this development.

Capture of Mowu Angami

The first batch of 300 Nagas under Thinsuelie trekked 1000 km to reach Yunan in China in January 1967. The second batch of 500 Nagas was led by Mowu Angami in December 1967. This batch, which was on its way back to Nagaland after training, had no knowledge of the crisis that had overtaken the underground during its absence. The army captured a part of this group numbering 165 under Mowu Angami in March 1969 with their arms and documents, which confirmed their Chinese links. The capture of Mowu's gang is still shrouded in conflicting explanations. The rival group accused Kaito's men of betrayal and helping the army in capturing Mowu and his gang.

The crisis in the underground had repercussions in the overground politics. The Naga National Organisation (NNO) led by Hokishe Sema split over the relationship with the RGN. SC Jamir defected from the NNO and joined the splinter group, which had formed the United Democratic Front (UDF) considered pro underground. There was an attempt on the life of Hokishe Sema on August 8, 1972, when the convoy of vehicles in which he and his family were travelling was ambushed on Dimapur-Kohima road. Fortunately, Hokishe and his family survived, but the driver and two bodyguards were killed and Hokishe's daughter was injured. The Government of India banned NNC and FGN and lifted the cease-fire on September 1, 1972. The RGN was dissolved on August 16, 1973 and 335 armed cadres of this group were absorbed into newly raised 111 and 112 Battalion of Border Security Force (BSF). Zuehoto became a battalion commander and Scato Swu later became a Member of Parliament.[31]

The Shillong Accord

The defeat of Pakistan in the 1971 Indo-Pak war was a grievous blow to Naga insurgency. The insurgents lost their bases in East Pakistan. During the war self-styled General Thinsullie, chief of the underground Naga Army (Phizo Group), and self-styled Brigadier Nidellie were captured by the Indian forces inside Bangladesh. In a major development, a section of Nagas who were supporters of the underground and had formed a political party, the UDF, decided to confront the Government on a political plank. UDF contested the general elections of 1974 with the promise to bring genuine reconciliation between the underground and the Government of India. The election did not produce a clear majority but UDF formed a government with the help of some independents under a moderate Naga, Vizol. The government did not last long as there were defections from its ranks. Political instability forced the Governor to impose President's rule. The pressure on the underground was resumed. There was an attempt to send another gang of hostiles to China led by Issac Swu. The bulk of the gang was prevented from crossing the border into Myanmar and many were either killed or captured. A small number, however, succeeded in escaping the security dragnet.[32]

The imposition of internal emergency by Smt Indira Gandhi in 1975 gave a free hand to the security forces to flush out the insurgents from their jungle hideouts. Between April and August 1975, a spate of surrenders took place. A total of 1,214 surrendered.[33] The church leaders again took initiative to broker peace. A liaison committee, under Rev Longri Ao with Dr Aram among others, was formed to facilitate talks with the underground. The liaison committee held talks with Biesto Medom, Keviyalle (Phizo's brother), Ramyo and M Asa of the underground. When it became clear to the Governor, Shri LP Singh, that the agreement had a fair chance of success, he met the committee at Shillong. The Governor was assured that the underground on their own volition accepted without condition the Constitution of India and promised to deposit their arms at an appointed place. The agreement, which came to be called the Shillong Accord, was finally signed on November 11, 1975.[34]

Formation of National Socialist Council of Nagaland (NSCN)

When the Shillong Accord was being negotiated, Isak Swu and Muivah with a group of 150 hardcore rebels were on their way back from China. It may be recalled that a group had managed to exfiltrate and reach the Chinese territory towards the end of 1974. This group had begun to return in small batches. When Muivah and Isak Swu were informed about the developments, they rejected the Accord and termed it as betrayal by the NNC and swore to fight on. Chinese hand was discerned in the rejection of the Accord, as it was in their interest.[35] This group did not physically enter Nagaland but established itself in Myanmar's territory, where they had the support of Chin Nagas. They set up a camp on a mountain top, identified as Sapha camp. Soon cracks developed in the group. Isak and Muivah made derogatory remarks against Phizo and the policy adopted by the NNC. The UDF government of Nagaland had established a camp at a place called Pangshe on the Indian side of the border to negotiate with Isak-Muivah group but no progress was made till September 1979. As an interim measure, the dissident group had set up a military council. In March 1979, Isac-Muivah group called a National Assembly, which elected Khaplang, a Hemi Naga from Myanmar, as the Federal President. Isak and Muivah were able to convince Khaplang to break with the NNC. On February 2, 1980, the trio announced the formation of the NSCN, replacing the FGN[36]. The period leading up to the formation of NSCN was bloody. Those who had lived and fought together were engaged in killing each other, all in the name of ideology and the future of Nagaland. 20 top underground cadres lost their lives at the hands of their erstwhile colleagues. It was one of the darkest periods in Naga's struggle for self-determination.

The NSCN Manifesto

The manifesto of NSCN included the following: -

- Unquestionable sovereignty over every inch of Nagaland.
- Dictatorship of the people through NSCN.
- Socialist government to ensure fair equality to all the people.
- Nagaland for Christ.
- No illusion of saving Nagaland by peaceful means.
- Self-reliance.

Split in the NSCN

Sometime in 1985, feelers were sent through Rev Longri Ao for talks with the NSCN without pre-conditions. The Government of India agreed to hold talks but reportedly backed out. The government once again proposed talks but within the framework of the Indian constitution. The offer was rejected. Soon differences arose over the response to the Indian Government's persistent proposal to start dialogue. Rumours were spread that Isak and Muivah have sold out and planned to oust Khaplang.[37] An effort was made to patch up the differences but in a pre-emptive strike, Khaplang aided by Myanmar's troops attacked Muivah group on April 30, 1988. 140 men of Muivah group were killed while 230 others including women and children escaped and fled to the jungles pursued by Myanmar's troops. Many died but a handful under Muivah joined up with Isak and trekked to Konyak area. The NSCN formally split into two factions; the Konyak Nagas under Khaplang and Khole Konyak formed

NSCN (K) and the Thangkhul Nagas under Isak and Muivah formed NSCN (IM).

The split has led to bloody feuds between the two groups. The NSCN (IM) has made a strong comeback since the split in 1988. Over the years it has extended its influence to the Naga inhabited areas of Assam, and some parts of Meghalaya and Arunachal and has become the mainspring of insurgencies in the North-east. The NSCN (IM) has established a government-in-exile called the Government of the People's Republic of Nagaland; the name Nagaland has been replaced by Nagalim to include the areas claimed in Greater Nagaland.

The NSCN (K) areas of influence are in parts of Mokokchung district and Tuensang. It also has a government-in-exile and its headquarters is located in Myanmar. There are frequent raids and killings by both sides to extend their areas of influence. Elimination of rivals and betrayals has marked the course of events since the split.

Admission to the UNPO

The cause of NSCN (IM) received a boost after it was admitted to the UNPO, which is a Non Governmental Organisation (NGO) based in Hague and has nothing to do with the United Nations Organisation. Muivah has been attending the meetings of UNPO. He had also attended a UN Human Rights Committee session in Geneva in 1993 under a pseudonym. NSCN (IM) admission to UNPO has enabled it to open offices in a number of countries in South East Asia, Europe and North America.[38]

Drift in Naga Movement

Naga underground are now divided into three main groups: NSCN (IM), NSCN (K) and NNC. NNC still survives in Angami area but has split into two factions; NNC (A) under Phizo's daughter Adino and NNC (K) under Khadao Yanthan. Muivah group enjoys influence among Thangkhuls, Semas and Phoms in Zunheboto, Wokha, Ukhrul, Dimapur and Kohima, whereas Khaplang group among Konyaks and Aos in Tuensang, Mokokchung and Mon. In Angami and Chakesang areas the legacy of Phizo still lingers.

The character of Naga insurgency has undergone sea change over the years. What was predominantly a rural guerrilla movement is now mainly confined to towns and urban centres like Dimapur, Kohima and Mokokchung. The commitment to the cause, which illuminated the movement in the fifties and sixties, is now absent. Today, militancy is a way to make easy money. Extortion, kidnapping and killings of innocent civilians have replaced the guerrilla warfare. A nexus of corrupt officials, ministers and contractors siphon off funds for development. They in turn finance militants belonging to different factions. It is a vicious circle. The situation has turned worse by trafficking in drugs and gunrunning. Insurgency provides an ideal cover for such operations. Baptist Pastor Rev Nu laments "there is not a single MLA in 60 member assembly without links with Muivah or Khaplang faction."

A Fresh Peace Initiative

People of Nagaland are disillusioned and are fed up with violence and bloodshed. Fifty years of strife has taken its toll. It is this realisation that, perhaps, prompted NSCN (IM) to agree to a cease-fire and political negotiation with the Union Government. Talks began in February 1997 followed by a cease-fire agreement, which was first signed on August 1, 1997 and has been in force since then. Several rounds of talks have taken place, first with Swaraj Kaushal as the official interlocutor and subsequently with K Padmanabhaiah. The Naga delegation had laid down three conditions before talks could start: firstly, it shall be without any pre-condition; secondly, the talks shall be at the highest level; and thirdly, the venue shall be outside India. Three rounds of talks have taken place outside India since 1997. A cease-fire-monitoring cell was established at Dimapur, which had representatives of the centre, the security forces and the NSCN (IM). Despite differences in the interpretation of the provisions of the agreement, the cease-fire has held on. Some major differences are listed below:-[39]

- NSCN contends that the use of force was unauthorised only against the security forces, while the army's contention is that it includes everyone including civilians.
- NSCN's contention is that carrying of arms is permitted, except inside the prescribed areas. This interpretation is obviously illogical. No movement of arms was permitted outside the prescribed area.
- NSCN considers collection of taxes as legitimate on the plea that it is the Government, a formulation that no government can accept.
- Indian laws are not applicable to the underground, which obviously cannot be accepted by the Government.

According to Lt Gen Narahari[40], who visited Nagaland in 2000, the security forces insisted and enforced, as much as they could, the rule regarding carrying of weapons outside the prescribed area. The villagers whom he met during his visit confirmed that extortion and tax collection by the underground was going on.

During the talks in Amsterdam in July 2002, Isak and Muivah agreed to come to India to hold talks with the Indian leaders. To facilitate their arrival they were promised safe passage and the Government of Nagaland withdrew arrest warrants against them. So far, the talks have made little progress. During the talks held in New Delhi in January 2003, Muivah and Isak Swu made a significant statement and said that insurgency in Nagaland has come to an end and vowed to stop the campaign of guns. (Promise of Peace, *Frontline*, January 31, 2003) But subsequently, as the talks faltered on the question of Greater Nagaland, Muivah was ambivalent and in the 'Walk the Talk' interview with Shekhar

Gupta in June 2005, he was not very sure if the cease-fire would continue to hold. (*Indian Express*, June 21, 2005)

In April 2000, NSCN (K) announced a formal cease-fire with the Indian Government, which resulted in a meeting between the two sides in September 2001. During the meeting of the Cease-fire Supervisory Board on February 19, 2002, thc Khaplang faction agreed to shift its cadres to designated camps.

There is a view in the security forces that the cease-fire has given the insurgents a breather to enlarge their influence in the North-east. Despite the cease-fire both factions of NSCN have been indulging in extortion, levying taxes and killings. It has been reported that Muivah had visited Pakistan in January 2000, raising doubts about his continuing links with the ISI. It has links with almost all militant groups in North-east India. It has links with Hynnilwtrep National Liberation Council (HNLC) and A'chik National Volunteer Council (ANVC) of Meghalaya, National Democratic Front of Bodoland (NDFB), National Liberation Front of Tripura (NLFT), A'chik Liberation Matgrik Army in the Garo Hills and Hmar People's Convention in Mizoram. NSCN (IM) made a real breakthrough in extending its area of operation by gaining a foothold in the Imphal Valley. The Meiteis and Nagas have never had very friendly relations. So, when Namoijam Oken Singh left UNLF and formed Kangli Yawol Kanna Lup (KYKL), the NSCM (IM) promptly gave support and arms to this group and thus got a foothold in the crucial Imphal Valley. The extended linkages of NSCN (IM) with the insurgent groups in all the states of the North-east are extremely profitable for them. The small splinter groups have no ideology; they are in business of insurgency only for extortion, the major share of the extortion goes in the kitty of NSCN (IM). The organisation is also believed to have contacts with the LTTE of Sri Lanka and People's War Group in Andhra Pradesh. It has established network of contacts for arms procurement in Thailand, Myanmar, Bangladesh and other South East Asian countries.

NSCN (K) faction has an equally wide area of influence and is believed to enjoy the support of the former Chief Minister, SC Jamir. The organisation has been engaged in fratricidal feud with Muivah faction, which considers it as traitor. It has bases in Myanmar, Bangladesh and Bhutan. In May 2001, Myanmar launched a massive combing operation against NSCN (K) on their side of Naga Hills to flush them out. Many were injured in the firing between the two sides in Konyak region along the Indo-Myanmar border.

Demand for Greater Nagaland

The success of the current initiative hinges on the response to Naga's demand for the creation of Greater Nagaland comprising the present Nagaland and Naga inhabited areas of the neighbouring states of Assam, Manipur and Arunachal and in Myanmar. Whether the proposed Greater Nagaland will be an independent entity or part of the Indian Union has not been spelt out clearly by the NSCN. The demand has, nonetheless, raised the hackles of Manipuris, who fear that the Centre may agree to carve a Southern Nagaland comprising the Naga inhabited districts of Senapati, Ukhrul, Chandel and Tamenglong in order to appease the Nagas. Their fear is rooted in the unanimous resolution passed in the Nagaland Assembly in 1994, which favoured the establishment of Greater Nagaland. Manipuri suspicion was reinforced when in 2002, the cease-fire with Naga militants was extended without territorial limits; earlier extensions were only within the territorial limits of Nagaland. The announcement was a grievous blunder. It caused widespread resentment and shock amongst Meiteis cutting across all barriers. The anger of the people turned violent and for days Imphal was literally burning, forcing the government to withdraw Manipur from the ambit of cease-fire.

Appraisal

The Nagas remained isolated during 600 years rule of Ahom kings in Assam. The isolation continued even after the British annexation of Assam, which resulted from the Treaty of Yandeboo in 1826. The British devised the policy of 'Excluded Areas' to keep the tribes of the North-east isolated from the plains, primarily to prevent raids in the plantations.

The Nagas were first exposed to the outside world during the World War I when they were recruited in the labour corps for service in France. The World War II and particularly the Battle of Kohima were to have a profound effect on the psyche of Nagas. They were exposed to the war as a frontline state and became aware of the nationalist movements that were sweeping across most of South and South-east Asia.

The spread of Christianity gave the Nagas a sense of identity or "more specifically a sense of separateness" from the plainsmen. This sense of separateness was exploited by Phizo to politicise the Nagas on a separatist platform. Unfortunately, in the early years the church played a role, which willy- nilly encouraged this sense of separateness.

There is a widespread belief among the present day Nagas as also in the minds of many other Indians that there was unanimity amongst Nagas for separation from India at the time of transfer of power and in the years immediately after Independence. This is not borne out by facts. The speech given by T Alibaimti, president of NNC, in a public meeting in Kohima on December 6, 1948, where he exhorted, "I have but one word to say, our country is connected with India in many ways. We should continue that connection," underlines the differing approaches of leaders like Alibaimti and Sakhrie on one side and Phizo and his supporters on the other. Sakhrie was one of the founders of Naga movement and differed with Phizo on use of violence and had warned that Nagas were ill prepared for such a clash. His criticism of Phizo led to his brutal assassination by the followers of Phizo.

Clause 9 of Akbar Hydari Agreement proved one of the most contentious between the two opposing sides. Phizoite Nagas interpreted the clause as their right to declare independence after the expiry of ten years whereas the Government of India held the view that it only meant that Nagas could decide the changes in the administrative arrangement for the Naga Hills. In any case the Government of India held the view that after the adoption of the Constitution the agreement was subsumed in the Sixth Schedule.

Lt Gen Narahari in his book *"Security Threats to North-east India"* rightly observes that Nagas have psyched themselves that Naga Hills was never part of India. There are several parts of India that never came under one legislative or administrative authority, but they all came under one colonial authority. The Government of India Act of 1935 brought Naga Hills, which was under British rule, into British India and on August 15, 1947, under the Indian Union as successor state. It is worthwhile recalling that the Nagas recognised the overlordship of Ahoms and paid tributes to their kings. Ahoms on their part left the Nagas to live, as they liked, as long as they did not create any trouble for them. There is enough evidence to believe that Manipuris in earlier days penetrated Naga Hills and exacted tributes when they felt strong enough to do so.[41]

A few comments on Naga insurgency and counter-insurgency are called for. The harsh measures taken by the army in the face of violent guerrilla attacks in the fifties contributed to the sense of separateness even among that section of Nagas, who favoured a peaceful settlement. When insurgency started in 1956 neither the political leadership nor the army had any experience in fighting insurgency. The then Army Chief, Gen KS Thimaya, is reported to have candidly told Nehru that it required political wisdom rather than military muscle to solve the Naga problem.[42] It must, however, be said to the credit of Nehru that he had rightly grasped the nature of the problem, but the government failed to evolve a long-term politico-military strategy to deal with the situation. It will serve no purpose to deny that in the initial stages there were widespread violations of Human Rights and acts of vendetta in which innocent lives of civilians were lost and villages burnt. Torture to elicit information was quite common. Grouping of villages to deny the guerrillas public support was experimented for a while but wisely given up, as it proved counter-productive. However, the brutalities and violations of Human Rights by the underground have not been adequately documented. They have an unflattering record of assassination of dissidents and opponents. Sakhrie was kidnapped, tortured and then killed because he opposed Phizo. His erstwhile comrades physically liquidated Kaito Sema, who was one of the most charismatic underground military leaders, after he broke with Phizo and formed a separate party. He was shot dead in broad daylight in Kohima in August 1968. The underground opposed to any agreement with the Government of India and assassinated Dr Imkongliba Ao, who was the Chairman of Nagaland Interim Body pending elections to the first Assembly of the newly created State. Some assailants killed Kevichusa, who was the general secretary of NNC, in his house in Dimapur in June 1994. The treatment of captured Assam policemen by the underground was equally deplorable. Armed Nagas attacked the few police posts established by Assam Police, captured the bewildered policemen, stripped them of all clothing and ordered them to march back to the plains in nude. In fact in Satakha, 72 policemen were stripped by the rebels and ordered to start walking to the foothills.[43]

In the early years of insurgency the guerrillas were galvanised by idealism. There was romance in operating from jungle hideouts. There was a well-defined aim to fight Indian imperialism. The support of Pakistan and China boosted their morale and provided them a platform for anti-India propaganda. The charisma of Phizo kept the insurgency alive.

The Indian Army had no experience of counter-insurgency operations when it was sent to Nagaland but it soon learnt its lessons. It became better organised and developed tactics to keep the guerrillas on the run. It also realised that the insurgent war must be fought on two fronts simultaneously; one military and the other psychological, to win the hearts and minds of people. This realisation brought greater accountability and control over the actions of units in counter-insurgency operations. On the political front the creation of a new State of Nagaland and encouragement to over-ground politics took the wind out of the separatist movement.

The underground Nagas missed a historic opportunity to find a lasting solution to the Naga problem when they refused the offer of a settlement by Smt Indira Gandhi not within the Indian Constitution but within the framework of Indian Union, meaning thereby that the constitution could be amended to accommodate a settlement. The Shillong Accord was another turning point in the chequered history of Nagaland. The opportunity to usher in an era of peace was lost due to the refusal of a section of underground to accept the accord, ostensibly in the name of ideology but in fact due to external influence and personal egos. The failure also brought into focus the failure of the negotiators to enter into wider consultations with various factions before finalising the agreement. The split in NSCN complicated the situation further. Internecine war between the two groups has taken many lives. Although the divide may suit the security forces at the tactical level, but the rift makes the search for a lasting peace all the more difficult. The overground politics has also got mired into fractious rivalries. SC Jamir (former Chief Minister of Nagaland) is reported to be siding with Khaplang group whereas Rishang Keishing (former Chief Minister of Manipur) is reported to be supporting NSCN (IM).

Five decades of insurgency has taken its toll on many fronts. The Naga society is today beset with doubts and people are sullen and tired of senseless violence. The centre has pumped in crores of rupees year after year as central assistance. Unfortunately, over the decades a nexus between politicians, bureaucrats and contractors has developed which appropriates the major portion of the funds in the name of development projects.

The character of Naga insurgency has changed over the years. No longer the guerrillas contemplate a life in jungle hideouts. The scene of action has shifted to towns. In the early years the emphasis was on mass mobilisation and guerrilla tactics of hit and run. Now the emphasis is on extortion, kidnapping, arm-twisting and blackmail. The community is held to ransom by fear of militants who are running a parallel government. Every government employee including ministers pay a part of their salary to the underground as tax. So do professionals like doctors, traders and shopowners. For every contract, a commission is paid to one militant group or the other: The exchequer is part financing the insurgency.

Naga-Kuki confrontation has further complicated the problem. The insistence of Nagas to incorporate Naga dominated areas of Manipur in Greater Nagaland will prove to be a major hurdle in the final settlement of the Naga problem. The continuance of cease-fire is, however, a silver lining in an otherwise gloomy scenario. Muivah's acceptance of New Delhi as the venue for further talks and his travel on Indian passport are positive signs and give hope for the future. Perhaps, the realisation has dawned on him and his other colleagues that the Nagas do not have a strong case for demanding the inclusion of small pockets of Naga enclaves in Assam. His posturing suggests that he is looking for an honourable escape route. Even more propitious is the emergence of powerful non-political organisations like the Naga Hoho that represents 25 Naga tribes, the Naga Student Union and the Naga Mothers' Association. They are exerting great moral force on the polity of Nagaland today.

Notes and References

1. Alemchiba, *A Brief Historical Account of Nagaland*, (Kohima: The Naga Institute of Culture, 1970,) p. 26.
2. AM Mackenzie, *The North-east Frontier of India*, (New Delhi: Mittel Publication, 1979), p. 91.
3. A Mackenzie, *History of Relation of the Government with the Hill tribes of the NE Frontiers of Bengal*, (Calcutta: 1884), p 114. Quoted by Prakash Singh, *Nagaland*, (New Delhi: National Book Trust, 1972), p. 18.
4. Ibid., p. 116.
5. Ibid., p. 26.
6. Ibid.
7. Asoso Yonuo, *The Rising Nagas*, (New Delhi: Vivek Publishing House, 1974), pp. 105, 106.
8. L Wati, *Facts and Growth of Naga Nationalism*, 1993, Published in Mokokchung, p. 18.
9. Phanjoubam Tarapot, *Insurgency Movement in North-east India*, (New Delhi: Vikas Publishing House), p. 105 and SK Chaube, *Hill Politics in NE India*, Reprint (New Delhi: Orient Longman, 1999), p 157.
10. L Wati, n.8., p. 29.
11. Ibid, p. 30.
12. Governor of Assam Memo No 88-c/47, Shillong, dated June 22, 1948, addressed to the Deputy Commissioner Naga Hills, Kohima, and signed by Bordoloi, Akbar Hydari and NK Rustomji, advisor to the Governor, reproduced in L Wati, n. 8., pp. 31,32.
13. RD Palsokar, *Forever in Operations: History of 8 Mountain Division*, p. 24.
14. Asoso Yonuo, n. 7., p. 203.
15. L Wati, n. 8., p. 55.
16. Ibid, p. 60.
17. RD Palsokar, n., 13., p. 28.
18. Ibid, p. 31.

19. Ibid, p. 32.
20. Tungti Chang had formed the Naga Home Guard and Kaito had formed Naga Safe Guard. The two were later merged to form Naga Home Guard, which later became the underground army. Ao Senba, *The Naga Resistence Movement*, (New Delhi: Regency Publication, 2001), p. 54.
21. A daughter of Phizo married an Indian Army officer and embraced Hinduism and took a Hindu name, Radhika. Phizo's body was brought to New Delhi by British Airways plane on 10 May 1990 and was taken to his village where he was buried. .Kiran Shankar Maitra, *The Noxious Web: Insurgency in North-east India*, (New Delhi: Kaniska Publishers, 2001), p. 10.
22. RD Palsokar, n 17., p. 45.
23. Shankar Rao Deo did not take part in the deliberations due to ill health.
24. The extension of cease-fire was finally terminated in 1972 after an abortive attempt on the life of the Chief Minister, Hokise Sema.
25. YD Gundevia, *War and Peace in Nagaland*, (Dehradun: Palit and Palit, 1975), pp 129 -133. Chapter vii of the book describes the negotiating stance of the Naga delegation.
26. L Wati, n. 8., p. 112.
27. YD Gundevia, n. 25., p. 136.
28. Ibid, pp. 79-80, Gundevia gives an exhaustive account of Scott's bias against the Government of India.
29. DR Mankekar, *On Slippery Slope in Nagaland*, (Bombay: Manaktala, 1967), pp. 19-29.
30. BG Verghese, *India's North-east resurgent*, (New Delhi: Konark, 1996), p. 92.
31. NS Narhari, *Security Threats to North-east India*, (New Delhi: Manas, 2002), pp 217-18. Narhari is the former General Officer Commanding of Tezpur based 4 Corps and has done extensive research on North-east.
32. L Wati, n. 8., pp128-129. Also author's interaction with Brig N Bahri who was the Brigade Major of 56 Mountain Brigade at Mokokchung and played a major role in preventing the rebels to cross the border.
33. NS Narhari, n. 31., p. 118.
34. The underground leaders signed the Accord as individuals and not as representative of NNC. This was later used by a section of the underground to repudiate the Accord.
35. NS Narhari, n. 31., p. 119.

36. L Wati, n. 8., p. 164.
37. BG Verghese, n. 30., p. 95.
38. Ibid., pp. 99-100.
39. NS Narhari, n. 31., p. 126.
40. Lt Gen Narhari (Retd) toured extensively in the North-east in the year 2000 to collect facts and impressions for his book, which was published in 2002.
41. J Johnston, *Manipur and Naga Hills*, (New Delhi: Gyan Publishers, 2002), pp 41-43. Manipur's influence declined during its period of decadence just before and after the Burmese war of 1819-25. It was re-asserted during the time of Gambhir Singh, who reduced many villages, including Kohima, at which place he stood upon a stone and had his footprints sculpted on it as token of conquest. The Nagas greatly respected this stone and cleaned it from time to time.
42. Nirmal Nibedon, *North-east India: The Ethnic Explosion*, (New Delhi: Lancers, 1981), p. 28.
43. Nirmal Nibedon, *Night of the Guerrillas*, (New Delhi: Lancers, 1978), p. 74. Scato Swu confirmed this incident in an interview with Nirmal Nibedon.

4

Mizoram

There is no recorded history of Mizoram. The Mizos also called Lushais are of Mongolian stock and are believed to have migrated into the present habitat sometime in the 18th century from Upper Burma.[1] They inhabit the mountainous track along the India-Myanmar border known as the Mizo (formerly Lushai) Hills. The Mizos have many similarities with the Chins of Myanmar across the border. The Lushais form the main tribal group of Mizoram and most of the Mizo chiefs of old were Lushais. The other important tribes inhabiting Mizoram are Chakmas, Lakhers, Kukis, Riangs, Pawis and Hmars. Over a period of time the above tribal conglomerate adopted a more distinctive Mizo identity. The spread of Christianity, which came to the hills in 1894, and the adoption of Lushai dialect, Duhlian, with Roman script accelerated the process of consolidation of Mizo identity.[2]

A little known fact about the Mizos is the belief amongst some that Mizos were Jews and descendants of one of the lost tribes of Israel. This led to the formation of a Mizo-Israel Zionist Organisation (Mizo) in 1974, which addressed the Israeli Prime Minister seeking recognition of this newfound identity. Some have migrated to Israel. The 1991 census records 792 Jews in Mizoram and 373 in Manipur.[3]

Like the Nagas, the Mizos are spread in large areas in Mizoram, Manipur, Cachar, Tripura and extending into Arakan and Chin hills of Myanmar and the CHT of Bangladesh and again like Nagas who claim kinship with Nagas of Myanmar across the border, the Mizos claim kinship with the Chins of Myanmar and dream of a greater Mizoram extending into Myanmar and Bangladesh.

Physical Geography

The present state of Mizoram has an area of 21087 sq km and is sandwiched between Myanmar and Bangladesh. It has a 250-km common border with Bangladesh, which is inadequately policed. With Myanmar it has a common border of another 410 km, which constitute 70 percent of the total boundary length of the state. On its North is Churachandpur district of Manipur, whose Kuki tribes have affinity with the Lushais of Mizo hills. Mizoram has six parallel mountain ranges running North to South; between them are enclosed five deep river valleys. The average height of these ranges is about 3,000 feet, with higher peaks rising to over 7,000 feet. The Phawngpuri or the Blue Mountain in South Mizo Hills rises to a height of 7,100 feet. Nearly 65 percent of the high ranges and deep valleys are covered with dense forests, which provide safe hideouts to the insurgents. The more important rivers are the Dhaleshwari, Sonai, Tuival, Kolodyne and the Karnalphuli.[4]

The British Period

The Lushai Hills, as Mizoram was called earlier, was annexed by the British in 1890, much later than other hill areas of Assam. The British had administered the Lushai Hills as "Excluded Area" and no political activity was allowed in the Lushai Hills. The British in collaboration with the local chieftains administered the area. The area was excluded from Government of India Reform Act of 1919 and 1935 although some Mizos had expressed their desire for representation in the Assam legislature but the British put down all such suggestions with a heavy hand.

When it became clear that India would soon gain Independence, McCall, the district officer of Lushai Hills from

1932 to 1943 conceived a plan, which envisaged the grouping of hill areas in Eastern India and Northern Burma under the trusteeship of the League of Nations. McDonald who was the district officer after McCall towards the closing years of the British rule even floated the idea of an autonomous state comprising Lushai Hills and a portion of Burma extending up to the Bay of Bengal as a protectorate of the British.

Period Prior to the Transfer of Power

The first political party in the Lushai Hills came into existence in 1946. The Mizo Common People's Union (MCPU) later known simply as Mizo Union was formed on April 9, 1948. The first general assembly of the MCPU was held in 1946. The Union debated the three options open to the Mizos viz to join the Union of Burma, become independent or remain with India. The overwhelming response was in favour of remaining with India with a provision that the arrangement would be reviewed after ten years. The majority in the Mizo Union was in favour of abolition of chieftainship. This alarmed the chiefs *(Lal)*, the traditional elites, who parted company with the Mizo Union and formed a separate organisation called United Mizo Freedom Organisation (UMFO) in July 1947. The avowed aim of UMFO was to merge Lushai Hills with Myanmar. At this stage an alternative scheme was put forward by Professor Coupland, which suggested the creation of a Crown Colony of Eastern Agency, consisting of the hills of Assam and Myanmar, which in due course could be an independent state.[6]

The Constituent Assembly, which was formed to debate and draft the Constitution of India, had appointed an Advisory Committee to advise on the constitutional proposals for the governance of hill tribes of Assam. A subcommittee of the above headed by Shri Gopinath Bordoloi was formed. As the Mizos were not represented in the Constituent Assembly, the subcommittee popularly known as Bordoloi Committee invited the Mizo Union to send two representatives as co-opted members. The Bordoloi Committee visited Aizwal on 17-18 April 1947 to record the testimony of the Mizos with regard to their constitutional position. It is worth mentioning here that Phizo visited Aizwal during this period and canvassed for the separation of Lushai Hills from India, but his idea did not find support amongst the Mizos. The Mizo Union submitted a memorandum to the Bordoloi Committee on April 22, 1947, which underlined the case of the Mizos for the right of territorial unity and solidarity and self-determination within the province of Assam.[7] The memorandum demanded the following:

- Territorial unity and solidarity of the whole of Mizo population. Henceforth, Lushai people and Lushai Hills to be known as Mizo and Mizoram respectively.
- Retaining the sole proprietary rights over the land.
- Full autonomy within the State of Assam.

All the above provisions would be subject to revision according to the future trend of events even to the extent of secession after ten years.

The use of the term Mizo was innovative. Mizo is an indigenous term, which translated as Hillman or Highlander. It cut across tribal boundaries and had greater territorial connotation.[8]

On the eve of Independence L Peters, the last superintendent of Lushai Hills, took upon himself to convene a joint meeting on August 14, 1947 which was attended by representatives of both the Mizo Union and UMFO. The conference first enquired whether the option of joining Pakistan or Myanmar, apart from India was open. In the event such an option being closed the groups main demands were[9]: -

- The continuance of existing safeguard of their customary laws and land etc.
- Retention of Chin Hills, 1896 Regulation and Bengal Eastern Frontier Regulation, 1873.

- That the Lushai Hills will be allowed to opt out of the Indian Union, when they wish to do so, subject to a minimum period of ten years.

The fears of the Mizos about losing their identity and ethnic exclusiveness in the vastness of India were genuine. The founding fathers of the Constitution took special care to ensure that the fears of the Mizos were addressed and safeguards provided to protect tribal interests. The Sixth Schedule of the Constitution accommodated most of the demands of the Mizos. The creation of autonomous district councils was an important step in that direction.

Political Scenario after Independence

The Mizo Union participated in the first general elections of 1952 and won all the three seats to the Assam Assembly and obtained majority in the Autonomous District Council. UMFO led the opposition. As discussed earlier the political aim of UMFO was to merge Lushai Hills with the Chin Hills of Myanmar. The objective was later changed to the formation of a separate hill state in North-east India. This received support from Eastern India Tribal Unit (EITU), a political party of Garo-Khasi and Jaintia Hills, which wanted a separate hill state within Indian Union. The political proximity of UMFO and EITU led to their merger.[10]

The Mizo Union split before the second general election (1957). The official Mizo Union retained majority in the District Council but conceded two of the three seats of the Assam Assembly to the dissidents. Subsequently, in 1960 the Mizo Union participated in the formation of All Party Hill Leaders Conference (APHLC), an umbrella organisation for the hill people who propagated the creation of an Eastern Frontier State comprising hill areas of Assam, Manipur and Tripura within the Indian Union. The Mizo Union contested and won two seats to the Assam Assembly in 1962 elections; EITU nominee supported by Mizo Union won the third seat. On a directive from APHLC both the Mizo Union members of the assembly resigned their seats in October 1962. The bye-elections were held in 1963, in which Mizo Union lost both the assembly seats to MNF, the formation of which will be discussed later. The defeat of the Mizo Union candidates to MNF who were openly propagating secessionist demands triggered a debate in the party's rank and file about the advisability of aligning with the APHLC. Serious doubts were expressed about the status of Mizoram in the proposed Eastern Frontier State, the formation of which was the main political aim of APHLC. After the debate, it was decided to part company with APHLC and demand a separate Mizoram state under the Indian Union.[11]

Formation of MNF

The formation of MNF is linked to Mautam (rat famine), caused by destruction of crops by rodents. The astronomical growth of rodent population and death of bamboo plants characterises this ecological phenomenon that occurs every 50 years. The last had manifested in 1958. Due to delay in providing relief by the Assam Government an organisation called the Mizo National Famine Front (MNFF) was formed in 1959 to organise relief work among the people affected by the famine. The efficient relief work endeared MNFF workers to the people and they became very popular. The person who organised the relief was a man called Laldenga who had resigned his job in the district council. As Laldenga went about organising relief work, he took advantage of the discontent of the people to propagate his idea of an independent Mizoram. The strained relations between the Mizoram Autonomous District Council and the Assam Government encouraged the Mizo chiefs, whose privileges had been withdrawn, to incite the people against the Assam and Central Governments. MNFF dropped the word famine on October 12, 1962 and became a political party called the Mizo National Front (MNF), which was to spearhead the demand for separation of Mizoram from India. Laldenga, the MNF president and Lalnunmawia, the vice-president made a secret trip to East Pakistan to seek support for independent Mizoram and to secure arms and guerrilla training for MNF cadres. Both of them were arrested on their return but were later released on their giving a written undertaking of good conduct to the Chief Minister Chaliha.[12] But Laldenga was never serious about honouring the undertaking given in writing. Soon after his release from the prison, Laldenga began recruitment of volunteers and arranged for their training in guerrilla warfare in East Pakistan. By the beginning of 1965, the first battalion of MNF with 200 volunteers had been formed.

Even as these clandestine activities of the MNF were spreading in Mizoram, the Mizo Union had launched a movement for the creation of a separate state of Mizoram within India. To press their demand a delegation of Mizo Union met the Prime Minister, Lal Bahadur Shastri in October 1965, who promised that he would ask the Pataskar Commission, which was then examining the administrative arrangement proposed for the hill areas of Assam, to look into their demand. Unfortunately, Shastri died soon after in early 1966. When the commission visited Mizoram towards the end of 1965, the MNF submitted a memorandum to it demanding sovereign independence status for Mizoram.

MNF Prepares for Revolt

As stated earlier MNF had already formed its first battalion in early 1965. A group of guerrillas who had sneaked into East Pakistan took delivery of arms and ammunitions at Dohazari near Chittagong port. The arms and ammunitions were taken in boats to Ruma Bazaar from where it was transported by porters and hidden in deep forests half way between Aizwal and Lungleih.[13]

By early 1966 four battalions of the MNF had been formed. The battalions were grouped under five commands imitating the Indian territorial commands. What was of interest was the renaming of the central command as Aizwal Town Command, which reflected the emphasis on urban insurgency, quite unlike the Nagas who in the early years had concentrated on remote rural countryside.

Most of the leaders of Mizo National Volunteers, later renamed Mizo National Army (MNA), were ex-servicemen. Many of them like Biakchhunga had served in the Chin Rifles in the Burmese Army. Others had served in the Indian Army or Assam Rifles. Laldenga himself was an ex-Havildar of the Indian Army. Many who had been dismissed from the service from 2nd Battalion of Assam Regiment for indiscipline in 1954 joined the ranks of the MNA.

The Beginning of Insurgency: Operation Jericho

Soon after the visit of Pataskar Commission, MNF started an armed uprising on the night of February 28, 1966, which took the whole country by surprise. The MNF declared independence on 1 March and overran most of the area of Mizo Hills. It was a lightening guerrilla strike, code-named "Operation Jericho". In Aizwal the treasury, radio station and the police headquarters were overrun without any resistance. Aizwal - Silchar road which links Mizo Hills with rest of India was cut off near Vairengte. The strike by the guerrillas could not have come at a worse time for the Indian Government. The army had not yet got over the trauma of its humiliating defeat at the hands of the Chinese in 1962 and the inconclusive war with Pakistan had ended just a few months before in September 1965. The total collapse of the administration was a major embarrassment for both the central and the state governments. Field Marshal Manekshaw, who was then the General Officer Commanding-in-Chief, Eastern Command, admitted in a press conference at Fort William on June 14, 1966, "we were caught with our pants down."[14] For more than two days the government had lost all control over the Mizo Hills.

The Insurgent Plan

Self-styled Brigadier General Sawmvela commanded the underground MNA. It consisted of two main wings, the Dagger Brigade and the Lion Brigade, each with a number of battalions of variable strength. The plan of the insurgents was to capture three main Assam Rifles posts, Aizwal, Lungleih and Champhai by surprise attack on the night of 28 February and cut the road to Silchar by capturing Chinluang and other police posts. It was a well-conceived plan, the success of which hinged on the capture of Aizwal, which had the garrison of 1 Assam Rifles.[15]

The rebels' first target was the telephone exchange, which was destroyed thus disrupting all communication between civil and military and outside world. The next target was the treasury, which was guarded by armed constables. The guards were taken by surprise and surrendered without putting any fight. The rebels took away all arms and Rs. 20,000/- from the safe failing to detect the larger amount of Rs. 1,20,00,000/- in currency notes, which had been kept in a separate room.

The attack on 1 Assam Rifles in the heart of Aizwal town was not pressed home. On night 2/3 March, nearly 4,000 rebels encircled Aizwal; at that time the garrison was not aware of the magnitude of the threat. All the families including the family of the District Commissioner were moved inside the battalion area. The exchange of fire continued throughout the day on 3 March. The police post in the town and the jail had fallen. The garrison held by 1 Assam Rifles was the only force resisting the attack by rebels.[16]

Strikes by the Indian Air Force

The Indian Air Force attempted to land re-enforcements and supplies by helicopters but failed due to heavy and accurate sniping by the rebels who had by now surrounded the garrison from all sides. Ultimately, air strikes by fighter aircraft were called at 11:30 AM on 5th March. The air strikes were repeated in the afternoon, which forced the rebels to disperse. When another strike came on 6 March, the rebel guerrillas had melted away in the jungles. Many had fled across the border to East Pakistan.[17]

The Army is Called Out

The Indian Government responded by authorising the move of army to quell the rebellion. 61 Mountain Brigade was ordered to move from Agartala to Aizwal on 3th March. Earlier, on 2nd March the Government of Assam had declared the whole of Mizo Hills as "disturbed area" under the Armed Forces (Assam and Manipur) Special Power Act of 1958. By 8th March, Brigade Headquarters was established at Aizwal where 8 Sikh had arrived by 6th evening. 3 Bihar was dispatched to Lungleih and 2/11 GR to Champhai.

The rebels had launched simultaneous attacks and Lungleih at Champhai. At Champhai the quarter guard of Assam Rifles post was taken by surprise, which resulted in the loss of all arms, which were kept in the armoury. The soldiers surrendered and were taken prisoners. The post was recaptured much later by 2/11 GR on 17th March. The Assam Rifles post at Lungleih gave a gallant fight for four days against rebels who vastly outnumbered them. An attempt was made on 5th March to supply them by helicopters but failed. When water and ammunitions in the post ran out, Lieutenant Marwah and 66 men were taken prisoner. It must be said to the credit of the rebels that they treated the prisoners well.[18] The Indian Air Force strafed the rebel position from 9 to 13 March, forcing them to disperse. A column of 5 Para finally relieved the post on 17 March.[19]

The entire 61 Mountain Brigade with four battalions and supporting arms moved into Mizo Hills by 15th March. By the end of the month, the army was in full control of the situation in Mizoram. The bulk of the MNA had crossed over to East Pakistan and Laldenga had established his headquarters in CHT. In the west the rebels were hard pressed because the Burmese had refused sanctuary to the rebels in their territory.

Although the bulk of MNA had dispersed across the border, there were strong pockets of resistance. The rebels who had stayed back continued to ambush and raid army columns and isolated posts but they posed no great threat. In the crossfire between the security forces and the rebels, innocent civilians suffered the most. By the end of April 1967, 61 Mountain Brigade took firm control and began mounting combing operations both in the interior and the border areas. The number of hostile acts came down drastically. The induction of additional BSF battalions and armed police detachments changed the balance in favour of the security forces.

After a relative lull between 1967 and 1969, insurgency picked up again in early 1970 when 200 armed hostiles returned to Mizo Hills from their bases in CHT after training.[20] In a major incident the hostiles ambushed an army contingent and killed one officer and six jawans at Marpara in 1969. On July 2, 1970 the rebels killed a number of non-tribals in the border villages of Tripura and on August 15, 1970 a number of explosions occurred at different places in Aizwal.

Grouping of Villages: Operation Accomplishment

In the beginning of 1967 the controversial grouping of villages code-named "Operation Accomplishment" was undertaken as the main thrust of counter-insurgency operations. This was tried out by the British against the communist insurgents in Malaya to deny the insurgents contact with the local population and thus deny access to food, water, shelter and more importantly intelligence. Under this scheme scattered villages were shifted and relocated in bigger groups along the main road.

The grouping scheme covered a 30-km belt astride the main road. In the first phase, which was undertaken in January 1967, the regrouping was done along the main Silchar-Aizwal-Lungleih road. The grouped villages were called Protected and Progressive Villages (PPV). 18 PPVs were established in this phase. In the second phase the focus was shifted to the border areas, which were used by the rebels for ingress into Mizo Hills from their bases in East Pakistan and Myanmar. In 1969 the administration passed orders for regrouping 182 villages into 40 Voluntary Group Centres (VGC) in the border areas.[21]

There were allegations of villages having been set on fire and the grouping done under coercion, which caused widespread resentment amongst the villagers. The residents of regrouped villages had to carry identity cards at all times and no move was allowed after sunset. These restrictions virtually amounted to curfew.

The clustering of villages was undertaken to curb the hostiles initiative and freedom of movement. It allowed the army to undertake large-scale operations to scour the jungles and the hillsides. The rebels were forced to find sanctuary in East Pakistan; a few escaped to Arakan via the Kaladan Valley, which was inadequately administered and policed by Myanmar. But in the process, the Mizo economy was destroyed and the villagers had to undergo great hardships. The rebels, instead of being denied shelter, received even more support from the alienated villages.

Overground Politics: Mizoram becomes Union Territory

The insurgency continued, though at a low level, alongside the electoral process. A number of proposals for the reorganisation of the North-east were mooted, but none found favour with the Mizos. In the elections to the district council in 1970, no party obtained a clear majority. After considerable horse trading Mizo Union formed a coalition with the Congress and called it the

United Mizo Parliamentary Party (UMPP). This coalition formed the government and successfully negotiated the status of Union Territory for Mizo Hill District. Smt Indira Gandhi inaugurated the Union Territory of Mizoram on January 21, 1972 at Aizwal.

The Aftermath of 1971 War

The defeat of Pakistan in 1971 war gave a severe blow to Mizo insurgency. They lost a safe sanctuary and were deprived of material support and training from erstwhile East Pakistan. The escape of MNA hardliners from East Pakistan after the fall of Dhaka was dramatic. It was made good in seven motor launches, which were collected at Rangamati. Each boat could carry 100 people. The remnants of MNA with over 150 weapons, which included a large number of machine guns, were loaded in the boats. The convoy of boats steamed towards Myanmar on the morning of 17 December. The Indian Air Force helicopter flew over the convoy and gave the fugitives some anxious moments, but finally they reached Arakan coast and formed National Emergency Council on December 23, 1971. Many had headed back to Mizo Hills. Laldenga managed to contact the Pakistani Consulate in the coastal town of Akyab with whose help he procured false passports for himself and his close associates and managed to escape out of Rangoon on a KLM flight to Karachi on April 18, 1972.[22]

MNA Regroups and Strikes Back

After the loss of its bases in erstwhile East Pakistan, MNA was fighting for its survival across the border in the jungles of Myanmar. In Arakan, the Mizos tied up with the Burmese Communist Party and took part in joint operations against the Burmese Army. One such attack was on an army post at Tanthawng in June 1972. A month later a group of 70 battle-hardened rebels with some new recruits left for Yunan in China under self-styled Major Damkoshiak. Unlike the previous attempt to reach Yunan in August 1968 under Bualhranga, which had failed, the group reached Yunan for training by the Chinese.

There was a spurt of hostilities after the installation of UT Government in 1972. Shortage of food in the interior due to failure of monsoons forced the guerrillas to concentrate around towns, particularly Aizwal and Lungleih. There were dramatic killings and widespread looting of cash from government treasuries and rice from godowns. Mizoram was declared a disturbed area on March 3, 1973 and night curfew was imposed in Aizwal.

The MNA had organised assassination squads, which marked a change in tactics to urban terrorism. Although the number of encounters came down, there was an increase in the number of selective killings. Lalnunmawia, one time vice-president, was killed in his hospital bed on June 25, 1972. On March 10, 1973 there was an attempt on the life of the Governor, when his convoy was ambushed on Silchar-Aizwal road, but fortunately he escaped.

The guerrillas who at this stage numbered around 1,000 were armed with sophisticated Pakistani and Chinese weapons. An attempt was made to set up a continuous belt of insurrection all along the border from Manipur to the Arakan Hills in the East and the Jampui Hills in Tripura and CHT in Bangladesh in the West. The MNA also went on a feverish recruiting drive.[23]

The situation across the border in Myanmar was favourable for the Mizos. A parallel rebel government was functioning in the mountains of North Myanmar, particularly in Shan area and in the Chin Hills in South. The MNF was hopeful of support from U Nu who was trying to overthrow Ne Win government through insurrection. The pro-Beijing Burmese Communist Party was the principal ally of the MNF giving them sanctuary in the Arakan and the Chin Hills.[24] The Mizo rebels sneaked into Mizo Hills from their bases in Arakan in small batches and concentrated in Aizwal and Lungleih. The town commander of MNA was one self-styled Major Kapchhunga who levied and collected taxes from the residents including government officials.[25] Lalheila, code-named MC-351, was the official executioner of the MNF.[26]

The situation in Mizoram was fluid and there was a sense of drift and uncertainty. The most sensational and serious attack took place on January 13, 1975. The rebels killed the Inspector General of Police, the Deputy Inspector General of Police and Superintendent of Police in the Police Headquarters in the heart of the capital Aizwal. The government was forced to take notice of the grim ground realities in Mizoram. MNF was again declared unlawful, the previous notification having expired long back. Some effective steps to tone up the administration were taken. The killing of top police officials was a devastating experience for the Mizoram Police. When no police officer was willing to come forward to fill the vacant post of the Inspector General, Brigadier SS Randhawa was appointed to head the Mizoram Police. Randhawa proved equal to the task and within a span of six months brought the situation under control and put the police force back on its feet.[27]

Peace Moves and 1976 Agreement

Around 1973 there were some feelers from Laldenga seeking peace. [28] The Mizo Union, which had formally merged, with the Indian National Congress in early 1974 urged Laldenga to begin talks with the Governor, SP Mukherjee. Brigadier T Sailo, the highest-ranking Mizo officer in the Indian Army had retired and formed a new regional party called the People's Conference. In mid-1975 a group of MNA returnees from China, led by Dankoshiak surrendered to the Indian authorities. A whole set of circumstances were developing which prompted Laldenga to seek a settlement. He wrote to Mrs Indira Gandhi in August 1975 expressing his desire to come to a settlement with the Government of India. With the prospect of a settlement,

Laldenga returned to India in January 1976. In February, he signed an agreement by which he agreed to abjure violence, accept Mizoram as an integral part of India, seek a solution to the Mizoram problem within the Constitution of India and most importantly hand over all arms to the central government in a camp within a month. The agreement was ratified in a convention held at Calcutta in the last week of March 1976, which was also attended by Arakan based leaders. But some leaders harboured misgivings about the agreement. Laldenga proved indecisive in honouring the agreement. While the government wanted the surrender of arms by the MNF to precede political settlement, the MNF wanted it to be the other way round.

Progress of Talks under the Janata Government

Mrs Gandhi lost the parliamentary election in January 1977. The new Prime Minister, Mr Morarji Desai insisted that Laldenga must honour his commitment to surrender arms before arriving at any political settlement. The failure of talks led the government to ask Laldenga to leave India by June 6, 1977. On June 9, 1977 62 MNF and MNA personnel led by Sawmvela, ex-chief of MNA laid down their arms and declared that it was immoral to continue armed struggle after July, 1976 Accord. Laldenga, however, continued to stay on in Delhi and continued talks with the then Home Minister, Charan Singh.[29]

Mizo Union Ministry led by Chief Minister Chhunga resigned in May 1977, ostensibly to facilitate the progress of peace talks. The announcement by the Indian Government in August 1977 that it would end President's rule and hold elections in Mizoram came as a rude shock to Laldenga. He did not want Brigadier Sailo to gain political initiative from him. In a letter to the Home Minister, Mr Charan Singh, in November 1977, Laldenga indicated that the surrender of arms could be completed by January 26, 1978.[30] Laldenga feared that an election at this stage would lead to Sailo's victory, which would weaken his bargaining position with the government. Laldenga also hinted at an interim government with himself at its head, but the government found it unacceptable.

Laldenga had led the Central Government to believe that he had issued instructions to his headquarters for implementation of the agreement within a time bound programme. But his duplicity was exposed when security forces at Champhai arrested Zoramthanga, the MNF general secretary. It was revealed that he was carrying instructions, which were contrary to what he was saying to the government. This led to the talks being called off in March 1978.

Rift in MNF

By now MNF was riddled with factionalism. Biakchhunga, who had been stripped off his post as the chief of MNA by Laldenga for allegedly parleying with Sailo, got himself elected as the president of MNF ousting Laldenga. Laldenga tried to retrieve the situation by attempting to manipulate the arrest of Biakchhunga, but Biakchhunga intervened and prevented a bloodbath. For Biakchhunga and his followers this was the end of their lives as guerrillas. In August 1978, 201 MNA rebels led by Biakchhunga laid down their arms and joined the mainstream.

Sailo's Victory in 1978 Assembly Elections

Far reaching developments were simultaneously taking place in the overground politics. The rise of People's Conference founded by Brig Sailo was quite phenomenal. Sailo concentrated on exposing human rights violations by the security forces and won widespread acclaim for it. The People's Conference won an overwhelming majority in the assembly elections held in 1978 but Sailo's refusal to grant undue favours caused dissension in his party, which led to the fall of the government and imposition of President's Rule. In the mid-term poll held in May 1979, Sailo again won a majority but with reduced margin. The politics of Mizoram hereafter got polarised between supporters of Sailo and Laldenga. Laldenga now issued a fresh directive to revive insurgency. A quit order on *Vais* (outsiders) was served. Non-Mizos were ordered to leave Mizoram by July 1979. The law and order deteriorated to the extent that MNF and all its front organisations were declared illegal. Sailo persuaded New Delhi to place Laldenga under arrest. Between January and March 1980, the MNF killed more than they had killed in the last ten years.[31]

Resumption of Talks after Return of Indira Gandhi to Power in 1980

The victory of Mrs Indira Gandhi in 1980 parliamentary elections gave Laldenga another opportunity to start negotiations with the Centre. On the advice of Congress leaders of Mizoram, Laldenga was released from prison, and all charges against him were withdrawn and counter-insurgency operations were suspended. G Parthasarthy was entrusted with the task of negotiating with Laldenga. During the talks, Laldenga made some unacceptable demands, which included giving Mizoram a status similar to Jammu and Kashmir, unification of Mizo-Kuki areas in Manipur and Tripura with Mizoram, delinking Mizoram from Sixth Schedule, incorporation of inner line as a constitutional guarantee and ouster of Sailo as the Chief Minister and installation of Laldenga in his place as the head of the interim government. The Government was amenable to bestowing full statehood on Mizoram and making Laldenga the interim Chief Minister, but other demands were unacceptable. Talks continued throughout 1982, but the renewed escalation of violence, on instructions of Laldenga (according to intelligence reports), forced the government to call off further negotiations. Laldenga was asked to leave the country and he left for London on April 21, 1982.[32]

The government responded by inducting additional army brigades and intensification of counter-insurgency operations.

The suspension of operations in the previous years had given the people a taste of normal life and they began to yearn for peace. The church also threw its weight on the side of peace and made fervent calls for ending hostilities. The overground politics of Mizoram was also making a shift. The Congress party in Mizoram, which was aligned with Indira Gandhi's Indian National Congress, embarked on a campaign for the ouster of Brig Sailo, who was held responsible for the failure of peace talks with Laldenga. In the elections to the Mizoram assembly in 1984, the Congress under Lalthanhawla fought on the platform of ushering in peace and won with an overwhelming majority. Lalthanhawla, who was himself an ex–MNF man was successful in winning the support of his ex-MNF colleagues for the Congress. He became the Chief Minister in May 1984. In accordance with the election pledge, Laldenga returned to India on October 29, 1984 a day before the assassination of Mrs Gandhi, to resume talks.

Events after the Assassination of Indira Gandhi: Memorandum of Settlement

The victory of Congress in 1984 parliamentary elections after the assassination of Indira Gandhi came as a boon to Laldenga. The happenings in Punjab delayed the resumption of talks, but Lalthanhawla successfully persuaded Rajiv Gandhi to work out a plan for the final settlement. The talks were resumed in 1985 and a Memorandum of Settlement was signed on June 30, 1986. Under the provisions of the settlement, the MNF committed itself to end all underground activities, ensure surrender of insurgents with arms and ammunitions. The Centre on its part agreed to grant statehood to Mizoram and rehabilitate the rebels. It also guaranteed to safeguard the social and religious practices of the Mizos, customary laws and procedures, administration of civil and customary justice according to Mizo customary laws and regulation of ownership as well as transfer of land to Mizos.

In the unwritten part of the Accord it was agreed that the Congress (I) ministry in Mizoram would resign and there would be a coalition government with Laldenga as Chief Minister and Lalthanhawla as the deputy chief minister for six months after which elections to the newly created state assembly would be held. In the election held in 1987, the MNF won 25 seats, Congress 12 and People's Conference 3. Laldenga retained his Chief Ministership.

The corrupting influence of power soon caught up with the rebel leaders of yesteryears. It was not long before there were accusations of corruption, nepotism and favouritism. The former guerrillas had turned into modern day politicians and not surprisingly in subsequent elections to the assembly the MNF lost the mandate of the people of Mizoram.

Appraisal

The British kept Mizoram like other hill areas of Assam isolated from the rest of the country as a measure of colonial policy. Mizo Hills was annexed in 1890 and administered as 'Excluded Area'. Unlike the Nagas and other hill tribes of Assam, the majority of 15 tribes of Mizo Hills had assumed a Mizo identity early on after their annexation by the British. The spread of Christianity and the adoption of Lushai dialect with Roman script provided the stimuli for bonding. As Urmila Phadnis puts it, "Identity need not be ascriptive or given. It can also be created."[33]

Again, unlike Nagaland there were two streams of opinion among Mizos on the status of Mizo Hills. The left-wingers who were educated young Christians wanted the abolition of chieftainship, representation of Mizos in the Assam legislature and their socio-economic advancement. On the other hand, the chiefs supported by a segment of Mizo Union and backed by the British favoured Lushai Hills joining Myanmar. The Church in Mizoram played a positive role and did not support cessation from India. They had taken a stand against violence from the very beginning and had also told Laldenga that they were against seeking help from China.[34]

Grouping of villages in Mizoram, which took place during the period 1967-69, has been criticised by a number of analysts on the ground that the strategy caused large-scale alienation of Mizos and helped gain widespread sympathy for the underground. This is true, but in the short-term and in the circumstances prevailing then, insurgent activity declined appreciably and most of the insurgents took refuge in the forests of Sajek range in CHT.

The emergence of Bangladesh after 1971 war was a major turning point in the insurgency in Mizoram. Not only did the Mizo insurgents lose their bases in CHT, they also lost the active support of Pakistan, who in the immediate aftermath of their defeat in the war, wanted to develop a more cordial relation with India. Although Pakistan had given sanctuary to Laldenga in Rawalpindi, they arranged his flight to Geneva in August 1974 on a passport issued by them in the name of Peter Lee. Laldenga had seen the writing on the wall and wrote to Mrs Indira Gandhi that he was now willing to find a solution of the Mizoram political problem within the Constitution of India.[35]

What were the reasons for the success of Mizo Accord when other accords have failed to bring peace in Nagaland, Tripura and Assam? The most important factor was that Laldenga was the supreme leader of the MNF. Although his leadership was challenged in the late seventies, he was to quickly regain his position. Laldenga and his principal aide Zoranthanga were able to persuade their cadres to lay down their arms at specific locations, accept the Indian Constitution and return to civilian life. The terms of the agreement envisaged surrender of arms would follow the political accord and not precede it. The role of the Church was another significant factor. The church leaders had thrown their weight in favour of the peace process. The willingness of the Chief Minister, Lalthanhawla, to step down from the chief ministership to make room for Laldenga was an act of great statesmanship. In the larger context, there was always an influential political class that favoured autonomy within the Indian Union.

Notes and References

1. Animesh Ray; *Mizoram*, (India: National Book Trust, 1993), p. 23.
2. BG Verghese, *India's North-east Resurgent*, (New Delhi:, Konark, 1996), p. 135.
3. Ibid., p. 1.36.
4. For full description of physical geography of Lushai Hills see *Imperial Gazetteer of India*, Vol XVI, (Oxford: 1908), pp. 213-214.
5. VIK Sareen, *India's North-east in Flames*, (New Delhi: Vikas Publishing, 1980), p. 145.
6. Urmila Phadnis, *Ethnicity and Nation Building in South Asia*, (New Delhi: Sage Publications, 1990), p149. Chieftainship was abolished in 1954, when special privileges of the chiefs came to an end.
7. VIK Sareen, n. 5., p. 148.
8. Urmila Phadnis, n.6., p. 190.
9. Ibid., p. 150.
10. VIK Sareen, n. 5., p, 150.
11. Ibid., pp. 150-152. Also see Subir Bhaumik, *Insurgent Crossfire*, (New Delhi: Lancers, 1996), p. 146.
12. Subir Bhaumik, n. 11., p. 146.
13. Ibid., p. 148.
14. Ibid., p. 15.
15. DK Palit, *Sentinels of the North-east: Assam Rifles*, (New Delhi: Palit and Palit, 1984), p. 261.
16. Ibid., p. 261.
17. Ibid, p. 264.
18. Ibid, p. 262.
19. Ibid, p. 262.
20. At this time both Pakistan and China were giving moral and material support and training to Mizo rebels mainly in Sajek Range of Hills in

CHT. Ved Marwah, *Uncivil Wars: Anatomy of Terrorism in India*, (New Delhi: Harper and Collins, India, 1995), p. 240.

21. For critical examination of this scheme see Subir Bhaumik, n. 11., pp 159, 162, and Ved Marwah, n.20., pp 238-240 and DK Palit, n. 15., p. 271.
22. Subir Bhaumik, n.11., pp. 171-172.
23. Animesh Ray, *Mizoram*, (India: National Book Trust, 1993). p. 171.
24. Ibid, p. 172.
25. Ibid, p. 172.
26. Subir Bhaumik, n. 11., p. 174.
27. For a lucid description of the personality of Brig Randhawa see Ved Marwah, n. 20., p. 249.
28. Zoranthanga, a trusted ally of Laldenga was sent to Kabul to contact Indian officials in November 1973. Subir Bhaumik, n. 11., p. 174.
29. Vijendra Singh Jafa, "Mizoram: Contours of Non-military Intervention" in KPS Gill (ed) *Faultlines*, Vol 4, (New Delhi: Institute for Conflict Management, 2000).
30. For the text of Laldenga's letter to the Home Minister see Subir Bhaumik, n. 11.,, pp. 181-182.
31. Subir Bhaumik, n. 11.,, p 186, Quoting Animesh Ray, *Mizoram: Dynamics of Change*, (Calcutta: Pearl Publishers, 1982).
32. VS Jafa, n. 29., p. 91.
33. Urmila Phadnis, n. 6., p. 148.
34. RN Prasad, *Government and Politics in Mizoram*, (New Delhi: Northern Book Centre, 1987), p 195. Quoted by VS Jafa, n. 29., p. 70.
35. Nirmal Nibedon, *Mizoram: The Dagger Brigade*, (New Delhi: Lancers, 1980), pp. 208-9.

5

MANIPUR

Manipur has a total area of 22,356 sq km. The state is bound by Myanmar in the East and Nagaland in the North. The Cachar district of Assam is to its West, while Mizoram and Chin Hills of Myanmar are to its South. Nine-tenth of the state consists of almost parallel rows of hills, which rise up to 3000 meters above sea level. The average altitude of the valley is about 790 meters above mean sea level. The temperature varies between 2.8 - 33.3 degrees celsius. The rainy season extends from May to September with rainfall varying from 149 cm in the valley to about 380 cm in the Western hills. The Loktak Lake in Manipur is the largest fresh water lake in the North-east region.

Manipur is connected to other parts of the country by road and air. Manipur is ill served by two National Highways – NH 53 from Silchar through Jiribam to Imphal and NH 39 from Dimapur via Kohima to Imphal. The population of Manipur according to 2001 census is 23,88,634. Two-third of the population is concentrated in the valley and remaining one-third is scattered in the hills. The hilly areas of Manipur cover 90 percent of its geographical area. The valley area of Manipur is inhabited mainly by Meiteis, which according to oral tradition is composed of seven clans who speak a common language. There are differing views about the origin of Meiteis. The Meiteis differ from other hill tribes in that among most of the other tribes the clan is endogamous.[1]

Before the advent of Hinduism (Vaishnavism), the Meiteis worshipped Sanamahi and Pakhangba (the Almighty creator), as their supreme deities. By the end of 17th century, many local deities could be identified as belonging to the great Gods of Hindu religion. The present Meitei language spoken by the people has evolved from the language spoken in the valley and has its own script. In the ancient history of Manipur, there were no such tribes as Nagas and Kukis in Manipur. The British introduced the generic term Naga and Kuki for their own convenience to identify the tribes in the hills. The census of 1881 recognised Naga and Kuki as being two hill tribes and the Gazetteer of Manipur 1886 classified the population into two groups – the plains population and the hill tribes based upon geographical zones.

Historical Backdrop

Manipur literally means "the land of gem". The erstwhile kingdom of Manipur was known by different names in the past. The Burmese called it Kathe, the Cacharis called it Moglai, and other tribes of far Eastern region knew it by the name of Cassay.[2] It is claimed that the indigenous names of Manipur are Kangleipak, Poirei (Pak) and Meitrobak. [3] The present name Manipur was first officially introduced in early 18th century during the reign of Garib Nawaz (1709-48). The name Manipur is also linked to the great epic Mahabharata, in which Arjuna married Chitrangada, a princess of Manipur. The historians have yet to conclusively decide the origin of its name and its antiquity.

Very little is known of its pre-historic and early history. It is not known when the early settlements took place in the geographical area, now called Manipur. From the sketchy historical evidence and the physical characteristics of the people, it is surmised that Mongoloid races from North and East were the first settlers in the valley of Manipur.

Prior to 18th century, Manipur kings were often engaged in hostilities with neighbouring Burma. Although there is no definitive record of early relations between Burmese and Manipuris, later records reveal "a terrible relationship of plunder and devastation operating on both sides to the damage of both people."[4] Garib Nawaz, who ascended the throne of Manipur in 1714 AD, has been described as a brilliant leader of Manipur. [5] During his reign, Garib Nawaz inflicted many defeats on the Burmese forces. It was during his time that Vaishnavism spread in the Manipur Valley.

After the death of Garib Nawaz his successors fought amongst each other for supremacy. The palace intrigues and fratricidal feuds amongst the princes weakened Manipur to such an extent that the Burmese were prompted to invade Manipur, first in 1755, and then again in 1758, and inflict crippling defeat on it. The defeat proved so crippling that the King had to seek alliance of the British. The first formal treaty of alliance between Manipuris and the British was signed on September 4, 1762 during the reign of Jai Singh. Under the treaty Jai Singh was promised the help of British troops to recover territories lost to the Burmese. The force sent to assist Manipur was, however, recalled and after this there was little communication between the British and the state of Manipur for many years.[6]

Jai Singh died in 1799. After his death, the numerous sons of Jai Singh engaged in unsavoury intrigues, plots and treachery to gain supremacy. From about 1815, the Burmese excursions into Assam and Manipur began to alarm the British. In 1819, the Burmese intervened in a family feud of the royal family and captured Manipur. By now the relations between the British and the Burmese had become very strained. Finally, Lord Amherst, the then Governor General of India, declared formal war against Burma on February 24, 1824. Gambhir Singh supported by British forces under Lieutenant Pemberton marched from Sylhet on May 17, 1825 and reached Western limits of the valley. The Burmese fled from the valley and thus the valley was taken back from the Burmese control on June 10, 1825. Later

Gambhir Singh with the help of British forces under Captain Grant pushed out Burmese from the Kabaw Valley.[7]

The Defeat of the Burmese and the Treaty of Yandeboo

The fighting at many fronts had weakened the Burmese. When the British under Campbell occupied Yandeboo, a town within 45 miles of Ava, the capital of Burma, the Burmese sought peace and signed the Treaty of Yandeboo on February 1, 1826. By virtue of this treaty, the Burmese were to renounce all claims on Assam, Manipur and the states of Cachar and Jaintia. The King of Ava recognised Gambhir Singh as the ruler of Manipur. The British Government entered into another agreement with Gambhir Singh, which decided the Western boundary of Manipur.

After the defeat of the Burmese, Manipur regained its status as an independent state. Gambhir Singh died in 1834. On his death his son being at the time only one-year-old, Nar Singh, his uncle, was appointed regent. In the same year, the British Government decided to restore Kabaw Valley to Burma and agreed to pay to the Raja of Manipur an annual allowance of Rupees 6370/- in compensation for the loss of the Kabaw Valley[8].

In 1835, a political agent was appointed to act as a medium of communication between the State of Manipur and the British Government[9]. Although there was no clause in the agreement, which curtailed the sovereignty of Manipur, yet the State came under stifling British influence thereafter. The British influence is evident in the manner in which Kabaw Valley, under Manipuri control since 1826 by the right of conquest, was given back to the Burmese King of Ava in 1834 without the consent of Raja Gambhir Singh.

Annexation of Manipur

After the death of Gambhir Singh, his one-year-old son, Chandrakirti, was put on the throne with Nar Singh (cousin brother of Gambhir) as the regent. In a family intrigue reminiscent of the past events, Nar Singh proclaimed himself the king in 1844 and the minor king had to flee to Cachar in the care of his mother. Nar Singh died in April 1850 and was succeeded by his brother Debendra. But luck was not on his side. Chandrakirti had by now become an adult and in a swing of fortune he returned to Manipur in July 1850 and reclaimed his throne.

Chandrakirti Singh was a clever ruler. He knew that to remain in power he had to keep the British on his side. The opportunity to show his loyalty to the British came in 1879, when the Nagas killed Dumant, the British political agent in Kohima. He dispatched a contingent of 2000 soldiers under Johnstone, the political agent of Manipur, to suppress the rebellion and thus won the goodwill of the British.[10] But it also sowed the seeds of Nagaland - Manipur animosity, which was to manifest more than a 150 years later in the demand for Greater Nagaland.

Chandrakirti died in 1866 and was succeeded by his eldest son Surachandra. Interestingly, Chandrakirti had ten sons by his six queens. Tikendrajit, the king's half-brother was the *Senapati*, or Commander-in-Chief, who, it is alleged engineered an attempt on Surachandra's life. Surachandra fled to Cachar from where he sought British help to restore him to the throne. In the interim another prince Kulachandra, Surachandra's brother, declared himself the king. The real power seems to have been in the hands of Tikendrajit. The British decided to recognise Kulachandra's claim to throne provided Tikendrajit, was removed from the state and was punished for his lawless conduct.

Fearing trouble, the Viceroy of India ordered JW Quinton, the Chief Commissioner of Assam to personally supervise the events that were to take place. After much deliberation, it was decided by the Chief Commissioner to hold a durbar, at which the orders of the Government of India were to be announced and the *Senapati* arrested. The latter, however, refused to appear, and it was decided to arrest him on March 24, 1891. But Quinton arrogantly made the mistake of keeping the regent Kulachandra waiting outside the residency for hours in the sun, which hurt the pride of Manipuris and they were seething with anger.[11]

When the plan to arrest Tikendrajit Singh without the use of force failed, Quinton made another mistake of ordering his arrest by sending armed soldiers to raid his house. The raid resulted in an exchange of fire, which continued for the whole day, but in the evening a truce was agreed to. Quinton, thereafter, informed the regent and Tikendrajit that he wanted discussion with them directly. The *Senapati* invited the Chief Commissioner to meet him at the fort. After the assurance of safe passage, Quinton accompanied by other British officers proceeded to the fort, where he met the *Senapati* but no agreement was reached. The sequence of events after the Chief Commissioner had reached the fort is not clear. There appears to have been total disorder. As the Chief Commissioner's party was leaving, their way was barred and in the misadventure one officer was killed and another wounded but Tikendrajit could not be arrested. The Chief Commissioner and other officers were detained for two hours, and then marched to an open square where they were beheaded by the public executioner. Some escaped to Burma and Cachar.

On receiving the news of the rebellion, the British launched a full-scale attack on Manipur with three columns: one each from Kohima, Silchar and Tamu (Burma). The main fighting took place at Thoubal and Khongjam. In the Battle of Khongjam a Manipuri officer, Major Paona Brajbari, fought a valiant battle till the last and became a hero for Manipuris for all times. By the time the British troops arrived at the palace on April 27, 1891 the *Yubraj* (the Prince) and the *Senapati* had fled. They were, however, captured; the *Senapati* and some others were hanged while Kulachadra and other ringleaders were deported to the Andamans. Thus the revolt in 1891 against the British led to a complete take over of the administration by the British. Churachand, a boy belonging to the collateral branch of the royal house, was placed on the throne. During his minority the political agent administered the state. In 1907, the Maharaja, who was educated at the Ajmer College, was formally installed on the throne *(gaddi)*.[12]

The young Maharaja was subjected to the advice of a durbar (council) headed by a British officer, who virtually became the administrator of the hill areas. Subsequently, the Government laid down the doctrine that the hill areas were merely dependent on Manipuri rajas. In 1917, there was a Kuki revolt against recruitment of labour for service in France as part of war effort. After the suppression of the revolt, far-reaching changes were made in the administration of Manipur. The Maharaja became responsible for the administration of Manipur with the advice of the durbar but had to keep the British political agent apprised of the differences between the Maharaja and the durbar. The Governor of Assam became the appellate authority. The British president of the durbar became *de facto* administrator of the hill areas. The bifurcation of the administration of the valley and the surrounding hills had the effect of separating hill and plain politics of Manipur.[13]

Politicisation of Manipur Politics

The politicisation of Manipur administration can be traced back to 1934 when a group of Manipuri intellectuals formed the Nikhil Hindu Manipuri Mahasabha with the patronage of the ruler. The king was the president and Haijam Irabot was the vice-president. The guiding light was however Irabot who was himself a member of the royal family. Under his influence the words "Hindu-Manipuri" were removed and it was renamed simply Nikhil Manipur Mahasabha in 1938. One of the demands of the Mahasabha was a combined administrative unit of hills and plains.[14]

Radicalism of Haijam Irabot

Haijam Irabot was one of the earliest political leaders of Manipur who devoted his life to achieve an independent Manipur. He had radical views and was a tireless campaigner against injustice. Early in 1940, he campaigned against the export of rice from Manipur. The hoarding of rice by businessmen for selling it outside at exorbitant price had created an artificial shortage. His campaign against such unethical practices landed him in jail for three years. When he demanded jail reforms, he was transferred to Sylhet jail, where he met many Marxists and was exposed to communist ideology. He was released after his prison term but was denied entry into Manipur. By now the war with Japan had advanced to the doors of India and consequently the ban on Irabot was lifted in 1946. On return to Manipur he formed a political party called Praja Sangha, which was in opposition to Manipur Congress (not a unit of the Indian National Congress).

Events Immediately Prior to Independence

When it became clear that the British would soon depart granting Independence to India, the Maharaja signed the Instrument of Accession on August 11, 1947 entrusting defence, communication and foreign affairs to the Government of India. A Standstill Agreement was also entered into in respect of other matters. In the same year, influenced by Pearson, the President of the Durbar, a liberal constitution for the state was formed. Under the Manipur Constitution Act 1947, elections were held towards the end of 1948 to a new 53 member state assembly on the basis of adult franchise. Both the plain and the hill areas took part in the elections. A coalition government was formed without Manipur Congress. The Manipur Congress had launched a movement for merger of Manipur with India whereas the coalition government headed by Maharaj Kumar Priobarta Singh, influenced by Irabot, was opposed to it. In 1948, International Communist Congress was held at Calcutta, which had adopted Zhdanov line of proletarian revolution that had also attracted the youth in many parts of Asia. The communists were making rapid ingress into Burma. The fear of instability along the Eastern borders of India was real. It was in these circumstances that Maharaja Bodhchandra Singh signed the Instrument of Merger on September 21, 1949.[15] A Chief Commissioner took over the administration of the state on October 15, 1949. The Council of Ministers and the Legislative Assembly was dissolved. On January 26, 1950 Manipur became a Part C state in the Union of India.

The merger was followed by crackdown on communists. Irabot escaped to Burma, where he sought help from the Communist Party of Burma. Irabot established himself in Kubaw Valley and with the help of Burmese communists set up "Manipur Red Guard" to fight for an Independent Socialist Republic of Manipur. But he soon fell ill with typhoid and died of illness on September 26, 1954 in Tangbo, a village in Burma.[16] Thus ended the life of a remarkable man who became a legend in the history of contemporary Manipur.

The Growth of Secessionist Movement and Insurgency

The idea of a separate state had made an impact on the thinking of some Manipuri intellectuals. After the death of Irabot, they decided to carry forward the idea left behind by him. Thus was born a Pan-Mongoloid movement, which nurtured the idea of creating a new nation of Mongoloid people of the entire North-east region of India. In due course the idea crystallised in the formation of the United National Liberation Front (UNLF) on November 24, 1964 under the leadership of Arambam Somorendra. By the end of 1960s UNLF had established itself as a well-knit underground organisation. But soon differences cropped up between Somorendra and Oinam Sudhir, the two top leaders on UNLF. Oinam Sudhir wanted immediate armed revolution whereas Somorendra preferred to wait and prepare the people politically before launching a full-fledged armed struggle.

The Genesis of Insurgency

There were many causes of discontent amongst the Meiteis of Manipur. They had a sense of greatness and looked upon themselves as inheritors of a past of which they were justly proud. Although Manipur was geographically small, it had a distinct history, culture and political entity. They had, therefore, hoped for a full-fledged state right after Independence, which was granted only in 1972.

Manipur rulers had sought retrocession of Kabaw Valley from Burma on a number of occasions. After Independence the Government of India continued to pay Kabaw compensation to Manipur Durbar till 1953, when Nehru waived the claim in favour of the Burmese during a joint visit to Manipur with U Nu. The unilateral act was seen as arbitrary and rankled the Manipuri mind.

The Meiteis entertained a sense of discrimination by the Central Government. In order to woo the rebellious Nagas of the hills, the government granted them many concessions. Whereas tribals can freely buy land in the Imphal Valley, Meiteis are debarred from acquiring land in the hills. Again hill people are categorised as Scheduled Tribe, which gave them an advantage over Meiteis of the valley in recruitment to All India Services. The situation was rectified after job reservations were given to Meiteis as other backward caste in the All India Services in 1990s.

Yet, another cause of discontent was the perception amongst Meiteis that they were discriminated for being Hindus, whereas the government in its bid to woo the Naga militants pampered them. The exclusion of Manipuri language, which boasts of a well-developed literature and is the *lingua franca* in both the hills and the valley, from the Eighth Schedule of the constitution till 1992 was another irritant in Manipur relations with the Centre.

Spread of Insurgency

Sometime in 1968 a group of UNLF cadres under Oinam Sudhir went to Sylhet in East Pakistan to seek their support.[17] This was the time when the internal situation in East Pakistan was getting explosive due to the agitation launched by Sheikh Mujibur Rehman. The Pakistanis did not want to put their relations with India under further strain and to show that it was not supporting the secessionists, handed over the Meitei youths to the Indian Army.[18] While still in East Pakistan Oinam Sudhir and Somarendra fell apart and Sudhir was expelled from the party. Sudhir needed an organisation behind him to make an impact on the Pakistanis. He was a skilful organiser and soon set up "Revolutionary Government of Manipur (RGM)" in Sylhet, sometime in 1969. He organised a handful of Meitei youths and made an impression on the local Pakistani commander, who began training the Meitei youths in the use of weapons. The rebels put their training to use during the 1971 war. They attacked isolated Indian Police posts at Cachar, Dharamnagar, and Karimganj.[19] When Pakistan suffered a crushing defeat, Oinam Sudhir with his group returned to Manipur but was apprehended in Tamenglong district by the local police. After some months in jail, they were released under the general amnesty. Thus, ended a chapter in the attempt to stoke the fire of rebellion in Manipur. But only temporarily. Soon another organisation, more radical than UNLF, rocked the state with violence.

Formation of People's Liberation Army (PLA)

In an attempt to bring about peace, Manipur was granted statehood in 1972. This had been a long-standing demand of the Manipuris and was one of the causes of their discontent. With the grant of amnesty peace returned to Imphal Valley for some time. After the announcement of amnesty Sudhir with his other colleagues, Bisheshwar and Sanajaoba, set up a farm at

Kondong Lairenbi in Chandel district. But their life of tranquility was only short-lived. Differences surfaced between them. Bisheshwar wanted to continue the struggle whereas the other two were not very enthusiastic. Relationships in insurgent groups are fragile. As it so often happens in insurgent movements, supporters of Bisheshwar gunned down Sudhir and Sanajaoba.[20] Bisheshwar was now heading the group that wanted to continue the fight.

Pakistan's help had dried up after its defeat in 1971 war. Bisheshwar had left leanings and was influenced by Maoist thoughts. The group decided to seek China's help. On June 14, 1975 Bisheshwar, along with 16 others left Imphal for Lhasa.[21] It took them 15 days to reach Kathmandu from where they crossed the Tibetan border at Tatokpani and reached Lhasa. The group was given lectures on Maoist thoughts and communist ideology and later trained in guerrilla warfare.

On its return from Lhasa to Imphal the group formed a new organisation called the PLA (Eastern Region) in 1978 with Bisheshwar as its Chairman. PLA's main object was to wage an armed struggle for separation of Manipur from India and establish a society based on Maoist thoughts. The China returned guerrillas spread out in different parts of the valley and established secret cells. This was the beginning of the second phase of insurgency by Meitei youths this time charged with communist ideology.

The PLA started ambushing security forces in order to acquire arms and create panic. The guerrillas selected their targets in crowded areas in broad daylight and escaped on cycles. They enjoyed the sympathy of a large section of Meitei population. They sought assistance from Bangladesh and Kachins in Burma. The guerrilla activities rose with the formation alongside the PLA of People's Revolutionary Party of Kangleipok (PREPAK) led by Tulachandra. Lesser insurgent groups sprouted but soon faded away. The NSCN was active in the hills to further the Naga cause whereas MNF kept the pot boiling in the Mizo Hills.

Terrorism peaked in the years between 1979 and 1981. Small bands created terror on an unprecedented scale. Their effectiveness was all the more remarkable since they did not have many arms and their numbers were small. The Meiteis had mastered the art of urban terrorism. They killed three CRPF men in an ambush at Patsoi on April 26, 1980. In the shoot-out CRPF killed four persons, which included two women. The incident was blown out of proportion to project CRPF as trigger-happy. But the security forces had begun to get their act together. They raided a PLA camp at Choro in October 1980 and killed at least four Lhasa trained guerrillas, but Bisheshwar and some others escaped.

The number of persons killed in incidents of violence was going up year by year. The numbers killed went up from two in 1972 to 14 in 1979, 36 in 1980 and 50 in 1981.[22] Alarmed at the rise in violence, Imphal Valley was declared as disturbed area in September 1980 and the state was brought under the Armed Forces (Assam and Manipur) Special Powers Act. The army swung into action and relentless operations under Maj Gen VK Nayyar, GOC 8 Mountain Division, were undertaken, which soon yielded results. In July 1981, on a tip-off, the army surrounded the underground camp at Tekcham. Almost all the top leaders who were inside the camp were killed. The army captured Bisheshwar on July 6, 1981.

After the capture of Bisheshwar, Kunjbihari took on the leadership. But the army kept up the pressure. On April 13, 1982 the army surrounded remaining hardcore guerrillas, at Kadampokpi 10 km from Imphal. In the ensuing encounter Kunjbihari and eight others were killed. The decimation of Lhasa trained guerrillas was a major setback for the PLA. Although sporadic low level terrorist acts continued, but the momentum had been halted.

Bisheshwar was persuaded to work overground and join politics. He contested the elections for Manipur Assembly as an independent. He won but his election was subsequently set aside. Bisheshwar later paid the price for joining the mainstream when his followers shot him dead in August 1984.

Resurfacing of UNLF

The UNLF maintained a low profile for nearly two decades while spreading its ideology. Raj Kumar Meghen alias Sana Yaima, great grandson of Tikendrajit, was now heading the organisation as its general secretary. The mainstay of UNLF's campaign was the issue of Manipuri identity. His refrain was: "Manipur was and has never been a part of India." The UNLF's main ideological goal is to fight for restoration of independence and free Manipur from the shackles of Indian colonialism.[23] The other main objective of the UNLF is to unite the feuding insurgent outfits in different parts of North-east India. It had established contact with NSCN in April 1985 and set up camps in upper Burma near the headquarters of NSCN and KIA.

Formation of Indo-Burma Revolutionary Front

UNLF, NSCN (K), ULFA and KNA formed the Indo-Burma Revolutionary Front (IBRF) in May 1990 to "build up a united struggle for the independence of Indo-Myanmar". However, each group had its own axe to grind in the coalition. The KNA and NSCN (K) had its common enemy in NSCN (IM), while both ULFA and UNLF sought the support of NSCN (K) to set up sanctuaries in Myanmar. Soon after the formation of IBRF, UNLF launched its next phase of armed struggle when it ambushed a CRPF patrol in Loktak hydal project area on December 15, 1991.

Restructuring of PLA

After a series of setbacks suffered by the PLA in its encounter with the army in the early 80s and the virtual elimination of all its important leaders who had been trained in Lhasa by the Chinese, it decided to keep a low profile. It set up a camp in the Eastern Naga Hills in early 1983 close to NSCN headquarters. The group later contacted KIA, the Burmese insurgent group, for training and other assistance.

During it's time in wilderness in Myanmar, PLA cadres were trained and supported by NSCN and KIA. But it was not a cohesive group and lacked leadership. Soon Irengbam Bhorot assumed the leadership of PLA and started a new chapter in its struggle. The majority of its members returned to Imphal in early 1989 and on 13 February launched their first attack on a CRPF patrol in the area of Moirang Bazaar. Four CRPF men were killed and their weapons taken away. The PLA had announced its homecoming. In early 1990, it set up a base in Sylhet where PREPAK had already set up its camp. The PLA now under its new leader joined PREPAK and KCP in forming a Revolutionary Joint Committee (RJC) to work together. Irengbam Bhorot, who was the commander of PLA, revived its political wing, the Revolutionary People's Front. Under his leadership the PLA forged links with the armies of Bangladesh and Pakistan.[24]

Upsurge in Violence and Political Instability in the 1990s

There was relative peace after the decimation of PLA hardcore in the 1980s but the decade of 1990 saw an upsurge in violence and political instability. The eruption of clashes between the Nagas and Kukis in 1992 added a new dimension to insurgency. The NSCN (IM) and the KNA triggered the violence primarily for gaining control of the town of Moreh, a nodal point for the smuggling of narcotics, arms and other contraband on the Burmese border. The violence escalated in 1993. In a well-executed ambush on June 29, 1993 on NH 39, NSCN (IM) killed 26 army jawans and eight civilians. Between May and September 1993, NSCN (IM) killed 120 security forces personnel; 200 Kukis were killed between July and September 1993.[25] Naga-Kuki problem will be discussed in greater detail a little later.

Politics in the state is divided on ethnic lines. While the Meitei underground operate mainly in the Imphal Valley, Tangkhul Nagas are dominant in the hill districts. Muivah, himself a Tangkhul, has established a base in Ukhrul district. The underground Nagas have been collecting taxes to finance their activities.

The distinction between overground and underground politics in Manipur has blurred. Political leaders maintain close liaison with the underground. Lieutenant General VK Nayyar in his report to the Central Government in December 1993, advocating President's Rule, had noted that the overground and underground politics had got so intermingled that it was difficult to draw a clear line between them. He expressed his apprehension that the Chief Minister Dorendra Singh was aiding the Meitei extremists whereas his deputy Rishang Keishing was abetting the NSCN (IM). The Chief Minister was also suspected of aiding Kukis in the fratricidal war. There was a difference of opinion between Lieutenant General Nayyar, the Governor and the Central Government, which resulted in the Governor tendering his resignation.[26] Political instability resulted in imposition of Governor's rule on December 31, 1993. The situation improved temporarily, but in mid-1994, two army officers and one Assam Rifle's jawan were killed in Ukhrul. In a successful operation the army cleared a joint NSCN (IM)-Lim Guard camp in Senapati district.[27]

Fresh elections were held in 1995. Rishang Keishing (Congress I) was able to form a coalition government but failed to improve the law and order situation. The high point of the new Assembly was the passing of a unanimous resolution, which rejected the concept of Greater Nagaland. It may be recalled that Nagaland

Assembly had passed a resolution, which sought to create Greater Nagaland.

1995 witnessed a phenomenal increase in militancy. There was an explosion in the Raj Bhawan and an attempt on the life of Deputy Chief Minister Chaoba Singh in August 1995. On July 31, 1995 the NSCN (IM) attacked 9th Battalion of Manipur Rifles at Kangohud in Senapati district and looted 22 weapons and 3784 rounds of ammunition. On June 25, 1995 the militants took away weapons of the guards posted at the official residence of a minister in Imphal. A fortnight later, the militants again took away 10 weapons from the police. In all the above cases, the police offered no resistance. The army's suspicion of collusion between police and underground could not be easily dismissed.[28]

The period between 1990-95 proved to be bloodiest for Manipuris. According to Chief Minister Rishang Keishing 504 persons were killed in extremist related crimes and 479 were injured. A total of 314 security personnel were killed and 408 were injured during this period.[29]

The coalition Government at the Centre led by Shri IK Gujral took the initiative to start the peace process and declared cease-fire with the NSCN (IM) in August 1997. The NSCN (IM) has been demanding the extension of cease-fire to hill districts of Manipur, and Naga inhabited areas of Assam and Arunachal. There have been violent demonstrations by Meiteis against extending the cease-fire to Manipur. The Manipuris are very sensitive to any suggestion by the government to bifurcate Manipur to meet the demands of NSCN (IM). The battle lines are drawn, as, Ninglokrone, the convener of Naga People's Movement for Civil Rights says, "Unification of all Nagas is irreversible."[30] Meiteis have taken an equally hard line and say, "If the hills are cut away, the blood will flow into the valley."[31]

The Naga-Kuki Conflict

Although the Naga-Kuki conflict is of recent origin the seeds of conflict were sown during the British colonial period. To understand the genesis of the conflict, a brief historical perspective is necessary. Broadly, there are four ethnic groups in Manipur: Meitei, Nagas, Pangal (Muslims) and Kuki-Chin-Mizo. The so-called Kuki Chin groups are again subdivided into old and new Kukis. According to CA Soppit, old Kukis migrated to Manipur in the beginning of 11th century, whereas migration of new Kukis is fairly recent i.e. during the first half of 19th century.[32]

Nagas occupy large parts of the five hill districts of Ukhrul, Senapati, Tameglong, Churachandpur and Chandel. The Kukis are settled in the Eastern and Southern parts of Chandel district, scattered in the whole of Churachandpur district and some pockets of Ukhrul district. Kangpokpi subdivision of Senapati district has the largest Kuki population.

Colonel McCulloch, who was the British political agent in Manipur in the early part of 19th century, settled the new immigrant Kukis on the exposed frontiers of the state as a barrier against Burmese invasion and also to use them against Nagas or vice versa. In 1840, McCulloch brought in a large number of Kukis and let them loose in Naga Hills with rations and firearms to fight against the Nagas. He consciously exploited the ethnic differences between Nagas and Kukis. The Nagas were enrolled in the punitive actions to suppress the Kuki rebellion in 1917-19. Again the Kukis in the service of the King of Manipur were used by the British to put down the Naga uprising in Kohima in 1879. That was probably when the first seeds of conflict between Nagas and Kukis were sown.

Political Mobilisation of Kukis[33]

The earliest Kuki organisation, the Kuki National Assembly was formed in 1947. It is a political party and takes part in elections. There is also a Kuki "Inpi" which is the apex organisation of the Kukis. It works for the welfare of the Kukis, but has not been very active. There is another organisation called the Kuki National Front (KNF), which was formed in 1987 by Nehlun Kigpen. The Front seeks a separate Kuki land within India consisting of the districts of Sadar Hills, Churachandpur and parts of Tamenglong and Ukhrul. Yet, another organisation called the Kuki National Organisation (KNO), with its armed wing the Kuki National Army (KNA) has the objective of setting up a Kuki state exclusively within Myanmar. The President of KNO, Mr Hanglen, makes no claim on Indian territory. Besides the above many Kuki militant outfits had come up in 1990s and faded away.

The Beginning of Naga-Kuki Clashes

The Naga-Kuki clashes started in 1992 and soon the feud took the form of fratricidal war. The genesis of the fratricidal war lies in the NSCN (IM) campaign to control Moreh, a trading centre on Myanmar border. NSCN (IM) goal is to cleanse the area of Kukis so that the underground Nagas have full control of the area. The smuggling of narcotics and other contraband have been a source of considerable income for the Kukis. The Nagas want the major share of the income from the illegal trade, which the Kukis are not prepared to part with.

Most of the killings and violence have taken place along NH 39. The total number of Kukis killed so far (till 1993) exceeds 1,000.[34] Lt Gen VK Nayyar, the former Governor of Manipur, was of the view that the clashes were an extension of NSCN (IM)'s design to dominate Southern Nagaland and alter the demographic complexion of the region through a process of ethnic cleansing. In a scathing indictment of political parties in his report to the President, the Governor aired his suspicion that the Chief Minister was aiding Meitei extremists while his deputy, a Tangkhul Naga, was abetting the NSCN (IM).[35]

Present Situation in Manipur

In 2001, the Central Government announced the extension of cease-fire with Naga militants without territorial limits which caused a massive outburst of anger in Manipur. For weeks Imphal was beset with violence, the type of which it had not seen before. The announcement was subsequently withdrawn, but not before 18 young Manipuris had lost their lives in the agitation.

Meiteis are afraid that their centuries old state would disintegrate and their rich cultural heritage would be lost. Fear, of course, is the key, which keeps manifesting at the slightest provocation. In July 2005, Manipur was once again on the boil as All Naga Students' Association of Manipur (ANSAM) had blocked NH 39 and NH 53 – the two lifelines of the state. The blockade was triggered by an announcement made by Okram Ibobi Singh, Chief Minister, declaring June 18 as State Integration Day and a public holiday to commemorate the popular uprising on June 18, 2001 by the Meiteis in which 18 young men had died. The blockade in July 2005 caused widespread scarcity of food items in Manipur and extreme hardship to the population. The Centre was forced to withdraw its decision of extending the territorial limits of cease-fire beyond Nagaland.

Appraisal

The idea of an independent sovereign Manipur is not a post independence development. In the forties, Haijam Irabot had propagated the idea of an independent Manipur and led a campaign for it with the help from the Communist Party of Burma. The idea was carried forward by a group of radical intellectuals, which in 1964, crystallised in the form of UNLF. The idea of an independent Manipur never took deep roots mainly because there was no charismatic leader to give shape to it. Besides, the Meiteis of the valley and the tribes of the hills of Manipur had always had antagonistic relationship.

The Manipuris have nursed a grudge against the Central Government for what many perceive as coercion in forcing the Maharaja to sign the Instrument of Accession.[36] In retrospect had Manipur not acceded to India, the princely state would have fallen into chaos and anarchy. But the Manipuris were not treated fairly after they became part of India. Although Manipur was geographically small, they had a distinctive history, culture and political entity for centuries and a literature as old as 2,000 years. And yet, it was given the status of a full-fledged state only in 1972, nearly a decade later than the Naga Hills, which was just a district of Assam. The exclusion of Manipuri language from the Eighth Schedule of the constitution till 1992 was another act of insensitivity by the Centre. There is a perception amongst Meiteis that they have been discriminated for being Hindus, whereas the Nagas have been rewarded with many concessions at their cost even though they (Nagas) openly rebelled against the Indian Government. The demand for Greater Nagaland, which includes the Naga inhabited districts of Manipur and the Centre's ambivalent attitude to this demand has further made the Meiteis suspicious of the Centre.

The corruption in the elected state government and the financial profligacy has resulted in total loss of its credibility as an instrument for governance. Despite central assistance, the grants were not utilised for projects, which could generate employment, resulting in yet further increase in the numbers of educated unemployed for whom joining the insurgents seem a better and lucrative alternative.

Even more alarming than the insurgency is the effect of narcotics. Trafficking in narcotics is one of the major causes of narco-terrorism in the State. A large population of Manipur has been addicted to drugs. The use of shared needles to inject heroin has resulted in the phenomenal rise of HIV (+ve) and AIDS cases in the state.

The scene in Manipur is bleak. The alienation of Meiteis for reasons already discussed, the emergence of Naga-Kuki clashes, the effect of narco-terrorism and the ever growing nexus between the insurgents and the politicians have all added to an explosive situation. The demand for Greater Nagalim by NSCN (IM) and the Centre's ambivalence will only deepen Meiteis fears. There are reports that Naga-Kuki clashes were instigated by central intelligence agencies to counter NSCN (IM). While it may yield results in the short-term but in the long-term it can only be counter-productive.[37]

Notes and References

1. KS Singh, ed., *People of India: Manipur*, (Calcutta: Seagull Books, 1998), pp.1-5.
2. Gangmumei Kabui, "Glimpses of Land and Peoples of Ancient Manipur" in Naorem Sanjaoba ed., *Manipur Past and Present*, Vol 1, (Delhi: Mittel Publication, 1998), p. 3.
3. Ibid, pp. 3-4.
4. WS Desai, *A Pageant of Burmese History*, p. 109, Quoted by Phanjoubam Tarapot, *Insurgency Movement in NE India*, (New Delhi: Vikas, 1993), p. 4.
5. EW Dun in "*Gazetteer of Manipur*" observed "nothing of any importance recorded in the meagre annals on Manipur from 1475 to 1714 AD, the date of accession of Raja Garib Nawaz."
6. *Imperial Gazetteer of India*, vol xvii, New Edition, (Oxford: 1908), p. 186.
7. Tarapot, n. 4., pp 11,12. Also see *Imperial Gazetteer of India*, Vol xvii, n. 6. pp. 186, 187.
8. *Imperial Gazetteer of India*, vol xvii, n. 7., p. 187.
9. Ibid.
10. Ibid.
11. Tarapot, n. 4., p. 20. Quoting *Statistical Account of Manipur* by J Roy, p. 119.
12. *The Imperial Gazetteer of India*, Vol xvii, nb, pp 188-89. The account of the battles at Thobal and Khogjam have been described by Tarapot in his book referred to earlier.

13. VIK Sareen, *India's North-east in Flames*, (New Delhi: Vikas Publishing, 1980), pp. 110-11.
14. Phanjoubam Tarapot, *Insurgency Movement in North-eastern India*, 1994 (second reprint), (New Delhi: Vikas Publishing House, 1994), p 27; quoting Soyam Chhatradhari, *Manipur Itihas*, p. 11.
15. The merger of Manipur is shrouded in controversy. Some Manipuris are of the view that the Maharaja was kept under house arrest at Shillong where he had gone to meet the Governor, and coerced into signing the Instrument of Merger. There is some truth in the allegation. This is how Nari Rustomji records the meeting he and Sri Prakasa had with Sardar Patel: "Sri Prakasa and I sat along the edge of the second bed in a state of nervous tension. The Sardar alone was completely relaxed, quietly listening and watching us. When Sri Prakasa had said his piece and voiced his apprehension that the Maharaja might not comply with his advice, the Sardar simply inquired whether he had a Brigadier in Shillong and it was clear from the tone of his voice what he meant" See Nari K Rustomji, *The Enchanted Frontiers*, p 109. Also Nilanjana Kishore, *Sri Prakasa: A Political Diary;* (New Delhi: Uppal Publishing House, 1999), p. 211.
16. Tarapot, n. 14., op cit, p. 39.
17. Tarapot, n. 14., p 41. There is a fairly large Meitei population in Sylhet, where they had fled during the war with Burma many decades ago.
18. Ibid, p 42. They were ultimately released from Dharamnagar jail in Tripura in 1972 as part of general amnesty granted by Manipur Government after 1971 war.
19. Ibid., p. 14.
20. Sanajaoba was brother-in-law of Bisheshwar.
21. Tarapot, n. 14., pp 54-55. Also see Ved Marwah, *Uncivil Wars: Anatomy of Terrorism in India* (New Delhi: Harper and Collins, India, 1995), p. 291.
22. Ved Marwah, n. 21, p. 291.
23. Tarapot, n. 21., pp. 65-66.
24. In 1991, the relations between India and Burma were strained as the Burmese suspected India of sheltering the followers of Aung San Suu Kyi following military crackdown on her supporters.
25. Ved Marwah, n. 21., p. 294.
26. VG Verghese, India's North-east Resurgent, (New Delhi: Konark, 1996), p. 121.
27. Lim Guard is an armed vigilance force of the Nagas mainly Tangkhuls. See Ved Marwah, n. 21., p. 295.
28. Ved Marwah, n. 21., pp 296-297. Marwah, who was the Governor of Manipur, has described the incidents of 1995.

29. *Times of India*, New Delhi, August 29, 1995. Quoted by Ved Marwah, n. 21. p. 297.
30. "Centre Extends Cease-fire in Nagaland," *Times of India*, New Delhi, October 10, 1997.
31. R Parasnnan; Watching the Nagas, *The Week*, July 27, 1997.
32. James Johnstone, *Manipur and Naga Hills*, (New Delhi: Gyan Publishing House, 2002), p. 45.
33. For a lucid account of Naga-Kuki conflict refer to a paper "An Introduction to Ethnic Problem in Manipur" by Gam a Shimray, Shimreichon and Tapan Bose and a reportage on Naga-Kuki clash "A prose in Counter-insurgency' by Sanjay K Singh published by Solidarity Group in Support of the Restoration of Civil and Democratic Rights in the North-east, (New Delhi: K14 (1st floor) Green Park).
34. Ved Marwah, n. 26., p. 294.
35. BG Verghese, n. 26., p. 124.
36. The meeting has been described in Note 15.
37. According to reports, Kuki militants received moral support from official sources of both the State and the Central governments. The President of KLO has claimed he met the Army Chief in New Delhi on December 24, 1992. (*The Hindu*, April 8-9, 1993). According to the news published in the *Hindustan Times* of July 22, 1993 the KNA is reported to have asked for Rupees Seven Crores from RAW. It had also asked for arms and ammunition to start a fight to the finish war with NSCN. The then Chief Minister of Manipur, RK Dorendra Singh, is reported to have given Rupees One Lakh to Kukis while his finance minister is reported to have donated Rupees Two Lakhs to Chin-Kuki Revolutionary Front. (*The Telegraph*, October 27, 1992). Quoted by Sanjay K Singh in a reportage on the Naga-Kuki clash published by Solidarity Group in Support of Restoration of Civil and Democratic Rights in the North-east; K 14 Green Park Extension, New Delhi.

6

TRIPURA

Tripura is the smallest state in the North-east. During the British rule the whole geographical area of Tripura was known as Hill Tipperah. It covers an area of 10,477 sq km. The Cachar district of Assam and Mizo Hills of Mizoram bind it on the East, Comilla and a part of Noakhali district of Bangladesh on the West and South, the Chittagong district of Bangladesh and a part of Noakhali on the South-east, and the Sylhet district of Bangladesh on the North-west.[1] It has 832 km of international boundary with Bangladesh.

The lie of the country is similar to that of CHT. Six principal ranges of hills, increasing in height towards the East, run North and South, with an average interval of 20 km. The hills are covered for the most part with bamboo jungle, while the low ground has abundance of canebrakes and thatching grass. The principal hill ranges, beginnings from East, are the Jampai (highest point Betling Sib 3,200 feet), Sakhantlang, Langtarai, Atharamura, Baramura and Destamura. Each successive range towards East is higher than the previous one. The principal rivers rise mostly from the hills and run through the valleys. Innumerable tributaries in their respective catchments areas feed them. The major rivers are Longai, Juri Deo, Manu, Dhalai, Khowai, Haora, Gomti, Mahuri and Feni.[2] These are neither very deep nor broad and flow into the Bay of Bengal, passing through Bangladesh.

Tripura has tropical climate. The temperature varies between 10-35 degrees celsius. The highest temperature is reached in

April/May and the lowest during January. It lies in the South-west monsoon belt and hence receives heavy rainfall in June-July. Two-third of the geographical area of Tripura is covered with hills, forests and swamps. In spite of this, the state has second highest density of population among North-east states. The population of Tripura as per 2001 census is 3,1,91,168, which is 0.31 percent of the total population of India.

Historical Background

The origin of the name Tripura is uncertain. There are many versions and there is no unanimity amongst historians and scholars. According to one version the name Tripura has been coined from the words *Tui* and *Pra*. In local dialect *Tui* means water and *Pra* means nearness; thus Tripura meant land adjoining water bodies. Some historians are of the view that the name was derived from one of the kings known as Tripur. Yet another set of scholars opines that Tripura is a sanskritised form of Tipera, the name of the tribe to which the ruling family belonged.

The early history of Tripura, particularly prior to 15th century is shrouded in legends and traditions. Thus the state's history has two distinct periods; the traditional period as recorded in 'Rajmala' (chronicle of Tripura Rajas). According to Rajmala the rulers of Tripura were the descendents of Druhya of the lunar dynasty. The legends claim that he was contemporary of Yudhistir of Mahabharata.[3] While the mythological accounts of Tripura trace back its history to epic age, eminent scholars have questioned the claim to antiquity. Those who believe in the historicity of Rajmala claim that Tripura was mentioned in Allahabad Prasasti of Samudragupta. Others have dismissed this claim as of no value in an article published in the Journal of Asiatic Society wherein the ancient Tripura has been identified to be modern Tewar in Madhya Pradesh (copper- plate inscription of King Vijya Manikya of Tripura by DC Sarkar of ARS vol XVII, 1951)[4]. Whatever may be the historical fact, the area now known, as Tripura was once an established kingdom cannot be lightly dismissed. The romantic tales contained in Rajmala about some of the kings conjure up a vision of past glories.

The ancient kingdom of Tripura at various times extended its rule from the Sunderbans in the West to Burma in the East, and Northwards as far as Kamrup[5]. As long as Hindu Rajas ruled Bengal, Tripura was safe from attacks and annexation. Bengal served as a barrier that kept the aggressors away. With the fall of Bengal to the Muslims in the early part of 13th century, annexation started. The history of Tripura from 1240-1765 AD was mainly the history of conflict with the Muslims. The state was overrun by Muslims under Tughril in 1279, and was again invaded by Ilyas Shah in the middle of 14th century and by Nawab Fateh Jung in 1620. [6] The plains portion (the district of Tipperah) was not, however, annexed to the Mughal Empire until 1733. Hill Tipperah proper was never assessed to revenue and remained outside the sphere of Muhammadan administration, although influence was usually exercised in the appointments of the Rajas.[7] The military prestige of Tripura Rajas was at its peak during the sixteenth century, when Bijoy Manikya defeated the Muhammadan troops who defended Chittagong, and occupied part of Sylhet and Noakhali.

It was during the reign of king Ratna Manikya in the later part of 13th century that Tripuris first came to be influenced by Hinduism. Ratna Manikya is believed to have settled nearly 10,000 Bengalis belonging to various professions in his kingdom, prompted by the desire to introduce plough cultivation and reorganise the archaic state administrative machinery on the model followed by the Muslims in Bengal. The King's policy of importing Bengali professionals had another far reaching consequence on the Tripura society; it left a lasting influence of Bengali religion and culture both on the royal family and the Indo-Mongoloid people of the kingdom. The influence of Hinduism gained momentum during the reign of Dhanya Manikya, who was a devout Hindu. He made Bengali, for the first time, the official or court language of Tripura. As Hinduism took roots in Tripura society, the traditional religion of the tribal people did not disappear. [8]

There are 18 tribes in Tripura, of which 12 are indigenous and the others are tribals, who were brought from other parts of India to work in tea gardens. Tripuris are the largest forming 55 percent of the tribal population (1971 census), followed by Reangs (14 percent). The ruling family belongs to Tripuri tribe, who were privileged class and treated non-Tripuris as second-class citizen and they paid additional taxes.

After the East India Company secured the *Diwani*, (the revenue rights), of Bengal from Emperor Shah Alam II in 1765, they placed a Raja on the throne, and since 1808 each successive ruler received investiture from the then British Government. In 1838, it was held by deputy governor of Bengal that, owing to his unchallenged possession from at least 1793, the Raja had obtained a prescriptive right to the territory within the hills. But from various accounts Hill Tipperah, i.e., the present state of Tripura was under British suzerainty. Between 1826 and 1862, the Eastern part of the state was constantly raided by Kukis, resulting in plunder and massacre of its peaceful inhabitants. The British had to take action to put an end to Kuki depredations. [9]

The Raja of Hill Tipperah, besides being the ruler of his kingdom, also held a large landed property called Chakla Roshanabad, situated in the plains of the districts of Tripura, Noakhali and Sylhet. This estate covered an area of 570 sq miles and was the most valuable possession of the Raja; it yielded larger revenue than the whole of Hill Tipperah.[10] In 1871, an English officer was first appointed as political agent to protect British interests and to advise the Raja. In 1878, the post was abolished and the magistrate of the adjoining district of Tipperah was appointed ex-officio political agent of Hill Tipperah [11]

The traditional life and culture of tribes of Tripura, like tribes in other parts of India, is centered round their land.

Independence and Merger of Tripura with India

The rise of communal politics, which preceded the partition of the country, resulted in one of the worst carnages in Noakhali in East Bengal in 1946. Thousands of Hindu refugees from East Bengal poured into Tripura. Raja Bir Bikram, the last sovereign of Tripura, gave shelter to the refugees. Rulers of Tripura had constituted tribal reserves for the settlement of five specific tribes. The reserved areas formed 42 percent of the total area of the state that is about 5050 sq km. The Regency Council de-reserved 1,500 sq km to rehabilitate these refugees. The tribes suspected the hand of the Bengali Dewan in the de-reservation of their land, which became one of the main reasons for tribal discontent, and rise of militancy directed at the Bengali refugees in later years.

The Rajah, who died on May 17, 1947 left behind a minor to succeed him on the throne. The Maharani's regency council acceded to India on August 13, 1947. With accession, responsibility for defence, foreign affairs and communication passed to the Union. Tripura Durbar finally decided to merge with India on October 15, 1949. But the two-year period after the Maharaja's death caused great uncertainty and anxiety for the Union, as elements in East Pakistan and in the royal palace itself made an abortive attempt to incorporate Tripura into East Pakistan.

Durjoy Kishore, a member of the royal family was conspiring with Abdul Barik, the richest businessman of Tripura at that time, and a supporter of the Muslim League. Durjoy was frustrated in his efforts to seize the throne after the death of the Raja. The queen, Rani Kanchanprabha, acting with great alacrity declared herself the regent and with the help of Delhi aborted Durjoy's designs of a "possible Kashmir type operation in Tripura."[12] State merged with India on October 15, 1949. Tripura became a Part 'C' state on January 26, 1950, a union territory in November 1956 and a full-fledged state in January 1972.

The Early Tribal Unrest and the Communist Revolt

The unrest in Tripura's tribal society surfaced in early 1940s, triggered by food shortages. As the Japanese Army knocked on the doors of the Eastern frontiers of India, the Raja put the entire resources of the state at the disposal of the allied war effort.[13] The prices of paddy and rice rose four-fold throughout the state and the level of food stock fell drastically below the minimum requirement. The tribals under the influence of tribal ascetic Ratanmoni Noatia revolted against the revenue collections and refused to be recruited in the army. The revolt lasted for nearly a year but petered out in the face of massive coercive power of the princely state. Ratanmoni was beaten to death in the palace prison at Agartala.[14] The rebellion has been described by the Marxists as " the first major peasant struggle in the state in Tripura."

The Communists have had a long presence in Tripura. In the 1930s they formed part of an underground movement active in neighbouring Bengal. Slowly, they began to expand their base in Tripura and positioned themselves in organisations like the Janamangal Samity (People's Welfare Organisation), which had begun to demand responsible government by popular vote. Yet another organisation, the Janshiksa Samity (Mass Literacy Group) was formed in 1945 to spread education amongst the masses. This organisation was not a communist front, but the Communists had developed and maintained firm links with it through their sympathisers.

The Communist Party was banned in India after it decided at its historic party Congress in Calcutta, to launch an armed struggle on the Chinese pattern to capture power. Tripura delegates decided to form a tribal organisation committed to the advancement of the tribal people. Thus was born an organisation called the Tripura Rajya Mukti Parishad in May 1948. The man behind its formation was a committed communist, Biren Dutta, who did not join its executive committee, because the Parishad was conceived as an organisation for the tribals[15]. Dasrath Debbarma emerged as its president, a position he held for nearly five decades.

The Mukti Parishad rapidly gained strength, mainly in Khowai, Sadar and Kamalpur areas. It attracted large numbers of young tribals to its rank and file. After the partition in 1947, the state received a large influx of refugees (at the rate of 10,000 per day) from East Pakistan. In order to settle the refugees the state government sought permission to denotify the tribal tract reserves. The proposal was bitterly opposed by the Mukti Parishad. A protest rally was organised in Agartala on August 15, 1948 to demand, amongst other things, a government by popular vote and end to Dewani rule and police atrocities. The successful demonstration on the Independence Day was a stunning event. It galvanised the youth, mostly tribals and some Bengali Muslims.

A month later, in October 1948, an incident of police firing on tribals took place to prevent, according to police records, a violent mob of tribals from seizing boatloads of paddy belonging to a wealthy *mahajan* (trader). The trader had returned after the harvests to take away the bulk of local produce to redeem his credit with interest. The incident was soon to turn into militancy: unfortunate fallout of the incident was a surge of anti-Bengali sentiments. One Rajchandra Debbana was to comment: "The tribals killed at Golaghati fell to bullets fired by Bengali policemen, the order to fire was given by a Bengali officer, the police were called by a Bengali moneylender who had been cheating us for a long time and it is a Bengali Dewan (AB Chatterjee) who had unleashed the reign of terror on tribals."[16] But it must be said to the credit of the tribal leadership of Mukti Parishad that they prevented the incident degenerating into Tribal-Bengali feud. The resistance offered by the Mukti Parishad leadership in containing an anti-Bengali backlash was crucial for the subsequent growth of the communist party in Tripura.

Soon after the firing incident, the Mukti Parishad leadership took a decision on armed resistance. A large number of former soldiers of Maharaja's army, with rich experience of jungle warfare in the Burma front during the war, had joined the Mukti Parishad. They proved an invaluable asset in the growth of guerilla organisation.[17] Five large guerilla units were formed, one each on the West and East banks of Khowai river, one in Kamalpur, and one each in North and South Sadar area. Dasrath Debbarma became the overall commander of the guerillas.

Counter-insurgency operations were started in early 1948 and by the beginning of 1949 they were in full swing. After a notification in Tripura State Gazetteer, entire Khowai subdivision was handed over to the military on March 9, 1949. Throughout 1949 and 1950, clashes were reported between the security forces and the guerillas. By the beginning of 1950, the guerillas had begun to attack stray patrols to keep them confined to camps. It was at this stage that *Shanti Sena*, the military arm of the Mukti Parishad came into existence. The Parishad held its first annual conference in 1949 when some important decisions were taken. It drew up a social code for Tripura society and decided to enforce tenant-sharecropper relationship in keeping with leftist ideology. [18] The code of conduct helped the Parishad to create a parallel government in the hills of Tripura. In a letter to Sardar Patel dated June

15, 1950, Jairamdas Daulatram, the Governor of Assam, acknowledged:

> *"But as in the meantime the situation in Tripura has deteriorated and the latest search report shows that they have set up a kind of parallel government at Khowai and they are as good as administering the country on the line of Telangana."* [19]

Most of the guerilla actions of the Mukti Parishad took place between March 1949 and November 1951.[20] As per police records, in that period there were 63 ambushes, 17 attacks on police camps, 44 kidnappings and 48 desertions from the ranks of police and para-military forces. Over 70 percent of major guerilla actions were in Khowai subdivision. This partly explains the reason why the movement was successfully contained.[21]

By early 1950, the Mukti Parishad leadership realised that it could not continue the campaign of armed resistance without the support of a national party. Mukti Parishad merged with the Communist Party of India (CPI) in mid-50s. But before it merged with the Communists, internal rift had surfaced in the organisation over the issue of land for the tillers. Dasrath Deb, the veteran leader, opposed this on two grounds: first, the class divisions in Tripura were nowhere as sharp as in Bengal; and second, most landowners in tribal areas were small landholders, while many soldiers, widows and poor small peasants could not till their land and resorted to sharecropping. In the wider context the tribal autonomy claimed by the Mukti Parishad remained a contentious issue even in the late 80s.

Advent of Electoral Politics

The coming of Nripen Chakraborty, a senior member of Bengal CPI, to Tripura in 1950 was to change the course of Left politics of Tripura in a profound way. On his arrival in Tripura, Nripen Chakraborty reviewed the situation. He described the armed resistance by the Mukti Parishad a spontaneous peasant war but cautioned that as the Mukti Parishad had grown up mainly in areas inhabited by Tripuri peasantry, the government has successfully projected its struggle as a war against the Bengalis or an attempt to dominate the minor tribes.[22] Nripen Chakraborty laid "the ideological basis for the growth of Tripuri communist party out of the movement that provided a home for resurgent Tripuri nationalism but never degenerated into ethno-communal sectarianism.."[23] Mukti Parishad was slowly integrated into the communist movement.

Mukti Parishad decided to contest the first parliamentary election in 1952. Both the communist candidates, Biren Dutta and Dasrath Deb won the parliamentary seats and the party also won the 17 of the 30 seats in the electoral college formed to return the Rajya Sabha candidate. The defeat of the Congress compelled it to rethink upon its strategy. It stood no chance unless Communists' stranglehold in tribal areas was broken. The Congress began to propagate that the Mukti Parishad, followed a policy of *Bangla Kheda* (drive away Bengalis), while to the smaller tribes it propagated Tripuris attempt to dominate lesser tribes. The shortsighted policy of the local Congress leaders sharpened ethnic differences and set the stage for subsequent tribal insurgencies in the years to follow. After Tripura became a Union Territory in 1956, Tripura Land Revenue and Land Reform Act, 1960 (TLR&LRA) came into force, which laid restrictions on transfer of land from the hands of tribals to non-tribals. However, the Act had no provision for the restoration of illegally transferred land. The Congress government amended the TLR&LR Act in 1974 to provide for restoration of illegally transferred land. It covered cases prior to January 1, 1969 but restoration work was never taken up and became a major cause for the ethnic divide between the tribals and Bengalis.

The Communists repeated their performance again in 1962 parliamentary elections but with reduced margin. The 1962 border war with China had put the Communists in a dilemma. When the party split, the Communists in Tripura became CPI (M). The Congress in Tripura painted them as agents of China and got an opportunity to crush the Communists. The Congress government of the state began settling new immigrants in tribal areas indiscriminately.[24] New immigrants gripped by a sense of insecurity voted en-block for the Congress and both its candidates won the parliamentary election of 1967. The CPI (M) won only three of the thirty seats in the state assembly.

Formation of Tripura Upjati Juba Samity (TUJS)

The electoral defeat suffered by the Communists in 1967 parliamentary elections disillusioned the educated tribals leading to the formation of TUJS. Its main objectives were to secure the creation of Autonomous Tribal District Council under the Sixth Schedule (by amendment of the constitution), restoration of tribal lands alienated to non-tribals and recognition of '*Kok Borok*' in Roman script as one of the official language of the state and its introduction as the medium of instruction.[25] Initially the TUJS had communist backing but their priorities were different; TUJS asserted its tribal identity whereas CPI (M) was unwilling to relinquish its two-community political strategy. Now that CPI (M) was committed to electoral politics, its over-emphasis on tribal issues would be politically suicidal. The neglect of party organisation in the tribal areas left the CPI (M) loosing its hold on the tribals. As the CPI (M) had begun to concentrate on students and employees, the marginalisation of Upjati Gana Mukti Parishad (as the Mukti Parishad had been renamed) was inevitable.

The Return of Sengkrak (Clenched Fist)

With the marginalisation of Mukti Parishad, the stage was set for the return to Sengkrak, a militant tribal organisation, which had surfaced in Agartala in 1948. Sengkrak had a chequered history. It was set up by the royalist pretender, Durjoy Kishore

Debbarman at the time of Independence and was active in and around Agartala, trying to gain support for his opposition to merge with India. The organisation was banned but resurfaced in 1967. It is believed that the second Sengkrak was formed by one Ratnasen Reang who was its self-styled president. In November 1967, leaflets were found pasted in parts of Kanchanpur and Chaumanu along Tripura's northern borders with Mizoram and CHT. The leaflets gave notice to all non-tribals to leave Tripura by November 25, 1967 or else they should be prepared to die at the hands of Sengkrak activists. The inspiration for the formation of Sengkrak came from the MNF in the neighbouring Mizo Hills. Ratnasen Reang driven in desperation to seek support had contacted some MNF functionary who promised to help him. The MNF was only too willing to expand its area of operations and stretch the security forces to their limits. In Reang, the MNF had found an opportunity; by mid 1968 it started training Sengkrak.

Nearly seventy Sengkrak cadres were given full time guerilla training by the MNF. But Sengkrak lacked the type of leadership and organisation, which could ensure a prolonged guerilla campaign. It was active during 1968-69. Their acts of violence included raids on village markets, post offices and other symbols of authority; attack on Bengali settlers and occasionally on security forces.[26] The MNF and Meitei insurgents were already getting support from erstwhile East Pakistan. But the defeat of Pakistan in the 1971 war was a grievous blow to fledgling Sengkrak. It died a natural death after Bangladesh was born in December 1971.

From Sengkrak to Tripura National Volunteers (TNV)

The circumstance under which TUJS was formed has already been described. Unprecedented influx of Bengali refugees united the tribes of Tripura and they soon grasped the consequences of the problem. The fear of marginalisation drew members of all tribal groups into the fold of TUJS. The TUJS was following a two-pronged political strategy; on the one hand, it started a campaign of mass mobilisation to build a support base and on the other it had begun to raise a guerrilla force. The decision of the Congress led government of Tripura after the 1971 war, to de-notify the 150 sq miles of tribal reserve tract for refugees, gave TUJS an issue it was looking for to mobilise the tribes.

The Communists won an absolute majority in 1977 assembly elections and stayed in power for ten years. The Congress failed to win a single seat. TUJS won all the four reserved tribal seats, which was a cause of worry for the Communists, who had nursed the tribes so assiduously earlier. This also provided an opening for TUJS to expose the lack of commitment of CPI (M) to tribal interests. Nonetheless, the Communists provided good administration and ensured the passage of Tripura Tribal Areas District Autonomous Council (TTADAC) under the Seventh Schedule 1979.

Bejoy Hrangkhwl, who was very active in TUJS, formed Tripura National Volunteers (TNV) in 1978 after having failed to win 1977 parliamentary elections. The year 1978 proved very propitious for Hrangkhwl. The breakdown of peace talks between MNF and the Indian Government, the resurgence of Meitei insurgency in Manipur and the anti-foreigner agitation in Assam and Meghalaya provided the ideal condition for the start of the next phase of insurgency in Tripura. TNV cadres were trained by MNF at Chhimtalang, near the tri-junction of the CHT, Arakan and Mizoram in the beginning of 1979. The joint TNV-MNF group began to indulge in attacks on the police and para-military forces. But when the involvement of Hrangkhwl with the TNV was revealed after the capture of a top TNV leader in October 1979, he went into hiding. Chief Minister Nripen Chakraborty was eager to neutralise the TNV, and in order to snuff out the fledgling militancy he withdrew all charges against Hrangkhwl and his fellow TNV members who were in jail. Though Hrangkhwl continued his links with TUJS as a member of the party, he broke links with TNV and let it go into oblivion.[27]

The rivalry between the CPI (M) and TUJS to win the support of the tribals came into play once again after the passage of the TTAADC Bill in the state assembly in 1979. The election to the council was due in June 1980. With the fulfilment of autonomous district council demand by the CPI (M), TUJS was left with no alternative but to exploit the issue of deporting foreigners, which was already gaining momentum in Assam.

The Formation of *Amra Bengali* and Polarisation of Tribals and Non-Tribals

When the TUJS decided to launch an agitation for the deportation on non-tribals from Tripura, the Bengalis formed a militant organisation called *Amra Bengali* with Anand Margi antecedents. *Amra Bengali* was opposed to the autonomous district council idea, whereas TUJS viewed it as central to their polity. The battle lines were drawn. The stand off between *Amra Bengali* and TUJS lead to widespread riots on June 4, 1980; the fuse was lit, as so often happens, by a drunken brawl and a rumor that a tribal boy had been knifed by a non-tribal, triggering a chain reaction. A committee was set up by the Centre under Dinesh Singh to look into all aspects of the carnage. As per the committee's report, citing official records, up to July 31, 1980 550 were killed, which included at least 69 tribals.[28] The report observed that "according to Chief Minister himself, 1,800 were reported missing; many of them might be dead." Over 34,660 huts were burnt and the loss of property was tentatively estimated at around rupees 21 crores.[29]

In the aftermath of the riots, a large number of TUJS leaders including Hrangkhwl and tribal youths were taken into custody. The predominantly Bengali police force was accused of complicity in the massacre. The Mandai riots, therefore, gave a fresh lease of life to tribal insurgency. But even as tribal insurgency was getting a fresh momentum, Hrangkhwl disbanded the TNF after he was released from prison in December 1980.[30]

Formation of All Tripura People's Liberation Organisation (ATPLO)

Just as Hrangkhwl disbanded the TNV, another organisation, ATPLO, came into being under the leadership of Binanda Jamatia at Thangnan with over 125 tribal youths. Chuni Koloi, who was earlier with TNV, had joined the new organisation and was one of its most feared underground leader. But the ATPLO had a short life. It became a victim of tribalism and inflated egos of leaders. There was soon a rift between the leaders. The breakaway group under Chuni Koloi joined Hrangkhwl to revive TNV. The much weakened ATPLO under Binanda Jamatia could not stand up to security forces too long and surrendered in 1993. [31]

A daring raid on September 3, 1982 facilitated the revival of TNV by a group of guerillas under Chuni Koloi armed with only five rifles and eight country made guns on Manu police station in North Tripura. The guerillas broke into the police station and decamped with 16 rifles, five revolvers and one matchlock gun. With this, the tribal insurgency in Tripura entered its final and most virulent stage. During this stage TNV had close links with the MNF. Bangladesh was initially reluctant to provide direct help to TNV but later it provided some help, which was channeled through MNF.

Insurgency in Tripura peaked between 1984-85, briefly ran out of steam in early 1986, regained momentum by the end of the year and reached unmanageable proportion in 1987-88, before a tripartite settlement between TNV, the Central and State Government resulted in TNV giving up its armed struggle.[32] The 1988 assembly election in Tripura was most violent and as many as 91 people were killed, mostly non-tribals.[33] The Centre acted decisively and brought the whole state under Disturbed Area Act and called in the army to control the situation.

The Accord

Hrangkhwl had seen the writing on the wall. The Mizos had negotiated peace with the centre. He saw the futility of war and realised that the tribals would gain more by peaceful means. On August 12, 1988, a tripartite agreement was signed between TNV leaders, officials of the Union Home Ministry and Tripura Government. A month later 437 TNV guerillas (150 hardcore activists) surrendered with 106 weapons at an official function at Gobindbari. A faction of TNV, which refused to surrender, was later forced to surrender by the army supported by erstwhile TNV leaders.[34]

The tribals gained much from the peace accord. The TTAADC, which was aborted in June 1980 due to riots, had finally come into being in 1982, but since a structure under the Seventh Schedule did not fulfill the aspirations of the tribals, this was dissolved and a new autonomous council under the Sixth Schedule was established in March 1985 (prior to the accord) through a constitutional amendment. The Sixth Schedule prohibits sale of land to non-tribals.

Some may say that TNV gained very little; but the tribals gained. The TNV became a legitimate political party in December 1988 by amending its constitution. The government agreed to implement the Representative of Peoples Act, 1950, to reserve three additional seats for scheduled tribes in Tripura State Assembly (total 60 seats). The government also agreed to expedite implementation of development projects for tribal people.

Post Accord Scenario

It was hoped that the agreement with TNV would end the violence but some former TNV collaborators led by one Kala

Debbarma formed a new organisation, the National Liberation Front of Tripura (NLFT) and have been indulging in violence and criminal acts. Yet, another group consisting of former TNV cadres was formed named All Tripura Tiger Force (ATTF). These organisations have no ideology and are motivated by the prospect of making quick money by indulging in criminal acts. A disturbing trend in the recent years has been the political patronage provided to these criminal groups by recognised political parties. While CPI (M) is said to support ATTF, a political party called Independent People's Front of Tripura (IPFT) is suspected to have links with NLFT.[35] TTAADC was ruled by the Left Front from 1985 to 1990 and thereafter by the TUJS-Congress combine over the next five years. In the election to TTAADC in August 1995, the TUJS, an ally of the Congress since early eighties, lost to the Left Front. The defeat of a tribal party in a tribal area by a party dominated by Bengalis is indicative of the fissures in tribal polity. The tribals have fragmented into many parties, and their armed wings have made the situation even worse by indulging in extortion and criminal acts. 65 percent of abductions in the north-east are occurring in Tripura. In 1999, at least 2,000 people were killed due to militant actions; 21 people were killed up to March 2000.[36] Militants frequently launch forays into Indian territory from safe havens in Bangladesh to exploit the porous border. However, imaginative employment of security forces has kept the militants at bay.

Appraisal

The main reason for insurgency in Tripura has been the large-scale influx of Bengali refugees after the partition of the country and the consequent alienation of tribal land. The Tripuri kings themselves started the process of Bengali immigration in the 13th century. King Ratna Manikya settled a large number of Bengali Hindus to reform the archaic administration of Tripura on the pattern of Muslim rulers of Bengal. Subsequently, professionals and tradesmen were encouraged to settle, as there were not many who had those skills. After the World War I, when the prices went up, entrepreneurs were encouraged to clear forestland to set up tea gardens. This brought in labourers, mostly tribals, from Bihar, Orissa, erstwhile Central India and Madras provinces. The tribal population as percentage of total population had already decreased from 63.77 percent in 1875 to 53.16 percent in 1941. However, the demographic shift took place gradually and therefore, did not create any social tension. The refugee influx after the partition was not a trickle but a flood, which tore apart the fragile demographic balance. In the next decadal census, the tribal population dropped to 37.23 percent and in the 1981 census it dropped further to 28.44 percent of the total population of the state. With increasing refugee population, there was a great temptation to encroach upon the reserved tribal tracts. TLR&LR Act was amended in 1974 to facilitate restoration of illegally transferred land. The Act caused dissatisfaction on two counts; first, the cut off point, which legalised transfer of tribal land that had taken place before January 1, 1969, and second, the progress of restoration of post January 1969 cases had been very tardy. The conflicting interests of tribes and Bengalis led to large-scale ethnic clashes in 1980.

The tribes of Tripura have agitated for an autonomous district council for long, which was constituted first under the Seventh Schedule in July 1979. The non-tribes opposed the Act on grounds that the "council would cover an area of 7131 sq km out of a total area of 10,447 sq km, which was three-fourth of the territory of the state, to serve the interests of no more than one-fourth of its population." Eventually, the Centre constituted an autonomous council under the Sixth Schedule during Rajiv Gandhi's prime ministership in June 1995.[37] By then, the two contending ethnic groups had spilled much blood.

Insurgency in Tripura was sustained by tacit support of Bangladesh government, which reciprocated by supporting

Tripura militants as a tit for tat for the encouragement given to Chakma's *Mukti Bahini* by the Indian government.[38] The continuance of militancy has continued even after the Accord mainly because of slow implementation of its provisions. The slow pace of development, the proximity of safe bases in Bangladesh, the spread of insurgency in the whole of north-east and the easy availability of arms in the open markets of Thailand, Cambodia and Myanmar are other causes. Political parties abetting one or the other militant group have only aggravated the situation.

Notes and References

1. KS Singh ed, *People of India*: Tripura vol XLI, (Anthropological Survey of India and Seagull Books, Calcutta, 1996), p1. Also see *Imperial Gazetteer of India, Vol XIII, (New Edition)*, (Oxford: 1908), p.117.
2. KS Singh, ed., n 1, pp.1-2.
3. Ibid., p. 3.
4. Quoted by VIK Sareen, *India's North-east in Flames*, (New Delhi: Vikas Publishing House, 1990), p. *126.*
5. *Imperial Gazetteer of India*, Vol XIII, (New Edition), (Oxford: 1908), p. 118.
6. Ibid.
7. Ibid.
8. VIK Sareen, n. 4., p. 128.
9. Imperial Gazetteer of India, Vol. XXIII, n. 5.,, p. 118.
10. Ibid., pp. 118-119.
11. Ibid., p. 119.
12. Subir Bhaumik, *Insurgent Crossfire*, (New Delhi: Lancer. 1996), p . 70.
13. "*War Supplement to Tripura Gazette*," January 14, 1942.
14. Subir Bhaumik, n. 12., p. 68.
15. Ibid., p. 94.
16. Ibid., p. 101.
17. Ibid., p. 97.
18. For code of conduct of guerillas, social conduct and tenant-sharecropper relationship, see Subir Bhaumik, Ibid., p. 102, 107-109.

19. See Durga Das, ed, *Sardar Patel Correspondence* 1949-50, Vol 9, (Ahmedabad: Navjivan Trust, 1974), pp, 200-202.
20. Subir Bhaumik, n. 12., p. 115.
21. Ibid, p. 116.
22. Saroj Chanda, *Tripuray Communists Party Gorar Yuger Duiti Aprakashito Dalil*, (Agartala Tripura Darpan Prakashan, 1983, Quoted by Subir Bhaumik, n. 12, p. 118.
23. Subir Bhaumik, n. 12., p. 118.
24. A fresh wave of Bengali refugees had poured into Tripura after riots in East Pakistan in 1964.
25. BG Verghese, *India's North-east Resurgent*, (New Delhi: Konark, 1996), p. 172.
26. Subir Bhaumik, n. 12., p. 135.
27. Ibid., pp. 208-209.
28. BG Verghese, n. 25., p. 175.
29. Ibid.
30. Subir Bhaumik, n. 12., p. 225.
31. Ved Marwah, *Uncivil Wars: Anatomy of Terrorism in India*, (New Delhi: Harper and Collins, India 1995, p. 300.
32. Subir Bhaumik, n. 12., p.
33. Ved Marwah, n. 31., p. 300.
34. Subir Bhaumik, n. 12., p. 240.
35. NS Narhari, *Security Threats to North-east India*, (New Delhi: Manas, 2002), p 191. NLFT has links with NSCN (IM), whereas ATTF with NSCN (K).
36. Ibid., p. 191.
37. The Sixth Schedule prohibits sale of land to non-tribals.
38. Sanjoy Hazarika, *Strangers of the Mist: Tales of War and Peace from India's North-east*, (New Delhi: Penguin, 1994), pp. 276-290.

7

The Quest for Swadhin Asom

Assam is one of the Easternmost states of India, lying between the foothills of the Eastern Himalayas and Patkai and Naga Ranges. It is connected with the rest of India by a narrow corridor in West Bengal. From the geographical point of view, Assam can be divided into two physical regions, the highlands of the frontier tracts to the North and East and the plains below. The plains comprise the Brahmaputra and the Surma or Barak Valleys.

Today's Assam is much smaller from its past size and is divided into ten administrative districts; districts of the Brahmaputra Valley are Goalpara, Kamrup, Darrang, Nowgang, Sibsagar, Lakhimpur and Dibrugarh, whereas Barak Valley has only one district, Cachar. The highland of Assam consists of two districts, Karbi Anglong and North Cachar Hills. Assam has a composite population. Through long periods of history people of different parts of the land and beyond migrated to Assam and got integrated with the native population and their culture.

The early history of Assam is very obscure. The country that is now known as Assam is mentioned in the Hindu epics and legends of Gangetic India. There is no doubt that Aryans had found their way in the country but unfortunately they left no reliable record behind them. Khasis and Jaintias, who are of Austric stock, are believed to be the earliest inhabitants of Assam. They are termed as Proto Austroloid because they are said to be descendants of migrants from Australia and other islands of the Pacific Ocean to the Asiatic mainland. The beautiful megaliths or pillars of stones, which they created over the graves of the dead, are found in Meghalaya. After Austrics, Mongolians entered Assam from the North and the North-east. The larger group had come from China and Tibet; some had come from Burma. Among the Mongolians, the Bodos established themselves in the Brahmaputra Valley and expanded to North and East Bengal and North Bihar. They occupy North of the Brahmaputra Valley even today. It is speculated by some that the first Mongolian migration took place long before 1000 BC. About the same time when Mongolians were entering Assam from North-east, the Aryans appeared from the East, and it is believed that between the 6th and 7th century BC they migrated to the East of Karatoya River, which in ancient time was the Western boundary of Assam. In the early Aryan literature Eastern India is referred to as Mlechha country. It is generally believed that the number of Aryans was never large in Assam. Racially, Assam is always known as the land of non-Aryans. Although the Aryans were not numerous in numbers, yet they established their cultural supremacy over the country. However, many of the non-Aryan races like the Nagas and Mizos continued to live a secluded life in the inaccessible mountain abodes and did not come under the Aryan influence. On the other hand, the North Indian Brahmins called Kalitas were successful in assimilating into Hinduism all the plain tribal people including the Ahoms.

Pragjyotisa and Kamrup

In the ancient Sanskrit literature both Pragjyotisa and Kamrup are mentioned as names for Assam. In Kalki Purana and Yogini Tantra, Kamrup also appears as the name of this land. Till the conquest of the Ahoms, Pragjyotisa was known as Kamrup, which occurs for the first time, in so far as epigraphy is concerned, in the Allahabad pillar inscription of the Gupta Emperor Samudragupta.

According to Mahabharata, the kingdom of Pragjyotisa extended Southward as far as the Bay of Bengal and the Western boundary to river Karatoya. The Puranas written much later than Mahabharata, mentions ancient Assam as Kamrup. According to Kalki Purana, the temple of Kamakhya was in the centre of Kamrup. The Vishnu Purana describes that Kamrup extended around the Kamakhya in all directions for 450 miles. Thus Kamrup must have incorporated Assam, East Bengal and Bhutan. The Yogini Tantra, composed much later than Purana, also records extensive boundary to Kamrup. It is said that Kamrup included the whole of Brahmaputra Valley, Bhutan, Rangpur district (Bangladesh), Cooch Behar, part of Mymensingh district of Bangladesh and possibly Garo.[1]

The Origin of the name Assam

The name Assam does not appear in ancient sources, either literary or inscriptional, dating earlier than 16th century. Abul Fazal, a great scholarly protégé of Akbar, in his well-known book *Ain-i-Akbari*, refers to the name for the first time as Asham.[2] Till the conquest of the Ahoms, Pragjyotisa was known as Kamrup. During the Ahom rule, it was called Asama or unparalleled or peerless. The modern name 'Assam' seems to have been derived from the appellation 'Asama.'[3] There is no finality about the origin of the name Assam except that it had something to do with Ahoms.

Early History

Reliable history of Assam is derived from the narrative of the Chinese pilgrim Huien Tsang, who visited Kamrup about 640 AD during the reign of King Kumara Bhaskaravarman (594-650 AD). He was contemporary of the great king Harsha of North India. Not much is known of the next few centuries, but the recent discovery of inscribed copper-plates, which appear to have been prepared between the 10th and the middle of 12th centuries, throw some light on those days. The primary object of these inscriptions was to recite the grant of land to Brahmins.[4] It would seem that soon after Huien Tsang's departure, the country fell into the hands of aboriginal chiefs who were subsequently converted to Hinduism. Then followed a dynasty founded by one Pralambha; the sixth in descent from him was Balavarman, in whose time the copper-plates documents above referred to were executed. These kings called themselves Lords of Pragjyotisha. Early in 11th century, a fresh line of kings, who claimed descent from the mythical Naraka, succeeded them. The area ruled by these kings varied greatly from time to time. Sometimes it stretched as far west as Karatoya River and as far south as the sea coast, including within its limits the Surma Valley, Eastern Bengal and occasionally Bhutan; at other time it did not even comprise the whole of what is known as Brahmaputra Valley; sometimes again, and perhaps this was the most usual condition, the country was split up into small principalities each under its own chief. The Surma Valley, at any rate, was independent of Brahmaputra Valley.[5]

According to Mahapurushias, Lower Assam & the adjacent part of Bengal subsequently formed a kingdom called Kamata, and its ruler in the 14th century was Durlabh Narayan. The third and last of this line, Nilambar, was overthrown in 1498 by Husain Shah, the Muslim King of Bengal, who took the capital Kamatapur, by a stratagem. A few years later Biswa Singh laid the foundation of the Koch Kingdom with its capital at Cooch Behar. Koch tribe at that time was probably purely Mongolian, but later intermixed with local Dravidian stock. Biswa Singh's son Nar Narayan extended his kingdom in all directions, and even defeated the Ahom king. By mid 16th century the Koch kingdom had begun to decline and finally dismember.

In the other part of Brahmaputra Valley, an event occurred which was to change the course of history of Assam. The Ahoms, a branch of the Shan race, who occupied the upper portion of

Irrawady Valley, crossed the Patkai Hills and entered the North-eastern extremity of the Brahmaputra Valley in 1228 AD. The Ahoms, who were led by Sukapha with barely 1,000 followers, had left behind their womenfolk as being incapable of undergoing the hardships of an unfriendly terrain. They were thus compelled to increase their numerical strength by incorporating non-Ahoms in their fold and inter-marriage with local women.[6]

The Ahoms entered Assam in the area that now forms part of Lakhimpur and Sibsagar districts, which at that time was inhabited by Bodos, who were easily subdued. From the 13th to 16th centuries, the Ahoms were mainly busy in consolidating their power and in adjusting their relationship with the neighbouring principalities of Kamata that was subsequently transformed into the well-known Cooch Behar kingdom, Cachar, Jayantia, Darrang, Chutiya and Kamrup. The principality of Kamrup, a part of much greater kingdom of the same name was contiguous to the Mughal territories, and thus became the theatre of many a long drawn battles between the Mughals and the Ahoms.[7]

The history of 17th century Ahoms was the history of Assam-Mughal conflicts. Mir Jumla, the trusted and tried commander of Aurangzeb and the uncrowned King of Golkonda and Carnatic, entered the borders of Assam in 1662 and occupied the Ahom capital Gargaon. [8] By the Treaty of Ghilajari of 1663 between the Ahom King Jayadhwaj Singha and the Mughal General Mir Jumla, Kamrup was transferred to the Mughals and a heavy war-indemnity was levied on Ahoms. But four years later in August 1667, Kamrup was taken back from the Mughals by the Ahom General Lachit Barpukhan, during the reign of Chakradhwaj Singha, the successor of Jayadhwaj Singha. Aurangzeb, rattled by the defeat sent another force under Raja Ram Singh of Amber to recapture Guwahati, the capital of Kamrup. The Ahoms inflicted a crushing defeat on the Mughal

Army in the Battle of Saraighat, in the vicinity of Guwahati, in March 1671. The Mughal army retired to their garrison at Rangamati where it waited till 1676 for another opportunity to attack Assam. However, internal troubles and conspiracies did to Ahoms what the Mughals had failed to do. In a brief space of eleven years there were no less than seven Ahom Kings. The Mughals took advantage of this rotten state of affairs and recovered Guwahati, but they were finally driven out in the reign of Gadadhar Singha, who ascended the throne in 1681. [9]

Gadadhar Singha ruled his kingdom for fifteen years from 1681 to 1696 AD. Rudra Singha (1696-1714) who succeeded his father was more statesman like than his father. His reign is memorable for the final triumph of Hinduism over the religion of Ahoms.[10] He planned for greater conquests and hoped to unfurl the flag of victory in the neighbouring Mughal territories and dreamt of seizing the throne of Delhi.[11] He mobilised a force of 4,00,000 men at Guwahati, which planned to enter into Mughal territories in November 1714, but unfortunately as the preparations were afoot for the march, Rudra Singha died in September of the year.[12]

The kings who succeeded Rudra Singha lacked his courage and vision. Siva Singha (1714-1744) was initiated into tantric cult and had no flair for kingship. His successors, Pramatta Singha and then Rajeshwar Singha, though not brilliant, were capable rulers. Jai Singha, the king of Manipur, sought his help to expel the Burmese usurpers from Manipur, which was given.

As time went by the Ahoms lost much of the old martial spirit and pride of race with which they had till then been animated. Moamarias rose in revolt during the reign of Laxshmi Singha, who had succeeded Rajeshwar Singha.[13] The insurrection was put down but to rise again during the reign of Gaurinath Singha (1780-1795). The rebels defeated the royal troops in 1786 and took the capital by storm. Gaurinath fled to Guwahati and sought aid from the British, who had succeeded the Mughals in Sylhet and Goalpara. Lord Cornwallis sent Capt Welsh with a small force in 1792, which subdued the rebels, reoccupied Rangpur and Gaurinath Singha was placed on his ancestral throne. Capt Welsh returned to Calcutta in 1794 after having enacted a treaty for the promotion of commercial intercourse between Assam and the East India Company.[14]

Gaurinath was succeeded by Kamleshwar Singha who successfully subdued the beginnings of rebellion in other parts like Nowgong, Kamrup and North Lakhimpur. This was due to the timely actions of Purnanda Burgohain. Chandrakanta (1811-1818) succeeded Kamleshwar Singha who at the time of accession was only fourteen-years-old. Purnanda Burgohain was all in all with unlimited powers, which caused jealously among Chandrakanta's favourites and sycophants. A conspiracy was hatched to assassinate Purnanda. Badanchanda Barphukan, Assam's viceroy at Guwahati was suspected of being one of the conspirators. Purnanda deputed emissaries to apprehend Badanchanda, who came to know of it in advance, and fled from Guwahati to Calcutta for his safety. In Calcutta, Badanchanda met the Burmese envoy who was then at Calcutta and went with him to Ava, where he persuaded the Burmese king to send an expedition to Assam. In March 1817, an army of 8000 men was dispatched, which entered Assam through the Patkai Pass, occupied the country as far as Jorhat and reinstated Badanchanda as the Governor of Guwahati. Through the instrumentality of Badanchanda, Chandrakanta entered into peace terms with the Burmese, and the Burmese force thereafter returned to Burma. But soon fresh dissensions started; Badanchanda was assassinated; Chandrakanta, who was suspected of being instrumental in inviting Burmese to Assam by deputing Badanchanda to Ava, was deposed by the new Burgohain Ruchinath (son of Purnanda) and one Purandar Singha was installed in his place.

The king of Burma regarded the murder of Badanchanda and deposal of Chandrakanta as an affront and deputed a fresh army to punish the enemies of Chandrakanta. Purandar Singha was defeated and fled to Bengal. Chandrakanta was once again placed on the throne after which the Burmese left but not before perpetrating extreme barbarity and atrocities upon all those suspected to have sympathy for Purandar. Having recovered his throne, Chandrakanta made preparations to counter future Burmese designs on Assam. When this was conveyed to the Burmese king, he sent an army again to punish Chandrakanta, who fled to Guwahati. The Burmese placed one Jogeshwar Singha on the throne but the Burmese Commander-in-Chief was the virtual ruler of Assam. In the meantime, the Burmese had come into conflict with the British in Manipur, Cachar and Jayantia, where sporadic fighting had broken out. The British, in order to neutralise Burmese influence, marched their troops from Goalpara towards Guwahati. The Burmese resistance lasted for ten months from March 1824 to January 1825, but in the end the British defeated the Burmese and occupied Rangpur, the Assamese capital. The Burmese promised not to interfere in the affairs of Assam and by the Treaty of Yandeboo enacted in February 24, 1826, Assam finally passed into British hands.[15] Scott, the Commissioner of Rangpur was appointed to administer the country.

In parts of Assam outside Brahmaputra Valley, the decline in Ahom power had eased the pressure on Kachari kings, whose capital was now at Khaspur in the plains of Cachar.[16] But Manipuris on their Eastern frontier threatened the Cacharis and they had been appealing to the British for help against Manipuri threat since 1817, which were rejected until early 1824, when the British received intelligence of a possible invasion of Cachar and Jayantia by the Burmese. The first collision with Burmese troops occurred on the Cachar plains, but by then the main scene of action had shifted to Assam in the Brahmaputra Valley.[17]

In Cachar, the Raja was replaced on the throne but was forced to relinquish a portion of his domain to a rebel, Tukaram, who in 1830, assassinated the Raja. In the absence of a lawful heir, Cachar was annexed to the British territory. In 1835, the Raja of Jayantia was dispossessed of his territory in consequence of the repeated abduction of British officers. The Khasi Hills to the West was conquered in 1833 as the result of an attack made on a party engaged in the construction of a road through the hills; but the people were left in a state of quasi independence under their own chief. Shillong was however, fully taken under the British control and became the capital of the province.[18] The occupation of Naga Hills commenced in 1866 and the last addition was made in 1904, when the Eastern Angami region was formally annexed. By 1869, Garo Hills was annexed and formed into a district with headquarter at Tura. Lushai Hills was finally annexed in 1890.[19]

After the British annexed Assam in 1826, a British agent, representing the Governor General, administered it. A separate province of Assam along with the East Bengal district of Sylhet was created in 1874 and its administration came under a Chief Commissioner, with its capital at Shillong. This added a new twist to the politics of Assam; Bengali speaking population outnumbered Assamese.[20]

Assamese Nationalism and the Growth of the Idea of Swadhin Asom

The idea of a *Swadhin Asom* is not a recent idea; it has a long history going back to the British annexation of Assam by the Treaty of Yandeboo. After the brutalities committed by the Burmese in the last days of the Ahom rule, the British annexation was a great relief and was welcomed by the people. But the honeymoon was not to last long; dissatisfaction against the British rule, which was focused mainly on revenue collection, began to grow. The steep rise in revenue rates and the investment in the tea and oil industries at the cost of agriculture impoverished the people further. This resentment was reflected in the rebellion against the British led by Peali Barphukan, son of Badanchandra Barphukan. Although the rebellion did not succeed, it was nonetheless the first attempt to consolidate the public opinion against the British.

The 1857 uprising had its repercussion in Assam, which took the form of a revolt led by Maniram to restore the Ahom scion Kandarpeshwar Singha on the throne. Maniram was made the Dewan of the Assam Company in 1839 in recognition of his services to the British during the campaign against the Burmese.[21] When Maniram fell from grace and was stripped of much of his powers, he resigned and turned against the British. Although the revolt did not succeed, Maniram became a martyr and a rallying point for the nationalist forces.

The events of 1857-58 and the peasant uprising of Phulagari[22] in Nowgong district in 1861 consolidated the nationalist sentiments, but it was the pull of Assamese language, which gave impetus to the Assamese nationalism. Bengali as the official language had replaced the Assamese language in 1837, which had greatly hurt Assamese sensibility. Christian missionaries who had brought out the Assamese journal *Orunodoi* (1847-83) played a deciding role in getting the rightful place for Assamese as the official language and the medium of instruction in schools in Assam in 1873.

Asamiya Bhasa Unnati Sadhani Sabha (ABUS) was formed in 1988, which worked to make Assamese the richest language in the world. ABUS brought out a journal *Jonaki*, whose contributors focused on Assam's glorious past and called upon people to draw inspiration from the old kingdom of Kamrup. Though only a few of the contributors in the journal were explicit in expressing the idea of an independent Assam, yet the general tone of the articles seemed to suggest that '*Swadhin Asom*' was the answer to the present misfortune of Assam.[23] The contributors harked back to the time of Bhaskarvarman and

Ahoms, which symbolised prosperity. Assamese linguistic nationalism or Asamiya Jatiyabad found manifestation in poems like *Mor Desh* and *Asom Sangeet*. Written in 1910, the poem *Mor Desh* eulogises Assam as a country of unparallel beauty. The song is sung at all public occasions in Assam along with the national anthem.[24] Two types of nationalism, regional and pan-Indian, existed side by side but when regional aspirations conflicted with pan-Indian interests, it was the regional nationalism that got the better of pan-Indian nationalism.[25]

The partition of Bengal in 1905 led to a massive opposition both in Bengal and Assam. The anti-partition movement brought the Assamese middle class in closer contact with the development in the rest of the country. But it was Gandhi's non-cooperation movement that introduced Assam to national politics. When the Congress Working Committee approved the setting up of Assam Pradesh Congress Committee in January 1921, members of Assam Chatra Sanmilan decided to take active part in Gandhi's non-cooperation movement, which led to politicisation of the masses. The rise in the level of political consciousness was reflected in the formation of a number of organisations like the Assam Sanghrakshni Sabha founded by Ambikagiri Roychoudhury (later turned into Assam Jatiya Mahasabha). Such organisations voiced regional demands, which included safeguard against unchecked immigration from Bengal.

Ambikagiri was among the first Assamese intellectual to put forward the idea of an Indian federation of linguistic nationalities with dual citizenship.[26] He was also amongst the first to spell out the relationship between Assamese and pan-Indian nationalism. He believed that after independence each nationality must be given the right to assert itself according to its own genius. As early as 1937, Ambikagiri wrote to Nehru on behalf of Asamiya Sanghrakshini Sabha and drew his attention to the growing feeling among a sizeable section of intelligentsia that if central leaders did not view the fears regarding the Muslim influx seriously then Assam should secede from India.[27]

Many other intellectuals shared the idea of *Swadhin Asom;* chief among them was Jnananath Bora. He argued that Assam's ills lay in joining the Indian Union. In an article 'Why should Assam stay in India?' Bora insists that Assam's regeneration would be possible only if separated from India. His view could not be taken as representative of Assamese middle class, yet a large section of the intelligentsia had sympathy for the cause of *Swadhin Asom.*

Roychoudhuri also formed Atmarakshi Bahini to save the Assamese homeland from the designs of Muslim League, which lobbied for inclusion of Assam into Pakistan. Roychoudhuri was totally opposed to it, so much so, that, after Independence when the Congress government failed to check the infiltration from East Pakistan, he in a meeting of the Jatiya Mahasabha held on January 1, 1948 declared that Assam should come out of the Indian Union and become an independent country like Burma[28] The courageous resistance put up by Bordoloi against the grouping scheme and the separation of Sylhet from Assam greatly assuaged the fears of Assamese of losing their identity. For more than two decades after Independence pan-Indian nationalism had an upper hand in Assam politics.

Centre-State Relations: Genesis of Assam's Alienation

The first major difference between Assam and the Centre manifested on the question of settling the refugees from East Pakistan. When Bordoloi expressed his unwillingness to continue settling refugees, mainly Hindus, from East Pakistan without limit, Nehru was furious. In a letter addressed to Bordoloi in May 1949 Nehru wrote: "You say there is no further land available in Assam. This is a question of fact, which can easily be determined. It is patent, however, that if land is not available in Assam; it is less available in rest of India."[29] Nehru in the same letter told Bordoloi: "If Assam adopts a policy of incapacity to help solve the refugee problem, then the claims of Assam for financial help would obviously suffer."[30]

Nehru was rattled when demands were made for dual citizenship from parties like the Assom Jatiya Mahasabha of Ambika Roychoudhury, about which reference has already been made earlier in the narrative. Nehru expressed his annoyance rather insensitively in a letter to Bordoloi: "I suppose one of these days we might be asked for the independence of Assam."[31] He further added rather bluntly "that Assam will have to be left out of consideration in our general scheme of progress." The veiled threat in the above comment was inescapable. Bordoloi responded in his letter to Nehru dated 24 August 1949: "You have done the people of Assam wrong in assuming that the people of Assam want dual citizenship. If some crank ventilates through press and literature, any fad of his, the blame should neither go to the people of Assam nor to the government." [32] Sardar Patel was equally insensitive to the problems faced by Assam in settling unlimited refugees, which is reflected in a letter written by Patel to Bordoloi in July 1950 saying that instead of falling prey to local prejudices he (Bordoloi) should appreciate the difficulty of the Centre.[33] It was such insensitivity towards Assam that initially sowed the seeds of discord, which ultimately manifested in secessionist demands in the 1970s.[34]

The feeling of step-motherly treatment of Assam in economic development by the Centre was accentuated by the decision to build the first oil refinery in public sector at Barauni in Bihar, which would process crude oil from Assam carried over hundreds of kilometres of pipeline from the Upper Assam oil fields. There was widespread resentment in Assam against the Centre's decision, which took the form of a satyagraha in 1950-57. Nehru visited Assam and declared at a meeting in Nowgong that there was no reason why the refinery should not be in Assam if it was technically feasible and economically viable. An expert committee which was set up to go into the merits of the case ruled that a refinery in Assam was both technically feasible and economically viable.[35] But finally a decision was taken to set up the refinery at Barauni on the advice of the defence chiefs, who held the view that they could not undertake to protect the refinery if it was situated in Assam or the pipeline if it went to Calcutta along the Pakistan border.[36] The decision came as a huge disappointment to Assam that was reflected in the letter that Chief Minister, Medhi, wrote to Nehru: "If defence cannot undertake to protect the refinery located in Assam, how will they protect the oil fields and the transport system in the Eastern region".[37] The Centre did not change the decision despite the forceful arguments by the Assam government and the public outcry but agreed to set up a much smaller refinery with a capacity of 0.85 million tonnes at Guwahati as against Barauni's capacity of 3.30 million tonnes. This was obviously done to placate popular feelings but the Assamese continued to harbour a feeling of discrimination.

Assam tea is one of the major foreign exchange earners of India, yet it had hardly any impact on the state's economy. The profit earned by the British and Indian companies were channelised outside the state and even in the matter of sales tax, Assam got only half the amount secured by West Bengal by virtue of the head offices of most of the large companies being in Calcutta. For example, according to a report published in the *Assam Tribune* of June 15-16, 1980, Assam that year got only Rupees 22 crores as sales tax on tea produced in the state whereas West Bengal got Rupees 42 crores.[38] The transfer of tea gardens from British to Indian hands has made no difference to Assamese. Outsiders hold most managerial posts in the tea gardens; head offices of the tea companies are still based in Calcutta and the main office of the Tea Board continue to be also in Calcutta.

The defeat of the Indian Armed Forces in 1962 India-China war was a traumatic experience for the Indians; for Assamese it was even more so. When it seemed that the Chinese would soon reach the plains of Assam after the army had started withdrawing from their defences in the mountains in Bomdila, Nehru's address to the nation, which virtually abandoned Assam to its fate, left a deep wound in Assamese psyche. Today, it is quoted as proof that Centre considers Assam as a colony.

Yet another cause for Assamese alienation was the territorial reorganisation of Assam in 1972. The agitation against the reorganisation of Assam on a federal basis was based on the view that those regions of Assam, which did not have a predominantly Assamese speaking population, were part of a bigger Assamese fraternity. But ironically Assamese had totally alienated non-Assamese by their language policy, which led to the break-up of Assam into a number of new states. Nari Rustomji makes a telling comment: "The dismemberment of Assam however inevitable under the circumstances came as a shock and trauma from which she (Assam) could not quickly recover. For Assam suffers from a sense of deep hurt that the Centre has been primarily responsible for her humiliating reduction to the status of a mini State, one amongst many under shared governors, and that, too, not *primus intu pares*, but a near equal."[39]

Assam Students Movement (1979-1985)

The Assam movement has its genesis in the illegal immigration of Bangladeshis, which was highlighted by the observation of Sakhder, the Chief Election Commissioner (CEC), who expressed serious concern at the fact that the names of foreign nationals were included in the electoral rolls of the state in large numbers.[40] The Chief Commissioner went on to say that in case of Assam the population in 1971 recorded an increase as high as 34.98 percent over the 1961 figures and this increase was attributed to the influx of a large number of persons from Bangladesh.

All Assam Students Union (AASU) took up the issue raised by the Election Commissioner and began to focus its attention to the dangers posed by the illegal immigrants, who threatened to change the demographic profile of the state. The updating of the electoral roll for the parliamentary bye-election to the Mangaldoi constituency caused by the death of the sitting member in 1979 finally set the stage for the Assam Movement. The tribunal set up to update the rolls found 45,000 voters in an electorate of six lakhs to be foreigners. On the initiative of AASU, the All Assam Gana Sangram Parishad (AAGSP) composed of several parties was formed at Dibrugarh in August 1979, which would spearhead the Assam Movement.[41]

When the Janta Government fell, mid-term election was held in December 1979. The CEC who had earlier taken a stand for removing the names of foreigners from the electoral rolls, now changed his stance obviously under pressure from the government, and decided that "a person whose name has been included shall be presumed to be a citizen of India." A press note released on September 18, 1979, said that no person who was included in the electoral rolls shall be eliminated on the ground of citizenship as the process of establishing citizenship was time consuming. The commission further advised scrutiny of electoral rolls after the election was over. This led to widespread protest against the unconstitutional verdict.

The election was boycotted except in Cachar district, which has a predominantly Bengali population. President's Rule was imposed in Assam on December 12, 1979; the legislature and the ministry was suspended but not dissolved. The assembly was later revived and by deft manipulation and encouraging defection by the Congress (I), which had only eight members in a house of 126, formed the ministry with the support of 43 defectors on December 6, 1980. It was one of the darkest chapters in the parliamentary history of the country.

Indira Gandhi who was swept into power at Delhi with an impressive majority in the parliamentary elections held in early 1980, opened negotiation with the student leaders. The students refused to budge from their demand of detection and deportation of illegal immigrants from Bangladesh. The government took recourse to coercive methods to subdue the agitators. It proved counter productive. The students now introduced a new weapon – closure of the pipeline that fed crude oil to the refinery at Barauni to strike at the heart of the Indian economy.

As Assam was reeling under the mass upsurge led by student leaders like Prafulla Kumar Mohanta and Bhrigu Phukan, Indira Gandhi made another political blunder. She decided to go through the assembly elections, which were due in 1983. It proved a watershed in the history of democratic India. Officials to conduct the elections were flown from Delhi and other places like Bihar and transported to the polling booths under heavy security. There were few candidates and fewer voters. In many constituencies there was no polling at all. The election was marred by state violence in which at least 130 persons were killed.[42] The Congress won a landslide victory, but it was a phyrric victory.

The Nellie Killings

The Nellie killings will be remembered as one of the worst ethnic cleansing in Assam. Lalung tribesmen inhabit the area and had lost their land to immigrants from East Pakistan and Bangladesh who had settled on land bought from illiterate tribes. There has been simmering discontent against the immigrants, mostly Muslims. When the Muslim settlers decided to defy the call given by AASU to boycott the election, the tribes were furious. As so often happens, the anger of tribes was ignited by the talk that Muslim settlers have molested tribal women. The anger and outrage led to the horrific carnage in which more than 1700 were killed. The violence spread across the state and one estimate put the total killed around 3-4,000. It was the worst pogrom in independent India.

The Assam Accord

The process of reconciliation started after the assassination of Indira Gandhi in 1984. Her son, Rajiv Gandhi, who succeeded her took advantage of not carrying any political past and opened negotiations with the student leaders and struck a deal with them, which finally resulted in the Assam Accord of 1985. The government agreed to drop all cases against AASU and other agitators; the draconian laws that gave sweeping powers to government officials and security forces were lifted; the Centre pledged to detect and deport illegal immigrants who had settled in the state after 1971 and agreed to hold elections to the state assembly and 14 Lok Sabha seats in the State in December 1985. Hitendra Saikia, the Chief Minister, was to step down before the elections. On its part AASU agreed to take part in the elections on the basis of the 1984 electoral rolls, which were prepared on the basis of 1971 list, the rolls AASU had opposed all along. Be as it may, the elections were held soon after the Accord in which Asom Gana Parishad (AGP), formed after the Accord, came out victorious.

The Rise of United Liberation Front of Asom (ULFA)

ULFA was born even before the students had consolidated their movement against the perceived discrimination of Assam by the Central Government. The Front was formally launched on April 7, 1979 at Rang Ghar pavilion in Sibsagar, once the seat of Ahom kingdom. Those present on that fateful day were Rajiv Konwar, better known as Arobindo Rajkhowa, Golap Baruah alias Anup Chetia, Samiran Gogoi alias Pradip Gogoi and Paresh Baruah. ULFA derived its inspiration from Asom Jatiyabadi Yuva Chatra Parishad (AJYCP), which was a semi militant organisation. Many of the ULFA founders were members of AJYCP. The Front determined to wage armed struggle to liberate Assam from the exploitation of India. Its declared objectives are: -

- To achieve Assam's independence by armed struggle.
- To safeguard Assam's interests
- To have full control over the natural resources of Assam
- To secure widespread support against Indian exploitation

ULFA maintained close links with AASU and during the first few years of its founding kept a low profile. It concentrated on building the organisation on a sound base, establishing foreign links and securing support of other militant groups of the North-east.[43] The formation of AGP Government in 1985 consequent to its victory in the assembly elections held after the signing of the Assam Accord facilitated the spread of ULFA. It is now established that the AGP Government and its surrogate organisations, such as, AASU, were closely associated with the ULFA. Not officially, of course, but at the village and local levels.[44]

ULFA first made contact with the Kachin Independent Army (KIA) and NSCN (IM) in Burma in 1986 and sought their help in training the cadres. KIA agreed to train and give them arms but at a steep price; they demanded one million rupees for arms.[45] To raise money ULFA went on a spree to rob banks and extort money from wealthy businessmen and tea garden owners. But the relationship between the KIA and ULFA was interrupted when Indian Research and Analysis Wing (RAW) threatened the KIA to send back pro-democracy Burmese fugitives if KIA did not stop training ULFA cadres. The threat worked; there was no further training by KIA. ULFA then turned to Muivah faction of the Nagas, but the split and fratricidal war between the two factions of NSCN forced ULFA to terminate its relationship with the Muivah group. After snapping its ties with Muivah group, ULFA came under the influence of Khaplang group, which then trained its cadres.

By 1990, the stock of AGP Government had hit rock bottom. A number of ULFA cadres were close to AGP and, therefore, during its first term in office, the government was not in a position to take tough measures against ULFA. Taking advantage of the situation, ULFA succeeded in infiltrating into the state's bureaucracy at all levels. As time went by ULFA's acts of extortion, killings, kidnappings and robberies became brazen. Businessmen paid large amounts as protection money and were reluctant to complain out of fear. Tea gardens paid quietly to buy peace with ULFA. The swiftness of capitulation of the tea industry surprised even the militants. " If we asked for something in terms of lakhs and crores, it would be paid within days, before the deadline that was set." [46] The Central Government was hesitant to take action, as AGP was at that time the coalition partner in VP Singh's government.

Operation Bajrang

On the fall of VP Singh's government at the Centre, Chandrasekhar, the new Prime Minister, dismissed Mohanta's government and imposed President's Rule. The immediate provocation came when ULFA demanded 3.5 million rupees from Unilever, which had seven tea estates at Doom Dooma, and fixed a deadline. Unilever's Headquarters in London brought the matter to the notice of the Indian High Commissioner, who advised the Centre to take strong action. The Assam Chief Minister had told the companies that " they were on their own and the government could do little to bail them out."[47] Doom Dooma incident provided a justification to the Centre to take strong action against ULFA.

The Army launched Operation Bajrang on November 28, 1990, but the word of the impending operation was leaked out to ULFA by their sympathisers in the government. A few low ranking cadres were caught but the top leadership escaped the dragnet. During the operations the army discovered mass graves at Lakhipathar camp of ULFA; the discovery shocked the people of Assam and demolished the Robin Hood image of ULFA.

Operation Rhino

Operation Rhino was launched in September 1991 with greater secrecy. The operation proved a success; most of the ULFA bases in the state were destroyed and nearly all the top ULFA leadership, namely, Manoj Hazarika, Andrew Giri, Bhaskar Baruah, ULFA general secretary Golap Baruah, vice president Pradip Gogoi and some others were captured. In November, Anup Chetia was apprehended at a guest house at Calcutta by the intelligence agencies. He gave valuable information about the inner working of the organisation. In late December 1991, Sunil Nath, the spokesman of ULFA was arrested. Next to fall in trap was Kalpjyoti Neog followed by another top ULFA figure Moon Ali, who was arrested from a hotel room. But the most important success was Hirakjyoti Mohanta, the deputy commander-in-chief of ULFA, who was shot while trying to escape after he promised to lead the army to a ULFA hideout. His death was a crippling blow to ULFA.

Within weeks of the start of Operation Rhino, the army had captured 4300 suspects; after initial screenings 1,700 were released. Apart from weapons, the army had recovered seven million rupees.[48] It was now clear that ULFA was fighting with its back to the wall. From the statements made by the captured leaders, it began to emerge that the leadership was changing its stance from *Swadhin Asom* to *Swadhikar* (autonomy). Arobindo Rajkhowa, the ULFA chairman, wrote a letter to Prime Minister, Narsimha Rao, declaring his willingness to end the hostilities and negotiate. The Indian Government wanted a written commitment from ULFA to accept a solution of the Assam problem within the Indian constitution, to abjure violence and to deposit arms at an appropriate time to be decided mutually.

In the new year (1992), ULFA gave the written statement, which should have set the stage for ULFA's capitulation. But events took a different turn. Following the written commitment, army operations were suspended temporarily to allow ULFA leadership to convene a meeting of their central council. Paresh Baruah, the C-in-C, who had taken refuge in Bangladesh, was opposed to any peace talks, and kept sending messages to his followers to reject government's overtures and continue the fight.

The top leadership tried to convince and persuade the cadres to accept the assurances given by it to the government but despite the extension of the suspension of army operations from one deadline to the other, the leadership failed to persuade the cadres. There was too much pressure from Paresh Baruah and his followers to abandon the peace initiative. In desperation Rajkhowa, Chetia and Pradip Gogoi told the Union Government that they would have to travel to Bangladesh to talk to Paresh Baruah. The Union Government obliged and gave them safe passage from Delhi. But it was only a ruse to flee India and join Paresh Baruah in Bangladesh. By the end of March 1992, the three had slipped out of India to Bangladesh not to return.[49]

Split in ULFA

In the absence of top leaders aligned to Paresh Baruah, Munim Nobis, the man who had initiated ULFA's Bangladesh connection, Sunil Nath and Kalpajyoti Neog signed a statement opposing armed struggle and advocating peace talks with the government. The ULFA had split between pro and anti-peace talk faction. The pro talks faction gave up their demand for

Swadhin Asom (independence) and favoured *Swadhikar* (autonomy). They were expelled from the organisation. Many came overground. The lure of a comfortable life after living the life of fugitives was difficult to resist. Those who came overground were given cash grants and soft loans to begin a new life. Many were recruited in police. A few bought tea gardens with ill-gotten money. The local police often turned a blind eye to their unlawful activities in return for their support in obtaining information about ULFA. Many became law unto themselves, which was resented by the public. They began to be derisively called SULFA, an acronym for Surrendered United Liberation Front of Assam.[50]

Shift in ULFA's Ideology

One of the reasons for the dwindling public support for ULFA has been its about-turn on the question of illegal Bangladeshi immigrants. In a 15-page booklet issued in July 1992, ULFA states that the immigrants from Bangladesh have now become a part of the national life and Assam's struggle for freedom can never be successful without them. Yet, another significant point made in the booklet is that English would be the link language of *Swadhin Asom*, thereby nullifying almost a century of struggle to give the Assamese language its rightful place in the state.[51] The document was also critical of AASU and termed the Assam Movement as one based on emotion. AASU struck back and denounced ULFA as anti-Assam. It pointed out that ULFA leadership was comfortably based in Bangladesh and that was the reason for its shift in ideology.[52]

Recrudescence of ULFA Violence

Paresh Barua's faction has training camps in Bangladesh where its cadres live and train. In 1992, Narsimha Rao handed over pictures and documents about the camps to Begum Khaleda Zia during her visit to Delhi. She as usual denied the existence of any such camps in Bangladesh.

Saikia completed his five-year term in 1995 and fresh elections were held for the Assam assembly in early 1996. AGP in alliance with five other parties formed the next government. AGP also joined the non-BJP coalition government at the Centre, which gave it considerable leverage. The AGP tried to assuage the feelings of ULFA by saying that it saw extremism in Assam as a result of "accumulated hurt" and criticised the policy of crushing insurgency by military means. But within hours of swearing in of Mohanta as the Chief Minister for the second time, superintendent of police of Tinsukia was shot down. Next day Parag Das, a civil rights activist and editor of *Ahomiya Pratidin*, was killed.

Illegal Migrants Detection Tribunal Act (1983)

The IMDT Act (1983) is an extremely controversial issue, which provokes extreme passion and has divided the politics of Assam. The act was passed in 1983 to prevent alleged harassment of religious and linguistic minorities under the Foreigners Act 1946. Indira Gandhi was instrumental in bringing the IMDT Act, applicable only in Assam, which provided for identification and determination of illegal migrants, mainly from Bangladesh, by judicial tribunals. Under the Act the onus of proving a person to be a foreigner rests on the complainant. Most Assamese feel that the above proviso makes the Act ineffective, whereas the minorities are of the view that it provides them protection against police harassment. The political parties are polarised on this issue. The Congress and the left parties are against its repeal, whereas, BJP and AASU favour repeal. AGP's position is ambivalent. Although it favours repeal, it is not vocal fearing adverse Muslim reaction; Muslims now form a sizeable percentage of its vote bank. AASU has been agitating for its repeal on the ground that the Act impedes the identification of illegal migrants.[53]

The Unified Command

A unified command was formed to better coordinate the political, administrative and military aspects of counter-insurgency operations. The system produced the desired result and contributed substantially in fighting insurgency more effectively. The structure of the unified command is discussed in greater detail in the chapter on counter-insurgency. The pro ULFA elements in the government claimed that under the unified command the state government was virtually handed over to the army.

AGP in Crisis

The compulsions of electoral politics brought the realisation to the AGP leadership led by Mohanta that given the demographic composition of the state, it would be imperative for the party to shed its image of a party purely of Assamese middle class. It has, therefore, tried to bring Bengalis, both Hindus and Muslims, to its fold. The dilution of its ideology has opened the party to the charge that it is going soft on the question of identification and deportation of illegal immigrants from Bangladesh. AASU has distanced itself from the AGP and is aggressively demanding the repeal of IMDT Act-1983, whereas the position of AGP is ambivalent.

The critics of Mohanta claimed that the army kept him in power, though it was ULFA, which helped him to come to power; it was widely reported that ULFA had canvassed for AGP in the 1996 assembly elections, but things did not go the way ULFA had expected. There was an attempt on the life of Mohanta in Guwahati in January 1997. Mohanta had come out strongly against the secessionist demand of ULFA, but there were allegations of complicity with ULFA against one of his cabinet ministers, Zoinath Sarma. Although Mohanta denied the report, he accepted that a section of the government employees were paying regular taxes to ULFA. It became quite evident that not only the government employees but some political leaders were also providing moral and material support to ULFA.[54]

The Current Scenario

There have been reports of links between tea companies and ULFA. In a sensational revelation, the Assam government made serious charges of clandestine links between Tata Tea and ULFA. Although the medical expenses of Pranati Deka, ULFA's cultural secretary, in Jaslok Hospital which were paid by Tata Tea in August 1997, was explained by the company as non-discriminatory under its special medical aid programme, the controversy highlighted the fact that almost all tea companies in Assam were paying protection money to ULFA. The army justifiably claimed that unless the source of funding to the militants is choked, it would be difficult to wage an effective fight against them.

There were attacks by ULFA on oil pipelines in November 1997, which were more to demonstrate their presence rather than a part of a planned strategy. The senseless killing of a social activist, Sanjoy Ghosh, in mysterious circumstances in July 1997 outraged all sections of Assamese society.

During the 1999 Kargil War, it was reported by the army intelligence that insurgents of Assam, especially ULFA, have been used by the ISI to spy for Pakistan on the movement of troops from Assam.[55] There were also suspicions that the series of attacks on the railways in Assam during the period of the Kargil War were intended to disrupt troop movements. These anti-national activities of ULFA have not gone down well with the Assamese and have been widely condemned. People have responded with anger against ULFA leadership. There was enthusiastic upsurge of patriotic feeling not only in Assam but the whole of the North-east and people are overwhelmed with pride for the sacrifice of soldiers belonging to the North-east. ULFA has lost much of its support amongst the Assamese.

The total dependence of Paresh Barua, ULFA's Chief, on ISI and DGFI has had a marked effect on the organisation's activities in Assam. Paresh Barua is now a virtual prisoner in the hands of ISI, and unlike in the past when he overruled ISI suggestions to damage economic assets like oil pipelines, he now bows to similar ISI pressures. It may come as a surprise to many that ULFA has seldom targeted illegal Bangladeshi migrants. The killings of non - Assamese and Hindi speaking Assamese by ULFA in 2000 was at the behest of ISI.[56] As per Annual Report of the Ministry of Defence 2003-2004, 312 insurgents were killed, 930 apprehended and 1356 weapons recovered in the period under report. More importantly, 3457 insurgents and their sympathisers surrendered.

Destruction of ULFA Camps in Bhutan

In the nineties, ULFA decided to shift its camps from Bangladesh to the forests of Southern Bhutan for a number of reasons. Sheikh Hasina and her Awami League had come to power in Bangladesh in 1995 and were sensitive to India's security concerns. She began to put restrictions on the activities of ULFA and others and pressed them to close their camps located inside Bangladesh. Bhutan's attitude to Assamese militant groups setting up camps inside Bhutanese territory was ambivalent in those days. The 1988 census in Bhutan had turned up tens of thousands of illegal Nepalese migrants in Bhutan, which had the potential to change the demography in Southern Bhutan. Illegal migrants, mostly Nepalese, who had come over to Bhutan in the 1960s and stayed on without acquiring citizenship, were told to leave forthwith. The situation turned violent and there were clashes between Bhutanese and Nepalese.[57] This was the situation when ULFA and other militant groups shifted their camps to Southern Bhutan. It is speculated that someone in the Royal Bhutan Government decided to use ULFA and National Democratic Front of Bodoland (NDFB) as foils against Nepalese settlers in Southern Bhutan.[58] ULFA and NDFB were only too happy as the situation suited them. Having established their camps in the forests in

Southern Bhutan close to the Assam border, ULFA and Bodo militants began to strike at targets in Assam and withdrew to their sanctuaries in Bhutan. This was an intolerable situation for the Indian security forces. When the Indian Government complained to the Bhutanese, the Indians were told that they would talk to the Assamese insurgents and ask them to leave Bhutan but refused to consider offensive action jointly with the Indian Army.

The talks between the Assamese insurgent groups and the Bhutan Government dragged on for six years. In the meantime, the situation worsened for the Indian security forces, as they could not take retaliatory action against the insurgents. The situation was no better for the Bhutanese either. ULFA and NDFB had assumed that the Bhutanese were not in a position to force them out of Bhutan by force. They became too cocky, took the law in their own hands and became a threat to Bhutan's sovereignty. Finally, the Royal Bhutan Government in consultation with India decided to take military action to destroy the insurgent camps located inside Bhutanese territory.[59] The operation started on December 15, 2003 in which nearly 6,000 troops of the Royal Bhutan Army (RBA) took part. The Indian Army provided logistic support and sealed the Indo-Bhutan border to prevent militants from escaping. In all 30 camps of ULFA, NDFB and Kamatpur Liberation Organisation (KLO) were destroyed and important leaders of the three insurgent groups were either killed or captured. Of more than 2,000 insurgents who were in these camps, 100 were killed and 200 were either captured or surrendered.[60] A large quantity of weapons and ammunition was also recovered. The operation was a great blow to insurgents in Assam. Although it is reported that the insurgents have begun relocating in Bangladesh, security analysts believe it will take a long time before they recover from the loss suffered in Bhutan.

Emergence of Islamic Fundamentalism in Assam and North-east India

In the recent years, Islamic fundamentalism has grown in Assam and other parts of the North-east. PK Mohanta, the then Chief Minister of Assam, in the report he presented to the State Assembly on April 6, 2000 disclosed the contours of an emerging Islamic militancy in Assam. The report laid bare the nexus between the ISI and the Islamic militant groups, which had come up after the destruction of Babri Masjid in 1992. The nexus was revealed after the arrest of 31 suspects, which included four important members of the network, in Guwahati on August 7, 1999. The 16- page report revealed the ISI strategy aimed at promoting indiscriminate firing, creating new militant groups based on communal and ethnic lines, supplying arms and explosives to militants, causing sabotage of oil pipelines and promoting communal tension.[61]

The rise in Islamic militancy in India's North-east is linked to the rise of Islamic fundamentalism in Bangladesh. As Bertil Linter of the *Far Eastern Economic Review* opines: "A revolution is taking place in Bangladesh that threatens trouble for the region and beyond if left unchallenged. Islamic fundamentalism, religious intolerance, militant Muslim groups with links to international terrorist groups, a powerful military with ties to the militants, the mushrooming of Islamic schools, churning out radical students, middle class apathy, poverty and lawlessness - all are combining to transform the nation." [62]

This phenomenon has gained ground after the American intervention in Afghanistan. It was reported in both national and international print and electronic media that remnants of Taliban and *al Qaeda* escaped to Bangladesh and have been consolidating their position there. The present government headed by Begum Khaleda Zia of the Bangladesh National Party, which is in alliance with fundamentalist Jamaat-e-Islami, Islamic Oikyo Jote and Jatiya Party, has facilitated their consolidation. Indian intelligence analysts believe that advance guard of Islamic fundamentalists have been scouting for sympathisers in Assam.

The dangers of illegal immigration have already been highlighted earlier. So far Assam is concerned almost one hundred percent of the immigrants are Muslims. "Although the indigenous Muslims of Assam continue to remain loyal to the secular fabric of the region, the agent provocateurs among the illegal immigrants from Bangladesh with active aid from ISI and DGFI could engineer situations that could adversely affect communal harmony in the region." [63] To this emerging danger the abdication of its original ideology by ULFA, which came into prominence for its opposition to illegal immigrants, has added a new dimension. ULFA is now fraternising with the same people it wanted to be deported. It is now clear that Islamic fundamentalists are trying to usurp the separatist mantle from ethnic militant movements by piggy-backing onto them.[64]

Muslim militant groups have shunned publicity and have avoided direct confrontation with the security forces and have not openly spelt out their ultimate objective, that is, to create a Greater Bangladesh. For the time being they are focussing on religious propaganda and enlarging their membership and area of influence. Almost all of them have links with the ISI, which along with DGFI of Bangladesh has propped these groups to further the agenda of Islamisation of the region. To achieve the aim of a Greater Bangladesh, Muslim militant groups have a long-term plan: " to wait for an opportune moment, which will be the demise of the ethnic militant movements and the demographic change that will soon be upon the region." [65]

THE BODO INSURGENCY

Historical Backdrop

The Bodos belong to Indo-Mongoloid tribe who migrated to their habitat in North-cast India through Patkai Hills from

China and Tibet and gradually spread over the whole of modern Assam, North Bengal, and parts of East Bengal. They ruled over a vast tract of land in the North-east under various tribal names, namely, the Chutiyas, the Kacharis, the Koch etc, at different times in the historical past.[66] Bodos are known by the name of Kacharis and Mech in the plains of Assam. They are called Mech in North Bengal and West of Goalpara district. The name Mech is derived from the name of river Mirchi in North Bengal.[67] In the North Cachar Hills they are called Dimasa; in North Lakhimpur and Nowgong districts they are Sonwals. The Bodo race includes Rabhas, Mech, Koch, Dhimal, Saraniyas, Lalung, Hajong, Dimasas, Garos, Hill Tipperas, Chutiyas and Morans.[68] It is probable that the Bodos spread in several directions; one group went up to Cachar and was called Cacharis; the others went along the Brahmaputra and established themselves in the whole of modern Assam up to Goalpara and parts of Jalpaiguri and Cooch Behar under the name of Bodo. By whatever name they prefer to be identified, all of them may originally be traced back to the same root, the great Bodo race.

At the time when Ahoms entered Assam in the 13th century, the Caharis ruled over the Brahmaputra Valley stretching from Cooch Behar to Naga Hills with their capital at Dimapur.[69] There were many clashes between the Kacharis and the Ahoms for supremacy. Finally, the Kacharis were defeated in 1536 and the capital Dimapur was annexed. The Bodos-Cacharis thereafter got scattered and went in to decline. They are today mainly concentrated in the foothills of Arunachal Pradesh and Bhutan. Apart from these, they are inhabited in the neighbouring areas of Assam, namely, North Bengal, Meghalaya, Tripura and Nagaland. They are also to be found in Myanmar and parts of Nepal.

Political Awakening

The Bodos were relegated to the margins of history for nearly hundred years after the British annexed them, till they were politically organised in 1833 under the Tribal League. Hordes of immigrants from East Bengal had been settled on tribal land under the Muslim League ministry headed by Saadulla, which was formed after the 1935 elections. The League tried to bring all the tribal communities on a common platform and focus on their socio-economic problems, mainly the alienation of tribal land. Bordoloi promised protective measures and was thus able to win their support in a bid to topple Saadulla ministry.

The Bodos were optimistic that they will get a fair deal after Independence and, therefore, transformed the Tribal League in a socio-cultural organisation, the Tribal Sangha. But they were soon disillusioned. Bordoloi, as the chairman of the sub committee of the constituent assembly that developed tribal policies, described Bodos as no different from the Assamese mainstream unlike the Nagas and other hill tribes, who were given special dispensation. This perception of Bordoloi created differences between the Congress and the Bodos.

Formation of Plain Tribal Council of Assam (PTCA) and the Movement for Autonomy

The Assam Land Revenue Regulations provided for creating tribal belts and blocks in tribal majority areas where non-tribals would not be entitled to possess or buy land. Despite this restriction alienation of tribal lands continued. Tribal youths were denied jobs on the pretext that suitable candidates were not available amongst them. It was in such circumstances that PTCA was formed in 1967, and became the first organisation to demand a separate homeland for the Bodos.

The PTCA boycotted the general election in 1967. Their boycott of the bye-election to the Kokrajhar Lok Sabha constituency in 1968 was so effective that in as many as 117 of 138 booths not a single vote was cast. PTCA now raised their demand and called for the formation of a separate state for the Bodos, to be named Udayachal. The newly formed All Bodo

Students Union (ABSU) gave support to the formation of Udayachal.

The language policy of Assam further antagonised the non-Assamese and tribals. The boycott of the general election in 1967 had one positive outcome for the Bodos; it gained for the Bodo language the status of the medium of instruction at the secondary stage of education in all Bodo–dominated areas. Simultaneously, ABSU and the Bodo Sahitya Sabha jointly launched a movement during 1974-75 for the adoption of Roman script for Bodo language, which was being written in Assamese script. As a spoken language, Bodo language had no script of its own. The Assam government tried to crush the agitation by strong-arm tactics, but it only made the Bodos more determined. Ultimately, after persuasion from the Centre, Devnagri script was accepted for the Bodo language on the promptings of Indira Gandhi. This further widened the gulf between the Assamese and the Bodos.

In the 1978 Assembly Elections, which was the first after the imposition of emergency, the Janta Party came to power in Assam with PTCA as its coalition partner. One of the leaders of PTCA, Samar Brahma Chaudhury, became a minister in Assam Janta Government. But the Janta Government at the Centre fell only after 18 months, causing political instability in the State. In 1983 Assembly Elections, which was held at a time when the Assam movement led by AASU was at its peak, the Congress won a pyrrhic victory. PTCA won three assembly seats, and once again Samar Brahma was taken in the ministry. In the elections to the Assam Assembly held after the signing of the Assam Accord in 1985, PTCA did not win many seats; nonetheless, it cast between 70 to 80 percent votes in the proposed Udyachal area. However, its leaders soon lost credibility amongst the Bodos, as they were seen feathering their own nests and betraying the tribal cause. PTCA split into two factions on the question of a separate state for the Bodos.

Divide Assam Fifty-Fifty

The failure of PTCA leaders to make any headway in the demand for a separate homeland for the Bodos brought about a new turn in Bodo politics. During Assam agitation, ABSU had taken an active part in it; the Bodos now expected the AGP Government, which had taken office after the 1985 Assembly Elections, to reciprocate by restoring the land taken away from them in the past, but the AGP Government did nothing to implement Clause 10 of the Accord, which said that existing laws will be enforced to prevent illegal occupation of tribal land and eviction of those in illegal occupation. As nothing much was done by the AGP, bitterness developed between tribals and non-tribals.

The leadership of tribal youth had by now gone to ABSU led by Upendra Nath Brahma, who was elected its president in 1986. A new movement was started under his leadership with the slogan 'Divide Assam Fifty-Fifty'. It demanded the Northern half of Brahmaputra Valley, leaving the area South of the river for Assamese. The slogan 'Divide Assam Fifty-Fifty' was given up in November 1988 and a call was given for a separate state of Bodoland. ABSU adopted a 92-point charter of demand but agreed to drop 89 of the 92 demands after meeting of its leader Upendra Nath Brahma with the Chief Minister of Assam in January 1989. The three substantive demands, which now formed the basic plank of ABSU agitation were: -

- Creating a separate state having the status of UT for the plain tribals in the Northern Brahmaputra Valley, making the river the natural boundary.
- Creating District Councils in the tribal compact areas in the Brahmaputra Valley South of the river.
- Creating a regional council for Bodos, Rengma and non-Karbi plain tribes within Karbi Anglong Autonomous District Council, because the non-Karbi plain tribes such as Bodos did not enjoy constitutional safeguards as tribals in Karbi Anglong Autonomous District.

The Beginning of Insurgency[70]

The Bodo movement took to insurgency after January 1988 incident when nine Bodo women were gang-raped by some Assam policemen. The movement slowly began to turn violent in the face of apathy by the AGP Government. In the first phase, small wooden bridges connecting village roads were burnt to prevent police access to villages. Simultaneously, village schools were burnt to deny police and CRPF from establishing camps in the school buildings. In the second phase, Assamese officials and policemen were harassed and terrorised and railway tracks and government buildings were targeted. In the third phase, ABSU tried to set up a parallel administration with its own police – the Bodo Police Force (BPF). Unfortunately, tribal violence was met by unprecedented brutality by Assam police, hardening attitudes further.

The untimely death of Upendra Nath Brahma in 1990 was a grievous blow to the Bodo movement. It was mainly due to his leadership that the Bodo demand for autonomy was brought to the national agenda. It was also mainly due to his efforts that the Centre agreed to take part in the tripartite talks. After his death the movement slowly passed into the hands of a militant outfit, the Bodo Security Force (BdSF), which had a secessionist agenda. It is alleged that BdSF was propped by the intelligence agencies to counter both ULFA and AGP.

Formation of Bodoland Autonomous Council (BAC)

After the death of Upendra Nath Brahma the leadership of ABSU had passed on to Sugwai Bwasumatari and S Brahma. A series of tripartite talks between ABSU, Central and State Governments were held in 1992-93 as part of the peace initiative started by the then Minister of State for Internal Security, Rajesh Pilot. An expert committee was formed to give recommendations on the administrative, legislative and financial powers to be granted to the proposed BAC. The recommendations of the expert committee were rejected by ABSU and Bodo People Action Committee (BPAC), mainly due to the insistence of ABSU-BPAC on inclusion of additional villages, which were scattered all over the nine districts in the proposed Bodoland area. After some give and take, an accord was signed in February 1993 between the Centre, the State Government, ABSU and BPAC, which paved the way for the formation of BAC, covering nearly 2,300 sq km in the lower Assam districts of Kokrajhar, Bongaigaon, Barpeta, Nalbari, Darang, Mangaldoi and Sonitpur.

Ethnic Cleansing

From the outset, the BAC has been mired in controversy. In the name of contiguity, a faction of ABSU demanded the inclusion of 515 additional villages over and above 2570 villages agreed to by the government. The government rightly pointed out that the demand was unreasonable since the Bodo population in the villages being additionally demanded was less than two percent of the total population. Soon after the accord was signed extremist groups such as BdSF, later renamed National Democratic Front of Bodoland (NDFB) and Bodo Liberation Tigers (BLT) became active. They vehemently opposed the accord and let loose a reign of terror and brutally attacked non-Bodos, particularly the Bengali settlers from erstwhile East Pakistan, Muslim minorities, Koch Rajbongshi and Santhals from Bihar and Orissa. Their demand is a liberated Bodoland for Bodos only. Since 1994, the extremists have indulged in senseless and brutal violence with a view to change the ethnic composition in the BAC. The Bodos in the BAC area do not constitute more than 40 percent of their total population of about 20 lakhs.[71] The extremists have also been trying to grab the vast tracts of land owned by non-Bodos, which were sold to them by the tribals three to four decades ago, on the pretext that no outsider had a right to own land in Bodoland. The 1996 ethnic riots, in which Bodo militants killed 100 Santhals, forced a large number of Santhal families to move to relief camps. The BLT created terror on a large-scale in 1995; it blew up several coaches of Brahmaputra Mail near Kokrajhar by placing explosives and damaged railway tracks, bridges and oil pipelines. Forced against the wall, non-Bodos have organised themselves in self-defence and have started retaliating.

The Second Peace Initiative: Bodoland Territorial Council (BTC)

The creation of BAC quite obviously did not satisfy the Bodos. Since its creation, it has been a non-functioning political entity. Even the election to the BAC to replace the nominated administrative unit has not been held in the last ten years. The BAC area has for all practical purposes remained under the *de facto* rule of insurgent groups like the BLT and the NDFB. However in a turn of events, the BLT announced in early 2000 its readiness to enter into a cease-fire agreement with the government, which was negotiated by the Centre on March 29, 2000. Subsequently, the ground rules for enforcing the cease-fire were framed in tripartite talks between the representatives of the BLT and the Central and the State Governments. The BLT agreed to abide by the constitution and the laws of the land. A joint monitoring group, on the lines of the cease-fire monitoring group operating in Nagaland, was set up.

Finally, on February 10, 2003, the BLT signed an accord with the Centre and the Assam Government, which paved the way for the creation of 46-member BTC, an autonomous district in Assam. Though ABSU and BPAC leaders were present at the signing ceremony, they did not sign the accord. Having been signatories to the earlier BAC accord, they obliviously could not sign the latest accord. The Memorandum of Settlement (MOS) was signed at New Delhi in the presence of Deputy Prime Minister LK Advani, Assam Chief Minister Tarun Gogoi and the Ministers of State for Home ID Swami and Harin Pathak. The MOS proposes to abolish the existing BAC formed in 1993, as soon as the BTC comes into existence. The Centre will move a constitution amendment bill to include the BTC in the Sixth Schedule. As many as 3,082 villages have been identified to be included in the BTC, which will be divided into four contiguous districts after reorganisation of the existing districts of Lower Assam.[72]

There is renewed optimism amongst Bodos, but the non-Bodos in the BTC under the umbrella of Sanmilita Janagosthiya Sangram Samiti (SJSS) have opposed the BTC and threatened to launch an agitation to demand the scrapping of the accord. Non-Bodos constitute 80 percent of the population in the area. The outlawed NDFB has also opposed the BTC and has vowed to continue the fight for a sovereign Bodoland.[73]

Kamatpur Liberation Organisation (KLO)

There is a sizeable Rajbongshi population in parts of North Bengal. Koch Rajbongshi was one of the major tribes in India, and historically belonging to the same stock as Bodos but now a caste Hindu community classified as OBC. Some Rajbongshi also live in Assam. The community has been demanding a separate state – Kamatpur, since 1995, to be carved out of North Bengal and Assam. The encouragement for the demand has come mainly from ULFA.

Rajbongshi community, who broke away from the All Kamatpur Students Union, to wage an armed struggle to form a separate country, raised KLO in December 1995. KLO's areas of operation include six districts in North Bengal; South and North Dinajpur, Coochbehar, Jalpaiguri, Malda and Darjeeling – and four districts in Assam – Dhubri, Bongaigaon, Kokrajhar and Goalpara. However, most of their activities have been centred around Alipurduar and Jalpaiguri. To begin with, KLO cadres were trained in ULFA camps, but in 2003 they set up their independent camps inside Bhutanese territory. The KLO has been raising funds mainly through extortion from small tea garden owners and businessmen of the region. It has close links with Kamatpur People's Party.

The KLO has been dealt a mortal blow by Operation Flushout, which was launched by the Royal Bhutan Army (RBA) in mid December 2003. The RBA destroyed its camps in Bhutan along the 150-km border with West Bengal and captured five of its most wanted leaders. The RBA handed over Tom Adhikari and Milton Burman alias Mihir Das and others to the Indian authorities on 21 December. Tom Adhikari was its executioner, who was greatly feared among the business community. The self-styled KLO chairman Jiban Singha alias Tamir Das, however, managed to evade capture and is believed to have escaped to Bangladesh. The interrogation of the captured leaders revealed that contrary to the general view that the KLO was financed by the ISI, it turned out that the organisation was propped up by ULFA. More important, Indian intelligence found evidence of KLO's links with Maoist groups in Nepal. It was discovered that KLO in West Bengal provided cover to Nepal Maoists, which in turn had links with Bhutan Communist Party (BCP).[74] After the setback suffered by the KLO in the operation by RBA against Indian insurgent groups camped in Bhutan, the organisation does not have enough resources to regroup and stage a comeback.

Karbi-Dimasa Movement

The Karbis, earlier known as Mikirs, are the predominant tribe of the Karbi-Anglong district. The Dimasas are in majority in North Cachar Hills district. These two are autonomous districts enjoying the status under the Sixth Schedule of the Constitution from the very beginning. There is a long-standing demand in both the districts for their elevation to an autonomous state (but with the existing district councils intact), under the provisions of Article 244-A.[75] The genesis of the demand lay in Assam Official Language Bill –1960. The Hill States were born in reaction against the Language Bill. The Karbi-Dimasas were also influenced by a similar kind of identity crisis. The movement for the first time gathered momentum with the emergence of the Autonomous State Demand Committee (ASDC) in 1986. The ASDC split in 2000 with the emergence of UPDS, which is the dominant militant outfit of Assam's Karbi-Anglong district. UPDS, whose base extends to the adjacent North Cachar Hills, has again split into two factions; one led by Kathar and the other by Heresing Bey. The faction led by Heresing Bey agreed to a cease-fire with the Centre, but Kathar group has remained intransigent. Kathar, in his latest statement, appeared to be willing to talk and is reported to have said: " We are not for secession from India. What we want is a federal state, by limiting the federal government's powers to a handful of subjects like defence, external affairs, currency and communications and some residuary powers."[76]

Appraisal

The idea of *Swadhin Asom* is not a new idea. The historical memory of Assamese goes back to their glorious past to the old kingdom of Kamrup and Ahoms, which had held sway up to the borders of present day Bihar. They hark back to the reign of the Ahoms, which symbolised prosperity and power. Equally significant has been the Assamese linguistic nationalism, which found manifestation in poems like *'Mor Desh'*, written in 1910, the poem eulogises Assam as a country of unparalleled beauty. The song is sung even today at all public functions along with the national anthem.

The partition of Bengal on communal lines in 1905, which amalgamated Assam and East Bengal, was a grievous blow to Assam's identity. Not only Assam lost its identity, but also the creation of a new province of East Bengal and Assam had disastrous consequences for the subsequent historical, political and economic development of Assam. The amalgamation initiated large-scale influx of land hungry immigrants from East Bengal districts to Assam. Although the partition was undone in 1912 but by that time large-scale immigration had already become a serious problem, which the census commissioner in his report of 1931 compared to an invasion by an army of ants. In the decade prior to Independence, Assam alternated between the Muslim League and Congress governments. The Muslim League government of Saadulla made a planned effort to change the demography of Assam by encouraging Muslim immigrants into Assam and settling them on government lands in the hope that Assam would become part of East Pakistan. What shocked the Assamese was the acceptance by the Congress of the Cabinet Mission Plan of 1946, which had provided for three categories; one each for Hindu and Muslim majority provinces and the third group comprising Muslim majority Bengal and Hindu majority Assam. Bordoloi correctly assessed that thc grouping would lead to Assam becoming part of East Pakistan. At the expense of opposing Nehru and Patel, Bordoloi revolted against the acceptance of the plan and with the support of Gandhi succeeded in getting it shelved.

The relationship between Bordoloi and Nehru was further soured when Bordoloi expressed his unwillingness to continue settling refugees, mostly Hindus, from East Pakistan without limit. Organisations like the Jatiya Mahasabha were even more critical and recommended: "if the Congress Government failed to check the infiltration from East Pakistan, then Assam should come out of the Indian Union and become an independent country like Burma or any other country." The insensitivity of the Centre sowed the seeds of discord, which in later years manifested in alienation and finally to secessionist demands. In the economic development too, Assam felt discriminated. The decision to build the first oil refinery in Bihar, ignoring the claim of Assam, was widely resented. The head offices of major tea companies are located outside Assam, which again is resented by Assamese, cutting across party line.

In the wake of Chinese attack in NEFA in 1962 and Indian Army's withdrawal, Nehru's address to the nation, which was perceived by the Assamese as virtually abandoning Assam to its fate, left a deep scar on their sense of belonging to India. Yet, another cause of their alienation was the territorial reorgansation of Assam in 1972, which created separate states like Meghalaya, Mizoram and Arunachal. Assam suffers from a sense of deep hurt that the centre was primarily responsible for the dismemberment of Assam. But ironically, the Assamese were themselves to blame, for they had totally alienated the non-Assamese by their chauvinistic language policy of 1960, which imposed Assamese language on non-Assamese and acted as the catalyst that led to Assam's break up into a number of states.

The formation of ULFA preceded the Assam Movement. Although it derived its inspiration from AJYCP, ULFA had close links with AASU and AGP. The rise of ULFA as a secessionist organisation coincided with the formation of AGP Government (1985-1990). Most of its recruits were drawn from AASU cadres. Mohanta's government had abdicated most of its responsibilities, which resulted in ULFA infiltrating every organ of the state apparatus. The imposition of President's Rule, though short, and Operations 'Bajrang' and 'Rhino' blunted ULFA's capabilities, but it shifted base to Southern Bhutan and regained its strength. When negotiations failed to persuade ULFA to vacate Bhutanese territory, the RBA had to launch military operations in December 2003 to drive them out by force. The operations delivered a grievous blow to ULFA and it will take some time before it recovers fully from the dismantling of its camps and the killing/surrender of its cadres.

The popularity of ULFA is on the downslide. One of the reasons for the diminishing public support is the dichotomy in its role as the champions of Assamese aspirations and its views on Bangladeshi immigrants. In a booklet issued in 1992, it declared that immigrants from East Bengal had become an inseparable part of the toiling people of Assam. This shift in its ideology has not gone down well in Assam. The majority of

Assamese do not believe in independent Assam. This was amply demonstrated during the Kargil War when the Assamese patriotism was on full display. Their complaint is against the economic neglect of Assam and the perception, to a large extent justified, that the Centre is not adequately responsive to their concerns, particularly with regard to loss of identity. ULFA continues to garner some support amongst the middle class Assamese because they fear that they will be marginalised unless the ULFA phenomenon is kept alive.

The terrorist attack by *al Qaeda* on the Twin Towers in New York on September 11, 2001 has changed the way the world looks at terrorism. The biggest threat to plural societies comes from global Islamic fundamentalism, which has cast a shadow on India's North-east too. The insurgency in Assam is slowly but perceptibly being taken over by Islamic fundamentalists. They are not very active today, but are waiting in the wings for an opportune situation to develop to unleash their concept of *jihad*.

The Bodo insurgency is the result of Assamese chauvinism and lack of vision on the part of their leaders. There was a callous disregard and neglect of Bodo grievances by both the Congress and AGP governments. The Bodos were already fearful of Assamese hegemony because of the imposition of Assamese language. When the Assam Accord was signed in 1985, the Bodos had expected that their lands, which were earlier taken away from them, would be restored. But the AGP government did nothing to implement the promises made in the accord. The Bodo insurgency started under these circumstances. To add fuel to the fire, it is widely believed in Assam that the Bodoland agitation was created, encouraged and even financed by the Congress (I) with a view to creating problems for the AGP government, which had successfully challenged the hegemony of the Congress.[77]

The earlier accord signed on February 20, 1993, was flawed and was signed in haste owing to pressure from Rajesh Pilot. Saikia had wanted the boundary of the proposed BAC to be clearly demarcated before the accord was signed as he feared ethnic clashes if it was not done. Unfortunately, Saikia's fears came to be true. One of the major flaws was that villages that were non-Bodo in character were placed in the BAC. The present accord signed on February 10, 2003 has greater acceptability, having secured the support, though qualified, from a cross-section of political parties. It also provides for the application of the provisions of the Sixth Schedule to the BTC. Another reason for optimism is that BLT leaders have expressed their commitment not to provoke confrontation with the broader Assamese society.

Notes and References

1. NN Acharya, Brief *History of Assam: From Earliest Times to 1983*, (Guwahati: Osmos Publication, 1987), The book traces the history of Assam from the earliest times to the present times in an easy narrative form.
2. Ajay Mitra Shastri, *Ancient North East India: Pragjyotisha – A Pan-Indian Perspective*, p. 5.
3. Ibid.
4. *Imperial Gazetteer of India*; Vol vi, New Edition, (London: Oxford, 1908), p. 24.
5. Ibid, p. 25.
6. SK Bhuyan, *Tungkhunga Burunji or A History of Assam 1681-1826* AD, (Calcutta: OUP, 1933), p. xviii.
7. Ibid.
8. Ibid.
9. *Imperial Gazetteer of India*, vol vi, n. 4., p. 29.
10. Ibid., p 30. The Ahoms were not merely animists of the type found among the aboriginal tribes of India, but had a regular pantheon of which the leading members were, in later times at least, identified with Hindu Gods and Goddesses.
11. SK Bhuyian, n. 6., p. xx.
12. Ibid., p. xx.

13. Moamarias are a Vaishnavite sect; most of whose members are drawn from lower Hindu castes and were concentrated in Upper Assam. They did not worship idols or acknowledge the supremacy of upper castes. The struggle of the Moamarias became one against the feudal structure of Ahom rule, which finally accelerated the downfall of Ahom monarchy.
14. SK Bhuyian, n. 6., p. xxiii.
15. For a brief account of Tungkhungia period of Ahom rule (1681 to 1826) see SK Bhuyian, n. 6., pp xx–xxiv. *Also Imperial Gazetteer of India*, pp. 23-35.
16. *Imperial Gazetteer of India*, n. 4., p. 33.
17. Ibid.
18. Ibid, p. 34 .
19. Ibid.
20. Udayon Misra, *The Periphery Strikes Back: Challenges to the Nation State in Assam and Nagaland*, (Shimla: Indian Institute of Advanced Studies, 2000), p. 78. Sylhet had a population almost equal to that of whole of Assam comprising Hill districts, Brahmaputra and Surma Valleys. The Bengali speaking population outnumbered Assamese-speaking population till 1947, when Sylhet went to Pakistan.
21. Ibid., pp. 68-70. For a sketch of Maniram's life see Udayon Misra. Maniram collaborated with Kandarpeshwar but Maniram's letter to Kandarpeshwar was intercepted, which led to his arrest and trial resulting in his being hanged.
22. Ibid., p. 71. In September 1861, about 15,000 peasants marched to Phulagiri in Nowgong district and demanded that the taxes on betel nut be withdrawn.
23. Ibid., p. 80.
24. Ibid., p.81.
25. Sudhir Chandra, *Economic and Political Weekly 1982*, quoted by Udayon Misra, n. 20., p. 81.
26. Ambikagiri was initially a staunch supporter of the Congress and tried to balance Assamese nationalism with pan-Indian nationalism. But after Independence, he moved away from his earlier views, and propagated separation of Assam from India. Udayon Misra, n.20., pp. 86-87.
27. Amlendu Guha, *Planter Raj to Swaraj; Freedom Struggle and Electoral Politics in Assam 1826-1947*,(New Delhi: 1977), p. 252. Quoted by Udayon Misra, n. 20, p. 86.
28. Girin Phukan, *Assam's Attitude to Federalism*, (New Delhi: 1984), p. 62. Quoted by Udayon Misra, n. 20., p. 87.
29. S Gopal. ed., *Collected Works of Jawaharlal Nehru*, Second Series, Vol II, letter to Bordoloi dated May 18, 1949, p. 70.

30. Of about 20 lakh refugees who entered India from East Pakistan during 1947-50, undivided Assam rehabilitated some three lakh. Udayon Misra, n. 20., p. 111.
31. Selected works of Jawahar Lal Nehru, Second Series, Vol 12 (New Delhi: Project of Jawahar Lal Nehru Museum and Library Fund, 1991), p 264.
32. Letter from Bordoloi to Nehru, Shillong, August 24, 1949. Quoted by Nirode K. Barooah, Gopinath Bordoloi: Indian Constitution and Centre-State relations 1940-50 (Guwahati 1990).
33. Nirode K Barooah, *Gopinath Bordoloi: Indian Constitution and Centre-State Relations*, (Guwahati: 1990), p. 33. Quoted by Udayon Misra, n 20 p. 113.
34. Udayon Misra, n. .20, p. 115.
35. Amiya Kumar Das, *Assam's Agony*, (New Delhi: Lancers, 1982), p. 223.
36. Nehru's letter to Fazal Ali, Governor of Assam, Number 459-PMO-57 New Delhi dated June 12, 1957. Reproduced by Udayon Misra, n. 20, p. 205.
37. Quoted by Udayon Misra, n. 20, p. 118.
38. Ibid., p. 124.
39. Nari Rustomji, *Imperilled Frontiers*, (New Delhi: Oxford University Press, 1983), p. 12 .
40. Statement made by the Chief Commissioner in the Conference of the Chief Electoral Officers of the states held at Ootacamund from October 24 to 26, 1978. Quoted by Amiya K Das, n. 35., p. 62.
41. AAGSP was made up of AASU, the Assam Sahitya Sabha, the Purbanchal Lok Parishad, the Assam Jatiyabadi Dal, the All Assam Tribal Students Union, the Plain Tribal Council of Assam, the Bodo Sahitya Sabha and the All Assam Karamchari Parishad.
42. Udayon Misra, n. 20, p. 133. Quoting Narayan Sarmah's, *Nirbachan Pratirodh Sangramar Itihas*, (Guwahati: 1983), pp. 147-155.
43. Udayon Misra, n. 20., p. 135.
44. Sanjoy Hazarika, *Strangers of the Mist: Tales of War & Peace from North-east*, New Delhi, Penguin, 1984), p. 178.
45. Ibid., p. 179.
46. Ibid., p. 192.
47. For a full account of the sequence of events of Doom Dooma episode see Sanjoy Hazarika, n 44, pp. 192-98.
48. Ibid., p. 217.
49. Ibid., p. 226.
50. Bez Baruah, editor of *Sentinel* published from Guwahati, once told Lt Gen Narhari, that if one wants a good living, it is better to invest in

an old weapon, get into police record, do something as an ULFA cadre, and surrender. Then the person's life is made. NS Narhari, *Security Threats in North-east India,* (New Delhi: Manas, 2002), p. 22.

51. MS Prabhakara, "ULFA's links with Bangladesh," *The Hindu*, New Delhi, September 8, 1992.
52. For a more comprehensive analysis of ULFA's ideology see Udayon Misra, n. 20., pp. 140-145.
53. The BJP led NDA Government at the Centre introduced a bill in Parliament to repeal the IMDT Act (1983), but the Lok Sabha was dissolved consequent to the defeat of NDA led alliance in the Parliamentary Elections held in 2004. The ruling Congress-led UPA alliance in an affidavit filed in the Supreme Court supported the continuation of the act. A three-member bench of the Supreme Court in a unanimous decision declared the IMDT Act and rules framed in 1984 as *ultra virus* of the constitution while hearing a writ petition of AGP parliamentarian Sarbananda Sonwal.
54. The army had filed a FIR against Zoinath Sarma for his links with ULFA.
55. "Assam's Militants Spying for Pakistan, says Army," *The Times of India*, New Delhi, June 26, 1999.
56. *The Hindustan Times*, New Delhi, December 2, 2000 gives month wise breakdown of killings of non-Assamese in the year 2004. The figures of 2003-2004 are taken from the Ministry of Defence Annual Report for that year, p. 30.
57. Sanjoy Hazarika has described the background to the problem arising from the notice served on illegal Nepali migrants in Southern Bhutan in detail in his book '*Strangers of the Mist*' in the chapter titled, 'Neighbours, Secret Affairs'.
58. Jaideep Saikia, 'Bhutan's Tryst with Assamese Separatists', *Border Affairs*, New Delhi, April-June 2001.
59. King Jigme Wangchuk had discussed the impending military operation against Assamese insurgent groups with the Indian Prime Minister during his visit to India on September 14, 2003. *The Indian Express*, New Delhi, December 15, 2003.
60. Ashok K Mehta, Bhutan's All Clear, *The Pioneer*, New Delhi, December 31, 2003.
61. Jaideep Saikia, *Terror sans Frontiers: Islamic Militancy in North East India*, (Urbana-Champaign (USA), University of Illinois, ACDIS Occasional Paper, July 2003), p.20. Saikia gives the profiles of the four main leaders; one belonged to Sind (Pakistan), two were residents of UP (India) and one was from Kupwara (Kashmir), pp. 48-49.
62. Bertil Linter, "Bangladesh: A Cocoon of Terror," *Far Eastern Economic Review*, April 4, 2002.

63. Jaideep Saikia, n. 61., p. 2.
64. Ibid, p. 17. Saikia has analysed in Chapter 2 of the monograph the strategy adopted by ISI of Pakistan and DGFI of Bangladesh in hijacking ULFA and converting it into an accomplice for the furtherance of their long-term plan of creating Greater Bangladesh.
65. Ibid., p. 52.
66. BK Barua, *A Cultural History of Assam*, First Edition, (New Delhi: National Book Trust, 1972), p. 72.
67. CC Sanyal, *The Mech and Totos of North Bengal*, (University of West Bengal: 1973).
68. Chutiyas and Morans have been added by Sidney Endle, *The Kacharis*, (Delhi: Cosmo, 1973), p. 5.
69. Chandana Bhattacharjee, *Ethnicity and Autonomy Movement: Case of Bodo-Kacharis of Assam*, (New Delhi: Vikas Publishing House 1994), pp 64-69.
70. For the background to the Bodo Insurgency, see Barun Dasgupta, "Bodo Agitation: Background and Prospects", *Mainstream*, New Delhi, June 24, 1989
71. Kalyan Chaudhuri, "Turning to Peace", *Frontline*, New Delhi, March 14, 2003, p. 47.
72. Ibid., p. 47.
73. NDFB signed a cease-fire agreement with the Centre and the Assam Government on May 25, 2005. The agreement according, to which the NDFB agreed to suspend its two-decade-old violence activities, will be in operation initially for one year. In turn, security forces will not carry out any operations against NDFB. A joint monitoring group will be constituted to oversee the implementation of the agreement. *The Hindustan Times*, May 26, 2005, p. 6.
74. Praveen Swami, 'The View from Delhi', *Frontline*, New Delhi, January 16, 2004.
75. This article was incorporated in the constitution as the 28th Amendment to enable the creation of Meghalaya as an autonomous state within Assam in 1969. Meghalaya was reconstituted as a full-fledged state in January 1972.
76. *Frontline*, New Delhi, January 17, 2003,
77. MS Prabhakara, "Promises and Problems," *Frontline, New* Delhi, March 14, 2003 pp. 50-51.

8

Meghalaya

The present state of Meghalaya consists of Garo, Khasi and Jaintia Hills.[1] Though there are a number of tribes living in Meghalaya, the three dominant tribes from West to East are the Garos, Khasis and Jaintias (Syntengs). The Garos are of Bodo-Tibeto-Burman stock whereas Khasis belong to Mon-Khemer group. Both Garos and Khasis have matriarchal society. The Garos have five major matrilineal clans; Sangmas and Maraks are amongst them. The Jaintias are said to have migrated to Meghalaya from South-east Asia. Like the Garos and Khasis, the Jaintias have no long recorded history or a script and use Khasi language. The Jaintia kings embraced Hinduism though the traditional belief system was akin to Khasi faith. All the three major tribes have increasingly adopted Christianity. The important immigrant communities are the Bengalis, the Muslims, the Nepalis, the Marwaris and the Mazhabi Sikhs; all came for economic reasons.

During the Ahom rule, the Garo, Khasi and Jaintia Hills were not a part of Assam. After the Treaty of Yandeboo in 1826, the British annexed Garo Hills first and then Khasi and Jaintia Hills. In 1874, when the Province of Assam was created under a Chief Commissioner, Shillong was made its capital. The British administration brought with it Bengalis and Nepalese; the Bengalis were absorbed in the administration whereas the Nepalese formed part of the military. The Marwaris then followed as traders. The Welsh Presbyterian Mission was established among the Khasis in 1841 and the American Baptist Mission in Garo Hills in 1864. Shillong became a major educational centre, summer resort and a military garrison.

With the approach of Independence, the Governor of Assam got the Khasi States to sign a Standstill Agreement with India on August 9, 1947 based on their broad willingness to accede to India. In March 1948, all the Khasi chiefs had formally signed the Instrument of Accession. On January 26,1950 the United Khasi-Jaintia and Garo Hills became part of the province of Assam in the Union of India.

Meghalaya has a total geographical area of 22,500 sq km and a population of 23,06,069 (2001 census). It receives heavy rainfall during summer months and has the distinction of including the area of highest rainfall in the world. The average altitude of Meghalaya varies from 1,500 metres to 1,800 metres above sea level. The State has five administrative districts, namely, East Garo Hills, West Garo Hills, East Khasi Hills, West Khasi hills, and Jaintia Hills.

Assam's language policy, which imposed the Assamese language on the tribals of the hills, caused apprehension amongst them and they began to fear the loss of their identity. Soon their apprehension fuelled the demand for separation from Assam, which was articulated by the newly formed All Party Hill Leaders Conference (APHLC). As the demand became very vocal and widespread, the Government of India constituted a Commission in 1965 on the reorganisation of the hill areas of Assam under HV Pataskar. The Commission made a number of proposals, which included further devolution of powers to the three district councils that governed the hill districts under the Sixth Schedule of the Constitution within a united Assam. As a result of the recommendation of the Commission, which were modified to meet the demands of the APHLC, Meghalaya was declared an autonomous sub-state within Assam in 1970.[2] Meghalaya became a full-fledged tribal state on January 21, 1972.

Areas of Discord

The movement against foreigners by AASU in Assam had repercussions in Meghalaya as well. In line with the Assamese, the Khasi Students Union launched a similar agitation with 1951 as the cut off year. Among Indians a distinction was made between old and new settlers. Unfortunately the agitation took a violent turn and rioting broke out between tribals and non-tribals. The flash point was Shillong, which has a population of 3,50,000 of which 40 percent is non-tribal consisting of Bengalis, Assamese, Nepalese, Marwaris and others.[3] There have been a number of major riots against 'dkhars' or outsiders since 1979. Unfortunately the distinction between outsiders and foreigners has got blurred, which manifests in violence against non-tribals who settled in the hills many generations ago. Another bone of contention has been the influx of foreign nationals in Meghalaya, particularly Bangladeshis and Nepalese. Although land sale to non-tribals is prohibited, tribals complain that Bangladeshis are in illegal occupation of a large area of land.

Pattern of Militancy

Rampant corruption in Garo Hills and discontentment among Garos in Goalpara and Kamrup districts in Assam, where Garos are not recognised as scheduled tribes, gave birth to Achik Liberation Matgrik Army (ALMA), which is a vigilante outfit, but not secessionist. The group was backed and inspired by NSCN (IM). At its peak in 1989, its cadre strength was no more than 30. ALMA's claim to prominence was banditry and robberies of banks. Unfortunately for them, the self-styled C-in-C, Gregorge Momin and his NSCN (IM) accomplice were killed in an encounter. Lack of public support further demoralised ALMA cadres, which led to their surrender in 1994.[4] It was hoped that the lenient terms of surrender would encourage the more radical and secessionist Khasi Hynniewtrep Achik Liberation Council (HALC) to follow suit, but that hope was belied. HALC is a Shillong based urban outfit, and serves the interest of NSCN (IM) by providing guides and other support to secure safe transit to Naga insurgents to Bangladesh.[5] High rate of unemployment has attracted many youths to alcoholism and drugs resulting in rise of AIDS. The dropouts from the schools and colleges are creating a class of lumpens, who are recruited by anti-social elements and militant organisations.

Present Scenario

Yet another organisation Achik National Volunteer Council (ANVC) came up with its headquarters in the Garo Hills, aimed at the creation of an Achik homeland comprising parts of some districts of Assam. This was another front organisation, which facilitated the passage of ULFA and other insurgent groups to and from Bangladesh through the Garo Hills. ANVC signed a tripartite agreement with the Centre and the Meghalaya governments on July 23, 2004, declaring suspension of armed operations for six months. Under the agreement, all 250 cadres of the outfit would be confined to two army camps and their movements regulated by the armed forces. With this agreement, it is hoped that the infiltration to and from Bangladesh through Meghalaya would be checked.[6]

Notes and References

1. SP Mukherjee first referred to the state as Meghalaya in 1936. This was officially adopted when it attained statehood in 1971. KS Singh, ed., *People of India: Meghalaya*, Anthropological Survey of India (Calcutta: Seagull Books, 1994), p.1,
2. This was done by amending the Constitution.
3. The Khasi Students Union estimate was that there were around 3,00,000 Nepalese in the then Meghalaya's population of 1.7 million.
4. BG Verghese, *India's North-east Resurgent*, (New Delhi: Konark, 1991), pp. 204-5.
5. Ibid.
6. *The Hindustan Times*, New Delhi, July, 24, 2004.

9

Arunachal Pradesh

Arunachal Pradesh, a Sixth Schedule state, is the largest amongst the hill states of the North-east. It has an area of 83,743 sq km and a population of 8,64,558 (1991 census) of which two-third is non-tribal. The tribal population is of Tibeto-Burman stock. There are 26 main tribes and more than 100 sub-tribes. The Apatanis are among the most advanced of Arunachal tribes inhabiting the small Ziro Valley in the mountains. Arunachal has evidence of both Hindu and Buddhist influence. If the inner fringe shows Hindu influence, Buddhist influence is evident along the Northern and Eastern perimeters inhabited by Monpas and Sherdukpens (Kameng), Membas (Siang) and Khamptis, Singphas and Tangsas (Lohit and Tirap).

There is no common language in Arunachal: Nefamese – a mix of Assamese and local dialects and Hindi have become the common *lingua franca* with Devnagari and Roman scripts. English is the official language. Unlike the other North-east hill states, Christian presence in Arunachal is minimal. A large number of people follow '*Donyi Polo*', a form of animism, which includes the worship of the sun and moon.[1]

Political Evolution

Arunachal's recorded history starts from the 17th century. The Ahoms did not interfere with the tribals and generally followed a conciliatory approach towards them. The British followed a policy of isolation and left the tribals alone. They administered the countryside through the indigenous system of village councils and started the practice of appointing village headman from among the influential members of the village council; *Gaonburhas*, as they were named, came to exercise considerable power and influence.

The Inner line regulation was applied in North-East Frontier Tract, as it was then called, in 1873. As the British political control over that tract expanded, they thought it prudent to define the border with Tibet, which they viewed as a buffer state between India and China. In a tripartite conference held in Shimla in 1913 with Tibet and China, the boundary with Tibet was defined, which came to be known as the McMahon Line.

In 1919 the entire area was divided into three tracts – the Balipura, Lakhimpur and Sadiya frontier tracts. Tirap Frontier Tract was created a little later. The plain areas all along the frontier tracts were placed under Assam in 1951; the rest was redesignated as NEFA in 1954. The Tuensang Division was detached and amalgamated with the Naga Hills in 1957.

North-east Frontier Tract was directly under the Governor of Assam as 'Excluded Area' and was administered by him under his discretion. After Independence its governance was vested in Assam Government and the governor was to act on the advice of the Chief Minister. After the adoption of the constitution in 1950, the administration of NEFA was restored to the governor as the agent of the Centre. What it meant was that NEFA was constitutionally part of Assam but administered by the governor acting as the agent of the President. The promise that NEFA would be united with Assam after it had attained a certain level of development did not materialise.

The government appointed the Daying Ering Committee, which recommended elected village councils at the base,

Anchal Samiti at block level under sub-division officer and a Zila Parishad under a deputy commissioner. At the apex each of the five Zila Parishads were to send four members to Agency Council. The recommendations were implemented in 1969.[2]

The status of NEFA underwent another change in 1971 when North-eastern Areas (Reorganisation) Act detached NEFA from Assam and proclaimed it a UT under a Chief Commissioner. The administrative headquarters of the Agency was shifted from Shillong to Itanagar and the name was changed to Arunachal. Although direct election to Pradesh Council was introduced in 1972, a formal Council of Ministers came into being in 1975. The Pradesh Council was converted into legislative assembly and a lieutenant governor replaced the Chief Commissioner. Arunachal Pradesh became a full-fledged state in 1986.

The Indian Frontier Administrative Service was created in 1956 for better administration of border areas. Verrier Elwin enunciated the approach to the administration of NEFA in 1957, which said: " We cannot allow matters to drift in the tribal area or just not take interest in them. In the world of today that is not possible or desirable. At the same time, we should avoid over-administering these areas and in particular, sending too many outsiders into tribal territory...It is between these two extreme positions that we have to function." The development activities were guided by the philosophy of Verrier Elwin. Arunachal has avoided the violence that has marked the politics of other North-eastern states. Much of the credit for this should go to Verrier Elwin, who had the full support and enjoyed the confidence of Nehru. Arunachal also had the good fortune of having administrators of the calibre of Nari Rustomji, who had the vision and commitment in keeping with the policy framework for NEFA.

Rumblings of Discord[3]

The genesis of the discord lies in the settlement of refugees in Arunachal. After the flight of the Dalai Lama from Lhasa to India in 1959, a large number of Tibetan refugees fled to India and were settled in different parts of the country. A small number, not more than 3-4,000 were given refuge in Arunachal. A few years later Chakma refugees, who were displaced due to the construction of Kaptai dam in CHT in erstwhile East Pakistan, were settled in Tripura and Mizoram and subsequently relocated in Arunachal because of its relatively low density of population. The local population believed that the settlement was temporary and Chakmas would eventually return to East Pakistan/Bangladesh. Their perception was reinforced by the recent repatriation of Chakmas from Tripura to Bangladesh. But Bangladesh refuses to accept Chakma refugees who had moved out of CHT before the emergence of Bangladesh. What disturbed the tribals of Arunachal was the insistent demand by the Chakmas for citizenship and its consideration by the Central Government. The All Arunachal Pradesh Students Union (AAPSU) have organised protests and served 'Quit Arunachal' notices on Chakmas, which resulted in sporadic violence and intimidation of Chakmas.[4]

There is the danger of insurgent groups like NSCN, ULFA and Bodo militants trying to take advantage of the unsettled conditions and whip up emotions. There are unconfirmed reports that some Chakma youths have received training in Myanmar and are in possession of AK 47 rifles.[5] There are also unconfirmed reports that militant organisations like United Liberation Army of Arunachal and Peoples Volunteers of Arunachal have come up in recent times. It will be unfortunate if peace is disturbed and violence erupts in Arunachal. An explosive situation could develop if the Centre does not take remedial measures in time.

Although insurgency has not taken deep roots in Arunachal so far, yet dark clouds are discernible. Intelligence agencies have reported that every government employee and businessman in Tirap is forced to pay 25 percent of his gross income as tax for the Republic of Nagalim.[6] Tirap and Chaglang districts, which are used by insurgents of both Assam and Nagaland as a transit route to Myanmar, are most vulnerable.

Notes and References

1. For a brief sketch of Arunachal and its problems see BG Verghese, *India's North-east Resurgent*; 1996; Konark Publishers, Delhi, Chapter 11 and Nari Rustomji, *Imperilled Frontiers*, 1983, Oxford University Press, Delhi.
2. Six Frontier Divisions of Kameng, Subansiri, Siang, Lohit, Tirap and Tuensang were created in 1954.Tuensang was transferred to Naga Hills in 1957.
3. BG Verghese, n. 1., pp. 225-228.
4. Ibid., p. 226.
5. Ibid, 229. Quoting *United News of India*, Guwahati, May 1994.
6. Ashok Krishna, 'Counter-Insurgency and Internal Security' in Ian Cordozo, ed., *The Indian Army: A Brief History*, (New Delhi: USI, Centre for Armed Forces Historical Research, 2005), p. 212.

10

The External Dimension

The extent of moral and material support by an external power(s) is one of the crucial factors for the success of any insurgency. The North-east insurgents have been particularly fortunate in having found sanctuaries or support in Bhutan and China in the North, Bangladesh in the South and Myanmar in the East. The insurgents have received moral and material support from China, Pakistan and Bangladesh at some time or the other. The sanctuaries in Bhutan and Myanmar have, however not been the outcome of any adversarial or hostile relations between them and India, but because of the inability of their governments to adequately administer the border areas or deal effectively with the hostile activities of the Indian insurgents inside their respective borders.

The Idea of a Crown Colony

The British on the eve of their departure from India had recognised the strategic importance of the North-east as a springboard for wielding influence not only in India and Myanmar but also in parts of China and Tibet. They tried to convert the tribal areas as a new bastion of imperialism. To give shape to this plan, Professor Coupland suggested the creation of the 'Crown Colony of Eastern Agency' consisting of the hill areas of Assam and Myanmar, which would in due course, be an independent state. When Naga leaders were consulted, they rejected the idea outright. Almost coinciding with the demand for the secession of Naga Hills from India, a group of Mizo feudal chiefs, known as 'sailos' under UMFO raised the slogan of integrating Mizo Hills with Myanmar. McCall, the District Commissioner of Lushai Hills (1932-43), initiated a plan for grouping of hill areas in Eastern India and Northern Myanmar under the trusteeship of the League of Nations. His successor Macdonald floated the idea of carving out an autonomous state comprising Mizo Hills and portions of Myanmar extending up to the Bay of Bengal, which was to be a protectorate of the British Government.[1] The scheme of separating the hills of the North-east from India could not fructify partly because of Myanmar's Prime Minister U Nu's attitude on the issue, and partly due to firm declarations of Indian leaders perceiving such move as hostile actions vis'-a-vis' the new government. [2] Although the above proposals did not fructify, the idea formed the breeding ground for the problems that confront the region today.

The Western Perception of North-east India

Equally significant was the perception held by other Western powers about North-east India. As early as 1966, reports were circulated by *Agencia International de Prensa* (International Press Service) datelined Dacca that there were reports to create a 'United Independent Bengal' comprising East Pakistan, West Bengal, Assam, Tripura, Sikkim and Bhutan. The report said:

> *"The separatists are counting on USA and other Western powers to give them necessary assistance. They are confident that these powers would be interested in establishing an independent state in South-East Asia, which could help to normalise conditions there and which could provide shield against the Chinese aggression..."*

It is in this context that the circular from United States International Communication Agency issued in June 1979 entitled 'Project Brahmaputra' is significant. The circular was sent to all their branches in Delhi and Calcutta informing that the special research cell of George Washington University, with the approval of the State Department had detailed several teams of investigators to conduct research in the North-eastern states, Sikkim and Bhutan. The purpose of the research was to 'throw light on the public opinion in the region to establish in what measure the present status of these states remain acceptable or whether there are indications that the formation of a new state is a current problem.'[3] Although the emergence of Bangladesh in 1971 and the rapprochement of relations between USA and China changed the geo-political scenario in this region, the Western perception of the tribal areas of India's North-east, which is predominantly Christian, as being inherently unstable persists. Such a perception has had a negative effect on the psyche of rebel outfits and indirectly encourages separatism.

Pakistan's Support to Naga Rebels

The Naga insurgency was Godsend for Pakistan, which had adversarial relations with India. It was almost a strategic compulsion for Pakistan to tie down maximum Indian troops in the North-east. When the Nagas rebelled against India, Pakistan found an ideal opportunity to take advantage of the situation. Naga rebels were the first to receive moral and material support from Pakistan, which had opened an office of assistant high commissioner in Shillong soon after Independence. Naga rebels used the office to establish contact with Pakistani officials in Dacca. Eventually, the commission's office in Shillong was closed.

Pakistan's support to Naga insurgency started after Phizo's escape to East Pakistan. Phizo first attempted to sneak into East Pakistan through Burma in December 1952, but was captured by the Burmese. He was sent back to India, where he was taken into custody but was later released on compassionate grounds, as his wife had met with an accident. Phizo eventually crossed into East Pakistan on December 6, 1956 from North Cachar Hills. Phizo's visit paved the way for others like Zhekuto Sema, director intelligence in the underground set up, Thungti Chang, an important Konyak underground leader, and Mowu Angami, then a young leader who later became the chief of the underground army, to visit East Pakistan in 1957. Mowu Angami was intercepted and arrested on August 10, 1957 on his way back, but was released soon after on amnesty. Assam Police intercepted Zhekuto and Thungti on their way back in July 1958 but Zhekuto was killed in that encounter.

The groundwork for receiving moral and material support from East Pakistan was done during these visits. Pakistan had created a special liaison cell for contact and coordination with Naga and Mizo rebels. Between 1962 and 1968 at least ten groups of Nagas had crossed into East Pakistan. Kaito Sema, then commander of the underground Naga Home Guards, led the first big gang of Naga rebels to East Pakistan in early 1962. This gang returned to Nagaland in March 1963 through the Chin Hills in Myanmar with loads of arms and ammunition. To demonstrate their strength they blew up the railway track between Rangapahar and Dhansiri railway stations on April 9, 1963.[4] The next big gang of hostiles led by Dusoi Chakesang crossed into East Pakistan in October 1963, taking the longer Chin Hills route. The gang returned in May 1964 with Rupees 30,000 in Indian currency and military hardware. Another gang of 300 under Yeveto Sema went to Pakistan for training in May 1964. Zuheto Sema led the biggest and most successful expedition to Pakistan in October 1964, after the suspension of hostilities brokered by the Peace Mission had come into effect. The gang consisted of 1,000 hostiles.[5] They were given training on modern lines, after which they returned to Somra tract in Myanmar in March 1965, where they held on for a few months before trickling into Nagaland in August/September 1965. India was then engaged in a war with Pakistan. Pakistanis were reported to have put pressure on hostile Nagas to open another front in their war with India, but the Nagas did not indulge in any violence; their decision was governed by political expediency as also the fact that the cessation of hostilities between security forces and underground Nagas was operative in Nagaland and they did not want to openly violate the provisions of the agreement. But to make amends, the FGN protested against the use of Naga troops in conflict with Pakistan.[6]

The subsequent efforts to send Naga rebels to East Pakistan were not successful. In November 1965, a gang of nearly 1,000 led by Mowu Angami, the chief of underground army, was intercepted by the Myanmar's Army and was forced to re-enter India in Manipur. However, in another attempt in June 1966, a gang of 200 Naga rebels under Nedelie Angami exfiltrated through Mizo Hills and returned after training in November 1966 via Churachandpur and Tamenglong in Manipur.[7]

China's Support to Naga Rebels

China's motivation to support Naga insurgency converged with Pakistan. Both had antagonistic relations with India. China had border dispute with India and it claimed Arunachal as its territory and refused to accept McMahon Line as the boundary between them. It had fought a border war with India in 1962. The mid sixties was the period when ideological war between the communists and the Western democracies was at its peak. China viewed India as its rival in Asia and was giving full support to Naxalites in India. The tribes of the North-east were ideal targets for fanning insurgencies and keeping Indian troops tied down.

The Indian security forces had by 1966 greatly intensified surveillance of Indo-Pak border and it was becoming increasingly dangerous for the Naga rebels to cross the border into East Pakistan. The alternate route through Myanmar was also dangerous because the Myanmar's Army had become very active and was alarmed by the nexus between Indian and Myanmar's insurgent groups. But the increased surveillance of the Indo-Pak border was only one of the reasons for seeking Chinese support by the Nagas. Phizo had become disenchanted with the West and had begun to despair about their lack of support. He was desperately seeking to internationalise the Naga problem with the help of a powerful foreign ally. China was the obvious choice. The Chinese support to Naga rebels started towards the end of 1966. The first gang to China, about 100 strong, was led by Thinuselie and Muivah. It crossed the border in Tuensang in November 1966 and trekked 1,000 km through Myanmar's territory before reaching Yunan province in mainland China in January 1967 and returned in January 1968 with arms, ammunition and equipment. They set up a camp at Jotsoma, which was turned into a regular training camp for the underground army.[8]

The second batch of 500 led by Mowu Angami and Isak Swu crossed the international border in middle of December 1967. By this time the peace talk was deadlocked, but the suspension of hostilities continued. While the gang was undergoing training, China offered to support a Naga government in exile. The proposal neither found favour with the underground leadership in Nagaland, nor did Phizo approve of it.[9] In Yunan the Nagas were trained at Tengchung and Fuking. In April 1968, another gang of 450 under Dusoi Chakesang crossed the border in Tuengsang area but Dusoi lost direction and was taken captive. The main body wandered in the jungles: tired, hungry and hunted by Myanmar's forces, they returned to Nagaland in small batches. Dusoi and 76 other Naga hostiles were handed over by Myanmar forces to the Indian Army at the border town of Moreh on April 11, 1969.

According to official estimates, a total of 1650 Naga hostiles went to China during 1967 and 1968 out of which about 700 had returned till the end of 1969, and out of them 275 were captured.[10] About 150 of the apprehended lot, were released on 31 December 31, 1969 and January 1, 1970. Only the hardcore guerillas were tried for anti-national activities, violation of Passport and Arms Acts.[11]

Chinese support to Nagas began to taper from early 70s. There were many reasons for it. The security forces had tightened the cordon along the international border, making both ingress and egress hazardous. There was greater coordination between the Indian and Myanmar's forces following the meeting between Indira Gandhi and General Ne Win in March 1968. The border was sealed more effectively, night patrolling was intensified and intelligence on rebel movement was exchanged more frequently. The Chinese had also begun to have second thoughts about the ability of Naga rebels to wage a prolonged guerilla war against India. The Chinese were also alarmed by the large-scale surrenders by the Naga rebels. Based on the Governor's address to the 1970 Budget Session of Nagaland Assembly, 1,049 Nagas had surrendered in 1969 alone. The capture of the entire gang led by Mowu Angami which was on its way back from Yunan (China) not only demoralised the underground but the dissension amongst the leadership based on tribal loyalties put a question mark on their ability to put up a united front. The Chinese were naturally alarmed at this turn of events, but continued their support through much of 70s. In April and July 1971, fresh groups of underground were reported to have gone to the Yunnan via Chin Hills of Myanmar. The defeat of Pakistan in 1971 war with India, however, altered the geo-strategic situation dramatically. The insurgent groups lost their bases in Bangladesh, but only temporarily.

The loss of safe sanctuaries in Bangladesh did not deter the Naga rebels from sending another gang to China. Sometime in August 1974, a decision was taken to send a gang under Muivah. The journey started on September 5, 1974 with 73 gang members including nine women. The security forces prevented the majority from crossing the border, but about 30 odd crossed over to Myanmar. This was the first time that an outgoing gang was hotly pursued and mauled.

The number that had crossed over to Myanmar was not large enough to proceed to China, and possibly the Chinese had laid down the minimum number that should report for training. So another attempt was made to send additional strength in December of that year. But this time the army was well prepared to foil their attempt. The bits of information that were trickling in suggested that the gang was likely to cross Chanki-Mokokchung Road between Chungtia and Khensa on night 4/5 January 1975. Between 18 and 23 January, 23 hostiles were apprehended at Mokokchung. 10 Assam Rifles apprehended another seven on 23 January. In the next few days another 72 were apprehended. Thus ended the rebel's last attempt to send a gang to China. The troops under command of Maj Gen 'Ganjoo' Rawat had achieved a remarkable success. The units and formations and the staff of 56 Mountain Brigade, particularly the Brigade Major, Maj N Bahri, played a very important role.[12]

The cooperation between Pakistan and China to lend support to various insurgent groups operating in the North-east was even more serious. The trek to Yunan was proving to be long, arduous and dangerous. On return from China, underground Brigadier Thinusellie was sent to East Pakistan in late 1968 to coordinate arrangements for training of guerillas in bases in Pakistan. The Chinese, therefore, opened a guerrilla-training centre in East Pakistan to train North-east insurgents. A small airstrip was constructed at a place near Rangamati in CHT to train insurgents in air operations. On July 26, 1970 the Government of India sent a strong protest note to the Chinese against arms supply and guerrilla training to Naga and Mizo rebels. The note also referred to a meeting of hostile Nagas and Mizos held on February 15, 1969 in CHT, which was attended by representatives of the Governments of Pakistan & China and where discussions centered on developing East Pakistan as a centre of inter-tribal coordination.[13] But the emergence of Bangladesh after Pakistan's defeat in 1971 war changed the situation altogether.

Pakistan's Support to Mizos

Pakistan's support to Mizos was more crucial. Mizo guerillas had an ideal sanctuary in CHT across the border. The long border of Mizoram with East Pakistan provided many ingress and exit routes. Laldenga and his associates had crossed the border in the first week of December 1963 and established contact with Pakistani officials, who were only too willing to help. The secret plan to send Mizo guerillas to East Pakistan was delayed due to Laldenga's arrest on his return journey by Assam police, but was revived immediately after his release. Within weeks of Laldenga's release from the prison in early 1964, a group of 20 Mizos crossed the border to finalise the arms supply deal with Pakistan. They took delivery of arms from Pakistan's military intelligence at Dohazari, a railway station near the port city Chittagong, from where the supplies were taken up in boats to Rumabazar and thence to the border village of Hmunmuan. The entire cache was hidden in deep forests near a Mizo village on the Indian side of the border half way between Aizwal and Lungleih. The support given by Pakistan was crucial in the success of Mizo uprising on February 28, 1966.

Months after the Indian Army launched counter-insurgency operations, large number of Mizo youths, many studying in Shillong, headed for East Pakistan, where Pakistan's covert intelligence agencies had set up facilities for their training. Soon after, in the first week of July 1966, Laldenga left for Dacca to seek international support for the Mizo cause.

In the aftermath of 1971 war with Pakistan, Mizos lost a secure sanctuary in East Pakistan. After the defeat of Pakistani forces on December 16, 1971 the MNA organised a brilliant escape from East Pakistan to Arakan. On 17 December Biakchhunga organised seven motor launches at Rangamati; each boat could carry over hundred people. Thus began the great escape to Arakan, which met resistance en route by *Mukti Bahini* units, but the ordeal ended successfully and was one of the high points of Mizo resistance movement.[14]

The emissary of Laldenga contacted the Pakistani Consulate in March 1972 in the coastal town of Akyab (Myanmar), which helped Laldenga and his retinue in obtaining fake passports. Finally, in April 1972 Laldenga flew to Pakistan on a KLM flight from Rangoon under the assumed name of "Mr Zolkeps".[15] He would remain in Karachi to an uncertain future, till he was allowed by the Pakistani intelligence to go to Geneva sometime in 1975, again on a fake passport, to internationalise the Mizo problem.

Situation after Emergence of Bangladesh

After the liberation of Bangladesh, it was hoped that support to North-east insurgents would come to an end, but it was not to be. They lost their sanctuary but only temporarily. After the assassination of Sheikh Mujibur Rehman, Mizos regained some of the lost ground in CHT, not as associates of Chakma militants but as collaborators of the local authorities, helping them in settling Bengali Muslims in CHT and ensuring their own refuge in return.[16]

China's Support to Mizos

The first attempt to send Mizo rebels to China for training and procurement of arms was made in 1968. To pave the way for the smooth passage of the gang through Myanmar's territory, KIA was contacted for support. Earlier Lalhmingthanga, the MNA chief, had met Chinese diplomats in Dacca in preparation for the dispatch of 1,000 guerillas to Yunan (China) for training. Bualhranga, ambassador designate to China, led the gang. The gang met opposition from Myanmar's forces but despite that the gang reached Chindwin River in August 1968, only to find the river in spate. To add to their discomfiture Myanmar's troops had been alerted. The journey through Kachin territory to Yunan was, therefore, aborted.[17] Another attempt to send a gang to China was made in 1972. Unlike the earlier attempt, the second gang of nearly 70 led by Damkoshiak made it to Yunan through the Kachin corridor. But while returning from China, they surrendered to the Indian authorities, which was facilitated by an undercover operation by the Subsidiary Intelligence Bureau.[18] Unlike the Nagas, the Mizos were destined to fail in their efforts to forge a successful Chinese connection.

Pakistan's Support to Meitei Insurgents

As narrated earlier, by the end of sixties, UNLF had established a fairly wide network of supporters in the Imphal Valley. This was also the period when after Indo-Pak war of 1965 the relations between the two countries were strained. Pakistan was looking for an opportunity to start fresh ethnic trouble in the North-east. The Meteis were at the same time looking for sanctuary and material support from Pakistan to give a boost to insurgency in Manipur. In 1968, a group under Oinam Sudhir was sent to East Pakistan to seek help. The group established contact with the Meitei community at Sylhet.[19] But before Sudhir could convince the Pakistani intelligence, a group of 200 Manipuri youths landed at Sylhet prematurely, which upset the Pakistanis. They were not yet fully ready to give direct support to India's insurgent groups, so soon after the Tashkent Declaration. The group was apprehended and put in jail in Maulvi Bazaar for a month, and later handed over to the Indian Army at Tripura border. They were lodged in Dharampur Jail till their release in 1972, in a general amnesty by the Government of Manipur.[20]

A small group had escaped arrest and continued to stay in East Pakistan. Their leader, Sudhir, who by then had formed RGM, succeeded in getting Pakistani support and received guerilla training during the period 1970-71. They put their training to practice during the 1971 Indo-Pak war, engaging Indian security forces, particularly the police and paramilitary forces, in ambushes and raids on isolated police posts close to the border. But the outcome of the war forced them to return to Manipur. Some died in engagements while crossing the border, but three of them successfully slipped into Manipur, where they were finally apprehended at Nungba in Tamelgong District.[21]

China's Support to Meitei Insurgents

The Chinese trained Meitei insurgents not in Yunan but in Lhasa. The Meiteis under the charismatic Bisheshwar took an unconventional route via Kathmandu to reach Lhasa. They were ideologically left oriented and differed from Nagas whose ideological moorings were not very strong. The Meiteis were the ones to introduce urban guerilla warfare techniques and engage Indian troops in built up areas in the Imphal Valley.

Pakistan's and Bangladesh Support to Insurgents of Tripura

The seeds of insurgency were sown in Tripura soon after the Mizos had risen in revolt. But the defeat of the Pakistani Army in 1971 and the emergence of Bangladesh had changed the geo-political scene. There was a lull in insurgent activities for a while, but not for long. The Mizos began returning from their base in Arakan to Bangladesh in October 1976. MNF established its tactical headquarters in the Sajek ranges in CHT at a place called Langkor. Their headquarters was moved near the Tri Junction of Mizoram-Arakan-CHT to a place called Chhintalang in Bangladesh.

Sometime in 1977, Hrangkhwl sent two emissaries to Chittagong with a letter for Bangladesh President, Zia-ur-Rehman. The two emissaries were intercepted by Bangladesh Police, interrogated and sent back to Tripura, but it appears, Hrangkhwl's letter reached the president. The Bangladesh intelligence agreed to help TNV, but only through the MNF. The first group of TNV volunteers led by Chuni Koloi trekked to Chhintalang in the beginning of 1979, stayed with the MNF and took part in attacks on security forces jointly with them. The subsequent groups were given basic training and returned to Tripura. By the end of 1979, TNV had set up a camp in the jungles of CHT. After the ethnic violence that had erupted in Tripura in mid 1980, many young tribals took refuge in the jungles of CHT. The riots gave a boost to insurgency in Tripura. According to one estimate the MNF trained nearly 130 tribals between September and November 1980.[22]

After the disbandment of TNV in December 1980, All Tripura People's Liberation Organisation (ATPLO) was formed, but it was not supported either by Bangladesh or Pakistan. ATPLO received support mainly from the MNF, which trained nearly 100 of its volunteers. Chuni Koloi who was heading the ATPLO, made several attempts to contact Bangladesh officials between 1980 and 1982 but failed.

After the revival of TNV in November 1982, the links between TNV and MNF were revived. 60 TNV volunteers were trained by MNF in early 1983.[23] Hrangkhwl again tried to seek support from Bangladesh. Ananta Debbarma, TNV home secretary, met a Bangladeshi official at Mariswa, which was an important listening past for Bangladesh on the border with Tripura. In May 1983, Hrangkhwl himself contacted a senior Bangladeshi army official at Chittagong, who promised to give some ammunition but no weapons. Hrangkhwl made a secret trip to Pakistan in April 1985 with two ISI officials, who promised to help through Bangladesh, but the news leaked out. Bangladesh developed cold feet apprehending India might intensify support to *Shanti Bahini* guerillas.[24] The promised support to TNV did not materialise.

Insurgency in Tripura declined after the Mizos signed an accord with the Indian Government in 1985. This forced Hrangkhwl to negotiate with the government but even after signing the accord in 1988, the remnants of TNV have continued to operate from bases in Bangladesh. Ashok Tandon, Director General of Border Security Force (BSF), in his annual conference on November 27, 1997 admitted that both ATFF and NLFT continue to get support from Bangladesh. In spite of Indian protests, Bangladesh failed to close down rebel camps in its territory.[25]

Pakistani and Bangladeshi Support to ULFA

The credit for forging ULFA's connection with Pakistan's ISI goes to one Munim Nobis, who belonged to Guwahati. Before joining ULFA, Nobis was a member of Assam People Liberation Army (APLA), which was formed at Tezpur at the same time as ULFA. By 1983, APLA had formed a wide network of activists in Mangaldoi, Barpeta and Nagaon. Many APLA members were arrested and this forced it to merge with ULFA.

The first unsuccessful attempt by Nobis to contact ISI was made in 1988. He traveled to Karachi in the company of a Bangladeshi businessman who was well connected with both Bangladeshi and Pakistani intelligence operatives, but the businessman failed to put Nobis in contact with any important ISI functionary in Karachi. Nobis made the next attempt the following year but was told to come again with a more representative team. Senior ULFA leaders [26] flew to Karachi sometime in 1990 from where they were taken to Islamabad and then to Peshawar, which at that time was the headquarters of several Afghan mujahideen groups. The team was given intensive training in strategy, tactics, counter-intelligence, disinformation and use of weapons. The training lasted for one month after which they returned to Assam. No weapons were given at this stage.

The next visit of ULFA leaders comprising of Paresh Barua, the commander of the military wing and Sunil Nath, the publicity secretary took place in September 1991. They were taken to Darrah in North West Frontier Province that is one of the world's biggest open but illegal arms bazaar. The Pakistanis wanted ULFA to attack high priority strategic targets like oilfields and government buildings. ULFA rejected the suggestion fearing that it would turn the public against them. The Pakistanis also cautioned ULFA leaders not to confront the Indian Army directly. But ULFA had other ideas; it was confident of taking on the Indian Army head-on but rejected the suggestion to destroy economic assets, which would only alienate them from the general public.[27]ULFA, however, changed its tactics after Operations Bajrang and Rhino when they found the army too strong for them. Ironically, they subsequently began to target economic assets like oilfields and pipelines, which they had wisely spared fearing adverse public reaction.

In March 1994, the Assam Assembly was informed that ULFA militants had received training with the help of Pakistan's ISI, most of them in Afghanistan. ULFA also established contact with Bangladesh Field Intelligence unit in Dhaka and was allowed to establish training camps in Bangladesh in Mymensingh district at Bhemugach, Nilfarman and Dhami, all in Maulvi Bazaar area.[28] However, after the victory of the Awami League under Sheikh Hasina in the 1995 elections, the Government of Bangladesh decided to freeze all help to the North-east insurgents.

Sanctuaries in Myanmar and Bhutan

Following the crackdown by Bangladesh during the regime of Sheikh Hasina, many ULFA camps shifted from Bangladesh to Manas Reserved Forests in Assam and in the forests of South Bhutan close to the Indo-Bhutan border, from where they were physically removed in a military operation by the RBA in December 2003.

Appraisal

The support given by China and Pakistan to North-east insurgents was a consequence of antagonistic relations with

China and Pakistan. Unlike East Pakistan and Bangladesh, the sanctuaries of North-east insurgents in Myanmar are not the result of adversarial bilateral relations between the two countries, but due to the inability of the Myanmar Government to effectively administer their hilly areas along India's border.[29] The abetment of insurgency in Tripura was partially *quid-pro-quo* for the support India was extending to Chakma insurgents the *Shanti Bahini*. In the case of sanctuaries in Bhutan, the king tried to get the ULFA camps vacated from Bhutanese territory through talks, but when ULFA refused to vacate the camps even after an ultimatum, the RBA in a swift and well-planned operation in December 2003 destroyed the camps and forced them to flee. The action taken by Bhutan should be taken as an example of cooperative approach to effectively fight insurgencies in South Asia.

Notes and References

1. VIK Sareen, *India's North-east in Flames*, (New Delhi: Vikas Publishing House, 1980), p. 145.
2. Urmila Phadnis, *Ethnicity and Nation Building in South Asia*, (New Delhi: Sage Publications, 1990), p. 150.
3. Urmila Phadnis, n.2., p. 235. Also VIK Sareen, n. 1., pp. 24-27. Sareen gives a lucid account of CIA's activities in the North-east in early 1970s.
4. Prakash Singh, *Nagaland*, (New Delhi: National Book Trust, 1972), p. 122. Prakash Singh was then posted in the Intelligence Bureau in Nagaland.
5. Ibid.
6. Ibid., p. 124.
7. Ibid., p. 123.
8. RD Palsokar, *Forever in Operations: History of 8 Mountain Division*, 1992, pp. 63-64. and Prakash Singh, n. 4.,, pp. 131-132. The army raided Jatsoma camp in June 1968. 25 hostiles with Chinese arms and ammunition were captured. The underground Nagas had clearly violated the agreement on cessation of hostilities. BK Nehru, who had become the Governor of Nagaland in April 1968, forced the Nagas to adhere to the agreement on suspension of hostilities.
9. *The Hindustan Times*, New Delhi, July 18, 1968. Quoted by Prakash Singh, n.4., p.136.

10. Statement made by the Defence Minister in the Lok Sabha on December 3, 1969.
11. Prakash Singh, n. 4., p. 138.
12. Col Palsokar has vividly described the conduct of the whole operation. See RD Palsokar, n. 8., Ch 10, pp.136-157.
13. Asoso Yonuo, *The Rising Nagas*, (New Delhi: Vikas Publishing House, 1974), p. 305.
14. Subir Bhaumik, *Insurgent Crossfire: North-east India,* (New Delhi: Lancers, 1996), p. 171.
15. Ibid., p. 172.
16. *Times of India*, New Delhi, October 1, 1984. Quoted by Urmila Phadnis, p. 235.
17. Subir Bhaumik, n. 14., p. 166.
18. Ibid., pp. 173,176,177.
19. Sylhet has a large Meitei community, which had migrated from Manipur to escape from the Burmese attack in the early twentieth century.
20. For a more comprehensive account see Phanjoubam Tarapot, *Insurgency Movement in North-east India*, (New Delhi: Vikas Publishers), pp. 42-46.
21. Ibid., p. 46.
22. Subir Bhaumik, n. 14., p. 214.
23. Ibid., p. 222.
24. "Pak-TNV links Established," *The Telegraph*, Calcutta, October 1, 1985. Quoted by Subir Bhaumik, n. 14, p. 230.
25. *The Hindustan Times*, New Delhi, November 29, 1997.
26. Rajkhowa, ULFA president, Hirakjyoti Mahanta, the deputy commander of military wing, Predeep Gogoi, the vice president, Anup Chetia, the general secretary and Manoj Hazarika. For a fuller account of how ULFA made contact with ISI see Sanjoy Hazarika, *Strangers of the Mist: Tales of War and Peace from North-east,* (New Delhi: Penguin, 1995), pp. 170-175.
27. Ibid., p. 174.
28. Ibid., p. 235.
29. For a scholarly analysis of external factors in the spread of insurgency see Urmila Phadnis; *Ethnicity and Nation Building in South Asia*, (New Delhi: Sage Publications, 1989).

11

The Religious Dimension

Before the advent of Christianity, the hill tribes of Assam practiced animism. An important consequence of the spread of British administration in the hills of Assam was undoubtedly the arrival of missionaries, which led to many hill tribes converting to Christianity. People in the Brahmaputra and the Imphal Valleys had already embraced Hinduism before the advent of British colonialists in North-east India.

The spread of Christianity in the hill districts of Assam followed the British administration. The East India Company was more interested in expanding trade in India than spreading Christianity or civilising the tribes. In the early days of colonisation the European community in India was bitterly opposed to missionaries, chiefly because they might have a disturbing effect on Indians.[1] The Charter Act of 1813 laid down as a duty of the administration to introduce useful knowledge, help religious and moral improvement, reduce the powers of the East India Company and increase the control of the British Parliament over Indian administration. Christianity thus came to the hills of the North-east as a consequence of administrative policy.[2] The Welsh Presbyterian Mission introduced the Roman script and showed greater zeal for proselytising, as did the American Baptists, who encouraged the Assamese language and script. The abolition of East India Company's powers in 1833 gave a fillip to mission work. During the British rule, the administration supported the work of missionary and subsidised the cost of education, yet the North-east was not open house for missionary work. Mission work was prohibited in part of Garo Hills, unadministered area of Naga Hills, Arunachal and the plains of Manipur and until 1930 in Tripura[3]. Political and social factors decided the extent to which proselytising was permitted. The administration and the missionary worked hand in glove, one facilitating the work of the other. Interestingly, the spread of Christianity in the hill areas of North-east has been faster after Independence than before it.

David Scott, the first Commissioner of Assam, brought some English missionaries to preach Christianity to the Garos. Major Jenkins, who succeeded David Scott as the Commissioner of Assam invited American Baptists to come to Assam. In 1836, Rev Nathan Brown, Miles Bronson and OT Cutter came to Sadiya to take up proselytising work, but did not make much progress amongst the Hindus and tribals (animists) of the plains. From Sadiya they moved to Sibsagar where they established a mission but here again the missionaries did not meet with much success. Bronson then moved to Tirap, where he concentrated on establishing a mission school to teach the Gospel to the Nagas, but had to leave due to death of his sister.[4] By and large the American Mission remained confined to the Brahmaputra Valley, espousing the cause of Assamese language.

Christianity in Nagaland

It was only after the arrival of Rev EW Clark that proselytising began to have some success. Encouraged by Clark's success in baptising a few Nagas in November/December 1872, he was granted permission to open a permanent mission amongst the Ao Nagas. The first Christian village was founded at Molungyimsen in 1876, which was moved to Impur 10 miles North of Mokokchung in 1894. Clark served in Nagaland for nearly three decades and left Nagaland in 1911. He produced Ao-English dictionary and translated the gospels of Mathew and John in Ao language. Christianity spread well in Ao area but its progress was slow in the Angami and Lotha areas. In Angami area, Christianity spread much later in the beginning of 20th century.[5] Angami language was reduced to writing in Roman script and Biblical work was translated in Angami. The American Baptist Mission entered Naga Hills only after 1876, when the hills had come under some kind of administration. As late as 1891 AW Davis wrote that Nagas were not inclined towards Christianity. In 1947 only 20 percent of the population was Christian in Nagaland; as against nearly 85 percent in 2005. 1991 census put the Christians at 87.47 percent of the total population.

Spread of Christianity in Manipur

In Manipur missionary work was started by American Baptist Church in 1894 in Mao area, three years after the administration was taken over by the British. They met with much resistance from the animists; the Meiteis of the valley had already converted to Hinduism and were against missionary work. However, the missionaries found the Tangkhul Nagas in Ukhrul area more amenable. Schools were built primarily to convert the hill Nagas of Manipur.[6] By 1907 a strong foundation was laid in the hills of Manipur for the spread of Christianity. In the beginning of the 20th century, there was not a single Christian in Manipur but the decadal growth of Christians as a whole during 1961-71 was 83.66 percent. The Christian population of Manipur as per 1981 census was 34.11 percent of the total population.

Phenomenal Success in Mizoram

In Mizoram, Christianity came in the closing decade of 19th century close upon the heels of the administration in 1890. Two British missionaries came to Aijwal in 1894 and opened two missions – one by Welsh Presbyterian and the other by London Baptists. The spread of Christianity in Mizoram has been phenomenal. In 1901 census, Lushai Hills recorded only 26

Christians in a population of 82,434. By 1981, more than 80 percent of Mizoram population had converted to Christianity.[7] The Christian population of Mizoram as per 1991 census was 85.73 percent of the total population. The centenary of the coming of Christianity to Mizoram was celebrated with great fervor in 1994.

Christianity in Meghalaya

In Meghalaya, the first Presbyterian Church was established amongst the Khasis in 1841 and the American Baptist Mission in Garo Hills in 1864. Before the coming of Christianity, Khasis and Jaintias worshipped a formless God and referred to their religion as Niamtre, while Garos refer to their traditional religion as Sangrarek.[8]

The first Catholic Mission in the hills was German, which was opened towards the end of the 19th century but remained confined to Shillong. During the World War I, Italians replaced it. In 1933, the Catholic Church was opened in Tura in the Garo Hills. The Christian population of Meghalaya as per 1991 census was 64.58 percent of the total population. Incidentally, the influence of the Church of England in the hills is minimal.[9]

Leaving aside the Buddhists, the rest follow Hinduised version of the tribal religion. However, many local people have adopted Islam through marriage and at present there is a sizeable population of local converts to the religion. The Hinduised tribes, who inhabit the state, are greatly influenced by the Bhakti Movement. The Ramakrishna Mission and Brahmo Samaj have established their missions in Meghalaya but their influence has been minimal.

Arunachal: A Different Story

The situation in Arunachal was somewhat different from other hill areas of the North-east. The indigenous people of Arunachal practice a form of worship called *Donyi Polo*, which is really the worship of omnipresent, omniscient and omnipotent and is described as the cause of all creations including air, water, earth, soil, trees and flowers.[10] Because of the tensions and clashes, which the aggressive extension of missionary activities was causing in the area, the Arunachal Pradesh Freedom of Religion Act was passed in 1978. This Act prohibits conversion from one religion to another by use of force or inducement or by fraudulent means. While putting a ban on conversion from indigenous faiths to any other religion, the Act describes the indigenous faith as such religions, beliefs or practices including rites, rituals, festivals, observances, performances, abstinence, customs as have been found, sanctioned, approved, performed by the indigenous communities of Arunachal from time these communities were known and includes Buddhism as prevalent among the Monpas, Sherdupkens, Khampas, Khampatis and Singphos, *Vaishnavism* as practiced by Noctes and nature worship including *Donyi Polo* as prevalent among the indigenous people of Arunachal.

There is a suggestion that the Act extends protection to Buddhism and Vaishnavism as prevalent in Arunachal but Christians are kept outside the protective wing. But despite the Act, Christianity has made rapid progress; in 1971 less than 0.8 percent of the population of this area was Christian, by 1994 nearly one-eighth of it had been converted.[11] As per 1991 census, the population of Christians in Arunachal was 10.29 percent; the population of Hindus was 37.04 percent, Buddhists 12.88 percent, Muslims 1.38 percent, Sikhs 0.14 percent, Jains 0.01 percent, others 36.22 percent and not stated 2.04 percent of the total population.

Exposure to Hinduism

The impact of external exposure on tribal societies has been profound and manifested in the spread of religion. In pre-British days Hinduism had the most important influence in the plains of Assam. Sanskritisation and Aryanisation of Assam took place over a long period of time. Suniti Kumar Chatterjee is of the view that the Aryanisation of the ruling classes of Kamrupa was complete as early as 400 AD and by the end of the early medieval period, that is by 1200 AD, the Brahmaputra Valley had become a part of Aryan speaking India.[12] The process of Sanskritisation gathered momentum during the period of Sankaradeva (1449-1568), whose liberal brand of Vaishnavism brought thousands of tribal people of the Brahmaputra Valley within the fold of Hinduism. Islam had no place in the hills except through a few immigrants.

Hinduism was a great success in Hill Tipperah, where 1901 census recorded Hindus as 69 percent, Muslims 26 percent (almost wholly immigrant plains people), Buddhist 3 percent and animists 2 percent of the population.[13] Other Hindu communities in the North-east are the Meiteis in Manipur and the Kacharis. There are also Hindu Khasis on the Sylhet side. The influence of Hinduism was so great in this region that 1881 census report of Assam noted, "wherever they (the hill people) are not protected by mountains or jungles, the non-Aryan residents have invariably yielded, and are yielding, to the over powering fascination of the Hindu religion."[14]

The Brahmo Samaj came to Shillong in 1870s. In the summer of 1901, Vivekanand visited the Khasi Hills. In 1921, the Ramakrishna Mission opened a centre near Cherrapunji and later another in Shillong. The Ramakrishna Mission incidentally is the only Mission that has been allowed to open a school in Arunachal.

Situation after Independence

Until the end of 19th century, no significant progress in the spread of Christianity could be achieved in the hills. However, it began to make rapid progress from the beginning of the 20th century and picked up momentum soon after Independence. An integrated religionwise picture of the hills in 1961 furnished by the deputy registrar general of India is revealing. Among the

Mizos in Mizoram, Christians were 96.95 percent, Hindus 1.37 percent, Tribals 0.07 percent and Buddhists 1.54 percent of the population. Among Cacharis 93.63 percent were Hindus and 6.16 percent were Christians. In Manipur, among Hmars 99.21 percent were Christians; among Mizos 99.98 percent and among Paites 88.69 percent were Christians. In Naga Hills 56.12 percent of the population was Christian, 3.62 percent Hindu and 27.15 percent was tribal.[15] This indicates that the spread of Christianity has not been adversely affected after Independence. This also nails the allegation made by some missionaries that the community is being discriminated against in propagating the religion.

In Arunachal, the spread of Christianity has been minimal, as government policy discourages proselytising. The impact of Arunachal Pradesh Freedom of Religion Act 1978 has already been discussed earlier. Christianity came to Garo and Khasi Hills much earlier than Naga and Mizo Hills, yet its spread in latter has been more spectacular, possibly because the former were exposed to non-Christian influences more intensively than Nagas and Mizos.[16]

The Impact of Christianity on Tribal Societies

There is a view, some say misplaced, that the Christian missions alienated the tribes from their roots, indigenous culture and customs, which had many commendable traits. The loyalty of the converts was directed towards their own groups and the non-converts were regarded as sinners. SK Chaube, who has studied the subject in considerable depth, opines that the idea of groupness is germane to the type of teaching presented to the Nagas. But the Christians did not create the sense of medieval Christian unity. For example, when Baptist Church in Nagaland was nationalised, it was reorganised as Angami Association or Ao Association etc. That is why the charge that Church creates extra territorial loyalty does not stand.[17]

Verrier Elwin who influenced the policy of the Government of India towards the tribes after Independence was very critical of the cultural and traditional moorings of the Nagas becoming weak under the influence of Christian missions. This is what he had to say: "The activities of the Baptist mission among the Nagas have demoralised the people, destroyed tribal identity, and forbidden the joys and feastings, the decorations and romance of community life." Sir Robert Reid, who had been the Governor of Bengal, however, took a different view. He said: "But methods of proselytising had become modified as the years passed, and latter day missionaries sensibly tried to preserve all that was good in old tradition." [18]

The spread of Christianity in the 19th century, mainly through American Baptist Mission – although others like Presbyterian, Roman Catholics, Methodists, Seventh Day Adventists, and the Salvation Army etc also contributed – had both positive and negative impact on tribal societies. On the positive side, it forbade perpetual feuds, headhunting, encouraged abstaining from intoxicants, discouraged propitiation of the evil Gods and other licentious behavior. It is argued that the spread of Christianity brought the tribes out of isolation and introduced them to the other civilisations of the world. But this view is contradicted by the imposition of the Inner Line regulation, which was intended to keep the tribes isolated, particularly from the happenings in mainland India. What really exposed the tribes of the North-east to the outside world were the two World Wars, which brought them in contact with people of other nationalities and civilisations. Whatever may be the criticism of the work of Christian missions, it is hard to deny the many reforms introduced by them. The construction of living houses, segregation of animals from living quarters, personal hygiene and personal cleanliness, disposal of the dead through burial in community cemetery were introduced and/or encouraged by the missionaries.

Christian missions were pioneers in the field of education and health care but in one respect the Church education left a dangerous legacy: " The Mission carried out a uniform policy of imparting Roman script to the hill dialects, which were indeed enriched, but permanently alienated from the contiguous plain languages from which many hill dialects had drawn heavily. Thus Garos and Khasis are in the process of forgetting Bengali, just as Nagas are estranged from Assamese, despite the fact the *lingua franca* of Nagas is even today a broken form of Assamese."

On the negative side was the excommunication of unfaithful who broke the Sabbath and participated in traditional singing of folk songs. Christianity widened the barrier and the conflict between the hills and the plains. Professor WC Smith of the University of South California has drawn attention to the ill effects of the way in which Christianity was presented to the tribes: " There is a grave danger that Christianity as presented to the people (Nagas), comes to be little more than the adoption of another set of taboos, and taboo is no new element in the life of any group on a low cultural level. Under the old system the Nagas had to refrain from working on the fields on certain days, lest their God Lizaba curse the village with an epidemic or blight the rice crop; now they must refrain from work on the Christian Sabbath, lest Jehovah, the God of Israel smite them for their wickedness."[19]

Charge of Encouraging Secessionist Groups

There have been insinuations that Christian missionaries have encouraged secessionist groups in the North-east particularly in the years immediately before and after Independence. This gained credence from the activities of some of the colonial administrators, who wanted to carve out a 'Crown Colony' comprising of Arakan, CHT, Chin Hills, Lushai Hills, Naga Hills, Sadiya, Lakhimpur, Balipura Frontier Tracts and hill areas of Tripura and Manipur.

There is some truth in the allegation that Church leaders in Nagaland encouraged secessionist groups soon after Independence. The role played by Rev Michael Scott, a British national who was invited by the Church leaders of Nagaland to be one of the members of the peace mission, which facilitated the cease-fire in 1964, was clearly partisan and inconsistent with the role of a neutral facilitator during the negotiations. Even as Indira Gandhi had agreed to meet the Naga underground in 1966, Michael Scott was corresponding with the Burmese Government on behalf of the underground and was in touch with the United Nations pleading the case for Naga Independence. Consequently, Scott was expelled from India for activities inconsistent with his neutral status.[20] And perhaps it is not accidental that the leaders of the two early rebellions in the North-east, Phizo and Laldenga, were extended liberal patronage by the Church of England with all facilities for coordinating the activities of their followers.[21]

For over a hundred years, the Church functioned in tandem with the British administration. That kind of protection and cooperation was not possible after Independence. The Church, therefore, had to readjust its goal and its tactical devices.[22] The aim henceforth of an influential part of the Church was to carve out states, in which Christians would be in majority as Christians or, at the least, areas in which persons running the governments would be amenable to the influence of the Church. The effort has proceeded farthest in the North-east.[23]

There are intelligence reports with the government that establishes the link between specified missionary groups and secessionists groups in Nagaland and Manipur. Specific information points to their association with insurgent groups like the Naga National Council (A) led by Adino Phizo, daughter of AZ Phizo, and the NSCN (IM).[24] In Mizoram the role of the Church is overtly political. In 1988 two separate incidents involving Fathers of the Dengtol Mission and the Sarabil Centre pointed to their association with the Bodo activists.[25] In 1992, two British nationals were caught; they had been advocating separate Naga country through a Naga Vigil Organisation and had been receiving active support from the insurgent Naga National Council (A).[26]

"Religious nationalism is a significant feature of contemporary Asian politics. The birth of Pakistan is an outstanding example. There are similar movements associated with Christianity among Nagas in Assam, among Karens in Burma and Ambonese in Indonesia. When Indonesia became independent the Ambonese, most of whom were Christians, revolted against their own national Government. When Burma went out of the British Commonwealth, a good number of leaders of Karen, who revolted against the state of Burma, were Christians. Today some of the agitators for independent Naga state are also Christians."[27] The manifesto of NSCN (IM) has Nagaland for Christ as one of its objectives. The recent secession of East Timor, which is predominantly Christian, from Indonesia, has only aggravated the fears of many Indians about the separatist agenda of a section of Nagas.

The charge of alienation against the Christians has to be viewed in an objective manner. For more than one hundred years the missionaries denounced Hinduism for its caste system and painted it as a religion of superstition and devoid of any moral compass. No wonder as Christianity progressed in the hills so did the barrier widen between the people of the hills and plains. The impact of Christianity was not limited to the relations between the hills and the plains; it was more profound on tribal societies. Hutton, an ICS officer posted in Mokokchung was of the view that " role of the Baptist Mission among the tribal in general and Nagas in particular has been injurious and disruptive to their culture." But these are only one side of the coin. With the passage of time and devolution of political powers, the extra territorial moorings of hill tribes have irrevocably weakened. Although a section of the Church in both Nagaland and Mizoram had given moral support to insurgent groups, they played a constructive part in helping restore peace in strife torn tribal societies by providing a neutral forum between the insurgents and the Indian Union. This has been their most salutary role. In Meghalaya, Rev Nicholas Ray was instrumental in integration of Khasi states. A lobby among Khasi leaders led by Rev Gatoph advocated a separate entity outside India, but the plan did not get approval of the majority in the Church.

Assam's problem of identity to a large extent has been caused by the large-scale illegal immigration of Bangladeshi. They fear the prospect of immigrants from Bangladesh, most of who happen to be Muslims, outnumbering them. This has already been discussed in Chapter 2. Yet another dimension in the form of Muslim fundamentalism, which grew soon after the demolition of the Babri Masjid, and Islamic *jihad*, has been injected in the politics of Assam in the recent years.

Notes and References

1. SK Chaube, *Hill Politics in North-east India*, (New Delhi: Orient Longman, 1999), p. 52. Quoting EJ Thompson and Garrett, *The Rise and Fulfilment of British Rule in India*, (Allahabad: 1962), p. 192.
2. Ibid., p. 52. Chaube makes a distinction between the spread of Christianity in Bengal and the North-east; whereas in Bengal it came as an intellectual movement, in the North-east it came through administrative policy.
3. BG Verghese, *India's North-east Resurgent*, (New Delhi: Konark, 1996), p. 284.
4. Asoso Yonuo, *The Rising Nagas*, (New Delhi: Vivek Publication, 1974), p. 112.
5. Ibid., 114.
6. Ibid., p. 118.
7. Animesh Ray, *Mizoram*, (New Delhi: Book Trust of India, 1993), p. 137.

8. KS Singh, ed., *Meghalaya*, (Calcutta: Anthropological Survey of India and Seagull Books, 1994).

9. Chaube, n. 1., p. 55.

10. Rabjit Chaudhury, "Religious Overtones in Ethnic Issue in North-east India", in PS Datta, ed., *North-east and the Indian State: Paradoxes of a Periphery*, (New Delhi: Vikas Publishing House, 1997), p. 00.

11. Arun Shourie, *Missionaries in India*, (New Delhi: Asa Publications, 1994), p. 207.

12. Udayon Misra, *The Periphery Strikes Back:* Challenges to the Nation State in Assam and Nagaland, (Shimla: Indian Institute of Advanced Studies, Shimla, 2000), p. 5.

13. Imperial Gazetteer of India, Vol xiii, 1907, p. 119.

14. *Report of the Census of Assam, 1881*, Chapter v, paragraph 112. Quoted by SK Chaube, n. 1., p. 41.

15. SK Chaube, n. 1., p. 43.

16. Ibid.

17. Ibid. Quoting Moasosang, "The Naga Search for Self-Identity" in Rathin Mitra and Barun Dasgupta, ed., *A Common Perspective for North-east India*, (Calcutta: 1967).

18. Sir Robert Reid, *Years of Change in Bengal and Assam*, (London: 1994), p. 109. Quoted by Asoso Yonou, n. 4., p. 120.

19. Quoted by Asoso Yonuo, n.4., p. 120.

20. A detailed account of Rev Michael Scott's partisan role during the peace negotiations is given in YD Gundevia, *War and Peace in Nagaland*, (Dehradun: Palit and Palit, 1975), Ch. vii, pp. 101-126.

21. Rabijit Chaudhury, n. 10, p. 21.

22. Arun Shourie, n 1, p. 205.

23. Ibid., p. 205.

24. Ibid., pp. 205, 206.

25. Ibid., p. 206.

26. Ibid.

27. Excerpted from the book *Christianity and Asian Revolution*. Quoted by Amiya Kumar Das, *Assam's Agony*, (New Delhi: Lancers, 1982), p. 178.

12

The Role of Narcotics and Arms Trafficking

The illegal narcotics trade is one of the major reasons for the continuance of insurgencies in the North-east. The consequences of trafficking in narcotics are many; for one, it is a major source of funding for the insurgent groups, the other is the spread of AIDS in nearly all the states of the North-east. The linkage between arms, drugs and insurgency depends on three inter-related factors. First, to oppose and fight the government the insurgents need weapons. In the early stages, they procure them by snatching personal arms from complacent and ill-trained police and village guards; then as they become better organised they graduate to raiding isolated police posts, often in connivance with corrupt and sympathetic policemen. Next, as the struggle intensifies, the insurgents need more sophisticated weapons to challenge the firepower of the state for which they need funds. Very often illicit trade in narcotics is the best source to raise funds.

In the past, India's North-east was not a producer of narcotics; whatever little was produced was for local consumption and not for illicit trade, which is a post independence phenomenon. Unlike other insurgencies, for example the LTTE of Sri Lanka that is deeply involved in illicit drug trade, the insurgents of North-east India have so far relied on other means to raise funds. We have already documented in the Chapter on Assam how ULFA soon after its formation went on a rampage to rob banks and extort money from tea gardens to buy arms from the Kachin insurgents in Myanmar.

In Nagaland and Manipur insurgent groups routinely collect taxes from each household, government contractors and employees, transporters, businessmen and even government officials including ministers. But the situation is fast changing; insurgent groups have begun to trade in illicit narcotics to raise funds to keep the insurgency going.

KMT and the American Connection[1]

It will be interesting to digress a little to focus on how illicit trade started in this region. It all started with the American assistance to the KMT, the defeated nationalist forces of Chiang Kai Shek, which had retreated to Taiwan by May 1949. After the capture of Yunan by Mao's People's Liberation Army (PLA), stragglers from the defeated KMT fled to Myanmar. A part of this force under Chen-Wei trekked down to Mong Pong in the extreme South-east of Shan state and established contact with Taipei. Their declared intention was to regroup with some 5,000 other KMT remnants, who had fled to Laos and reconquer Chiang's lost provinces, starting with Yunan. Chiang decided to reinforce them.

At this stage the Korean war started. The North Koreans crossed the 38th parallel in June 1950 backed by China and as a consequence the Americans entered the war. Although officially the Americans were not involved with KMT in Myanmar, special covert operation was started to interfere with communist activities in South-east Asia. KMT forces were supplied by air from bases in Taipei and Bangkok with American assistance. Encouraged by the Americans, KMT made two abortive intrusions in Yunan in 1951, but the expected rebellion inside Yunan failed to materialise despite American support. Another attempt in August 1952 also failed that forced the KMT to hold the line against the communists in Myanmar.

The operations required finances. KMT was now controlling Trans-Salween highlands, where high quality opium grew. Yunan opium farmers flooded the highlands to escape Mao's ban on opium cultivation in China. Ironically, the opium traders were all Chinese. KMT imposed opium tax on farmers regardless of the type of crops they grew. Poppy cultivation with KMT encouragement spread to the hills including areas bordering India's North-east. The American sponsored secret war continued till January 1961, when the Burmese Army backed by the PLA took control of the KMT base at Mong Pa Lio and drove them to Laos. By now KMT decade long presence in Myanmar had created a thriving narcotics industry, which KMT continued to exploit from its bases in Thailand. When KMT stragglers had trekked to Myanmar in 1949, Rangoon was at war with six insurgencies. Almost no opium grew in areas of rebellion, and none of the rebels dealt in narcotics trade. By 1989 nearly all insurgent groups depended in some measure on the drug trade to finance their armies.

Linkages Between Narcotics and Arms Smuggling

The illicit trafficking in narcotics is often linked to arms smuggling, insurgency and organised crime. Illegal trade in narcotics and arms generate billion of dollars in the black market and is the major source of funding terrorism, insurgency and organised crime, which have international ramifications. It is inconceivable to fight them without fighting the menace of drug trafficking. Black money has given rise to money laundering, which is defined "as the conversion of profit from illegal activities into financial assets which appear to have legitimate origins." Money laundering has become far easier with international borders becoming more and more porous: the loopholes in the international financial system enabling traffickers to disguise the ownership, purpose, source and final resting place of drug money.

Narcotics Trade and the North-east

There are two major centres of drug production in Asia; the Golden Crescent comprising Afghanistan, North West Frontier

Province of Pakistan and the Central Asian Republics and the Golden Triangle comprising Myanmar, Thailand and Laos: these areas flank India in the North-west and North-east respectively. Myanmar has enormous lead over the other opium producing areas. There has been a sharp increase in the production of opium in Myanmar since 1989. This is mainly linked to the disintegration of the Communist Party of Burma in April 1989. The ex soldiers of the CPB are now involved in the drug trade. The Tatmadaw (the Burmese Army) has neither the ability nor the will to deal with the situation. Besides, the Military *Junta* in Myanmar takes a lenient view of drug trafficking in its rebellious ethnic states.

In India illicit cultivation of poppy takes place in the Himalayan foothills of Kashmir and Uttar Pradesh and in the North-east along India-Myanmar border but the production is insignificant and does not figure in the trafficking scheme. In India domestic heroin of choice is the heroin base or the brown sugar. This drug originates in India and is usually trafficked to Nepal, Bangladesh, Sri Lanka and Maldives. Since 1999, Indian officers have begun to seize small quantities of refined heroin destined for Sri Lanka and Europe. Government officials estimate that 30 percent of heroin seizure are of Indian origin and acknowledge India's emerging status as a heroin producing country.[2] Apart from poppy cultivation, India is a producer of Mandrax and other synthetic drugs like met amphetamines including 'ecstasy' produced in Myanmar that have found significant markets in India.

Earlier it was believed that states like Manipur, Mizoram and Nagaland are only links in the smuggling route, but it should be remembered that poppy cultivation in Manipur and Tripura is quite well spread. Ukhrul and Senapati districts of Manipur produce high-quality cannabis (Ganja), which moves in truckloads to Bihar and UP and thence to Nepal for its final destination in Western countries. Poppy cultivation is prevalent in Eastern Mizoram along Myanmar border. Over 100 acres under crop were destroyed between 1983 and 1987. Poppy cultivation is also prevalent in Lungleigh along the border with Bangladesh[3] There is evidence of poppy cultivation in Behiang in Churachandpur district of Manipur.[4] Poppy is also grown illicitly in Tirap, Chaglang, Lohit and Upper Siang districts of Arunachal Pradesh and Chandel district of Manipur.

Acetic Anhydride Seizure in India

A related problem is the illicit production of chemicals, which are required in the manufacture of narcotic drugs and psychotropic substance. Acetic Anhydride is used in the manufacture of heroin, which is the commonest drug abuse in South Asia. India is one of the largest manufacturers of acetic anhydride, which is smuggled from India into Myanmar and Pakistan. The chemical (called precursor) is required to convert raw opium into heroin. Ease of logistics has led to refineries being set up along the Indian border as well, and this explains the spurt of heroin supply into Nagaland and Manipur in recent years. The table below shows the quantity of acetic anhydride seized in India between 1992 and 1998.

Table 1: Seizure of Acetic Anhydride (1992-97)

Year	Amount in litres
1992	11, 530
1993	19, 758
1994	47, 740
1995	9, 282
1996	4, 627
1997	8, 311
1998	onwards data not available

Source: UNDCP Chemical Control in the *Fight Against Illicit Drug Production*, 1997. Quoted in Binalakshmi Nepram, *South Asia's Fractured Frontier; Armed Conflict, Narcotics and Small Arms Proliferation in India's North-east.*

Trafficking Routes in the North-east

Narcotics from Myanmar find their way into international markets, mainly to USA and the Western countries, via Thailand, China (Kunming), Myanmar and Eastern India. Both China and Thailand have cracked down on heroin smuggling in recent years. This has forced the drug cartels to find exit routes through North-east India. An official report prepared in August 1999 pointed out that Manipur, Mizoram and Nagaland together account for the smuggling of 20 kg of heroin everyday.[5] The above three North-eastern states have common border with Myanmar and, therefore, fall on the transit route of smuggling of narcotics, mainly to the Western countries. According to officials of narcotics cell in Manipur, the major routes in the region are Behiang on the Churachandpur-Imphal route, Moreh, Kanjong in Ukhrul district and Somrah. The International Narcotics Control Board in its annual report for the year 2000 has mentioned that Manipur, Nagaland and Mizoram bordering Myanmar are the most vulnerable areas along the new drug trafficking routes. The areas to watch are Moreh, Champhai and Mokokchung.[6]

Insurgents in the North-east are believed to be involved in narcotics smuggling from the Golden Triangle, although it is not yet all-pervasive.[7] A Home Ministry report says "- - as far as North-east states of India are concerned, there are clear intelligence reports to indicate that the Naga underground organisation is involved in trafficking of drugs and precious stones since 1981. The insurgent group of Manipur is also involved in trafficking of drugs." This assessment is backed by other analysts who see the violent clashes between Kukis and Nagas to control Moreh, a trading centre on Indo-Myanmar border, as a life and death struggle to control the trade in narcotics. However, a Manipuri researcher, Binalakshmi Nepram, disagrees and points out that the Manipuri insurgents in their anti-drug campaign have shot dead hundreds of drug addicts and drug peddlers.[8] This could be a ploy by insurgent groups to camouflage the illegal trade with social programme. Trafficking in narcotics and threatening drug users with dire consequences go on simultaneously. The result has been to drive addicts from the towns to the countryside and disperse urban concentrations, thus making surveillance difficult.[9]

1989 saw a change in the pattern of drug abuse in Mizoram from expensive heroin to cheap and legally available drugs such as Morphine, Cannabis, Pethadene, Diazepan, Nitrasum and Phensyde. The change in pattern was caused by two factors, first the crackdown on heroin smuggling in 1988 and the second, ban on Indian Made Foreign Liquor (IMFL) and introduction of prohibition in Mizoram in the same year.[10] This led to use of drugs, which were legally available in chemist shops. But the trend in Manipur had changed from morphine to heroin in the mid-eighties. Since then North-eastern states had over 1,10,000 drug addicts and over 6,871 HIV positive cases. Manipur had nearly eight percent of India's total HIV positive cases and ranked third in India. 76 percent of HIV positive cases in Manipur were intravenous drug users.[11]

Drug Abuse in the North-east

The prevalence of drugs has led to sharp increase in the spread of AIDS in the North-east. In Manipur the first case of HIV positive was detected in Imphal jail in July 1990. Sample HIV tests on two batches of 28 and 250 revealed as many as 80-85 percent positive cases. Soon after a few AIDS deaths were reported. The confessions of a drug queen with clientele reaching high places indicate that addiction has permeated all levels of society. It was initially believed that AIDS was mainly spread through shared needles in intravenous injection of drug but the role of permissive sex could not be ignored. In 1993-94 some 0.8 percent of pregnant women tested were found HIV positive against a nil finding in 1990.[12]. The prevalence of HIV positive cases is maximum in the Imphal Valley and in urban centres along the national and state highways. In Mizoram in a survey carried out in 1994, 1407 persons were found drug addicts, out of which 109 were females.[13] The prevalence of AIDS and HIV positive cases in Nagaland and Meghalaya is also widespread.

Arms Trafficking

A brief overview of illicit arms trafficking is now in order. After the split in the underground Naga movement in 1980 over the Shillong Accord (1975), the NSCN emerged as the most powerful insurgent group in the North-east. It has collected a formidable arsenal of small arms including AK rifles and rocket propelled grenades. Over the years, it has become the prime vector of proliferation of small arms in the region by virtue of its access to clandestine arms market of South-east Asia. Not only the access to clandestine market, it also controls the route through which such arms are smuggled into North-east. Most of the contraband weapons that flow into North-east originate in Cambodia, which has a surplus of such weapons from the Pol Pot days. South-east Asia arms cartels are also reported to buy weapons from erstwhile 'East Block' countries. Such weapons are then smuggled to the small islands off the South coast of Thailand-Myanmar border. It is believed that the route to South Asia begins in the Rangong Islands off the Thai coast from where contraband are shipped through Andaman Sea and landed in Cox Bazaar from where the arms are carried in smaller caches to different destinations in Myanmar and North-east India.[14] Some of the arms are taken to CHT from where they enter the North-east region via Mizoram, Tripura or further up through the North Cachar Hills and Karbi Anglong into Nagaland. Arms are carried even further up to Sylhet and enter Meghalaya through Dawki and Baghmara from where they pass into Assam through Mankachar in Assam's Dhubri district and then through Siliguri and Dooars into Bhutan.[15]

Appraisal

In the modern day insurgency, drug trafficking and gunrunning go hand in hand. While drug money is used to procure arms, arms sale in turn go to finance drug trafficking. Illicit cultivation of poppy crop benefit the whole of the population where it is grown; the profits help improve the daily life of the producer, the trafficker and the street peddlers. As a petty dealer in Moreh puts it: "It is good money, enough to find a wife."[16]

Although drug trafficking in India's North-east is yet to become a major problem and all-pervasive, yet North-east India is fast emerging as the single most important transit point in the smuggling of narcotics in South-east Asia. The temptation is too great to resist. A kilogram of heroin at Moreh costs relatively modest rupees 4,00,000 or so. A courier gets rupees 10,000 to transport the drug from Moreh to Imphal.[17] According to UNDCP, *World Drug Report, 2000,* the average retail price of one gram of heroin in India in 1999 was $ 5.2, while that in Netherlands was $ 42.5, in Canada $ 187.3, and in the USA $ 475.[18] The Narcotics Control Bureau Annual Report 2000-2001 puts the total heroin seizures in the North-east as 10,280 kg and 8,000 kg for the years 1999 and 2000 respectively.

The traffickers are often the leaders of insurgent groups across the border like the Zomi Revolutionary Army, which supply heroin in exchange for arms to fight against the army in Myanmar. Though local officials of narcotics cell in Imphal rule out the involvement of local groups, custom officials on the Indo-Myanmar border suggest the connivance of local groups. As observed earlier, the insurgent groups in Manipur depend mainly on extortion for raising funds, yet as the state coffers dry up, they look for alternate source of funding. It has been observed that both NSCN (IM) and NSCN (K) have been collecting 20 percent tax on the value of drugs passing through their area of control.[19] NH 39 has become a vital link in an increasingly important route leading out of the Golden Triangle.

The record of seizures by Narcotics and Border Affairs Cell at Imphal shows an increasing trend in heroin seizures. As other avenues for fund raising dry up due to greater accountability being called for in the spending of public funds, insurgent groups will begin to depend more and more on drug trafficking to fill their coffers.

Notes and References

1. For a comprehensive account of KMT-American connection in the secret war in Myanmar, see Shelby Tucker, *Burma: The Curse of Independence*, (London: Pluto Press, 2001), pp. 164-167.
2. US Strategic Report on Narcotic Drugs, 2001. Quoted by Soma Ghosal, *The Politics of Drugs and India's North-east*, (New Delhi: Anamika Publishers, 2003), p. 91 for Maulana Azad Institute of Asian Studies, Kolkata.
3. BG Verghese, *India's North-east Resurgent*, (New Delhi: Konark Publishers, 1996), p. 158.
4. Soma Ghosal, n. 2., p. 65. Quoting interview with officials of Narcotics and Border Affairs cell in Imphal.
5. Binalakshmi Nepram, *South Asia's Fractured Frontier: Armed Conflict, Narcotics and Small Arms Proliferation in India's North-east*, (New Delhi: Mittal Publication, 2002), p. 121.
6. "Indo-Burma Border could become a Major Drug Production Area", INCB, *News at Mizzima.com*. February 21, 2001. Quoted by Soma Ghosal, n. 2., p. 64.
7. Anindita Dasgupta, 'A View from North-east India' in Dipankar Banerjee, ed, *South Asia at Gun Point*, (Sri Lanka-Colombo: Regional Centre for Strategic Studies, 2001), p. 26.
8. Binalakshmi Nepram, n. 5., p. 123.
9. BG Verghese, n. 3., p. 133.
10. Ibid., p 158
11. Binalakshmi Nepram, n. 5., pp. 116.
12. BG Verghese, n. 3., p. 132.
13. Ibid., p. 156.

14. In February 1998, the Indian Navy in an operation code-named Operation Leech intercepted a major shipment of contraband weapons off the coast of Andaman Islands. In the encounter six members of Arakan Army, an ethnic insurgent group of Myanmar, were killed and 36 were arrested. 37 Thai fishermen who had assisted them were also taken into custody. Quoted by Anindita Dasgupta, n. 7., p. 37.
15. *The Sentinel*, Guwahati, February 15, 1997.
16. Anindita Dasgupta, "Small Arms Proliferation in North-east India: A Case Study of Assam", *Economic and Political Weekly*, January 6, 2001, p. 62.
17. Quoted by Soma Ghosal, n. 2., p. 64.
18. Quoted by Soma Ghosal, Ibid., p. 66.
19. Ibid., p. 65.

13

THE ETHNIC AND LINGUISTIC FACTORS

One of the most distinguishing features of the North-east is its ethnic diversity. The ethnic composition has already been discussed in Chapter 2. Here, the influence of ethnicity on the social, religious and political life of the North-east and how it has impacted insurgency will be examined. Broadly the area is inhabited by three groups of people – the hill tribes, the plain tribal and the non-tribal population of the plains. All the three groups are heterogeneous. Hills have more than 100 tribes of Mongoloid origin. There are ethnic groups with their origins in Indo-Burman, Indo-Tibetan, Austroloid, Kuki-Lushai, Meiteis-Chin-Kuki, Shan Tais and Indo-Aryan people.

The North-east was never a part of Mauryan, Gupta or Mughal empires, although there was interaction between the people of Assam and the empires in the Gangetic plains. The British incorporated the area into the Indian Empire, but much of the tribal territory was kept unadministered as a matter of tribal policy. Although Arunachal Pradesh (then NEFA) was more secluded than other parts of the North-east, yet it had larger contact with Tibetan people across the Himalayas and the plain tribals in the Brahmaputra Valley. The sanskritisation of Brahmaputra Valley was fairly extensive by the 12th century. Buddhism spread to parts of Arunachal not through Bihar in the west but from Tibet in the north. Hence, the Buddhist influences along the boundaries of Arunachal such as in Bomdila, Tawang, Tuting and Sikkim (Lepchas and Bhutias).

The Ahoms brought Tai faith in the 13th century. In due course they adopted Hindu faith, but it was Sankaradeva in the 15th century who spread the Vaishnavite movement across the land, particularly in Brahmaputra and Imphal Valleys. The various ethnic groups of Assam in the Brahmaputra Valley shaped themselves into a single entity during the 600 years rule of Ahoms, who fought back the Mughal invaders and kept them out of Assam.

But it was the advent of Christianity in the middle of the 19th century that gave a sense of distinct and separate identity to the tribal communities in the hills. The contribution of Christianity in the field of education and health is remarkable. Although the motivation was undoubtedly to proselytise, Christian missionaries gave the tribals a written language and script, often English and Roman script, which brought about awareness and a sense of group identity.

The other factor that brought fundamental change in the thinking of tribal leaders in the North-east, particularly in the Naga and Lushai Hills, was the World War II. The battles, which were fought by the British in Kohima and Imphal against the Japanese, left an indelible mark on the thinking of the people in this area. The period between 1942-45 would be a great watershed in the history of South-east Asia and ethnic belts stretching across international demarcations. The entire region, with Bangkok standing at the geo-political centre, was caught in the ethnic revival. By briefly occupying the region, Japan had willy-nilly, transformed the once docile millions of South-east Asia into freedom fighters.[1]

The ethnic explosion that took place soon after the end of the World War II was rooted in historical circumstances. European colonialism had caused much distress and deprivation in South-east and South Asia. So it was natural that there was strong resentment against the dominance, either by the white colonialists or by the local majority over ethnic minorities. For example, if the Nagas were generally anti-Indian and Ahoms anti-Bengali on the Indian side, the Kachins and Karens were anti-Burmese on the other side. "To go further, Indonesia's Sarekat Island was anti-Chinese rather than anti-Dutch in the first years, and the anti-Indian and anti-Chinese riots in Myanmar in the late 1930s, offers sharp contrast to the absence of comparable violence against the British nationals."[2]

There is a view, particularly amongst the plainsmen, that the sense of separateness amongst the tribals was caused by the spread of Christianity, which in due course took the form of insurgency. This view is refuted by authors such as Nibedon, who argue that ethnicity was the prime mover, the fundamental cause for the spread of insurgency.[3] In his view Christianity played a secondary role. It will, however, be fair to observe that the sense of ethnic separateness was indeed accentuated by Christianity.

In Mizoram, MNF aroused tribal symbolism to facilitate tribal fervour and solidarity. Christianity was also used for the same purpose. The missionary's contribution in providing the solidarity symbols to Mizos was significant in crystallising Mizo ethnicity. A promise of the land of Mizos also implied a land of Christians. This tribal symbolism and Christianity were blended into a new political religion of the MNF, which attracted not only the youth but others as well. [4]

In Manipur, the Meiteis who were converted to Vaishnavite Hinduism were exposed to Naga and Mizo ethnicity on their flanks. The Nagas were demanding Greater Nagaland comprising parts of Manipur, so were the Mizos demanding parts of Manipur and Tripura. The Meiteis found themselves in an unenviable position; three-fourths of their population would be concentrated in one-tenths of the land, while one-fourth of the tribal population would be covering nine-tenths of the land.

When the Naga and Mizo insurgencies were at its peak in 1960s, the Meiteis though sharing a common identity symbol, that of being Hindus with the rest of country, felt discriminated. It did not bring them any gain, on the contrary the Central Government showed marked preference for the Nagas living in the hills of Manipur. The perceived discrimination was the beginning of cultural revivalism amongst the Meiteis, who have since then tended to renounce their Hindu identity and revive old Sanamahi culture.[5]

The Assamese are threatened by the large influx of illegal immigrants from Bangladesh, the consequences of which have been discussed in Chapter 2. But the Assamese fear of the loss of their identity and culture stems not only from illegal immigration, but also equally from Bengali chauvinism and cultural imperialism. As a result Assamese began asserting their closeness to Mongoloid groups. The 3,00,000 Ahoms, mainly in Sibsagar district, have always been asserting their ethnic links with the Shans of Myanmar. There is a trend towards highlighting the ancestral link of the people of North-east with the people of South-east Asia. The nostalgia for finding socio-religious roots in a country from where a community (Ahoms) had emigrated 600 years ago is understandable but beyond a certain point it becomes a cause for concern. An All Assam Tai Sabha was formed recalling the Ahom's Mongoloid roots, which later became Ahom-Tai Mongolia Rajya Parishad – an ethno-political body in 1968.[6] The same year they put forward the demand for a separate state in upper Assam for Tai-Ahoms. A sense of alienation amongst Hindus of Mongoloid origin, though fully integrated with the Assamese society, has lately prompted them to discover a new identity and look for supplementary roots.

Besides ethnicity the language issue has been even more contentious and divisive. After the conquest of Assam in 1826, the British made Bengali as the official language of the province.

It was only after much struggle that Assamese was reinstated as the official language, the credit for which goes to a Baptist Missionary, especially a man called Miles Bronson, who prepared the first Anglo-Assamese dictionary and published the first Assamese newspaper *'Orundoi.'* Resentment against Bengali amongst most Assamese springs from Bengalese record of active collaboration with the British in suppressing Assamese.

Assamese resentment for Bengali language was manifested in many language riots after Independence. The first language riot took place in early 50s. The second widespread riots took place in the beginning of the 60s, triggered by the passage of Assam Language Act and the third in the 70s, triggered by the move to impart instructions in Assamese in the Universities of Guwahati and Dibrugarh.[7] According to the veteran journalist VIK Sareen: "The main objective of Assamese is to make Assam the land of the Assamese, in which Assamese language and culture would play the same dominant role that Bengali language and culture plays in West Bengal."[8] Ironically, Assamese fell prey to the same type of chauvinism that they accused Bengalese of. The language policy of Assam was one of the major causes of disintegration of Assam resulting in the carving out of smaller states like Meghalaya and Mizoram.

The Meiteis of Manipur have also nursed a sense of discrimination against Manipuri language. Among the North-east states, Manipur has a script that is more than a century old. It has been recognised as one of the advanced modern languages of India by the Sahitya Academy. Meteilon is the only medium of communication among various tribes of Manipur. And yet, the Manipuri language was not included in the Eighth Schedule of the Constitution. Manipur had to wait for 25 years before its language was included in the Eighth Schedule.

In Tripura, the question of script has aroused controversy since the Maharaja's days. Kok-Borok, a Tibeto-Burmese language in common use among a cluster of tribes including Tripuri, Reangs and Noatia, has been written in Bengali script. Recently, TTAADC decided to introduce Roman script for Kok-Borok. This has generated controversy and has divided the tribals and the Bengalese even further.

The Bodos have also used language for ethnic consolidation. As stated earlier the language policy of Assam was divisive. PTCA had boycotted the General Election in 1967 demanding the creation of tribal belts and blocks in tribal majority areas where non-tribals would not be allowed to possess or buy land. The boycott of 1967 election had one positive outcome for the Bodos; it gained for the Bodo language the status of medium of instruction at the secondary stage in Bodo majority areas. Simultaneously, ABSU and the Bodo Sahitya Sabha jointly launched a movement in 1974-75 for the adoption of Roman script for Bodo language, which was being written in Assamese script. As a spoken language Bodo language had no script of its own. The Assam Government tried to crush the agitation but it only made Bodos more determined. Ultimately, Devnagari script was accepted for the Bodo language on the promptings of Indira Gandhi. This further widened the gap between the Bodos and Assamese.

Language is closely linked with ethnicity. In Assam, it was one of the main issues to assert Assamese identity and to fight the perceived cultural imperialism of the Bengalese. In Manipur, the rejection for 25 years of the claim of Manipuri for inclusion in the Eighth Schedule was a major factor in the alienation of Meiteis from the Indian nationalism.

Notes and References

1. Nirmal Nibedon, *North-east India: The Ethnic Explosion*, (New Delhi: Lancers, 1981), p. 14.. Nibedon Biswas, the youngest son of late Dr K Biswas, Bishop of Assam, was correspondent for *Hindustan*

Samachar between 1968-72. Married to a Naga girl, he signs all his writings without his family name.

2. Ibid., p.15.
3. Ibid., p.16.
4. For a scholarly analysis of the role played by ethnicity in Mizo politics See Urmila Phadnis, *Ethnicity and Nation Building in South Asia*, (New Delhi: Sage Publications, 1989), pp. 148-164.
5. For greater insight See VIK Sareen, *India's North-east in Flames*, (New Delhi: Vikas Publishers, 1980), pp. 116-118.
6. BG Verghese, *India's North-east Resurgent*, (New Delhi: Konark Publishers, 1996), pp. 80-81.
7. For a fuller account of language riots and its role in ethnic consolidation of Assam See VIK Sareen, n. 5., Ch – The Spectre of Linguism.
8. Ibid., p. 70.

14

Counter-Insurgency Operations

Prior to 20th century guerrilla warfare was regarded as purely military form of conflict. It was the weapon of the weak against the strong. The guerrillas employed ' hit and run' tactics against their adversaries. This form of warfare was also applied to the role of irregular troops acting as partisans in support of conventional forces. Guerrilla warfare as a means to wage war came into prominence in the last century against colonial occupation. In the middle of the last century, guerrilla war took a new characteristic when political factors were grafted on irregular military tactics.[1] Dissident groups initially in minority and weaker than authorities, would seek power through a combination of subversion, propaganda and military action in the form of guerrilla warfare. The process came to be termed insurgency.[2] After the World War II insurgencies became the major threat to governments all over the world.

Contrary to experience, regular soldiers in most democratic armies believe that they exist primarily to fight conventional wars. Between 1960-63 John F Kennedy identified communist inspired insurgency as the predominant threat to American interests. Kennedy's National Security Action Memorandum No 124 of January 18, 1962 saw insurgency as a major form of politico-military conflict equal in importance to conventional warfare.[3] Modern British doctrine is heavily based on North-West Europe campaign of 1944-45. Yet, out of 94 separate operational commitments between 1945-1982, only 14 were not in some form of low intensity conflicts. Indeed, the British Army' only significant recent conventional experience has been 35 months of participation in the Korean War (1950-1953) when only five infantry battalions were deployed at any one time, followed by 10 days at Suez in 1956 and 24 days of land campaign in thc Falklands in 1982 and 100 hours of land operation in the Gulf (1990-1991).[4] The second Gulf War in Iraq has already turned into an insurgent war.

The Indian experience has been mixed. Soon after Independence the army fought a bitter war against the newly created state of Pakistan over Kashmir (1947-1948), followed by a short war of 21 days in 1965, once again over Kashmir, and finally the war with Pakistan in December 1971, lasting not more than a fortnight, but with a decisive victory over Pakistan, which resulted in the creation of yet another state - Bangladesh. In 1962, the Indian Army fought a border war with China, which lasted for about a month in October-November, resulting in India's humiliating defeat. But only a very small component of the Indian Army was involved in actual fighting. The air force was kept out of the war. In the closing year of the 20th century, India once again fought a conventional border war with Pakistan on the line of control in the Kargil sector of Jammu and Kashmir, lasting six weeks. The war was confined to a geographical area and only two divisions of the army were involved in combat. As against the intermittent commitment in conventional wars, the Indian Army has been fighting insurgency almost continuously since Independence. The army was called out in Nagaland to quell insurgency in 1956, and since then it has been involved in counter-insurgency operations not only there but in almost all of North-east in an ever widening area of operations. In 1984 the army was called out to restore order in the Punjab and launched the infamous Operation Bluestar, which led to virtual insurgency that was put down at great human and economic cost by the Punjab Police, assisted by the army and the para-military forces. By the time the situation in the Punjab was brought under control in the early nineties, Kashmir was aflame with insurrection aided and abetted by Pakistan. The proxy war in Kashmir continues till today. In between nearly four divisions of the army were deployed in Sri Lanka to fight the insurgent LTTE in accordance with the India-Sri Lanka Accord of 1987. The Indian Peace Keeping Force (IPKF) was finally pulled out in March 1990, but not before suffering about 1,100 dead and many more maimed for life in the fighting. The irony was that by the time the force was pulled out, it was detested not only by the LTTE but also by the Sri Lankan Government and the State Government of Tamil Nadu. The casualties suffered by the army in counter-insurgency operations far exceed the sum of figures in conventional wars.

Counter-insurgency operations have provided the staple operational fare for the Indian Army more than any other except, perhaps, the Israeli Army, and yet it has not received the attention it deserves. In most armies counter-insurgency operations are regarded unglamorous, where success cannot be easily measured in decisive battles won and results are not immediately visible. In the Indian Army this attitude is reflected in senior officers aspiring to command formations in areas where they have an opportunity to display their flair for large/small manoeuvres on maps and sand-models, which have lost much of their relevance in the changed world, or formations deployed for defence on the borders where there is little scope for experimentation or creativity. A few jockey to escape the daily rigours, hardships and uncertainties of a prolonged insurgent war. But the perspectives are changing and the role of the army is being re-defined. This is how General Shankar Roychowdhury, the former chief of the army and presently member of the Rajya Sabha, perceives the change: " The proxy war sponsored by Pakistan in Kashmir and its linkages with insurgency and violence in the North-east and elsewhere in the country had involved us in direct and indirect battlefield contact with Pakistan for over a decade now. These externally supported low intensity conflicts had completely redefined the traditional perception of external and internal threats, as also the categorisation of primary and secondary roles of the army, which was the main force dealing with them."[5]

Evolution of Counter-Insurgency Strategy[6]

When Naga insurgency broke out in Nagaland in 1956, neither the Indian Army nor the political masters had any experience of dealing with such situations. There was no lack of goodwill for the hill tribes of the North-east amongst the policy-makers of Independent India, which was profoundly influenced by its first Prime Minister, Jawaharlal Lal Nehru. Yet, when the unrest slowly spread to other parts and soon engulfed the whole of the North-east, the political leadership was slow to grasp the nature of insurgency and evolve a coherent policy, which took a tortuous path – from military solution to winning the hearts and minds of disaffected tribes.

Soon after Independence, Nehru enunciated what came to be called the 'Tribal Panchsheel': "People should develop along the lines of their own genius; Tribals rights in land and forest should be protected; train and build-up a team of their own people to administer and develop. Some technical help, from outside, will be needed. But we should avoid introducing too many outsiders into tribal areas; we should not over administer the area and overwhelm them with too many schemes. Work through and not in rivalry to their (tribals) institutions. Judge results not by statistics or the amount of money spent, but by the quality of human character that is involved."[7] The above broadly constituted the policy framework around which the development of the tribal areas was to be accomplished.

In a reversal of the British policy of keeping the hill tribes isolated from the mainstream of Indian life, Nehru was keen to develop national consciousness amongst the hill tribes of the North-east. There is a view that British deliberately kept the tribes isolated from the rest of the country to preserve them as 'museum specimens.' Verrier Elwin refutes this charge in his book 'Nagaland' and claims that this has no basis in fact. According to him, there was only one reason why the British did not bring the entire area under active administrative control: it was too much trouble. After Independence the tribal policy envisaged bringing the tribal population in the development process with the rest of the country as quickly as possible, but without any outside impositions and in conformity with their own cultural ethos. In the process of development Nehru did not want them "to be swamped by people from other parts of the country" and wanted them to "live their own lives according to their own custom and desires". He was also aware of the importance of keeping the tribes contented as "they live near the frontier of India and some of the same tribes live on the other side of the border, like the Nagas in Burma. They occupy thus a strategic position of great importance, which has grown in many years. Properly treated and encouraged, they can become a bulwark of our state. Otherwise, they are a danger and a weakening factor."[8] Nehru also visualised the pitfalls in implementing the tribal policy, which he had envisioned and articulated in letters he wrote to his cabinet colleagues and chief ministers. In a letter to CD Deshmukh Nehru commented, "They (Nagas) do not get on very well with the Assamese who, in the past treated them as inferiors. They are not prepared to tolerate any stigma of inferiority from anyone. As friends, they react well."[9] To his cabinet colleagues, he wrote," We are apt to judge people in various parts of India by the same standards and measure them by the same yardstick. The fact is that they differ in many ways in their customs, ways of life etc. This is particularly so in the North-east areas, where they have been cut off from India. They are a tough and a likeable people. They can be won over by friendly treatment and alienated by any attempt to suppress them or impose different ways on them. I am afraid not many people approach them with sympathy or understanding, we go with our own ideas and presume that they are the best."[10] Nari Rustomji, one of our ablest administrators who served in the North-east for long years, observed in his book, '*The Imperilled Frontiers*', that the unrest in the North-east has arisen not from any lack of goodwill on the part of the Indian Government but from want of understanding, empathy and sensitivity. His observation captured one of the many reasons for the tribe's alienation from the plainsmen.

Minimum Force

The operations against the rebels in the North-east have been undertaken with the understanding that they are fellow citizens and not enemies. The rebels have to be won over by actions designed to 'win their hearts and minds.' This implied the use of 'minimum force'. The training manual of the Indian Army emphasises minimum force as one of the cardinal rules of engagement when called out in aid of civil authority. This was originally formulated by the British to deal with situations like crowd control, communal rioting, unruly mobs and violent political demonstrations. The scope and meaning of internal security has, however, fundamentally changed over a period of time; it now encompasses aid to civil authority in situations vastly different, which include proxy war and low intensity conflicts where the protagonists are armed with sophisticated lethal weapons. The terms of engagement formulated in the past are no longer valid and needed to be redefined. General Shankar Roychowdhury, a former army chief, defines it as 'adequate minimum force, the adequacy of weapons and firepower for each situation to be determined by the field commander. This included heavier weapons like mortars or artillery whenever required.'[11]

Ordinary people are, however, to be protected not only from the violence of the rebels but also, to the extent possible, from the collateral damage that is invariably caused in the course of counter-insurgency operations by the security forces. This philosophy was a refreshing departure from the mindset of the colonists of the past. For example, following the massacre of an American company at Balangiga in Samav Islands in September 1901, Brigadier General Jacob Smith directed that no prisoner be taken and all males over 10 years of age be executed.[12] To be fair to the Americans, Smith was court-martialled while the situation in Batangas was the subject of Senate hearing.

Isolating the Populace from Insurgents: Grouping of Villages

Intelligence is the decisive factor in counter-insurgency operations. Conversely, it is equally important to deny information to the rebels, who depend heavily on the civil population not only for intelligence but also for logistic support. This meant isolating the rebels from population centres. The concentration of civilians in guarded areas to deny the guerrillas access to food or other support was not a new idea. The Russians had introduced slow strangulation against the Murids, the fanatical Islamic monastic order led by Shamil in Caucasus in 1840s, cutting guerrillas from population by a cordon sanitaire of military outposts.[13] Beckett observes that common approaches were emerging entirely independently in different armies faced with similar difficulties. Thus in the British campaign against the Boers in the latter stages of the South African campaign, the Spanish campaign in Cuba in 1895 and 1898 and the US campaign in the Philippines between 1899 and 1902, all three armies adopted what became known as reconstruction. Ironically, when faced with Filipino insurgency after occupying the former Spanish colony, the Americans themselves were forced to adopt reconstruction. Commanded by Douglas Macarthur's father, Arthur Macarthur, the American forces began to move the rural population into town in December 1900. In the province of Batangas, Brigadier General Franklin Bell reconstructed 10,000 people into protective zones and destroyed all crops, livestock and buildings outside the zones.[14] These measures may have been acceptable military means by colonial powers to quell insurgencies in the early decades of the 20th century in the subjugated and occupied territories, the political fallout of adoption of such measures against their own citizens would have been disastrous even in the times when human rights was not an issue as it is today.

Drawing on the British experience in Malaya, Indian Army tried the concept of grouping of villages as a means to isolate the rebels from the populace. It was tried out both in Nagaland and Mizoram. In Nagaland it was given up in the face of fierce opposition from moderate Nagas. In Mizoram the experiment produced mixed results. A study of the existing literature on the Indian experience leads one to conclude that the position of the army was some where in between. It was acutely aware of the hardship it caused to the innocent civilians but was desperate to gain information and simultaneously deny it to the hostiles.

Nature of Counter-Insurgency Operations

By its very nature counter-insurgency operations are restrictive, which place impositions on the free movement and daily life of the community. For example, area domination to restrict the freedom of movement of insurgents and to instil a sense of security amongst the populace, cordon and search to flush them out from their hideouts, road opening parties to keep the major roads open for traffic and imposition of curfew along the international border to prevent them crossing over to sanctuaries across the border are steps taken by the military to fight the insurgents. Each of the above type of operations cause impediment to smooth flows of daily life but could not be avoided in situations of active insurgencies.

Employment of Air Power

The use of air power against own people, even though they may be hostiles, has always been a debatable choice. It also went against the established principle of minimum force The Air Force was used in Nagaland for dropping supplies to beleaguered garrisons under threat from hostiles, but its use for strafing was quite another matter. In Nagaland and Mizoram air power was used defensively, even though for strafing rebel positions, in desperate situations as a last resort to save garrisons from being overrun by rebel forces. The specific situations when aircraft were used for strafing have been discussed later in this chapter. Since 1960s, helicopters have been used extensively for movement of troops, casualty evacuation and reconnaissance as integral pert of counter-insurgency operations.

Political and Diplomatic Initiatives

Counter-insurgency operations are politico-military in nature. Political mobilisation and military operations are undertaken side by side to achieve lasting results. In the context of North-east insurgencies, political initiatives have been taken at two levels, internal and external. At the internal level, negotiations have resulted in accords that granted greater political and economic autonomy to the disaffected tribes. At the external level, political and diplomatic steps have been taken to deny safe sanctuaries to the insurgents in neighbouring countries. For example, movement of insurgent groups have been restricted by increased cooperation between Indian and Myanmar security forces. The installation of the government headed by Sheikh Hasina in Bangladesh in 1996 augured well for India in its fight against insurgent groups. She denied them sanctuaries in her country and restricted their movement. But her defeat in the election held in 2001 and the victory of Bangla Nationalist Party of Begum Khalede Zia dramatically changed the situation in which the North-east insurgents once again established training and base camps in Bangladesh. The importance of sanctuaries across the international borders was highlighted in 1971, when after the defeat of Pakistani forces in Bangladesh, both Naga and

Mizo insurgents lost their bases in erstwhile East Pakistan, which forced both the groups to rethink their future. Loss of sanctuary in East Pakistan and hounded by the army in their renewed bid to send fresh recruits to China through Myanmar, a section of the Nagas, in fact, signed a peace treaty with the Government in 1975, known as the Shillong Accord. The Mizos also signed a peace agreement with the Government of India in 1976 but later reneged due to intense rivalry between the underground factions for supremacy.

Re-organising of Infantry Battalions for Counter-Insurgency Operations

One of the earliest attempts to reorganise the infantry battalions for counter-insurgency tasks was the creation of (I) Battalions in the 1960s by converting some of the existing battalions drawn from some selected regiments. These units were to be permanently deployed in the Naga Hills and Tuensang Area with their personnel being periodically turned over from within their respective regiments.[15] The (I) Battalions were to be lightly equipped having minimal motor transport but more radio sets. The battalions did good work but the experiment was given up for unknown reasons. The idea was revived again in the early 90s when the requirement of forces for internal security duties increased dramatically due to enhanced threat posed by Pakistan's proxy war after Operation Bluestar. It was envisaged to raise 'a paramilitary force with army's ethos under the MoD, designated as Rashtriya Rifles. Paramilitary forces and their lobby in the MHA vehemently opposed the idea, which was expected.[16] The Rashtriya Rifles had been conceptually visualised as a specialised internal security formation with units constituted of 75 percent ex-servicemen and balance from the regular army. But it didn't work out as originally conceived. Ever since its inception the force has 100 percent deputationists from the army and has been deployed exclusively in J&K except for a brief period in the North-east.

Composition of the Assam Rifles

Assam Rifles was raised primarily for deployment in the North-east and comprised men from these areas. Over the years, the force earned a well-deserved reputation as the *Sentinels of the North-east,* for its exemplary services in keeping peace and guarding our North-eastern frontiers. Some years ago, its composition was changed to all-India force and its distinctive character diluted to one of the many para-military forces. It has thus lost its excellent rapport with the local people, so essential for gathering intelligence. Gen VP Malik, the former army chief, recommends that the force should comprise 60 to 70 percent of its personnel from the North-east.[17] He also favours 'home and hearth' units or village guards of the type raised in Arunachal in the past. Such units with as many local ex-servicemen as possible should be raised wherever border-holding forces are thin on ground.[18]

Civic Action: Winning the Hearts and Minds

Military operations against insurgents by its very nature are bound to result in some harassment and grievance to the general public, despite the best efforts of the troops. They have therefore to be balanced by effective civic actions, which touched people's lives at the grassroots. A bridge over a rivulet connecting two villages, piped water supply and/or water storage tanks, improvement of village roads, construction of playing fields, repair of school buildings, visit by army doctors to inaccessible villages and treatment of patients in regimental polyclinics touched the lives of poor tribesmen and are parts of the campaign of civic action, which the Indian Army has been executing wherever it has been called upon to undertake counter-insurgency operations. The concept is, however, not an original formulation of the Indian Army. It can nonetheless take credit for implementing it in letter and spirit. It was practised in Malaya in counter-insurgency operations against the communist guerrillas in the sixties by the British forces under

General Templer. In the expanding American empire after 1898, civic action went hand in hand with military measures in the Philippines. In keeping with the American penchant for devising new exotic phrases, they called it the 'attraction' programme, which included a variety of public works projects to improve communication and health.[19] The experiences in communist countries have been different. The methods adopted by them against internal rebellions and dissents in colonies have been ruthless. The large- scale violations of human rights of national minorities and political dissenters during the Stalinist period in erstwhile Soviet Russia have been documented in many best selling novels by Russian authors, some of which have been made into classic movies by renowned western moviemakers. The operations of China's PLA in Tibet and Xinjiang are other examples. The crackdown on peaceful demonstration for the restoration of democracy by Chinese students in Tiananmen Square and the brutalities committed on them by soldiers armed with tanks are too recent to recall.

Psychological Operations (Psy Ops)

Psy ops are powerful weapons in the hands of protagonists in any insurgent warfare. The Naga insurgents scored hands down over the administration and the army in the conduct of psy ops. The NNC had developed an expert publicity department headed until the end of 1955 by the charismatic Sakhrie and later by others. The underground propaganda has often been brilliant, carefully crafted to address the psychology of the people, and in sharp contrast to the dull and pretentious publicity work of the government.[20] "An idyllic picture, for example, there is no communal feeling, or are there religious differences, no family ever pays tax (except perhaps to the underground), we do not arrest or imprison anyone, and murder is very rare (other than headhunting, of course), somewhat divorced from reality, of a what a free Nagaland was like, was created."[21]. In a booklet published in 1953, the villagers were told that in the plains, 'unlike our country land belongs to the state and the people have to pay taxes for land, for house-sites and buildings too, for fisheries and even for forest product. They have a water tax, latrine tax, entertainment tax and road tax. Everything has to be paid for if they have to live in this world. We Nagas pay no tax'.[22] The problem of how to raise finances for a separate state did not seem to bother anyone. In Mokokchung, there was a definite attempt to win over the churches by frightening them that the Hindu Government of India would ban Christianity and force the Nagas to become Hindus, and for a time many Christians became alarmed and joined the insurgents.[23] The Nagas are very fond of meat and their rice beer, which the insurgents exploited cleverly to gain their support by propagating that the campaign by the Hindus against cow slaughter and India's policy of prohibition would one day be applied to them.

The administration's attempt at psy ops was lackadaisical. Occasionally, pamphlets were produced setting out the protections provided to the tribes in the constitution and the many schemes formulated for the development of tribal areas. Even these never got distributed to the target audience and in many cases rotted in the government offices. Occasionally the government littered the jungles with leaflets announcing amnesty as in the Mizo Hills in January 1967. There was no policy to counter the specifics of insurgent propaganda, based on half-truths, other than announcing the allocation of large funds for the development of the North-east, which did not touch the daily life of the common people. The local factors and the peculiarities of different tribes were seldom factored in the formulation of policy. In the absence of transparency in the utilisation of the central fund, it was seen as bribe by the centre to the insurgents and their sympathisers. The politician-bureaucrat-contractor nexus came to define one part of the tribal scene. The army, however, made civic action an important part of their counter-insurgency operations. 'To the insurgents, Good Samaritan (name given to civic action programme in Manipur) was a dangerous psychological offensive by the army, which they tried to discredit with all means at their disposal including smear campaign in the local media.'[24] Learning from their past experience, the army has lately produced pamphlets, e.g., 'Bleeding Assam' that give factual accounts of the amoral life and debauchery which the top leaders of ULFA indulge in the safety of Bangladesh and the brutalities committed by its cadres on innocent people of Assam. Here again, the pamphlets are in English, which is not understood by ordinary Assamese.

Human Rights

Human Rights is a recent phenomenon, but it has been the cardinal principal for engagement for the army for long when called in aid of civil authority, which demanded strict compliance to impartiality, minimum force and good faith. When one looks at the record of human right violations in the last century, it is appalling to read that in the face of emerging guerrilla activity in Boer campaign in South Africa, General Roberts ordered that houses in the vicinity of any railway lines, bridges and telegraph lines that had been attacked should be burned down or blown up. Collective fines were also imposed and Boer civilians were forced to ride on trains as a deterrent against attack.[25] Indian Army's record was more humane and practical in similar situation in Nagaland. To avoid ambushes of vehicle convoys, 50 metres on both sides of main roads were cleared of vegetation and undergrowth, which gave road-opening parties a clear view and denied the insurgents ambush sites to hide. And yet, there were cases, fortunately few, when ambushed that resulted in death and injury, soldiers burnt houses, suspected to have sheltered the insurgents, and beat up innocent bystanders or used force that was not commensurate with the situation in the heat of the moment to avenge their dead comrades.

By the very nature counter-insurgency operations are restrictive and cause inconveniences to people and interfered with their daily chores. There was no way how vehicle searches, frisking of individuals, cordon and searches of villages or a group of houses, roadblocks and night curfews in selected areas could be avoided. It was possible to mitigate the inconveniences, but could not be fully eliminated. As the army gained experience, it did all it could to avoid inconvenience to innocent villagers. The insurgents exploited the collateral damage to civilian property and death or injury to innocent civilians in encounters with them to tarnish the image of soldiers as trigger-happy. In most cases the allegations of atrocities by soldiers were exaggerated, if not wholly false. This is how Verrier Elwin, who lived many years with the tribes of the North-east and influenced the tribal policy of Nehru, describes the situation: "From the very beginning the rebels made great play with the allegations of atrocities on the part of the police and other security forces. The booklet already quoted, which was issued in 1953 by the Naga Goodwill Mission to Assam, goes so far as to say that the government of India had instructed their Indian Armed Forces to rape Naga women whenever and wherever possible."[26] It also accuses them of stealing food and drink from Naga houses, fruit and vegetable from their gardens and grain from their fields and 'violating the sanctity of our religion and our custom.'

The Indian Army has come a long way since it was called out to meet the challenges of an extraordinary situation in Naga Hills in 1956. In the early years human right violations, as we understand the term today, were committed not out of any hostility or antipathy towards the Naga people, but soldiers reacted under grave provocation to avenge the death of their comrades, which were invariably spontaneous and seldom pre-meditated. One of the former Chief of the Army Staff, late General BC Joshi, issued the Ten Commandments for troops employed in counter-insurgency operations in Kashmir and the North-east:

- No rape.
- No molestation.
- No torture resulting in death or maiming.
- No military disgrace (Loss of arms, surrender, loss of post or imbibing un-army like culture).
- No meddling in civil administration (land disputes or quarrels).
- Competence in platoon/company tactics.
- Willingly carry out civic action.
- Develop media interaction (use it as force multiplier and not force degrader).
- Respect Human Rights.
- Only fear God, uphold Dharma (Ethical mode of life-the path of righteousness) and enjoy serving the country.

The National Human Rights Commission in its 1994-95 report noted: "The Commission welcomes the instructions of the Chief of the Army Staff and Corps Commanders as evidence of growing sensitivity amongst armed forces personnel to human rights matter.... the example of armed forces leadership (in the human rights matter) need to be followed at all levels."

Media Policy

In the 1950s when insurgency broke out in Nagaland, there was hardly any interaction between the army and the media. There were many constraints. The means of communication were very limited; the existing network of road and railways passed through the then East Pakistan, which became inoperative after partition. The Brahmaputra was bridged only in 1961. The radio and telegraph links were primitive. The existing government policy permitted the army interaction with the media, mainly print and radio (there was no television or multi media then), through the government's public relation officers, who were very few and not at all trained to handle news or analyse them. All that they did was to give news of ambushes and the encounters with the hostiles. Even these were reported in the national newspapers much after the events. The army itself depended on BBC for the latest news and political developments and their analysis. Mark Tully and Subir Bhaumik, the BBC correspondents who covered, (Subir Bhaunik still does) the happenings in the North-east from their base at Calcutta, became known names for radio listeners and enjoyed huge popularity even as some of their reporting was biased against the army. In the absence of news from the official channels, BBC Hindi service became extremely popular and also credible. The situation was redeemed later by reporters of some of the national and local newspapers, who went on to write excellent accounts of their reporting days in the North-east.[27]

The insurgents made better use of the opportunities to interact with the media. Fortuitously their access to BBC reporters helped them to freely project their views not only within the country, but more importantly to the western public, who had not yet got over the bias against their erstwhile colonial subjects. Some foreign journalists and newspaper correspondents were allowed to visit the principal towns of Naga Hills in December 1960 to see things for themselves, but the insurgent leaders described the visit as stage-managed.[28] Almost a year later Gavin Young, a British journalist, who was granted entry into Naga Hills wrote a one-sided perverted account of the situation in Naga Hills on his return to England.

As communications improved and North-east opened to the outside world and travel restrictions were relaxed, army's interaction with the media also became more frequent. But the old restriction of interacting through public relation officers continued. The army has felt circumscribed by the restriction on interaction with the media even for legitimate reasons to explain its viewpoint on issues for which the best spokesman would be the army itself. To get over the hurdle the army got around the existing orders and delegated responsibility for direct on-the-spot interaction with the media down to command and corps headquarters in respect of their own theatres and sectors on matters of internal security. Command headquarters, at their discretion, could delegate this responsibility down the line. This was not to the liking of the MoD, 'who had launched a sort of in-house guerrilla warfare with the army headquarters.' [29]

Unified Command

Counter-insurgency operations being politico-military in nature civil-military relationship have to be synergetic, which in the North-east has for most part been strained. In that context, the enhancement of army's public image as an instrument of social and economic change is viewed with suspicion and is opposed by both politicians and bureaucrats for it brings to light their inefficiency and the politician-bureaucrat-contractor nexus.[30] One of the cardinal principles of counter-insurgency operations is the unity of command, which was evolved by General Templer to fight the communist insurgency in Malaya in 1948. At the operational level it meant integrated civil-military operations under one military commander appointed by the civil government. It is obvious that the Malayan model could not be applied in the North-east, where all the states had elected popular governments. But the basic concept, suitably amended, could still be applied to maximise results.

The concept of unified command in counter-insurgency operations was first experimented in Kashmir where it functioned effectively to begin with, but soon lost its way in the turf war between the various security agencies and the bureaucracy. In Assam the concept had an inauspicious start. The newly elected coalition government headed by AGP in 1996 refused to take oath unless the army was withdrawn from counter-insurgency duties. The confrontation resolved itself when the very next day there were large-scale ethnic killings of Adivasis in the tea gardens in Bodo dominated area, which required army's presence to restore order.[31] Soon good sense prevailed and a modified Kashmir model of unified command was adopted in Assam. The Chief Minister agreed to associate himself with this group, but not formally head it. A three tier system was evolved; at the top was the Strategic Planning Group (ostensibly under the chief secretary) to lay down the policy; the second tier, the Operation Group, was headed by GOC 4 Corps, the senior military commander in Assam. It was here that key operational decisions were taken; the third tier was headed by the district collector supported by the battalion commander and the superintendent of police of the area. The strategic group at the top had GOC 4 Corps, State DGP and IGs of BSF and CRPF as members. GOC 4 Corps attended the meeting whenever the Chief Minister chaired it.[32]

In Manipur, the Chief Minister insisted that the DGP of the state head the unified headquarters, which resulted in the army keeping out of it. In Tripura the situation was different; there were no army formations in Tripura. The DIG of Assam Rifles, who, if he was a serving brigadier, had army battalions serving under him. Tripura too adopted a unified headquarters model headed by the chief secretary.

Formation of North Eastern Council (NEC)

The NEC was set up with its headquarters at Shillong to formulate and implement an integrated development plan for the North-east region as a whole. The NEC was given jurisdiction in all matters of common interest in economic and social planning, inter-state transport and communication, and flood control. The Governor of Assam heads the council. The chief ministers of all North-eastern states are its members.

Although the council's main focus was on infrastructure and economic development it also had a security component; the Director General of Assam Rifles functioned ex officio as the zonal security adviser to the North-eastern state governments. Regrettably, the security function of NEC was seldom activated despite this being pointed out by Gen Shankar Roychowdhury in his report to the government when he was the army chief.[33]

We will now turn to specific counter-insurgency operations in each of the states of the North-east.

Counter-Insurgency Operations in Nagaland

Situation in Nagaland Before Army was Called in

By the beginning of 1953, situation in Nagaland had turned volatile. Phizo toured the district and exhorted the people not to pay taxes. Assam Rifles men were ambushed and killed, government buildings and houses of loyal Nagas were set on fire, telephone lines were cut and bridges destroyed. One of the worst acts of violence, which took place in November 1954, was the massacre of fifty seven villagers of Yimpang by men of Pangsha village in Tuensang area in retaliation of the murder of a dak runner, who was the son of the village headman of Pangsha. The massacre was attributed to the Indian Army in a charge sheet produced by Phizo's followers and was widely circulated by Rev Michael Scott, about whom enough has been said earlier. Nehru in Parliament refuted the charges; while refuting he said that the massacre had nothing to do with any of the Indian security forces, which were not present there at all. The incident highlights the extent to which Phizo and his followers could manipulate and distort facts.[34]

Recourse to Force

As raids and ambushes, particularly in Tuensang Division, continued despite the induction of more platoons of Assam

Rifles and one battalion of the UP Special Armed Constabulary, it was decided to call in the army. In keeping with the understanding that the rebels are fellow citizens, the Chief of the Army Staff issued an Order of the Day in 1955: "You must remember that all the people of the area in which you are operating arc fellow Indians - - - and the very fact that they are different and yet part of India is reflection of India's greatness. Some of the people are misguided and have taken to arms against their own people, and are disrupting the peace of the area. You are to protect the mass of the people from these disruptive elements. You are not there to fight the people in the area, but to protect them. You are fighting only those who threaten the people. You must, therefore do everything possible to win their confidence and respect and help them feel that they belong to India."[35]

Troops of 181 Independent Infantry Brigade under Brigadier Sukhdev Singh, VrC were the first to move to Nagaland. The move began in July 1955 and by February 1956, all the four battalions of the brigade had moved to Nagaland. Two more brigades, 201 Infantry Brigade and 192 Infantry Brigade under Brigadiers Ram Singh and Niranjan Prasad, were moved to Mokokchung and Kohima sectors respectively.[36] With the induction of additional formations, Major General RK Kochar was appointed GOC Naga Hills and Tuensang in April 1956.

Siege of Kohima

By 1956, the rebels had formed the FGN; simultaneously a military wing called the Naga Home Guard was formed. The rebels armed themselves with arms and ammunition from the dumps left behind by the British and Japanese forces after the World War II. The hostiles attacked Kohima from three different directions on June 10, 1956. They cut off telephone lines and electricity[37] and besieged the town for nearly three days when Kohima remained cut off from rest of India and the greater part of the village remained under hostile control. Phizo had given instructions to assassinate men like Jasokie, who were moderate leaders. They were given protection inside army camps till Kohima was cleared of hostiles.[38] On June 14 the hostiles under Kaito Sema had a marked success when they ambushed and killed Lt Col JR Chitins, commanding officer of 1/3 GR near Zunheboto. Chitnis had, in April 1956, busted the headquarters of Kaito in Satakha area and had inflicted heavy casualties on the Semas.[39] Chitnis was the first officer recipient of Ashoka Chakra Class I in the Naga Hills. Army reinforcement were called forcing the hostiles to lift the seize and withdraw.

Initial Losses

Increased militant activities forced the government to declare Naga Hills as Disturbed Area. By the end of 1956 the army had recovered or captured large quantities of arms and ammunition at the cost of 135 killed and 442 wounded. This was a heavy price to pay for not firing first and lack of experience in fighting a guerrilla war.[40] In the early days of the counter-insurgency operations, the army suffered heavy losses. In one of the worst setbacks, a road protection party of 9 PUNJAB was ambushed by hostiles on April 1, 1957 on road Kohima-Jaluke. 32 men were killed. It was a grievous blow, but the units were learning fast; counter-ambush drills were perfected, convoy protection was better organised and greater emphasis was laid on minor tactics and the use of ground.

The Unfortunate Killing of Haralu

An unfortunate incident took place on July 2, 1956, which was to have far reaching effect on how the army conducted operations. Dr. Haralu, a respectable old doctor was killed by a patrol of the army in the early hours of that day.[41] The army patrol had mistakenly taken Haralu as a hostile. The insurgents made much of the incident to show the army as trigger-happy. The killing of Dr Haralu overshadowed the brutal killing of Sakhrie by the followers of Phizo. Nehru made a statement in the Parliament regretting the incident. The killing highlighted the difficult terms of engagement under which troops were operating.

Grouping of Villages: The Indian Experience in Naga Hills

During the period 1957-59, a number of measures, both military and political were taken to persuade the hostile Nagas to give up their struggle. One such measure was the grouping of villages that was adopted in early 1957. The villagers were allowed to go out during day and cultivate their fields under escort but had to return to the barricaded villages before nightfall. The grouping was intended to break the supply and intelligence network of the hostiles. It did have a positive effect on the counter-insurgency operations in the short term. But a large number of villagers were separated from their land and immediate surroundings around which their lives were built. Mr BN Mullick, the Intelligence Bureau Chief, who exercised considerable influence on the formulation of policy for the administration of frontier areas because of his proximity with Nehru, supported the grouping experiment wholeheartedly. In his assessment the grouping of villages was enough to break their (Nagas) spirit of defiance, if there was any."[42] But there are others who hold the view that the grouping produced more hostiles and added to their rank rather than breaking their spirit of defiance

Raising of Village Guards

Another step taken by the civil administration was to raise a force of Naga militias or village guards, who knew the ways of the hostiles. The government armed them with muskets and rifles and supplied them uniforms. The chiefs and headmen controlled the force. The hostiles considered them a greater threat than the army columns. There were several cases where the militia fought the rebels, and though there were a few cases of betrayal, on the whole they acquitted themselves well.[43]

Political Initiative: Creation of Naga Hills–Tuensang Area

The separation of Naga Hills district from Assam and forming it into a separate administrative unit along with Tuensang sub division of NEFA with effect from December 1, 1957 and placing it under the MEA to be administered by the Governor was a timely political initiative, which compromised the influence of secessionists amongst the Nagas. This was all the more important for the announcement of the separation from Assam and creation of an enlarged district as it came soon after a resolution was passed by the Naga People Convention held at Kohima in August 1957 and attended by 4,000 delegates and their supporters, opting for a settlement within the Indian Union, which substantially nullified the resolution of plebiscite adopted earlier by the NNC convention held in 1951.[44]

Even as the government took military and political initiative concurrently, violence continued sporadically. The Naga insurgency was far from being subdued. Army continued to operate aggressively. Large number of hostiles surrendered in 1957 and 1959. Their numbers had been greatly reduced but the hostile Nagas proved to be skilful guerrilla fighters and retaliated by ambushing army patrols whenever opportunity came their way. Nari Rustomji in his fascinating book *'The Imperilled Frontiers' wrote*: " it was soon a matter of doubt as to who was softening whom. It will serve no purpose to revive old memories, but it is recognised to everybody's shame, that it was the darkest chapter in the history of Naga Hills. - - - Fierce and relentless revenge was the main motivating force during the black and senseless period."

Action at Purr and Downing of the Air Force Dakota[45]

Although the strength of hostiles had been considerably reduced by relentless army operations, the guerrillas were still capable of raiding isolated army posts in inaccessible areas. They actually attacked Purr, an isolated post, some 166 km from Kohima, located at the northern tip of a high mountain range running North to South and parallel to the international border with Myanmar. The hostiles encircled the post with about 500 men of whom 125 were armed with three light machine guns and rifles of sorts and the rest with traditional weapons such as spears, bows and arrows and *daos*. They opened fire early in the morning of August 25, 1960 and kept it up throughout the day. They had destroyed the three bridges on the Tizu and placed 20 men on each to prevent reinforcement reaching the post, which was occupied by approximately 100 men. The firing continued the next day when they came to within few yards of the post, but withdrew when fired upon by the defenders of the post In the afternoon of the next day, two Dakotas dropped supplies, which fell into the hands of the hostiles. The Dakotas flew very low and one of them crash-landed between Meluri (near Purr) and Laphori, another small village to the east of Meluri. The ill-fated Dakota was hit by ground fire by the hostiles,[46] which forced it to land in a paddy field. It was piloted by Flight Lieutenant Anand Singha and had a crew of eight airmen. The pilot and the crew were captured by the hostiles and taken to their camp, where they were treated well. The defenders fought bravely till reinforcement from 4 Sikh Light Infantry arrived. Early on 28 August, five IAF fighters strafed the hostile positions inflicting heavy casualties, which forced them to lift the siege.[47]

Operations by the Assam Rifles

The depredations of the Naga hostiles included arson, loot and murder. There were a number of ambushes on road Kohima-Imphal. The Assam Rifles had a number of successful operations in 1960-61. In April 1961, in a memorable action against the hostiles, Subedar Kharka Bahadur Limbu of 8 Assam Rifles laid down his life while raiding a hostile camp in a jungle ravine, which was barricaded by a long palisade covered by bamboo stakes. The JCO, despite his injury due to hostile fire, led his men to the hostile hideout and killed three of them. He was posthumously awarded the Ashoka Chakra Class I for his exceptional courage.[48]

By the end of 1961, the total casualties among the security forces rose to more than 200 officers and men killed and 400 wounded. The figures do not include civilian casualties. The high casualty figures are indicative of the constraint under which the security forces were operating. On the other hand, the insurgents enjoyed the element of surprise. [49] The charge of being 'trigger happy' against troops by some critics is not borne out by facts and is misplaced.

The Pulling out of Troops to meet the Chinese Threat

1962 was a watershed in the history of the North-east. The Chinese attack in NEFA and Ladakh required army units in Nagaland to pull out to face the Chinese threat. 23 Mountain Division, which had taken over the counter-insurgency operation in Nagaland in 1960, moved out and its responsibilities were taken over by Headquarters of the Inspector General of Assam Rifles, which established its tactical headquarters at Kohima.[50]

Formation of the State of Nagaland

The new state of Nagaland was formed to take the wind out of rebel's demand for independence. The IB and the Government of Assam were against it because the precedent might encourage other tribes to raise similar demand. Besides, the constitution had not envisaged a state of the size of Nagaland having a population of just 5,00,000. BN Mullick, the IB chief, expressed his apprehension to Nehru. But a set of circumstances had developed which forced Nehru to accept the proposal. The Chinese were getting extremely belligerent and confrontation in NEFA had already taken place. The fear of a possible China-Pak nexus was ever present and it was considered prudent to tackle the volatile internal situation at the earliest.[51]

Raising of Headquarters 8 Mountain Division

After the 1962 war, it was decided to raise Headquarters GOC Nagaland, which would be specially trained for mountain warfare and counter- insurgency. The name Headquarters GOC Nagaland was changed to Headquarters 8 Mountain Division, which was raised at Ranchi in 1963.[52] The first GOC was Major General KP Candeth. The Division was responsible for counter-insurgency operations in Nagaland and Manipur.

Change in Tactics by Hostiles

In the beginning of 1963, the hostiles who had slipped across the border to East Pakistan returned to Nagaland, and brought modern rifles, machine guns and explosives. This introduced a new dimension to the conflict. The Pakistanis had advised them to change their tactics, not to attack army posts as it meant more casualties for them but to attack trains and such soft targets. On April 9, 1963, the hostiles blew up the railway track near Dimapur. Six passengers of the passing train were killed and 20 injured. This was only the beginning. In order to impede the peace talks, which had started in 1964, a series of explosions took place targeting North East Frontier Railway in Assam in February and April 1966.[53] The railway track in Dhansiri near Nagaland-Assam border was blown up, but fortunately there was no casualty. On February 17, 1966, a bomb exploded in a train at Farkating killing 37 passengers and injuring 50. On April 20, a time bomb exploded in a railway coach at Lumding railway station, killing 56 people and injuring 127. Three days later another explosion in a train standing at Dipha station killed 40 and injured 61.[54]

Agreement on Suspension of Hostilities and its Impact on Army Operations

As a consequence to the peace talks suspension of hostilities came into effect from midnight of September 5, 1964. The agreement was favourable to the hostiles and put the security forces at great disadvantage. According to the agreement, the security forces were not to undertake any jungle operations, raid camps, search villages, arrest anyone, take aerial action or patrol beyond 1000 yards of security posts and 100 yards astride roads. They were free to patrol the international border, but within three miles of it. The underground rebels were to refrain from sniping and ambushing, imposing fines, kidnapping and recruiting, indulging in sabotage, raiding or firing on posts, moving about in uniform or with arms and approaching within 100 yards of security post.[55]

The terms of agreement, which were loaded in favour of the hostiles, were violated blatantly. Taxes were imposed on civilian population and young boys were recruited in the underground army and sent to East Pakistan and China for guerrilla training. The army accepted the restrictions imposed on them but was not at all happy about these. In fact, Major General Candeth had warned the Governor that the agreement in the form it was proposed would result in hostiles gaining the upper hand and the prestige of the army would be lowered.[56]

After the cessation of hostilities, all was apparently quiet in Nagaland but the hostiles had stepped up their activities in Manipur, particularly in Ukhrul sub-division. A vehicle convoy of CRPF was ambushed near Mile 52 on Road Imphal-Tamenglong on July 12, 1967. Two JCOs and 21 other ranks were killed. Only one survived to tell the story. The hostiles who were 200 strong took away 19 rifles, two sten guns and 734 rounds of ammunition. In another incident, 16 JAT having received information from an apprehended hostile that a group was present in Tenjang in Tamenglong sub-division, despatched a column of one officer, two JCOs and 35 other ranks to deal with the hostiles. On reaching a nearby village, the local schoolteacher confirmed the information. But as night fell, the column was attacked by the hostiles and killed the officer, both the JCO and 17 other ranks. Nine were wounded. To add insult to injury, the hostiles took away four light machine guns, 18 rifles, three sten carbines, one pistol and two 2-inch mortars.[57] The one redeeming action during this period was by 9 BIHAR, which got the better of hostiles in an ambush and recovered one light machine gun, two rifles and large quantities of ammunition from them.

Operation at Jotsoma and Lessons Learnt

Thinousilie, who had led a gang of rebels to China, returned in mid-January 1968 with five 60 mm mortars, five rocket launchers, two medium machine guns, seven light machine guns, 400 semi automatic rifles, 750 mines, 750 grenades and five wireless sets.[58] They had established a camp near Jotsoma, in a bowl surrounded by steep hills, well covered so that it could not be spotted even from the air. The camp was raided by 9 BIHAR. Two companies of Assam Rifles had established stops on escape routes. 17 MADRAS was to lay a cordon in a semi circle, but were ambushed by hostiles who were fleeing from the camp. One officer, two JCOs and 23 other ranks of 17 MADRAS were killed. One officer and 18 other ranks were wounded. The same battalion had lost one officer, and 16 other ranks on March 20, 1968 in southern Manipur. It was time for introspection for the units, which had to lay greater stress on minor tactics, physical fitness and sub unit level drills.

The raiding party of 9 BIHAR had succeeded in approaching the camp perimeter stealthily but an alert sentry gave the alarm and most of the hostiles escaped the dragnet carrying their arms and secret documents. 9 BIHAR captured some hostiles and a diary in which the details of movements of the hostile gang to and from China were recorded. This confirmed the China link of Naga hostiles and was used by the Government to nail China's interference in Nagaland. The raid highlighted the skill of Nagas in guerrilla tactics, and at the same time it exposed the weakness of army units in training and minor tactics. There was another lesson. The cessation of hostilities had developed a sense of complacency amongst troops, for which they paid a heavy price.[59]

Split in Naga Insurgency

As it so often happens in most insurgencies, a split in the underground Naga ranks was inevitable. Power and money corrupts and Naga insurgents, who proudly proclaimed their revolutionary halo, were no exceptions. The genesis of the rift lay in personal ambitions and jockeying for power. Although Phizo had started the Naga movement, Sema tribesmen under Kaito Sema had borne the brunt of fighting ever since the army was called out. Kaito, the former head of the rebel army, was removed from his post of defence minister in the underground army in 1964 for his advocacy to forge links with China and criticism of the Peace Mission. When Mowu Angami was made the chief of the underground army, the injustice rankled Kaito. Both craved for a greater share of money and power and had their loyal followers amongst the rebels; personal ambition, the craving for power and tribal loyalties combined to create a situation, which led to the split in the underground on tribal lines. Kaito and his followers formed a parallel Revolutionary Government of Nagaland (RGN). The split, which came in 1967, was to have far reaching consequences for the underground movement. Kaito wanted to quicken the pace of settlement with the central government on the basis of giving up the demand for independence. The followers of Phizo blamed 8 Mountain Division for masterminding the bloodless coup.[60]

Capture of Mowu Angami[61]

When the split occurred, Mowu Angami was in China and had no inkling of the cataclysmic changes that had taken place in the underground movement. In the early 1968 it became clear that he with his gang were planning to return to Nagaland, additional troops were moved into Nagaland so as to capture them near the international border itself. Patrols were sent out to locate the gangs. The international border with Myanmar was sealed by deploying troops on likely routes of ingress. Reports started coming from mid-January 1969 about the move of gangs led by Isak Swu and Mowu Angami through Myanmar heading towards Nagaland.

Besides the army, supporters of Zuheto Sema, who was heading the breakaway RNG were also desperately looking out for Mowu Angami and his gang. Zuheto feared that if Mowu Angami succeeded in entering Nagaland and contacted his underground colleagues, the balance of power would shift in his favour. Mowu and his gang entered Nagaland on the night of March 6, 1969 in the area due East of Zunheboto. On March 8 two scouts of the gang were captured by a patrol of 14 RAJ RIF, who revealed the direction in which the gang was moving. 13 GUARDS, 22 Maratha Light Infantry, 8 MADRAS and two companies each of 13 RAJ RIF and 4 BIHAR were moved to lay a cordon around Lukhami area. Mowu Angami and his gang were trapped in the cordon and all escape routes were blocked by troops. One battalion surrounded the camp itself. The circumstances of Mowu's capture are still shrouded in mystery but from various accounts, the breakaway Kaito faction, led by Zuheto Sema, facilitated Mowu's capture. Mowu and his men were helpless as they were obviously tricked into handing their weapons to Zuheto. The followers of Phizo accused Zuheto and his followers for treacherously tricking Mowu and his gang, as they were unaware of the rift that had occurred in the underground during their long absence in China.

The capture of Mowu Angami and his gang was a dramatic event of the counter-insurgency operations in Nagaland. Notwithstanding the role played by Zuheto in the capture of

Mowu, the leadership of Major General Rawley, GOC 8 Mountain Division, was crucial. He not only coordinated the military operation but also simultaneously influenced the political, bureaucratic and administrative decisions.

After his capture Mowu was flown to Delhi in an IAF Dakota for interrogation. His gang totalling 169 including 22 Myanmarese surrendered with a rich haul of weapons and ammunition: five light machine guns, ninety 7.62 rifles, 47 sten guns, six 7.62 pistols, ten .303 rifles and four 60 mm mortars.[62] Isak Swu and his gang evaded arrest by breaking themselves into small groups, but around 90 of them were captured with their arms over a period of time.[63] Not wanting to risk the same fate as Mowu, they made their way to camps in Myanmar.

Another Attempt to Send a Gang to China Foiled

The army achieved a remarkable success in December 1974 in foiling the attempt of a large gang of Naga hostiles to cross the border with Myanmar and head for Yunan in China for training and bringing replenishments. The operation has already been described in Chapter 10.

Operation Golden Bird

In 1995, based on information informally shared with Myanmar Army, the Indian Army carried out Operation Golden Bird in the Mizoram-Chin Hills on Indo-Myanmar border to interdict a large consignment of weapons intended for NSCN (IM), PLA and ULFA, which was to be transported by porters from bases in the CHT in Bangladesh to Manipur in India. The weapons were being escorted by the NSCN (IM) through the ill defined Indo-Myanmar border in this region; a part of the consignment was to be delivered in Myanmar to anti-government insurgents in the Chin Hills. There was no formal contact between the two armies; only general information that Myanmar troops would be in the vicinity across the international border in the area. The operation had to be quickly coordinated under Eastern Command through its various subordinate headquarters. The Assam Rifles sector commander closest to the scene was nominated force commander and a scratch force of Assam Rifles and Sikh Light Infantry was quickly assembled and placed under the force commander. The operation was launched with speed and determination. The insurgent group was intercepted and engaged in a series of running clashes on both sides of the border by the Indian and Myanmar forces, resulting in a number of insurgent casualties and seizure of weapons. Golden Bird was a successful operation and an encouraging example of what even a little military cooperation between India and Myanmar could achieve.[64] However, the operation did not end as planned initially. With the Indian Government conferring the Nehru Award for international understanding on Aung San Swu Kyi right in the midst of the operations, the Myanmar Army was so outraged that it unilaterally withdrew from the offensive.

Counter-Insurgency Operations in Mizoram

While the Nagas were preparing for their journey to China, insurgency broke out in Mizoram, which took the country by surprise. In a swift, meticulously planned and executed guerrilla attacks the Mizo rebels overran virtually the entire territory of Mizoram. The insurrection was code named 'Operation Jericho'. The Indian response and some of the important counter-insurgency initiatives have been analysed here.

The Use of Air Power against MNF

The MNF launched Operation Jericho on the night of 28 February / 1 March 1966. By 3 March, 1 Assam Rifles at Aizwal was under siege by nearly 4000 MNF volunteers. It was decided to land reinforcement by helicopters, but the sniping by hostiles was so intense that the helicopters could not land. Air strikes by fighter aircraft were the only way out to break the siege. Fighters strafed hostile positions at 1130 hours on 5 March.

The strafing was repeated in the afternoon, which forced the hostiles to lift the siege.[65]

The Assam Rifles post at Lungleih was also attacked on 1 March. It put up a gallant fight and held out for four days before ammunition and water ran out. Attempts to supply the post by air failed and on 5 March, the post was overrun by the hostiles. One officer and 66 other ranks were taken prisoner.[66] At Demagiri in the South, the hostilcs gained control over the entire village except the Assam Rifles post, which held out with great courage. Here again, fighter planes had to be called to strafe the hostile position. From 9 to 13 March fighter planes of the IAF strafed the hostile positions, forcing them to scatter.[67]

Army Brigade Moves in

The entire 61 Mountain Brigade of four battalions and supporting arms moved into Mizo Hills by 15 March. Having secured the three major towns, the Brigade sent out columns to engage insurgent groups in other parts of the district. By the end of the month the security forces were in full control, but there were small pockets of insurgents who were capable of harassing actions and reprisals against loyal Mizos.

Besides 61 Mountain Brigade, additional troops from Assam Rifles were moved into Mizo Hills. 18 Assam Rifles was deployed in the South with its headquarters at Lungleih. By mid-April, 19 Assam Rifles was deployed in Mat River area with its headquarters at Serchip. 6 Assam Rifles, which was at Agartala, was also inducted into Mizo Hills by October 1966.[68]. In order to effect better command and control over large Assam Rifles component in Mizo hills, the DIG Range established his headquarters at Aizwal on November 21, 1966, by which time the army was well established and the chain of command was properly organised.[69]

In April 1967, a sector headquarters at Lunglawn named Lima Sector, was established and the DIG of Assam Rifles was made its commander. It had two Assam Rifles battalions, two regular infantry battalions and one BSF battalion under its operational control. At the same time the state's range headquarters retained administrative control over all Assam Rifles battalions in Mizo Hills, which it exercised from its main headquarters at Silchar.[70]

Operation Blanket

By April 1966, 61 Mountain Brigade was mounting numerous combing operations both in the interior and in the border areas. The MNA was on the run and a large number escaped to CHT. During the monsoons, the insurgents reorganised themselves and once the rains abated they infiltrated back into Mizo Hills. With the induction of a number of armed police detachments, new posts were established all over Mizo Hills. However, it was difficult to keep an eye on all the small villages; some willingly and some under coercion continued to give food and shelter to hostiles; so a new concept was evolved, code-named Operation Blanket, which envisaged each company or equivalent of Assam Rifles or army to establish two posts of about 20 men each next to villages within its area of responsibility. The sub-posts were to be self-contained for a fortnight and sufficiently mobile to reach remote villages threatened by hostiles. The aim was to instil confidence in small villages and gain information about the hostiles and terrain. The scheme proved a partial success; the villages were too numerous for the troops to keep an eye on all, and therefore, support to the hostiles could not be entirely cut off. [71]

Operation Accomplishment

The failure of Operation Blanket led to reappraisal of the situation. It was then decided that the only way to totally isolate the guerrillas from the inhabitants would be to group a number of villages into large hamlets, which could be easily protected. This would also enable the security forces to operate freely in the depopulated areas. Accordingly in the beginning of 1967, security forces began the task of grouping of villages, code-named Operation Accomplishment. Initially the hostiles did not react, but on February 3, 1967, one of the platoons of the Assam Rifles, while escorting the villagers from jhoom cultivation to Lungdai group centre, was ambushed in which six riflemen were killed.

The success of the grouping scheme is debatable. According to one view 'the insurgents, instead of being denied shelter, received more support from the people. They could get safe shelter and food more easily in the regrouped villages than from old ones, from where these people had been forcibly evicted. The insurgents were more welcome in the regrouped villages than the old ones.'[72] The grouping of villages had become so unpopular that when the orders for grouping in the central and South-western part of the hills was given, some Mizos challenged the order in the Guwahati High Court on the grounds that it was violative of the fundamental rights. The court immediately ordered a stay, which forced the government to withdraw the order for implementing the third phase of operation. In Nagaland the authorities had hurriedly degrouped all the Naga villages in the face of bitter opposition, yet those that had been regrouped would remain so in Mizoram.[73]

Political Initiatives

After the defeat of Pakistan in 1971 war, the insurgents lost their main support base. The government seized the opportunity and enacted the North-east (Reorganisation) Act, which among other things gave union territory status to the Mizo Hills. Indira Gandhi at Aizwal formally inaugurated the Union Territory of Mizoram on January 21, 1972. However, insurgency continued in Mizoram even after the elections to the newly formed legislative assembly, in which Mizo Union won an absolute majority.

Resumption of Operations in 1982

It may be recalled that Laldenga had opened dialogue after Indira Gandhi returned to power in 1980, which had led to suspension of operations from August 1, 1980. But Laldenga continued to make unreasonable demands and to put pressure on the government, he had issued instructions to escalate violence. The government, therefore, decided to end the talks in 1982 and resume operations.

On January 20, 1982, Laldenga was informed of the termination of talks, and as agreed he was lifted by IAF aircraft from Delhi to Silchar and then taken to Pavva in South Mizoram by helicopter, from where he was escorted to Bangladesh border.[74] MNF was declared an unlawful organisation and Unlawful Activities Act was promulgated.

At that time 57 Mountain Division had two brigades; 71 Mountain Brigade in the North and 311 Mountain Brigade in the South. The operations were launched on the night of January 20, 1982. In a matter of a few days a large number of MNF personnel were apprehended and arms, ammunition and cash were seized.[75] Two more mountain brigades i.e. 123 and 202 were inducted subsequently. 123 Mountain Brigade was deployed to prevent MNF personnel access to Jampui Hill Range to escape to Bangladesh.[76]

Counter-Insurgency Operations in Manipur

In 1978 two major insurgent groups - the PLA and PREPAK became very active in Manipur. In mid-1978 there was a sudden spurt in insurgency, which manifested in the abnormal rise in incidents of snatching arms from policemen in Imphal and in surrounding areas. In April 1979, the PLA took away one light machine gun, two self-loading rifles and one sten gun from BSF personnel in broad daylight in Imphal bazaar. On 6 August, it raided the Sainik School in Imphal and took away 53 drill-purpose rifles. In October 1980, a combined patrol of 11 JAT,

BSF and Village Volunteer Force encountered PLA guerrillas in Charo in Ukhrul area, which resulted in the killing of eight insurgents and injury to two; twelve rifles, some ammunition and documents were recovered. From the documents, it became known that PLA had collected Rupees 3,00,000, extorted from officials, contractors, ministers and businessmen.[77] Insurgency had taken roots in Imphal.

Force Level: Creation of Tactical Headquarters Manipur Sector

The spurt in violent activities by Meitei insurgents forced the government to invoke the provisions of the Armed Forces Special Powers Act, 1958, in September 1980. In October 1980, a new headquarters was created to take over the responsibility in Manipur less those with 9 Sector, i.e., Mao-Maram and Ukhrul. Major General KL Kochar established tactical headquarters Manipur Sector, popularly known as K Sector, at Imphal with its rear at Leimakong. 61 Mountain Brigade with its three infantry battalions and one CRPF battalion was placed under it. 181 Mountain Brigade was inducted on September 27, 1980, with its headquarters at Thoubal, south of Imphal.[78] It was hoped that by inducting a tactical divisional headquarters and one brigade into Manipur, insurgency in the valley would be crushed in three months. [79] But it did not happen that way. After the departure of Major General Kochar in December 1980, the entire area once again came under 8 Mountain Division. 61 Mountain Brigade was made responsible for Greater Imphal and the western and Northern parts of the valley, 181 Mountain Brigade became responsible for the southern part and the Manipur-Mizoram border, which was used by Mizos on their way from Myanmar to Mizoram. The North and east Manipur remained under the brigades in Nagaland. Besides the two brigades, there was 9 Sector at Imphal and a new sector headquarters, later designated as 11 Sector at Koirengei. This sector consisted of 95 and 96 BSF battalions, which were formed after converting 3 and 4 Manipur Rifles into BSF battalions in 1968 and 1969 respectively.[80]

Capture of Bisheshwar Singh at Tekcham

In the middle of 1981, there was again a spurt in both Naga and Meitei insurgencies. Major General VK Nayyar, who had taken over the command of 8 Mountain Division in May 1981, had introduced some effective counter-insurgency measures. Each battalion was ordered to keep one column ready to move at short notice. Officers and men of the column slept in uniform with their weapons by their side. The units established close contact with the local police to widen the intelligence network. Foot and bicycle patrols went round the city in civilian clothes or uniform, as the situation demanded. These innovative measures produced excellent results.

On July 6, 1981, 17 JAK RIF received information from one of its sources that some armed men were seen in Tekcham, a remote village around which the area was marshy. The armed men were hiding in two huts West of Tekcham. The commanding officer, Lieutenant Colonel RP Singh, decided to immediately cordon and search the area. Second Lieutenant CA Pithawala was tasked to take out a company column to trap the armed men. The column led by Pithawala left Thoubal at 1430 hours in vehicles, but debussed seven kms from the village in order to maintain surprise. The column was split into two groups; one half to cordon the huts from the North and the other led by Pithawala to block escape routes to the South and East. As the Northern column approached the huts, it came under fire from the huts. Pithawala attacked the huts from South. In the firefight he was hit in the right shoulder by a bullet, but he pressed on and as the attack progressed, one man from the hut tried to escape, but was captured. On interrogation it was found that the captured man was no other than Bisheshwar, the PLA chief.[81]

The column had been reinforced by now and the area was fully sealed. Next morning another man was caught alive. When the huts were searched, seven dead bodies were found. The search also resulted in the recovery of three 7.62 rifles, one sten gun, seven pistols, one radio set and some ammunition. It was a major success for the army and signalled the demise of insurgency in the days ahead. Pithawala was awarded the highest peacetime gallantry award, the Ashoka Chakra, and the commanding officer got a well-deserved Kirti Chakra.

The killing of Bisheshwar and his men had raised the morale of law abiding people of Imphal, but the end of insurgency was nowhere in sight. The Tangkhul Naga hostiles ambushed a convoy of 21 Sikh on February 19, 1982 at Mile 34 on Imphal-Ukhrul road and killed one officer, two JCOs and thirteen other ranks and wounded twelve. The Sikhs lost five 7.62 rifles, one sten, one light machine gun and some ammunition.[82]

Operation Kunjbihari

Kunjbihari, who had stepped into the shoes of Bisheshwar was still at large, but not for long. On April 13, 1982 at 1700 hours, 61 Mountain Brigade was telephoned by a source that 20 armed men were seen in Kadampokpi, a village 10 km South of Imphal. 14 BIHAR was ordered to establish a cordon round the village immediately. 17 RAJ RIF was to establish three stops and provide reserve. The Biharis were conversant with the area, so within an hour of the receipt of the order, the battalion cordoned off the village.

The village had ponds with high embankment around them, bamboo groves, haystacks and thatched huts, all of which combined to obstruct visibility and helped the Biharis to get close to the objective without being observed by the armed men. As the cordon moved closer, the trapped men opened fire from a double storied house and wounded an officer. The resistance by the armed men was violent, which indicated the presence of some very important leaders. A wounded hostile confirmed that Kunjbihari was also present in the village. By now both the GOC and the brigade commander had reached the scene of encounter. Brigadier Jhingon, having assessed the situation, decided to set the hut on fire, which forced the insurgents to come out firing. They were engaged with accurate fire by the troops and in the process were killed or captured. The firing was controlled and care was taken to evacuate men, women and children to safety. In the firefight seven hardcore insurgents, including Kunjbihari, were killed and six captured out of which five were wounded. The operation would have ended earlier had the battalion carried rocket launcher to blow up the hut. This was an important lesson from the encounter. [83]

Operation Blue Bird

In the eighties, after its formation, NSCN began a recruitment drive in the hills of Manipur, particularly in Senapati district. There were intelligence reports with the state government that NSCN cadres were planning to attack Assam Rifles posts in the interior of the district. One such report received by the superintendent of police, Senapati, from CID of Manipur government in the first week of July 1987 was passed on to 21 and 24 Assam Rifles, 39 CRPF, 7 Manipur Rifles and the Village Volunteer Force.[84]

Oinam is a remote village in Paomata sub division of Senapati district, 110 km North of Imphal; about four hours drive from the capital. During the monsoons, the village remains cut off from the rest of the state owing to the poor condition of 30 km long muddy road, which connects Oinam to Maram. Maram is situated along the NH 39 that runs from Kohima to Imphal. The remoteness of the village can be gauged from the fact there are people who were born, lived and died in the village without even seeing Imphal.[85]

Oinam was destined to hit the headlines in the middle of July 1987. On 9 July NSCN guerrillas attacked the post manned by 21 Assam Rifles after careful preparation, firing at the posts by automatic weapons and grenades. The attack came in broad daylight at 1130 hours and lasted for two hours, during which time two JCOs and seven other ranks were killed and three were seriously wounded. The guerrillas then looted the armoury and took away ninety 7.62 rifles, twenty sten guns, two light machine guns, two 2 inch mortars and ammunition.[86] Assam Rifles was slow to react; combing operations started only six hours later, which gave enough time to the guerrillas to make good their escape. Stunned by the loss of men and weapons, Assam Rifles assisted by units of the regular army launched a massive combing operation, code named Blue Bird, which was personally supervised by the Inspector General of Assam Rifles, Major General PL Kukrety. The massive search operation resulted in the recovery of almost 70 percent of the weapons taken away by the guerrillas. 14 civilians lost their lives during the combing operation, which lasted for a week.

There were allegations of large-scale human rights violations by the Assam Rifles, which was highlighted in the report by the Amnesty International. The incident had another fallout. In an unusual development the government of Manipur blamed the Assam Rifles for killing atleast eight civilian suspects in fake encounters; remaining six were killed while trying to escape from military custody. The Chief Minister, Rishang Keishing, sent a memorandum on behalf of his cabinet to the Union Home Minister charging the Assam Rifles of dereliction of duty and killing civilian suspects in fake encounters. In a scathing indictment he went on to ask why there were only 14 personnel in the post at the time of the attack when the post had the strength of a wing having atleast 122 weapons, which were reportedly taken away by the guerrillas.[87]

Operation Good Samaritan

The rationale for launching the ambitious civic action programmes for rural development in the most backward and undeveloped regions of the North-east, where army was the only agency with the manpower, equipment, training and above all the motivation, was to enhance and qualitatively multiply the Eastern Army's civic action activities. The focus was on development and repair of essential civic amenities, which were of immediate relevance to villages, whom the civil government had passed by. The Army Development Group (ADG) that had been created post 1962 for development in frontier regions, but had lapsed with the gradual spread of civic amenities, was revived. A sum of Rupees 20 crore, Rupees 10 crore each for projects in Nagaland and Manipur, was sanctioned by the Central Government.[88]

ADG functioned under Headquarters 3 Corps, and comprised integrated teams of construction engineers, medical and veterinary officers, electrical and mechanical engineers and education corps personnel. Under this programme, the army created networks of foot tracks linking villages on the hills with the nearest motorable roads, constructed or repaired local water supply schemes, carrying water up from springs and hill *nalas* to community water points, reactivated primary health centres and electricity supply that had not been functional for years. Football fields, village schools and churches were made. Army Education Corps personnel taught in village schools, Medical Corps manned village dispensaries and held medical camps, while soldier technicians taught vocational skills. The operation was launched in January 1995 and continued for three years; it wound up in June 1998. A variety of community-related works were completed, some of which were as under: -

Total length of track completed	201 km
Number of playgrounds constructed	72
School buildings repaired	34
Water supply schemes	45 villages
Bus stands constructed	10
Patients treated in medical camps	40,000
Animals treated in veterinary camps	40,000
Seeds distributed	3.5 ton

There were many other small works, which were undertaken at the request of village and community leaders.[89]

Counter-Insurgency Operations in Assam

The Assam Accord of 1995 led to fresh election in Assam and the installation of AGP government. It also heralded the rise of ULFA and the beginning of insurgency in the state. On the fall of VP Singh's government at the centre, Chandra Shekhar became the prime minister, whose first crucial decision was to dismiss Mohanta's AGP government and impose President's rule in Assam. ULFA was declared an unlawful organisation and banned.

Operation Bajrang

The army, as it so often happens, was called to restore order. It launched Operation Bajrang on November 28, 1990, but the word of the impending operation was leaked out to ULFA; the leak was at a high-level, for the information about the impending operation was known only to a handful of officials in the home ministry and the army command headquarters.[90] The operation resulted in the capture of informants, sympathisers and low ranking cadres; the top leadership escaped the dragnet and fled to Bangladesh. Operation Bajrang succeeded in locating and dismantling the major camps of ULFA; the main camp was at Lakhipathar, in the thick jungle of teak and bamboo, a short distance from both Digboi and Dibrugarh. There were seven satellite camps protected by improvised explosive devices (IED) and booby traps at the entrances to delay and warn the inmates. Lakhipathar and the satellite camps had been chosen for another practical reason; they were close enough to the Myanmar's border, about three hours via Khonsa in Arunachal for a quick getaway.[91]

The operation was conducted with many disadvantages: First, the AGP was hostile, and so was the local media. Second, the judiciary too was hostile to the army. Third, the state's administration was demoralised and its senior leaders had lost their confidence.[92] The army was criticised for calling off the operation prematurely without accomplishing the objective. Lieutenant General Ajai Singh, who was the GOC 4 Corps and overall commander for counter-insurgency operations in Assam, disagrees with the criticism. The bigger objective was to hold the assembly election without undue delay and restore the democratic process, for if the election had been delayed unreasonably, Assam would have gone the Punjab way. [93] Yet another unforeseen outcome of the operation was discovery of a mass grave with fifteen decomposed bodies, many with their hands and feet tied with ropes,[94] which debunked the reformist and Robin Hood image of ULFA and showed them for what they were, a band of killers, bandits and extortionists. The revelations produced shock and revulsion in the general public. Contrary to the prevailing view, the operation did adversely affect the support base of ULFA. With the assembly elections in hand, Operation Bajrang was called off, and the army was ordered to return to barracks in April 1991.

Operation Rhino

Within hours of Saikia having been sworn in as the Chief Minister on July 1, 1991, ULFA kidnapped 14 officials, including a Soviet engineer, Sergei Gritchenko and TS Raju-another engineer with the Oil and Natural Gas Commission from Assam oilfields in a well-planned operation. In return for the release of hostages, ULFA demanded the release of its 24 cadres, who were in prison. On July 9, Gritchenko was killed, which prompted the state government to release 11 of the wanted men in a bid to placate ULFA and declare a general amnesty in which nearly 400 suspects were freed from the prison. But ULFA was in no mood to relent. On 8 September, TS Raju was killed. Within 11 weeks as many as 166 persons were killed and 252 kidnapped.[95] The rapid deterioration in law and order forced the government to call the army once again to restore the situation.[96]

Operation Rhino was launched on September 15, 1991. Nearly 50,000 men were moved into positions over several days. Unlike Operation Bajrang the army this time had the political, administrative and intelligence backing that it had lacked the last time. The movements of ULFA leaders had been kept under surveillance and tracked when they had been allowed to move around during the election campaign. ULFA had set up camps in Namsai forests in Lohit district of Arunachal. Helicopters lifted troops and dropped them at suitable locations to seal all likely exit routes. 73 Mountain Brigade, which included troops of 13 PUNJAB, destroyed three such camps, but no cadres were killed or found. They had melted into the open countryside of Assam, where it became easier for the army to hunt them down.

After the initial strike, which was code-named 'Cloudburst', the second phase of the operation was launched, which resulted in the capture of 4300 suspects, unspecified quantities of weapons and Rupees 70,00,000 in Indian currency. After initial interrogations, 1,700 were released; the remainder were handed over to the police.[97]

The intelligence officials were for a change acting to a plan. Anup Chetia, who was under surveillance for some time, was picked up from a guest house in Calcutta in November. In late

December, the army in Guwahati nabbed Sunil Nath, the spokesman of ULFA. Next to fall in the army dragnet was another important leader, Kalpajyoti Neog, followed by the arrest of Moon Ali, a top ULFA man. The tightening noose had the desired effect on ULFA; the remaining hostages were set free. But the biggest achievement was the gunning down in Guwahati of Hirakjyoti Mahanta, the deputy commander-in chief, and an unwavering hardliner who opposed any solution under the constitution.[98] The loss of Hirakjyoti was devastating that forced Arobindo Rajkhowa to ask for cessation of operations.

Operation All Clear

The relentless operation by the army forced ULFA to flee and take refuge in Bangladesh and Myanmar. The victory of the Awami League and the installation of Sheikh Hasina's government in Bangladesh in 1996 was bad news for Assam insurgents. Sheikh Hasina was keen to develop friendly relationship with India and reluctant to give refuge to North-east insurgents in her country. It became dangerous for Indian insurgent groups to operate from Bangladesh. Assam insurgents like ULFA and NDFB shifted their bases to Bhutan from where they were finally driven out in December 2003 by the RBA in an operation code-named All Clear. RBA demonstrated the willingness of Bhutan not to allow anti-India activities from the Bhutanese soil and set an example of cooperative regional approach in the fight against terrorism.

Operation Leech

Weapons acquired illegally chiefly from arms bazaars in Bangkok and Cambodia are mainly Khmer Rouge surpluses. Their weapons have long been smuggled into India's North-eastern states by sea in fishing vessels and coastal craft and off loaded at two islets of the deserted Indian islands - St Martin and Landsfall islands – between the Burmese Coco Islands and the Indian North Andaman Island. The coastal areas around the harbour city of Cox's Bazaar in Bangladesh have become the den for smugglers of the region. The illegal weapons and other contraband are then carried in manpack columns to CHT from where they are smuggled into Indian territory, mainly Manipur, through either India-Bangladesh or India-Myanmar border. The army chief made a request to the Naval Chief if the Navy could mount anti-gunrunning operation to prevent the smuggling of arms reaching the insurgents in the North-east from the sea routes or from Thai ports and islands. Operation Leech, a tri-service operation, was initiated in the second week of February and May 1998 under the overall direction of the Chiefs of Staff Committee.[99] The control and direction of the operation thereafter became controversial and speculative; the story that emerged was a telling comment on the total lack of coordination between the intelligence operatives and the armed forces at the highest level, underlining the fact that no lessons had been learnt from the past. The operation resulted in the arrest of several Arakanese rebels by the Indian Navy in February 1998. In the early 1990s, New Delhi extended discreet support to the National Unity Party of Arakan (NUPA), a Buddhist faction on the Arakan coast (Rakhine State) that has long been struggling against the Burmese regime. In 1995, desirous of learning more about Chinese facilities along the Burmese coastline and in exchange of information on Sino-Burmese military activities, the Indian government allowed some NUPA rebels to use a few islets to the North of Andaman Islands, close to Coco Islands, where China appeared to have set up a surveillance base.[100]

Appraisal

Counter-insurgency operations of the Army have evolved over the past half-century. The Army has created a niche for itself and set a pattern of counter-insurgency operation based on winning the hearts and minds of the people. By its herculean efforts, it has established a tenuous peace in the region, which allows political dialogue to take place.

In the early days of army operations against the underground Nagas, despite continuous 'jungle-bashing', it was frustrated in its efforts to tame the rebels primarily because of inexperience, poor intelligence, inadequate understanding of the tribal ethos, unfamiliarity with the terrain, hostile neighbours and equally hostile foreign media and a civil administration, which though well meaning, had no idea of the nature of challenges the army was facing in the North-east. The Army learnt its lessons quickly and soon realised that its military operations had to be balanced by civic action campaign to win the trust and confidence of the local people. Troops were suitably oriented and trained to fight in small platoon and company groups without looking over their shoulders for directions from battalion and brigade headquarters. The opening of counter-insurgency and Jungle Warfare School at Vairengta, Mizoram was a major step in that direction.

It may be argued that the fifty years of army's counter-insurgency operations have failed to bring peace in the region. It is a cynical assessment. The army has approached the counter-insurgency operations as an exercise in nation building. It undertook civic action programme in some of the most backward and undeveloped areas in the North-east and 'was the only government agency in those isolated areas with the manpower, equipment and training and above all the motivation to do so'. While taking stock of the achievements of the last fifty years, it is no small achievement that today Mizoram is peaceful; in Nagaland there is a cease-fire and political dialogue is taking place; in Assam ULFA and NDFB have been marginalised and both have lost much of popular support and are propped by the Pakistan's ISI and Bangladesh, which is fast turning into a fundamentalist Islamic state. Having said that, the prognosis for the future is unflattering. The Islamisation of Bangladesh and the Maoist insurgency in neighbouring Nepal have frightening consequences for the North-east. It is facing a very hostile and uncertain neighbourhood, which will determine the direction of the future insurgencies there. The rise of Muslim fundamentalism in Assam coupled with unabated infiltration from Bangladesh; the expanding network of smuggling in narcotics and gunrunning in Manipur and Mizoram and the spread of AIDS will be the major concerns in the future. The external factors rather than ethnic impulses will fuel insurgencies and will keep them alive in the North-east in future.

Notes and References

1. Ian FW Beckett, *Modern Insurgencies and Counter-Insurgencies*, (London: Routelage,, 2001), p. vii.
2. Ibid., p.24.
3. Ibid., p.24.
4. Ibid., p. 25.
5. Shankar Roychowdhury, *Officially at Peace*, (New Delhi: Viking, 2002), p. 18.
6. Two articles, one by Rajesh Rajgopalan, "Restoring Normalcy: The Evolution of Indian Army Counter-Insurgency Doctrine" in *Small Wars and Insurgencies*, London, vol 2, No 1, Spring 2000, and the other by Shankaran Kalyanraman, "The Indian Way in Counter-Insurgency" in Efraim Inbar (ed), *Democracies and Small Wars; The Review of International Affairs*, Centre for Eurasian Studies, vol 2, Spring 2003, are noteworthy.
7. Verrier Elwin, *Nagaland*, 1961, Research Department Adviser's Secretariat, Shillong, p. 45.
8. Nehru's letter to CD Deshmukh in *Selected Works of Jawaharlal Nehru*, second series, vol 21, January 1, 1953 to March 31, 1953, a project of Nehru Memorial Library, p. 158.
9. Ibid., p. 158.
10. Nehru's letter to all Union Ministers dated March 1, 1953, n. 8., p.162.
11. Shankar Raychowdhary, n. 5., p. 98. The insurgent groups in the North-east, who in the early decades of 50s and 60s were armed with .303 and muzzle loading rifles, are today armed with AK assault rifles and automatic grenade launchers.
12. Beckett, n. 1., pp. 36-37.

13. Ibid., p. 36.
14. Ibid., pp. 36-37.
15. Shankar Roychowdhury, n. 11., p. 219.
16. Ibid., p. 220.
17. VP Malik, "Security on the Borderline", *The Indian Express*, New Delhi, September 18, 2004.
18. Ibid.
19. Beckett, n. 1., pp. 36-37.
20. Verrier Elwin, *Nagaland*, (Shillong: Research Department Advisors Secretariat, 1961), p. 73.
21. For the full text of the idyllic Nagaland, written by that master propagandist, Sakhrie, see Verrier Elwin, n. 20., pp. 73-75. Comments in brackets are Verrier Elwin's.
22. Ibid., p. 75.
23. Ibid., p. 75.
24. Shankar Roychowdhury, n. 11,, p.121.
25. Beckett, n. 1., p.
26. Verrier Elwin, n. 20., p. 77. The alleged atrocities by the Indian Army and the police forces have been catalogued by Mr Astorgchanger in his book *"Unforgettable Memories from Nagaland'*, Chapter 3. Published by Tribal Communications and Research Centre Mokokchung (Nagaland), 1993. The author without taking a definitive position on the atrocities believes that some of the events described could be true. The author served in Nagaland from December 1972 to mid-1974.
27. Journalists VIK Sareen, HK Sareen, DR Mankekar, Nirmal Nibedon, Sekhar Gupta and some others have written excellent books based on their reportings from the North-east.
28. Bendangangshi, *Glimpses of Naga History*, (India: Naga Patriots fzrom Soyim, Mokokchung (Nagaland), 1993), p.106.
29. Shankar Roychowdhury, n. 5., p. 99.
30. Ibid., p. 121.
31. Ibid., pp. 122-123.
32. Ibid., pp. 123-124.
33. Ibid., p. 105. Sikkim has recently been included as a member in the NEC.
34. YD Gundevia, *War and Peace in Nagaland*, (Dehradun: Palit and Palit, 1975), pp. 80-81. Also see Asoso Yonuo, *The Rising Nagas*, (Delhi: Vivek Publishers, 1974), pp. 211- 212. Asoso insinuates that the government may have had a hand in the massacre, which was the Naga version.

35. Quoted in Asoso Yonuo, n. 34., pp. 217-218.
36. RD Palsokar, *Forever in Operations: A Historical Record of 8 Mountain Division in Counter- Insurgency Operations in Nagaland and Manipur and in 1971 Indo-Pak Conflict, (56APO, Mountain Division, 1991)*, p. 30.
37. Aosenba, *The Naga Resistance Movement*, (New Delhi: Regency Publication, 2001), pp. 217-218.
38. RD Palsokar, n. 36., p. 31.
39. Ibid., p.31.
40. Ibid, p 32
41. The incident has been described in detail in Nirmal Nibedon, *Nagaland: The Night of the Guerrillas*, New Delhi, 1978, Lancers, pp 81-82. The army patrol had mistakenly taken Haralu as hostile.
42. BN Mullik, *My Years with Nehru: The Chinese Betrayal*, (New Delhi: Allied Publishers, 1971), p 313 and RD Palsokar, n. 36., p. 32.
43. BN Mullik, n. 42., p. 313.
44. The role of Intelligence Bureau, particularly that of SM Dutt who was deputy director of Intelligence Bureau in Shillong, in calling the Naga People's Convention was substantial. See BN Mullik, n. 42., pp. 312-322.
45. For detailed account of the action at Purr, see RD Palsokar, n. 36., pp. 35-36,
46. Nirmal Nibedon, *Nagaland, The Night of the Guerillas*, (New Delhi: Lancers, 1978), p. 224. In yet another incident, the helicopter carrying Maj Gen GN Sinha, GOC, 8 Mtn Div, was hit by ground fire of hostile Nagas, when the helicopter was over Theprezumi area on 12 July, 1974.
47. DK Palit, *Sentinels of the North-east: The Assam Rifles*, (Dehradun: Palit and Palit, 1984), p. 224.
48. Extracted from Subedar Kharka Bahadur Limbu's citation for Ashoka Chakra. Ashoka Chakra series I, II and III awards were later re-named Ashoka, Kirti and Shaura Chakra.
49. DK Palit, n. 47., p. 226.
50. GOC Assam was renamed 23 Mountain Division in 1960.
51. BN Mullik, n. 42., p. 329. The fear of Assam turned out to be true. Since the grant of statehood to Nagaland, Mizoram, Meghalaya and Arunachal Pradesh have been granted statehood and Bodos have taken up arms for a separatc state.
52. RD Palsokar, n. 31., p.41.
53. Ibid., p. 39.
54. Asoso Yonuo, n. 34., p. 286.The FGN blamed Kaito, who had been

removed from the post of deputy defence minister in the underground set up, for the explosions.

55. RD Palsokar, n. 36., p. 47.
56. Ibid.
57. Ibid., p. 62.
58. Ibid., pp. 63-64.
59. For description of the raid on Jotsoma see RD Palsokar, n. 36., p. 64. Also see Prakash Singh, *Kohima to Kashmir: On the Terrorist Trail,* (New Delhi: Rupa, *2002),* pp. 74-76. Prakash Singh was then the deputy director of Intelligence Bureau at Kohima.
60. RD Palsokar, n. 36., pp. 60-61. Kaito raided the underground armoury after the split and took away all the weapons without firing a shot.
61. For the accounts of various actions, which finally culminated in the capture of Mowu Angami, see RD Palsokar, n. 36., pp. 68-72.
62. RD Palsokar, n. 36., p. 72.
63. Ibid.
64. Shankar Roychoudhury, n. 5., pp. 295-296.
65. DK Palit, *Sentinels of the North-east: The Assam Rifles*, (Dehradun: Palit and Palit, 1984), pp. 262-264.
66. Ibid., p. 262.
67. Ibid.
68. Ibid., pp. 266-267.
69. Ibid., p.267.
70. Ibid., p. 268.
71. Ibid., pp. 269-270.
72. Ved Marwah, *Uncivil Wars: Pathology of Terrorism in India* (New Delhi: , Indus, 1995), p. 38 .
73. Nirmal Nibedon, *Mizoram, The Dagger Brigade*, (New Delhi: Lancers, 1980), p. 140.
74. Ashok Krishna,"Counter-insurgency and Internal Security" in Ian Cardozo (ed.), *The Indian Army: A Brief History*, (New Delhi: USI of India, 2005), pp. 205-206.
75. Ibid.
76. Ibid.
77. RD Palsokar, n. 3., p.164.
78. Ibid, p173. 181 Brigade remained under Tactical Headquarters M Sector till the end of December 1980.
79. Ibid.

80. Ibid., p. 172.
81. Ibid, RD Palsokar has described the account of the Tekcham in detail in his book, *Forever in Operations.*
82. Ibid.
83. Ibid., p. 158.
84. Phanjoubam Tarapot, *Insurgency Movement in NE India*, Second Print, (New Delhi: Vikas, 1994), p.163.
85. Ibid., p. 155.
86. Ibid., p.155.
87. Ibid, pp 157-158.Tarapot gives a detailed account of the entire operation including its political fallout. For Amnesty International report see *Operation Bluebird: A Case Study of Torture and Extra-Judicial Execution in Manipur* (London: , Amnesty international, UK).
88. The then Chief of Army Staff, General Shankar Roychowdhury, named the project Operation Good Samaritan. The General gives a detailed account of this operation in his autobiographical book *'Officially at Peace'*, n. 5., pp.118-121 .
89. *Defenders of the Dawn, A Panorama of Eastern Command*, (New Delhi: Lancers, 2000).
90. Sanjoy Hazarika, *Strangers of the Mist:* Tales of War and Peace from North-east, (New Delhi: Penguin, 1994), pp. 201-202 .
91. Ibid., p. 201.
92. Lieutenant General Ajai Singh in an interview with MS Prabhakara titled "Bajrang is Over" at the headquarters of 58 Mountain Division. *Frontline*, New Delhi, October 12-25, 1991
93. Ibid.
94. Sanjoy Hazarika, n. 90., p. 202.
95. "Bleeding Assam: The Role of ULFA" issued by the Ministry of Home Affairs, Government of India (undated).
96. For a more graphic account of the events leading to the resumption of army operations see Sanjoy Hazarika, n 99, pp 212-217
97. Ibid., p.217,.
98. Ibid., pp. 218-219.
99. Vishnu Bhagwat, Admiral (Indian Navy), *Betrayal of the Defence Forces: The Truth Inside;* (New Delhi: Manas, 2001), *p. 105.*
100. Renaud Egreteau, *Wooing the Generals: India's New Burma Policy*, (New Delhi: Authorspress De Sciences Humaines, 2003), p. 153. Egreteau, a French researcher, has done extensive research on security concerns in India's North-east.

15

Future Prospects

It is always difficult to predict the future course of events. Nonetheless, there are some trends that are discernible. One such is the illegal immigration from Bangladesh, which will continue to be the major concern. AASU has once again begun to highlight the failure of both the central and state governments to check infiltration. The recent (2005) judgement of the Supreme Court of India, which has held that IMDT Act - 1983 as ultra vires of the constitution, is a shot in the arm for those who have been demanding its repeal. But how this verdict is implemented on ground is still to be seen. Political parties in order to protect their vote bank have already started to find ways to subvert the verdict.

Illegal Immigration

Despite the partial fencing of the 4,096 km long and porous India-Bangladesh border, illegal infiltration continues. Unlike in the East, the Punjab border is fully fenced and lighted. The inter-post distance in Punjab is two km and each post has a minimum strength of two platoons. In West Bengal, Assam and Tripura the inter post distance is anything from seven to nine km and each post has only one platoon. There are a number of villages located right on the border and some even beyond the fence. The area in front is left wide open for the villagers and infiltrators to pass through. In Assam the construction of the fence was entrusted to the state PWD in the nineties. The then Chief Minister, who had won the elections on the immigrant vote, diverted the funds for the fence for other works, which delayed the construction of the fence for years.[1]

The continuance of infiltration will create social tension and conflict on a much larger scale than experienced before. One recent example will suffice. On April 24, 2005, members of a small club in Dibrugarh called Chiring-Chapori Yuva Manch (Chiring-Chapori is the name of an area in Upper Assam) distributed pamphlets to residents, urging them not to employ Bangladeshi migrants. It soon spread like a wild fire and turned into a campaign. Picking up from where Dibrugarh club left, local units of AASU in Tinsukia, Sibsagar, Golaghat and Jorhat issued statements asking Bangladeshis who came after 1971 to voluntarily leave; the result, over 5,000 that did not belong to these districts left. For Gogoi, the Chief Minister, all who left were Indian citizen. One doesn't require much foresight to see the contours of the emerging social conflict.

Islamic Fundamentalism

In the recent years, there has been a disturbing growth of Islamic militancy in the North-east. The phenomenon has gained ground after the American intervention in Afghanistan and Iraq. The juxtaposition of illegal Bangladeshi immigration that now consists mainly of Muslims, and the rising Islamic militancy is an emerging phenomenon, which has frightening consequences for India. North-east is profoundly affected by the events and trends in Bangladesh. According to Bertil Linter: "A revolution is taking place in Bangladesh that threatens trouble for the region and beyond if left unchallenged. Islamic fundamentalism, religious intolerance, militant groups with links to international terrorist groups, a powerful military with ties with militants, mushrooming of Islamic schools churning out radical students, middle class apathy, poverty and lawlessness, all are combining to transform the nation."[2] The world was put on warning when Islamic fundamentalists exploded bombs in 63 different towns and districts of Bangladesh almost simultaneously on August

16, 2005 killing two and injuring 138. The banned Jamaat-ul-Mujahideen with links to *al Qaeda* is suspected to be behind the explosions. The scale and coordination of the explosions have raised a number of questions for India's North-east.

The ethnic insurgencies are being slowly replaced or overtaken by Islamic militancy. The killings by ULFA of non-Assamese, mostly Biharis, in the last two months of the year 2000, points to a pattern; providing working space for Bangladeshi Muslims by replacing Biharis and other non-skilled workers from Orissa, West Bengal and Nepal.

Rise of Terrorism

The nature of insurgency has undergone profound changes in the past two decades. The romance of operating from jungle hideouts as revolutionaries no longer attracts the new generation of recruits. Insurgencies in the North-east are increasingly criminalised and terror has become the main weapon of the insurgents. Gone are the days when political mobilisation and guerrilla warfare defined the early insurgencies in Nagaland and Mizoram. In future, attacks on innocent civilians, explosions in trains and public transport, kidnapping for ransom and use of mines and IED will increase. The easy availability of arms and explosives will further facilitate this trend.

The Demand for Nagalim

Naga's demand for the creation of Greater Nagaland, called Nagalim, which will constitute not only the four hill districts of Manipur, but also parts of Assam, Arunachal and even Myanmar, is the major hurdle in the ongoing peace talks between the Centre and NSCN (IM). Neither Assam nor Manipur will allow any diminution of their present boundaries. The ongoing peace process is already faltering on this issue. The army has been warning that the Naga rebels are using the cease-fire for consolidating their position. In many parts of Nagaland and Manipur, the insurgents run a parallel government and have levied household taxes. The recent advertisement in the local newspapers for recruitment in the underground government is a clear violation of the cease-fire agreement and reinforces army's apprehension that NSCN (IM) has taken advantage of the cease-fire to spread its influence. The government will do well to prepare to cope with such a situation, if the talks fail.

Narco-Terrorism

The biggest challenge to the security of the North-east in future will come from narco-terrorism. No insurgent group can sustain itself for long without regular flow of funds. North-east has emerged as a major transit route for narcotics trade and gunrunning. An indicator of the scale of narco-trade is the high incidence of drug abuse, mainly in Manipur, Mizoram and Meghalaya. Most of the narcotics trade is through Moreh in Manipur; the Naga-Kuki clashes are direct consequence of insurgent groups trying to control the road from Moreh to Imphal to facilitate illegal trade. The demand for funds will fuel illegal trade in narcotics in a big way in future.

Pakistan's Alternative Proxy War

Pakistan's proxy war in Kashmir, which started in 1989, has run its course and failed in achieving its objective. But it hasn't given up hope. According to a recent study by the government, Pakistan has launched a new operation to redouble its destabilising work in India through Bangladesh. Pakistan was developing Bangladesh as the new base for its anti-India operations, and it is reported that it has already shifted almost 200 terrorist training camps from Pakistan Occupied Kashmir to Bangladesh.[3]

The Chinese Shadow

The Chinese stopped supporting insurgency in the North-east in 1979. But intelligence reports indicate that the Chinese support has not fully dried up. Speaking in the Parliament on

December 13, 2000, Minister of State of Home, Mr ID Swamy said that SULFA had disclosed that some of their colleagues crossed over to China from Bhutan and established contact with the Chinese in 1993.[4] A confidential IB report to the Home Ministry, the Chinese military have spread their area of operations in all seven states of the North-east and are running a parallel administration with the help of local militants. The report also said that 60 to 70 percent of illegal arms are being supplied to the rebels by the Chinese military.[5] Furthermore, in the year 2000, Indian intelligence disclosed that NSCN (IM) had revived the Chinese connection, which was believed to have snapped in the 1980s. Reports have also indicated that the NSCN (IM) has a full-fledged liaison office in Chinese territory across the border with Arunachal.[6] There are reports of ISI spying and collecting information about troops deployed in the North-east.[7] Who benefits from this intelligence? There is a view that China may be using channels established by the ISI for its own use. This cannot be easily discarded and needs to be carefully watched and analysed.

In India there is once again a new romanticism about China. In the prevailing geo-political scenario, China has inevitably to be an adversary. As long as India is silent about Tibet, it is fine with China. The day India shows any inclination to speak for the Tibetans, the Chinese are poised to destabilise the North-east.

Notes and References

1. EN Rammohan, "Bangladesh and India's Security", paper presented at the USI National Security Seminar 2004 on "India and its Neighbour other than Pakistan" at New Delhi on 9-10 November 2004.
2. Bertil Linter, "Bangladesh a Cocoon of Terror", *Far Eastern Review*, April 4, 2002.
3. Arun Shourie, *Will the Iron Fence Save a Tree Hollowed by Termites: Defence Imperatives Beyond the Military*, (New Delhi, Asa Publishers, 2005), p. 205.

4. *The Indian Express*, New Delhi, December 14, 2001.
5. *The Statesman*, New Delhi, December 20, 2000, p. 5.
6. *The Pioneer*, New Delhi, February 22, 2001.
7. Arun Shourie, n. 3, p. 204.

16

The Way Forward

As we have seen the nature of insurgency has undergone a dramatic change. It has moved from hardships of leech-infested jungles to the luxury of hotels in the urban centres. The young have been exposed to the outside world by better surface and air communications. The television had brought the world to their homes. No longer they contemplate a life in the thick jungles or being a fugitive from law. The romance of being a guerrilla fighter and a revolutionary is gone. They want employment and jobs and want to enjoy the 'good life.'

Reintroduction of Indian Frontier Administrative Service

The problem facing the North-east and the causes that fan insurgencies have been diagnosed. But all our efforts and good intentions have failed to achieve the desired results primarily because our policies are not implemented with vigour and commitment. For that we need efficient governance. Before anything else the administration in the North-eastern states should be vitalised. We need to create a pool of officers on the lines of the erstwhile 'Frontier Administration Service' for NEFA, who have a temperament for service in the tribal areas; officers who are adventurous and have an empathy for the tribes and would enjoy working in the North-east and not see their tenure there as a 'hard posting.'

Economic Development

The economic development of the North-east should top the priority list. But there are pitfalls in too rapid a transformation of undeveloped societies. In order to minimise the local populace from being overwhelmed by a workforce from outside the region, a massive programme to train tribes in skills which would enable them to be absorbed in industries and other developmental programmes envisaged to be set up in the North-east should be started immediately. In the past major thrust of investment in the North-east has been on building administrative infrastructure, which unfortunately has turned into 'Contractor Economy'. Time has come to strike a balance in investments that generate employment and infrastructure. The continuance of insurgency has held back adequate private investment despite 'tax holiday' for entrepreneurs in the North-east. Public sector investment in the North-east should therefore continue but the focus should shift to regional rather than on national priorities. Development of down stream industries should be given priority; for example, Numligarh refinery should be made into petro-chemical complex going down to the level of producing plastic granules, which would encourage local entrepreneurs to set up low capital plastic moulding and extrusion industries to meet the local requirement.

Special Package for the North-east

There is a view that enough resources have not been made available for the development of the North-east. Successive prime ministers have announced special packages for the region; first by Deve Gowda, who announced a special package for the North-east totalling Rs 6,100 crores in 1996. Four years later, Prime Minister Vajpayee increased it to Rs 10,000 crores with certain modifications. Vajpayee's package was an improvement – like the creation of a non-lapsable annual core fund of Rs 1,500 crore built up from the unspent balance of 10 percent allocation in various ministries for the North-east. The problem is that there is a great deal of corruption in the North-east, which eats up a fair amount of what is earmarked for development. That there is greater corruption in many other states is hardly an explanation for resource-starved North-eastern region. Jayantha Madhab, the region's foremost economist and chairman of North-East Financial Development Corporation, laments: 'elsewhere they are talking about downsizing the government, the reverse is happening in the North-east. The governments have become the sole agencies for employment; for example, Assam spends about 71 percent of total revenue on salaries and establishments. - - -there is a need for monitoring the utilisation of these funds, which are either being ill-spent, diverted or returned unutilised.'[1]

Border Trade

The economic prosperity of the people in the border areas will be greatly improved if border trade with Myanmar, Bangladesh and Tibet is liberalised and made free. Border trade between India and Myanmar was formalised through India-Myanmar Border Trade Agreement of January 21, 1994, which became operational on April 12, 1995. The trade will take place through Moreh (Manipur) on the Indian side and Tamu on Myanmar side. The second border checkpoint will be at Champhai (Mizoram). India has no formal border trade agreement with Bangladesh. However, considerable amount of border trade is taking place between Bangladesh and three North-eastern states of Meghalaya, Assam and Tripura, either through authorised custom check post or on an informal basis.[2]

Equally important is the development of road link between the neighbouring countries. Jaswant Singh inaugurated the 144 km road built by the Border Roads (India), linking the township of Tamu with the railhead at Kalemayo in Myanmar in December 2000 This road is designed to provide main access to Indian goods at important business centres in Myanmar like Mandalay. Moreh has goods coming from Myanmar, China and Thailand, and across the border in Myanmar shops have Indian made goods like cycles, pharmaceuticals and electric generators. The road will have little utility if we continue our restrictive trade practices.

Curbing Illegal Immigration

We have allowed the illegal immigration from Bangladesh to take place without taking any serious steps to minimise the influx if not to stop it altogether. In the short term, there are a number of steps that should be taken. The fencing of the border can be effective only if the fence is kept under constant surveillance. More BSF posts should be established to maintain round the clock surveillance. A parallel fair weather road/ track should be constructed in areas where this does not exist. More patrol boats for the riverine areas should be issued for the BSF. Residents of the border area must be issued identity cards; successive home ministers have announced that the scheme would be implemented soon, but nothing has actually happened on ground. The identity cards would also serve the purpose for identification during elections. A national registration system with thumb impressions of citizens should be introduced in the North-east to begin with and subsequently the whole country should be brought under its ambit. Detection and deportation of foreigners as envisaged in the Assam Accord of 1985 should be expedited. Border fencing started in Assam in 1992 and has not yet been completed.[3] Border fencing has commenced on other portions of Indo-Bangladesh border and is likely to be completed only in 2007. All these works must be expedited. Unfortunately, most of the above measures have got mired in the politics of 'vote bank' and unless political parties reach a consensus and see the problem from national perspective, no result can be achieved.

In the long run, the idea mooted by Atal Bihari Vajpayee to introduce 'work permit' for Bangladeshi nationals should be examined seriously. India should also work with other South Asian countries and donor nations in poverty alleviation schemes in Bangladesh and Nepal. [4]

Reorganisation of Assam

It is debatable whether the formation of new smaller states, carved out of Assam, on ethnic lines have been able to fulfil the legitimate aspirations of the people. The experience is quite the contrary. The formation of economically unviable smaller states has, in fact, fuelled demands for the creation of even smaller states by sub-state ethnic groups. The trend is manifest in the case of Bodos, who want a separate state and the tribes of Karbi Anglong, who want yet more autonomy. This trend is generated when ethnic groups in small legislatures develop an overbearing attitude towards smaller groups.[5]

Dhrubajyoti Borah has, however, argued that Assam was an artificially created state, a creation of colonial conquest. NEFA, though administratively separate, was tagged along with Assam. The British colonial administration kept annexing the surrounding areas, which were added on to Assam without any regard for history, ethnicity or social factors and in the process Assam proper got submerged into a multiplicity of different races over which it had no control. According to Borah, the State of Assam should comprise the plain districts of Brahmaputra Valley and two autonomous districts of Karbi Anglong and North Cachar Hills. The three Barak Valley districts of Hailakandi, Karimganj and Cachar should form a separate administrative unit. Historically, ethnically and linguistically separate, this area has the necessary infrastructure for a separate administrative unit.[6] The arguments are convincing, but it will open a 'Pandora Box'. It is author's considered view that this is not the opportune time for such an exercise; there should be no redrawing of boundaries and the existing boundaries should be frozen for the next three decades at the least, to allow people to find a balance with their neighbours and realise the interdependence on each other.

Control of Trafficking in Narcotics and Small Arms

The smuggling of narcotics and drugs through North-east to Nepal and Kolkata and then to western destinations can be stopped only with active cooperation of Myanmar. The government should make it clear to Myanmar that narcotics trade is a serious threat to India's security and society. The government should also strengthen the existing narcotics control organisation in the country and there should be greater interaction between the Narcotics Control Bureau at Imphal and other security agencies. It should be a national endeavour and not be seen as the responsibility of North-eastern states alone, as drug trafficking and addiction spreads like fire without regard to national or international boundary.

Rebuilding the Shattered Communications with Bangladesh

The partition of the country had totally shattered the communications and economy of the North-east. The main artery of communication, Inland Water Transport was severed but continued fitfully until altogether suspended after 1965 war with Pakistan. The entire inland water system was allowed to disintegrate. Just to give an idea of the dislocation, here are some facts. Before partition one could reach Dhaka from Agartala (Tripura) – a distance of 150 km in a few hours, drive down the 75 km distance to Chittagong port in an hour and touch Sylhet (90 km) and Comila (25 km) with ease. Now Kolkata is a distant city (1,645 km). In a significant move, beginning has been made in starting a bus service between Kolkata and Dhaka. The service began in April 1999 but has yet to become regular.

India should also take initiative to progress the idea of reviving the Asian Super Highway linking India, Bangladesh and Myanmar with the rest of Asia. In a meaningful step forward to establish a South-east Asian rail link, India and Myanmar have held preliminary discussions on a proposal to develop the rail link Silchar-Imphal-Moreh-Tamu (Myanmar)-Kalemeyo, where a railhead has recently been developed. India's Border Road Organisation has already developed the Moreh-Tamu-Kalewa-Kalemeyo road in October 2000. India has also agreed in principle to modernise and upgrade Myanmar's railways.

India-Myanmar Cooperation

The relations between the two countries deteriorated after India openly supported Aung San Swu Kyi and her National League for Democracy (NLD) and denounced the Military *Junta*, which had seized power in 1988. Myanmar's generals accused India for giving shelter to Myanmar's students who had fled the country in the wake of onslaught against supporters of the banned NLD. General Than Shwe, the number two in the *Junta*, accused India of providing support to rebel groups of Myanmar like Kachin and Karens. India-Myanmar relations were at its lowest ebb. India headed the list of countries accusing the military dictatorship of Myanmar. When the Military *Junta* refused to implement the election result of 1990, which gave the NLD an overwhelming majority, the international community other than China denounced it.

Myanmar has great geo-strategic importance for India; it abuts on our North-eastern states and portion of Bangladesh. It shares the border with China. Myanmar's northern borders also constitute the tri-junction of eastern frontiers of India, China and Myanmar. India-Myanmar cooperation is vital for fighting insurgency and drug smuggling in North-east India. It was therefore, only logical to mend our relations with Myanmar, which was started during the premiership of Narsimha Rao. JN Dixit's, the then foreign secretary, visit to Myanmar in early 1993 started the process of improving our relations with Myanmar. Since then the relations between the two countries have improved considerably; an agreement to control smuggling and illegal trafficking of drugs was signed. There are institutional arrangements in place for holding meetings between civil and military officials of both countries. In 2004 Myanmar Army carried out operations against rebellious Khaplang group and destroyed its headquarters located in Myanmar's territory. Both armies now share intelligence on regular basis.

India-Bangladesh Relations

Regrettably, our relations with Bangladesh have not been very cordial in the recent past. Some of the causes have been discussed elsewhere in the narrative. What is important to realise that it is in our interest to improve relations with Bangladesh; the development of North-east region is dependent on it. For example, India is eager to import gas from Myanmar through Bangladesh. On its part Bangladesh has agreed to let the gas pipeline run through its territory. Bangladesh has also agreed to give double entry visa for Indians in North-east who want to travel to Kolkata through its territory by road. In return Bangladesh wants India to address three major economic demands; first, the creation of a transport corridor in the small stretch of Indian territory, about 50 km across, that lies between Bangladesh on one hand and Nepal and Bhutan on the other, second, transmission of cheap electricity from Nepal and Bhutan to Bangladesh through Indian territory, and the third, India to address the massive trade imbalance in favour of India.[7] Although it is in India's interest to accede to these demands for the sake of cordial relations with Bangladesh, the internal politics within Bangladesh where Islamic fundamentalism and anti-India sentiments are on the rise, encouraged by fundamentalists, it is unlikely that there will be any improvement in the bilateral relations in the near future.

Shift in Counter-Insurgency Strategy

The nature of counter insurgency operation has also to change to meet the challenges of the new breed of insurgents who now operate from urban centres. The use of land mines and explosive devices to ambush road bound patrols and convoys have added a new dimension to insurgency. Terrorism is now the preferred weapon of insurgents. Railway coaches are blown up to spread fear among populace. Explosive devices are frequently used to cause death and injury to innocent civilians. Oil pipelines are blown up to give an impression of their ascendancy over the state security apparatus. There is no clear defined boundary for an insurgent group. The tactical alliance between various insurgent groups of the North-east makes it possible for their operatives to find shelter and safe bases anywhere in the North-east and even beyond. The arrest of ULFA vice chairman Pradip Gogoi in Kolkata on April 8, 1998 is a case in point. It also underscores the need for intelligence agencies operating in the northeast to coordinate their efforts not only amongst themselves but also with the neighbouring states of West Bengal and Bihar. Bhutan's action against ULFA camps located in their territory is an example of how neighbouring countries should deal with terrorism. The agreement between India and Myanmar's armies to coordinate their efforts to fight insurgency is a welcome step. We must also continue to seek cooperation of Bangladesh to close down training camps and bases of insurgent groups located in Bangladesh.

The security forces have to shift their focus from jungle hideouts to urban centres. Although the destruction of insurgent bases in jungle hideouts will continue to engage the attention of security forces they have to develop tactical doctrines to fight the militants in crowded urban centres where security forces will be provoked to open fire resulting inevitably in civilian casualties.

The security forces have recently suffered maximum casualties when mines and IED planted by militants have blown up vehicles carrying troops. Most of the improvised mixtures contain large quantities of nitrates, which can be detected by nitrogen vapour detectors. Infrared rays can be detected by electronic counter measures. Trained dogs and chemical sniffers are also useful. There has to be multiple approaches for detection. But in the final analysis, the alert eyes and specialised training of troops assisted by technology will produce the best results. Simultaneously with the use of latest technology, the security forces have to beat the insurgents in guile and cunning. Never following a routine, using unexpected routes, staggered timings, intelligent use of radio communications and creating uncertainty in the hostile camp would go a long way in wresting the initiative from the insurgents.

Legal Framework

Every democratic country faces the dilemma in striking a balance between protecting human rights and enforcement of law and order and enacts laws to deal with the cases of terrorism. Human rights activists have been leading protests against the Armed Forces (Special Powers) Act, AFSPA, and demanding its abrogation. The AFSPA, enacted by the Parliament in 1958, gives legal authority for troops to operate in insurgency areas of the North-east. AFSPA can be applied only in 'Disturbed Areas', which can be so declared by the governor of that state/union territory or the Central Government by official gazette notification. The declaration of the whole or affected part of the state as 'disturbed area' recognises the breakdown of law and order. It should be the responsibility of the elected governments to create conditions so that AFSPA is not enforced, and if enforced, it is withdrawn at the earliest. It is unfair of those who oppose abrogation of AFSPA to expect the armed forces to maintain law and order in extraordinary situations without legal cover. But defending the need for the AFSPA does not mean that custodial murder and rape or other human rights violations are condoned. However, some provisions of the Act could be reviewed and amended after very careful examination.[8]

Intelligence

Lack of timely intelligence has been the weakest link in counter-insurgency operations. Unfortunately, the many intelligence agencies in the North-east, as in other sectors, have more often than not acted at cross-purposes. The tendency to score over the other results in depriving the security forces, the intelligence they require to act decisively in time. Local police are better placed and experienced than central forces to gather information because of their intimate relationship with the local populace and better knowledge of the terrain. The Army has often failed to utilise this source to their advantage. The tendency to distrust the local police is overwhelming and at times even justified. In a given situation, the local police may be sympathetic to their own ethnic group, but with patience, tact and leadership, they can be motivated to act in impartial manner. In Assam, wherever the army has gained the confidence of the local police, they have provided valuable intelligence to the army.

Notes and References

1. *Times of India*, New Delhi, May 5, 1998, p.13.
2. As per 1994 Government of India Notification, there are 138 authorised land custom stations (LCS) along the land borders of neighbouring countries. Out of these, 100 LCS are with Bangladesh, Bhutan, China, and Myanmar. Out of the 100, 90 LCS are only with Bangladesh, which indicates the importance of India-Bangladesh trade. Our strained relations with Bangladesh does not give much optimism for opening authorised check points for border trade between the two countries. For more details see Gurudas Das and RK Purkayastha (ed), *Border Trade: North-east India and Neighbouring Countries,* (New Delhi: Akanksha Publishing House, 2000) p 28.
3. Remarks of the Governor of Assam during his address at the Conference of Governors in Jan 2003. Quoted by Shourie, *Will the Iron Fence Save a Tree Hollowed by Termites*, 2005, ASA New Delhi, p. 200.
4. Sanjoy Hazarika has suggested some very practical measures, which could be considered while issuing work permits. See Sanjoy Hazarika,

"Turn Migration to India's Benefit", *The Times of India*, New Delhi, April 27, 1999.

5. Smt CR Chibber, "A Viable Strategy to Fight Insurgencies in the North-east", *NDC Journal*, New Delhi, vol xxiii, 2001.
6. Dhrubajyoti Borah, 'Understanding Assam and the North-east' in PS Dutta (ed), *North-east and the Indian State: Paradoxes of a Periphery*, (New Delhi: Vikas Publishing House, 1995).
7. C Raja Mohan, 'Delhi Must Respond to Dhaka Concession on Yangon Gas', *The Indian Express*, New Delhi, January 18, 2005, p 3
8. Two articles, one by General VP Malik and other by Lieutenant General VR Raghavan, have focused on this issue. See VP Malik, "Act of Last Resort", *The Indian Express*, New Delhi and VR Raghavan, "Disarming the Fall Guys", *The Indian Express*, New Delhi.

Appendix 'A'

Nagaland Accord (1975)

The Shillong Agreement of November 11, 1975

The following representatives of the underground organisations met the Governor of Nagaland, Shri LP Singh representing the Government of India, at Shillong on 10th and 11th November 1975.

1. Shri I Temjenba
2. Shri S Dahru
3. Shri Veenyiyl Rhakhu
4. Shri Z Ramyo
5 Shri M Assa
6. Shri Kevi Yallay

2. There was a series of four discussions. Some of the discussions were held with the Governor alone; at other, the Governor was assisted by the two Advisors for Nagaland, Shri M Ramunny, and Shri. H Zopianga, and Shri ML Kampani, Joint Secretary in the Ministry of Home Affairs. All the five members of the Liaison Committee, namely Rev Longri Ao, Dr M Aram, Shri. L Lungalang, Shri Kenneth Kerhuo, and Shri Lungshim Shaiza, participated in the discussions.

3. The following were the outcome of the discussions:

4. The representatives of the underground organisations conveyed their decision, of their own volition, to accept, without condition, the Constitution of India.

   i. It was agreed that the arms, now underground, would be brought out and deposited at appointed places. Details for giving effect of this agreement will be worked out between them and representatives of the Government, the security forces, and members of the Liaison Committee.

   ii. It was agreed that the representatives of the underground organisations should have reasonable time to formulate other issues for discussion for final settlement.

Place: Shillong,

Dated: November 11, 1975

Sd/- (I Temjenba)

Sd/- (S Dahru)
Sd/- (Z Ramyo)
Sd/- (M Assa)
Sd/- (Kevi Yalley)

On behalf of the Representative of the Underground organisations.
Representative of Government of India

Sd/-
(LP Singh)
On behalf of the
Government of India

Supplementary Agreement of January 5, 1976

Implementation of Clause II of the Shillong Accord of November 11, 1975.

1. It was decided that the collection of arms, initially at collection centres, would commence as early as possible, and will be completed by 25th January, 1976. Initial places of collection to be decided through discussion between Commissioner, representatives of underground organisations and the members of the Liaison Committee.
2. Once all arms are collected, these will be handed over to Peace Council team at the respective places of collection.
3. Peace Council team will arrange to transport the arms from collection centres to Chedema peace camp and arrange guards, etc., for safe custody of arms.
4. Similar arrangement at agreed place/places will be made in Manipur with the concurrence of the Manipur Government.
5. The underground may stay at peace camps to be established at suitable places, and their maintenance will be arranged only by the Peace Council. Any voluntary contribution from any source will be made to the Peace Council who will utilise the fund according to necessity.

Sd/-
(LP Singh)
Governor

1. Sd/-
(Biseto Medom Keyho)

2. Sd/-
(Pukrove Nakru)

3. Sd/-
(Z Ramyo)

4. Sd/-
(I. Temjenba)

Place: Shillong
Dated January 5, 1976

Appendix 'B'

Memorandum of Settlement with MNF

Text signed in New Delhi between the MNF leader Laldenga and the Government of India, 30 June, 1986

Preamble

1. Government of India have all along been making earnest efforts to bring about an end to the disturbed conditions in Mizoram and to restore peace and harmony.
2. Towards this end, initiative was taken by the late Prime Minister, Smt Indira Gandhi. On the acceptance by Shri Laldenga on behalf of the Mizo National Front (MNF) of the two conditions, namely, cessation of violence by MNF and holding of talks within the framework of the Constitution of India, a series of discussions were held with Shri Laldenga. Settlement on various issues reached during the course of the talk is incorporated in the following paragraphs.

Restoration of normalcy

3.1 With a view to restoring peace and normalcy in Mizoram the MNF party, on their part, undertakes within the agreed timeframe, to take all necessary steps to end all underground activities, to bring out all underground personnel of the MNF with their arms, ammunition and equipment to ensure their return to civil life, to abjure violence and generally to help in the process of restoration of normalcy. The modalities of bringing out all underground personnel and the deposit of arms, ammunition and equipment will be as worked out. The implementation of the foregoing will be under the supervision of the Central Government.

3.2 The MNF party will take immediate steps to amend its Articles of Association so as to make them conform to the provision of law.

3.3 The Central Government will take steps for the resettlement and rehabilitation of underground MNF personnel coming overground after considering the scheme proposed in this regard by the Government of Mizoram.

3.4 The MNF undertakes not to extend any support to Tripura/ Tribal National Volunteers (TNV), People's Liberation Army of Manipur (PLA) and any other such groups, by way of training, supply of arms or providing protection or in any other manner.

Legal, administrative and other steps

4.1 With a view to satisfying the desires and aspirations of all sections of the people of Mizoram, the Government will initiate measures to confer Statehood on the Union Territory of Mizoram, subject to other stipulations contained in this Memorandum of Settlement.

4.2 To give effect to the above, the necessary legislative and administrative measures will be undertaken, including those for the enactment of Bills for the amendment of the Constitution and other laws for the conferment of Statehood as aforesaid, to come into effect on a date to be notified by the Central Government.

4.3 The amendments aforesaid shall provide, among other things, for the following:-

I. The territory of Mizoram shall consist of the territory specified in Section 6 of the North Eastern Areas (Reorganisation) Act, 1971.

II. Notwithstanding anything contained in the Constitution, no Act of Parliament in respect of

a. Religious or social practices of the Mizos

b. Mizo customary law or procedure

c. Administration of civil and criminal justice involving decisions according to Mizo customary law

d. Ownership and transfer of land, shall apply to the State of Mizoram unless the Legislative Assembly of Mizoram by a resolution so decides:

Provided that nothing in this clause shall apply to any Central Act in force in Mizoram immediately before the appointed day.

III. Article 170, Clause (1) shall, in relation to the Legislative Assembly of Mizoram, have effect as if for the word 'sixty' the word 'forty' has been substituted.

5. Soon after the Bill for the conferment of Statehood becomes law, and when the President is satisfied that normalcy has returned and that conditions conducive to the holding of free and fair elections exist, the process of holding elections to the Legislative Assembly will be initiated.

6a. The Centre will transfer resources to the new Government keeping in view the change in status from a Union Territory to a State and this will include resources to cover the revenue gap for the year.

6b. Central assistance for Plan will be fixed taking note of any residuary gap in resources so as to sustain the approved Plan

Outlay and the pattern of assistance will be as in the case of special category states.

7. Border trade in locally produced or grown agricultural commodities could be allowed under a scheme to be formulated by the Central Government, subject to international arrangements with neighbouring countries.

8. The Inner Line Regulations, as now in force in Mizoram, will not be amended or repealed without consulting the State Government.

Other matters

9. The rights and privileges of the minorities in Mizoram, as envisaged in the Constitution shall continue to be preserved and protected and their social and economic advancement shall be ensured

10. Steps will be taken by the Government of Mizoram at the earliest to review and codify the existing customs, practices, laws or other usages relating to matters specified in clauses (a) to (d) of para 4.3 (II) of the memorandum, keeping in view that an individual Mizo may prefer to be governed by Acts of Parliament dealing with such matters and which are of general application.

11. The question of the unification of Mizo-inhabited areas of other States to form one administrative unit was raised by the MNF delegation. It was pointed out to them, on behalf of the Government of India that Article 3 of the Constitution of India prescribes the procedures in this regard but that the Government cannot make any commitment in this respect.

12. It was also pointed out on behalf of the Government that as soon as Mizoram becomes a State

    i. the provisions of Part XVII of the Constitution will apply and the State will be at liberty to adopt any one or more of the languages in use in the state as the language to be used for all or any of the official purposes of the State;

    ii. it is open to the State to move for the establishment of a separate University in the State in accordance with the prescribed procedure;

    iii. in the light of the Prime Minister's statement at the Joint Conference of the Chief Justice, Chief Ministers and Law Ministers held at New Delhi on 31st August, 1995 Mizoram will be entitled to have a High Court of its own, if it so wishes.

13a. It was noted that there is already a scheme in force for payment of ex-gratia amount to heirs/dependents of persons who were killed during disturbance in 1966 and thereafter in the Union Territory of Mizoram. Arrangements will be made to expeditiously disburse payment to those eligible persons who had already applied but who had not been made such payments so far.

13b. It was noted that consequence on verification done by a joint team of officers, the Government of India had already made arrangements for payment of compensation in respect of damaged crops; buildings destroyed/ damaged during the action in Mizoram, and rental charges of building and lands occupied by the Security Forces. There may, however, be some claims which were preferred and verified by the above team but have not yet been settled. These pending claims will be settled expeditiously. Arrangements will also be made for payment of pending claims of rental charges for lands/ buildings occupied by the Security Forces.

(Signed)
LALDENGA
On behalf of Mizo National Front

(Signed)
RD PRADHAN
Home Secretary
Government of India

(Signed)
LALKHAMA
Chief Secretary
Government of Mizoram

Date: 30 June 1986
Place: NEW DELHI

The Memorandum of Settlement contemplates the following sequence of events:

1. Coming overground of MNF personnel and depositing of arms, ammunition and equipment by them in accordance with the time bound programme as already agreed upon between the Ministry of Home Affairs and the MNF delegation.
2. The MNF Party should take immediate steps to amend its Articles of Association to make them conform to the provision of law.
3. Government will initiate steps for rehabilitation of MNF personnel coming overground.
4. After completion of action under paragraphs (1) and (2) above, a Constitution Amendment Bill will be introduced in Parliament of the grant of Statehood and other consequential legislative measures to be taken up.
5. After the bill becomes law, preparation of delimitation of constituencies and holding elections of the State Legislature will be taken on hand when the President is satisfied that normalcy has been restored.

Appendix 'C'

Memorandum of Understanding with TNV (1988)

The following is the text of the "Memorandum of Settlement" to end insurgency in Tripura.

Preamble

Government of India has been making efforts to bring about a satisfactory settlement of the problem in Tripura by restoring peace and harmony in areas where disturbed conditions prevailed.

The Tribal National Volunteers (TNV) through their letter dated 4 May, 1988 addressed to the Governor of Tripura and signed by Shri Bejoy Kumar Hrangkhwl, stated that keeping in view the Prime Minister Shri Rajiv Gandhi's policy of solution of problems through negotiations, TNV have decided to abjure violence, give up secessionist demand and to hold negotiations for a peaceful solution of all the problems of Tripura within the Constitution of India. The TNV also furnished its bye-laws, which conform to the laws in force. On this basis a series of discussions were held with representatives of TNV.

The following were the outcome of the discussions:

1. Deposit of Arms and Ammunition and stopping of underground activities by TNV
2. The TNV undertakes to take all necessary steps to end underground activities and to bring out all underground of the TNV with their arms, ammunition and equipment within one month of signing of this memorandum. Details for giving effect to this part of settlement will be worked out and implemented under the supervision of the Central Government.
3. The TNV further undertakes to ensure that it does not resort to violence and to help in restoration of amity between different sections of the population.
4. The TNV undertakes not to extend any support to any other extremist group by way of training, supply of arms or providing protection or in any other manner.

Rehabilitation of undergrounds

Suitable steps will be taken for the resettlement and rehabilitation of TNV undergrounds coming overground in the light of the schemes drawn up for the purpose.

Measures to prevent infiltration

Stringent measures will be taken to prevent infiltration from across the border by strengthening arrangements on the border and construction of roads along vulnerable sections of the Indo-Bangladesh border in Tripura sector for better patrolling and vigil. Vigorous action against such infiltrators would also be taken under the law.

Reservation of seats in the Tripura Legislative Assembly for tribals

With a view to satisfying the aspirations of tribals of Tripura for a greater share in the governance of the State. Legislative measures will be taken including those for the enactment of the Bill for the amendment of the Constitution.

The Constitutional amendments shall provide that notwithstanding anything contained in the Constitution, the number of seats in the Legislative Assembly of Tripura reserved for scheduled tribes shall be such number of seats as bears to the total number of seats, a proportion not less than the number, as on the date of coming into force of the constitutional amendment, of members belonging to the scheduled tribes in the existing Assembly bears to the total number of seats in the existing Assembly.

The Representation of the People's Act, 1950 shall also be amended to provide for reservation of 20 seats for the scheduled tribes in the Assembly of Tripura. However, the amendment shall not effect any representation in the existing Assembly of Tripura until its dissolution.

Restoration of alienated lands of tribals

It was agreed that the following measures will be taken:

i. Review of rejected application for the restoration of tribal land under the Tripura Land Revenue and Land Reform Act, 1960;

ii. Effective implementation of the law for restoration;

iii. Stringent measures to prevent fresh alienation;

iv. Provision of soil conservation measures and irrigation facilities in tribals areas; and

v. Strengthening of the agricultural credit system so as to provide for an appropriate agency with adequate tribal representation to ensure easy facilities for both consumption and operational credit to tribals.

Redrawing of the boundaries of Autonomous District Council Area

Tribal majority villages, which now fall outside the autonomous district council area and are contiguous to such area will be included in the autonomous district and similarly placed non-tribal majority villages presently in the autonomous district and on the periphery may be excluded.

Measures for long-term economic development of Tripura

Maximum emphasis will be placed on extensive and intensive skill formation of the tribal youth of Tripura so as to improve their prospects of employment including self-employment in various trades such as motor workshops, pharmacies, electronic goods, carpentry, tailoring, stationary, weaving, rice and oil mills, general stores, fishery, poultry, piggery, horticulture, handloom and handicrafts.

Special intensive recruitment drives will be organised for police and paramilitary forces in Tripura with a view to enlisting as many tribal youth as possible.

All India Radio will increase the duration and content of their programme in tribal language or dialects of Tripura. Additional transmitting stations will be provided for coverage even of the remoter areas of the State.

The demands relating to self-employment of tribals, issue of permits for vehicles for tribals for commercial purposes, visits of tribals and women to such places in the country as may be of value from the viewpoint of inspiration, training and the experience in relevant fields will be considered sympathetically by the government.

At least 2,500 jhumia families will be rehabilitated in five centres or more in accordance with model schemes based on agricultural, horticulture including vegetable growing, animal husbandry, fisheries and plantations, with a view to weaning them away from jhum cultivation. The scheme would also provide for housing assistance.

In the autonomous district council area of Tripura, rice, salt and kerosene oil will be given at subsidised rates during lean months for a period of three years.

Conscious effort will be made for effective implementation of the provisions of the Sixth Schedule of the Constitution in so far as it relates to Tripura.

Memorandum of Settlement on Bodoland Territorial Council (BTC)

On February 10, 2003 the Assam government, the Union government and the Bodo Liberation Tigers signed the Memorandum of Settlement on Bodoland Territorial Council (BTC), in New Delhi. The jurisdiction of the BTC shall extend over 3082 villages and the BTC has been given legislative powers over 40 subjects. The accord provides for an Executive Council comprising of a maximum of 12 Executive Members, including a Chief and a Deputy Chief, with adequate representation to the non-tribal population. Presented below is the full text of the accord.

1. The Government of India and the Government of Assam have been making concerted efforts to fulfil the aspirations of the Bodo people relating to their cultural identity, language, education and economic development. Towards this end, a series of talks were held between Government of India, Government of Assam and Bodo Liberation Tigers (BLT) since March 2000. As a result, it is agreed to create a self-governing body for the Bodo Areas in the State of Assam as follows:

2. **Objectives**

The objectives of the agreement are: to create an Autonomous self governing body to be known as Bodoland Territorial Council (BTC) within the State of Assam and to provide constitutional protection under Sixth Schedule to the said Autonomous Body; to fulfil economic, educational and linguistic aspirations and the preservation of land-rights, socio-cultural and ethnic identity of the Bodos; and speed up the infrastructure development in BTC area.

3. **Area**

3.1. The area of proposed BTC shall comprise all the 3082 villages and areas to be so notified by the State Government. The above mentioned villages and areas shall be divided into 4 contiguous districts after reorganisation of the existing districts of Assam within a period of 6 months of the signing of the agreement on the lines of the proposal given by BLT subject to clearance of the Delimitation Commission.

3.2. A committee comprising one representative each from Governments of India & Assam and BLT will decide by consensus on the inclusion of additional villages and areas in the BTC from out of 95 villages and areas on the basis of the criteria of tribal population being not less than 50%, contiguity or any other agreed relevant criteria within a period of three months of signing of this MoS.

4. **Status of Bodoland Territorial Council**

The provision of the Sixth Schedule and other relevant Articles of the Constitution of India will apply to BTC, *mutatis mutandis* in terms of this agreement. The safeguards/modifications for the non-tribals in BTC area, inter-alia, will include the following:

4.1. Provision of para1 (2) of Sixth Schedule regarding Autonomous Regions will not be applicable to BTC.

4.2. A provision will be made in para 2(1) of the Sixth Schedule for increasing the number of members for BTC up to 46 out of which 30 will be reserved for Scheduled Tribes, 5 for non-tribal communities, 5 open for all communities and 6 to be nominated by Governor of Assam from the unrepresented communities for BTC area of which atleast two should be women. Nominated members will have the same rights and privileges as other members, including voting rights. Election from the 40 constituencies of BTC shall be on the basis of adult franchise. The term of the elected members of BTC shall be for 5 years.

4.3. Safeguards for the settlement rights, transfer and inheritance of property etc. of non-tribals will be suitably incorporated in para 3 of the Sixth Schedule. Any such law as may be made by the BTC in this regard will not, in particular:

(c) Extinguish the rights and privileges enjoyed by an citizen of India in respect of their land at the commencement of BTC, and

(d) Bar any citizen from acquiring land either by way of inheritance, allotment, settlement or by way of transfer if such citizens were eligible for such bonafide acquisition of land within the BTC area.

4.4. Provision will be added in para 6 of Sixth Schedule that in BTC area, language and medium of instruction in educational institutions will not be changed without approval of the State Government.

4.5. Provision of para 8 of Sixth Schedule regarding power to assess and collect land revenue and impose taxes shall be applicable to BTC.

4.6. Para 10 of the Sixth Schedule will not be applicable to BTC area.

4.7. Provision of Article 332(6) of the Constitution will be so modified that the existing status of representation of BTC area in the State Assembly is kept intact. After the creation of BTC, the Parliamentary & Assembly Constituencies shall be delimited by the Delimitation Commission in accordance with the provisions of the Constitution.

4.8. In the event, Panchayati Raj system ceases to be in force in the council area, the powers of the Panchayati Raj Institutions in such matters shall be vested with the Council.

The Amendments to the Sixth Schedule shall include provisions in such a manner that non-tribals are not disadvantaged in relation to the rights enjoyed by them at the commencement of BTC and their rights and privileges including land rights are fully protected.

5. **Power and Functions**

5.1. The Council shall have legislative powers in respect to subjects transferred to it as enumerated below. All laws made under this paragraph shall be submitted forthwith to the Governor and until assented to by him, shall have no effect. The BTC shall have executive, administrative and financial powers in respect of subjects transferred to it.

Subjects to be entrusted to BTC by Assam Government

1. Small, Cottage and Rural Industry; 2. Animal Husbandry & Veterinary; 3. Forest; 4. Agriculture; 5. PWD; 6. Sericulture; 7. Education (Primary Education, Higher Secondary including vocational training, Adult Education, College Education (General); 8. Cultural Affairs; 9. Soil Conservation; 10. Cooperation; 11. Fisheries; 12. Panchayat and Rural Development; 13. Handloom and Textile; 14. Health & Family Welfare; 15. Public Health Engineering; 16. Irrigation; 17. Social Welfare; 18. Flood Control; 19. Sports & Youth Welfare; 20. Weights and Measures; 21. Library Services; 22. Museum & Archaeology; 23. Urban Development – Town and Country Planning; 24. Tribal Research Institute; 25. Land & Revenue; 26. Publicity/Public Relations; 27. Printing & Stationery; 28. Tourism; 29. Transport; 30. Planning and Development; 31. Municipal Corporation, Improvement Trust, District Boards and other local authorities; 32. Welfare of Plan Tribes and Backward Classes; 33. Markets and Fairs; 34. Lotteries, Theatres, Dramatic Performance and Cinema; 35. Statistics; 36. Food and Civil Supply; 37. Intoxicating Liquors, Opium and Derivatives etc.; 38. Labour and Employment; 39. Relief and Rehabilitation; 40. Registration of Births and Deaths.

5.2. There shall be an Executive Council comprising of not more than 12 Executive Members, one of whom shall be the Chief and another one the Deputy Chief of the said Executive

Council. There shall be adequate representation for the non-tribal members in the Executive Council. The Chief and the Deputy Chief of the Council shall have the status equivalent to the Cabinet Minister and the other Executive Members equivalent to the Minister of the State of Assam for protocol purposes in BTC area.

5.3. The BTC shall have the full control over the officers and staff connected with the delegated subjects working in the BTC area and shall be competent to transfer officers and staff within the BTC area. ACRs of these officers shall also be written by the appropriated BTC authority.

5.4. BTC shall also be competent to make appointments for all posts under its control in accordance with the rules of appointment followed by the Government of Assam. However, the posts, where recruitment is made on the recommendation of APSC, shall not be covered under this provision. The Council may constitute a Selection Board for appointments to be made by it and may also make rules, with the approval of the Governor of Assam to regulate appointments and to ensure adequate representation for all communities living in the Council area.

5.5. No posts shall be created by BTC without concurrence of the Government of Assam and it shall also abide by the decision of the Government of Assam in respect of abolition of/temporarily keeping vacant any post.

5.6. Development functions and bodies within the competence of BTC shall be transferred to BTC. In respect of DRDA, concurrence of Government of India will be obtained.

5.7. The offices of the Dy. Commissioner and Superintendent of Police will be outside the superintendence and control of BTC.

5.8. The State Government would provide an amount; to be decided every year on population ratio basis, as grants-in-aid in two equal instalments to the BTC for executing development works. The proportionate share for the BTC shall be calculated on the basis of the plan funds available after setting aside the funds required for earmarked sectors and the salary. This amount may be reduced proportionately if the state plan allocation is reduced or there is plan cut due to resource problem. In addition, the Council will be paid a suitable amount of plan funds and non-plan funds to cover the office expenses and the salaries of the staff working under their control. The BTC shall disburse the salaries of the staff under their control and would ensure strict economy in the matter.

5.9. BTC authority shall prepare a plan with the amounts likely to be available for development works, both under State share and Central share, covering any or all the activities of the departments under their control. The Council shall have full discretion in selecting the activities and choosing the amount for the investment under the same in any year covering all groups of people in a fair and equitable manner. This plan will be a sub set of the State plan and would be treated as its integral part. Once the plan of the State, including BTC plan, gets the approval of the Planning Commission the BTC authority will start execution of their plan in the BTC area. Modifications, if any, made by the Planning Commission in the BTC proposal, shall be binding on the BTC authority. The State Government shall not divert the funds allocated to the BTC to other heads and also ensure its timely release. BTC may have Planning Department to prepare the plans for BTC area to be submitted to Planning Commission through the Government of Assam.

5.10. The executive functions of the BTC shall be exercised through its Principal Secretary who shall be an officer of the rank not below of Commissioner/Secretary to Government of Assam. The sanctioning powers of the Government of Assam shall be vested with the Principal Secretary of BTC and sanctioning powers of head(s) of the Department(s) including for technical sanction shall be conferred on the seniormost officer of that Department preferably not below the rank of Additional Director, who may be designated as Director of BTC for that department. The Principal Secretary and other officers shall exercise their powers under the overall guidance and supervision of BTC.

6. **Law and Order**

To strengthen the Police Administration, Government of Assam shall appoint an IGP for 4 districts of BTC and the jurisdiction of the DIG Kokrajhar shall also be modified to cover these 4 districts.

7. **Revision of list of ST**

Consequent to the inclusion of BTC area into the Sixth Schedule, the list of ST for the State of Assam shall be so modified so as to ensure that the tribal status of Bodos and other tribals living outside the BTC does not get affected adversely.

8. **Grant of ST status of Bodo Kacharis of Karbi Anglong and NC Hills districts**

   The Government of India agrees to consider sympathetically the inclusion of the Bodo Kacharis living in Karbi Anglong and NC Hills Autonomous Council area in the ST (Hill) List of State of Assam.

9. **Development of Bodo Language**

   9.1. The Government of India agrees to consider favourably the inclusion of Bodo Language in Devnagari Script in the Eighth Schedule of the Constitution.

   9.2. Bodo language shall be the official language of BTC subject to the condition that Assamese and English shall also continue to be used for official purpose.

10. **Additional Development Package for BTC**

   10.1. The State Government, within the limitation of financial and other constraints, may offer or allow the Council to offer, possible and sustainable additional incentives for attracting private investment in the Council area and would also support projects for external funding.

   10.2. In order to accelerate the development of the region and to meet the aspirations of the people, the Government of India will provide financial assistance of Rs 100 crores per annum for 5 years for projects to develop the socio-economic infrastructure in BTC areas over and above the normal plan assistance to the State of Assam. The size of the Corpus will be reviewed after a period of 5 years. Suitable mechanism will be built in the system to ensure that the funds are transferred to BTC in time and at regular intervals. An illustrative list of projects which may be considered to be taken up in BTC is given below:

List of projects:

1. To establish a centre for development and research of Bodo language; 2. Upgradation of existing educational infrastructure by way of renovation/addition of buildings, providing modern facilities for teaching such as computers, science laboratories etc. from primary level to college level in BTC area; 3. A cultural complex to be established at Kokrajhar to promote and develop Bodo tradition and cultural heritage; 4. To establish a super-specialty hospital with all modern facilities at Kokrajhar Government Hospitals shall be established in all district, sub-divisional and block headquarter; 5. To establish sports complexes in all the district headquarters; 6. Food processing plants and cold storage facilities at Kokrajhar, Kajolgaon, Udalguri

and Tamulpur; 7. Construction of a bridge over river Aai to connect Koilamoila, Amguri etc. with the rest of the district; 8. To build a Bodoland Bhawan in Delhi; 9. To set up integrated agro-processing park and textile-cum-apparel park; 10. Revitalisation of Kokilabari Agricultural Farm; 11. To develop adequate infrastructure to promote Manas sanctuary as an international tourist spot; 12. To complete Champa, Suklai and Dhansiri irrigation projects; 13. To construct a highway on the Indo-Bhutan border from Jamduar to Bhairabkunda to connect remote places located adjacent to the border; 14. To set up model dairy, fishery, horticulture and poultry farms/training centres at different places in all the 4 districts to encourage youth for self-employment; 15. To enhance the existing facilities in veterinary hospitals in BTC area.

10.3. Government of India will provide necessary one time financial assistance required for development of administrative infrastructure in the newly created district headquarters, sub-divisional headquarters and book headquarters, besides the BTC Secretariat Complex at Kokrajhar

11. **Centrally Funded University**

11.1. A centrally funded Central Institute of Technology (CIT) will be set up to impact education in various technological/vocational disciplines such as Information Technology, Bio-Technology, Food Processing, Rural Industries, Business Management, etc.

11.2. The CIT will be subsequently upgraded to a centrally funded State University with technical and non-technical disciplines to be run by the BTC.

12. **Relief & Rehabilitation**

12.1. The BLT would join the national mainstream and shun the path of violence in the interest of peace and development. After the formation of the interim council of BTC, BLT will dissolve itself as an organisation and surrender with arms within a week of swearing-in of the interim council. The State Government would provide full support to relief and rehabilitation of the members of BLT who would surrender with arms in this process in accordance with the existing policy of the State. Financial support in such cases however shall be limited to be provisions of the scheme prepared and funded by the Government of India. Withdrawal of cases against such persons and those related to overground Bodo movement since 1987 shall be considered according to the existing policy of the State of Assam.

12.2. The Government of India will initiate steps for review of action against the Bodo employees of Government of India and subordinate officers as well as in respect of Central Government Undertakings. Similar action would be taken by the Government of Assam.

12.3. Bodo youth will be considered for recruitment in Police, Army and Paramilitary forces to increase their representation in these forces.

13. **Special Rehabilitation Programme for the people affected by ethnic disturbances:**

The Special Rehabilitation Programme (SRP) for the people affected by ethnic disturbances in Assam, who are at present living at relief camps in Kokrajhar, Bongaigaon etc. shall be completed by the Government of Assam with active support of BTC. Necessary funds for their rehabilitation shall be provided by the Government of India and lands which are free from all encumbrances required for such rehabilitation shall be made available by the BTC.

14. **Interim Council**

Immediately after signing of the agreement, Interim Executive Council for BTC shall be formed by Governor of Assam from amongst the leaders of the present Bodo movement, including the signatories to this settlement, and shall include adequate representation to the non-tribal communities in BTC area. The Interim Council shall not continue for a period beyond 6 months during which period election to the Council shall be held. Government of Assam shall dissolve the Bodoland Autonomous Council (BAC) and repeal the BAC Act.

15. Government of Assam will consider inclusion of all tribals including Bodos in RHAC/MAC/LAC in consultation with leaders of these Councils.

16. The Implementation of the provision of the Memorandum of Settlement shall be periodically reviewed by a Committee comprising representatives of Government of India, Government of Assam and BTC.

Signed on February 10, 2003 at New Delhi in the presence of Shri LK Advani, Hon'ble Deputy Prime Minister of India and Shri Tarun Gogoi, Chief Minister of Assam.

(Hagrama Basumatary) Chairman Bodo Liberation Tigers (PK Dutta) Chief Secretary Govt. of Assam (RCA Jain) Secretary (BM) Ministry of Home Affairs Government of India.

Select Bibliography

Reports and Documents

- Ministry of Home Affairs, Government of India, *Basic Statistics of North-east Region*, 1995, North-East Council, Shillong.
- Ministry of Home Affairs, *Census of India*, Series 1, Paper 2, 1992.
- Ministry of Home Affairs, *Census of India*, 2001.
- Operation Bluebird: *A Case Study of Torture and Extra-judicial Executions in Manipur*, 1990, Amnesty International, London.
- "Army in Nagaland, Report of Justice Sen", Published in *Economic and Political Weekly*, August 24-31, 1996 .

Books

- Acharya, NN, *Brief History of Assam from Earliest times to 1983*, Guwahati: Osmos Publication, 1987.
- Atsongchanger, Mar, *Unforgettable Memories from Nagaland*, India: Tribal Communication and Research Centre, Mokokchung (Nagaland), 1994.
- Alemchiba, *A Brief Historical Account of Nagaland*, Kohima: The Naga Institute of Culture, Nagaland, 1970.
- Aosenba, *The Naga Resistance Movement: Prospects of Peace and Armed Conflict*, New Delhi: Regency Publication, 2001.
- Asoso Yonuo, *The Rising Nagas*, New Delhi: Vivek Publications, 1974.
- Bendengangshi, *Glimpses of Naga History*, Mokokchung: Naga Patriots from Soyim, Nagaland, 1993.
- Bhagwat Vishnu, Admiral (Indian Navy), *Betrayal of the Defence Forces: The Truth Inside*, New Delhi: Manas, 2001.
- Bhattacharya, Chandana, *Ethnicity and Autonomy Movement: Case of Bodo-Cachari of Assam*, 1996, Vikas Publishing House, New Delhi.
- Bhattacharya, KK, *North-east India: Political and Administrative History*, 1983, Cosmo Publication, New Delhi.

- Bhuyan SK, *Tungkhunga Burunji or A History of Assam 1681-1826*, 1933, Oxford University Press, Calcutta.
- Brajpujari HK, *India's North-east: Problems, Policies and prospects since Independence*, 1998, Spectrum Publications, Delhi.
- Bhaumik, Subir, *Insurgent Crossfire: North-east India*, 1996, Lancers, New Delhi.
- Beckett, Ian FW, *Modern Insurgencies and Counter-insurgencies*, 2001, Routelage, London (UK).
- Barua, BP, *Ethnicity and Nation Building in Bangladesh: A Study of Chittagong Hill Tracts*, 2001, HarAnand, New Delhi.
- Banerjee, Dipankar (ed), South Asia at Gun Point, 2000, Regional Centre for Strategic Studies, Colombo, Sri Lanka.
- Cardozo, Ian, Maj Gen (Retd), *The Indian Army: A Brief History*, 2005, United Service Institution of India, Rao Tula Marg, New Delhi.
- Chaube, SK, *Hill Politics in North-east India*, Orient Longman, New Delhi.
- Das Amiya Kumar, *Assam's Agony*, 1982, Lancers, New Delhi.
- Datta, PS (ed), *North-east and the Indian State; Paradoxes of a Periphery*, 1995, Vikas Publishing, New Delhi.
- Dev SC, *Nagaland: The Untold Story*, 1988, Published by Mrs Gowri Dev, 106, Regent Estate, Calcutta (WB).
- Dhar, Pannalal, *Ethnic Unrest*, 1998, Deep Deep publishers, New Delhi.
- Egreteau, Renaud, *Wooing the Generals*, 2003, Authorspress, Centre De Sciences Humaines, 2 Aurangzeb Road, New Delhi.
- Elwin, Verrier, *A Philosophy for NEFA*, 1959, Government of NEFA.
- Elwin, Verrier, *Nagaland*, 1961, Research Department Advisers' Secretariat, Shillong, (Meghalaya), India.
- Gundeviya, YD, *War and Peace in Nagaland*, 1975, Palit and Palit, Dehradun (UP).
- Gopalakrishna, R, *Insurgent North-east region of India*, 1995, Vikas Publishers, New Delhi.
- Ghosal Sona, *Politics of Drugs and India's North-east*, New Delhi: Anamika Publishers, 2003.
- Gurudev Das and RK Purkayastha (ed), Border Trade: North-east India and Neighbouring Countries, New Delhi, Akanksha

Publishing House, 2000.

- Hazarika, Sanjoy, *Strangers of the Mist: Tales of War and Peace from North-east*, 1995, Penguin, New Delhi.
- Kumar BB, *Tension and Conflict in North-east India*, 1995, Cosmo publication, New Delhi.
- Krishna, Ashok, Maj Gen (Retd), *India's Armedforces: Fifty Years of War and Peace, 1998, Lancers*, New Delhi.
- Marwah, Ved, *Uncivil Wars: Pathology of Terrorism in India*, 1995, Harper and Collins, India.
- Mitra, Subrata, K, and Louis, DR Alison (ed), *Sub-National Movement in South Asia,* 1998, Segment Books, New Delhi.
- Maitra, Kiranshankar, *The Noxious Web: Insurgency in North-east*, 2001, Kaniska Publishers, New Delhi.
- Misra, Udayon, *The Periphery Strikes Back: Challenges to the Nation State in Assam and Nagaland*, 2000, Indian Institute of Advanced Studies, Rashtrapati Bhavan, Shimla (HP).
- Ministry of External Affairs, *The Naga Problem*, 1960, External Publicity Division, Government of India.
- Nibedon, Nirmal, *North-east India: the Ethnic Explosion*, 1981, Lancers, New Delhi.
- Nibedon, Nirmal, *The Night of the Guerrillas*, 1978, Lancers, New Delhi
- Nibedon, Nirmal, *Mizoram: The Dagger Brigade*, 1980, Lancers, New Delhi.
- Nayyar, VK, Lt Gen (Retd), *The Threat from Within: India's Internal Security Environment*, 1992, Lancers, New Delhi.
- Nayyar, VK, Lt Gen (Retd), *Low Intensity Conflict*, 2003 .
- Narhari, NS, Lt Gen (Retd), *Security Threats to North-east India*, 2002, Manas, New Delhi.
- Nepram, Binalaxmi, *South Asia's Fractured Frontiers: Armed Conflict, Narcotics and Small Arms Proliferation in India's North-east,* 2002, Mittal Publications, New Delhi.
- Palsokar, RD, *Forever in Operations*, 1991, 8 Mountain Division, c/o 56 APO.
- Palit, DK, Maj Gen (Retd), *Sentinels of the North-east: The Assam Rifles*, 1984, Palit and Palit, Dehradun.
- Phukan, Girin and Dutta, NL (ed), *Politics of Identity and Nation Building in North-east India.*

- Phadnis, Urmila, *Ethnicity and Nation Building in South Asia*, 1989, Sage Publication, New Delhi.
- Ray, Animesh, Mizoram (New Delhi: Book Trust of India, 1993).
- Rustomji, Nari, *Imperilled Frontiers*, 1983, Oxford University Press, Delhi.
- Rai, Baljit, *Demographic Aggression Against India*, 1993, BS Publishers, Chandigarh.
- Sema, Hokishe, *Emergence of Nagaland*, 1986, Vikas, New Delhi.
- Shastri, Ajay Mitra, *Ancient North-east India: Pragjyotisha*, 2002, Aryan Books, New Delhi.
- Sinha, AC, *NE Frontier of India*, 1994, Indus, New Delhi.
- Sharma, SC, *Insurgency or Ethnic conflict*, 2000, Magnum Business Associates, New Delhi.
- Singh, Prakash, *Nagaland*, 1972, National Book Trust, New Delhi.
- Singh BP, *The problems of Change*, 1989, Vikas Publishers, New Delhi.
- Sareen, HK, *Insurgency in North-east India: A Study of the Sino-American Role*, 1980, Sterling publishers, New Delhi.
- Sareen VIK, *India's North-east in Flames*, 1980, Vikas Publishers, New Delhi.
- Shourie, Arun, *Missionaries in India*, 1994, ASA Publishers, New Delhi.
- Shourie, Arun, *A Secular Agenda*, 1993, Harper Collins Publishers India, New Delhi.
- Shourie, Arun, *Will the Iron Fence Save a Tree Hollowed by Termites: Defence Imperatives Beyond the Military*, ASA, Rupa & Co, 2005, New Delhi.
- Saikia, Jaideep, *Terror Sans Frontier*, 2003, University of Illinois, USA.
- Tarapot, Phanjoubam, *Insurgency Movement in North-east India*, Vikas Publishers, New Delhi.
- Verghese, BG, *India's North-east Resurgent*, 1996, Konark Publishers, New Delhi.
- Wati, L, *Facts and Growth of Naga Nationalism*, 1993, Published by the author, Mokokchung (Nagaland).
- Weiner, Myron, *Sons of Soil: Migration and Ethnic Conflict in India*, 1978, Princeton University Press, Princeton (USA).

Magazines

- Biswas, Sontik, "Kuki-Naga Conflict; Living on the Razor's Edge", *India Today*, October, 15, 1993.
- Bayan, Rana A, 'West by North-east', *Sunday*, Calcutta, January 29-February 4, 1995.
- Bhaumik, Subir, 'Herculean Task', *Sunday*, *20*-26 July 1997.
- Barun, Dasgupta, 'Bodo Agitation: Background and Prospects' *Mainstream*, June 19-24, 1989.
- Barun, Dasgupta, "Difficult Task Ahead", *Frontline*, July 25, 1997.
- Chaudhuri, Kalyan, 'Separatist Terror', *Frontline*, September 12, 2003..
- Chaudhuri, Kalyan, 'Turning to Peace', *Frontline*, March, 14, 2004.
- Chaudhuri, Kalyan, 'Territory Tussles', *Frontline*, February 28, 2003.
- Chaudhuri, Kalyan, 'In the Mood for Talks', *Frontline*, January 17, 2003.
- Chattopadhyay, Surhid Sankar, 'A Ruthless Hit Squad', *Frontline*, January 16, 2004.
- Ghosh, Santanu, 'On the Guard', *Sunday*, February 5-11, 1996.
- Gokhale, Nitin A, 'A Suspect Brew', *Outlook*, September 29, 1997.
- Gokhale, Nitin A, 'Handing Out an Olive Branch', *Outlook*, May 7, 1997.
- Gokhale, Nitin A, 'Big Brothers and Seven Sisters', *Outlook*, March 5, 1997.
- Grewal, RS, Brig, 'Ethno Nationalism in North-eastern India', *USI Journal*, New Delhi, Apr-Jun 2003.
- Hazarika, Sanjoy, 'Far Eastern Himalayas; Search for Distance and Dignity', *Himal*, May/June, 1995.
- Prabhakara, MS, ' The Foreign Hand; ISI Nexus in the North-east', *Frontline*, February 11, 1994.
- Prabhakara, MS, ' State of Emergency, *Frontline'*, February 11, 1994.
- Prabhakara, MS, 'Now, Operation Rhino', *Frontline*, September 28-October 11, 1991.
- Prabhakara, MS, 'Bargaining is Over; Lt Ajai Singh', *Frontline*, October 12-15, 1991

- Prabhakara, MS, 'Chasing a Mirage', *Frontline*, July 4, 2003.
- Prabhakara, MS, Promises and Problems, *Frontline*, March 14, 2003.
- Prasannan, R, 'Watching the Nagas', *The Week*, July 27, 1997.
- Rammohan, EN, 'Uneasy Borders Distant Neighbours' *USI Journal*, New Delhi, January-March, 2003.
- Ray, Tapas, 'Bodo Setback, *Frontline*, November, 29 1996.
- Ray, Tapas, 'ULFA's Anger', *Frontline*, August 9, 1996.
- Ray, Tapas, 'Tension in Mizoram', *Frontline*, November 1, 1996.
- Ray, Tapas, 'Conflict in Tripura', *Frontline*, July 26, 1997.
- Ray, Tapas, 'Trail of Violence', *Frontline*, August 23, 1996 .
- Ray, Tapas, 'Terror Campaign', *Frontline*, January 24, 1997.
- Saikia, Jaideep, 'Bhutan's Tryst with Destiny', *Aakrosh*, vol 7, Number 23, April 2004.
- Sinha, SP, Brig (Retd),' Insurgency in NE India: The External Dimension', *USI Journal*, New Delhi, July-September 1998.
- Sinha, SP, Brig (Retd),' Insurgencies in North-east India: An Appraisal, *Aakrosh*, New Delhi, vol 3, Number 7, April 2000.
- Sinha, SP, 'Tinderbox: The North-east is at its most vulnerable at this moment, *Force*, New Delhi, vol 2, no 6, February 2005.
- Sinha, SK, Lt Gen (Retd), " Insurgency in Assam', *USI Journal*, New Delhi, July-September 1998 .
- Special Report, 'Myanmar; Lifting the Shroud', *India Today*, January 31, 1994.
- Swami, Praveen, 'The View from New Delhi', *Frontline*, January 16, 2004.

Newspapers

- Banerjee, Nirmalaya, ' Nagas are fed up with Gun Culture', *The Times of India*, New Delhi, November 16, 1996.
- Correspondent, "From IV to HIV", *The Asian age*, Calcutta, May 1, 1997.
- Hussain, Wasbir, 'Ominous Sign in the North-east, *The Hindu*, New Delhi, September 9, 2002.
- Karmakar, Rahul, 'North-East in Flames', *The Hindustan Times*, New Delhi, October 5, 2004.
- Pubby, Vipin, 'Neglected North-east', *The Indian Express*, November 20, 1990.

- Prabhakara, MS, 'Losing a Privilege', *The Hindu*, Madras, September, 1993.
- Prabhakara, MS, Continued Unrest in the North-east', *The Hindu*, Madras, June 6, 1993.
- Prabhakara, MS, ' Manipur: Insurgents Active again', The Hindu, Madras, March 23, 1993.
- Prabhakara, MS, 'Welcome Changes in ULFA Stances', The Hindu, New Delhi, January 18, 1992.
- Prabhakara, MS, 'Shifting stances of ULFA', *The Hindu*, New Delhi, February 21, 1992.
- Prabhakara, MS, ' Assam's Poser on Liberalisation', *The Hindu*, Madras, 1993.
- Roy, Ash Narain,' At War With Itself", *The Hindustan Times*, March 7, 1997.
- Ram, N, 'Identity Crisis', *The Economic Times*, New Delhi, October 8, 1991.
- Rajeshwar, TV, 'Migration or Invasion', *The Hindustan Times*, Patna, February 7, 1996.
- Rajeshwar, TV, 'Unpalatable Options' *The Hindustan Times*, Patna, February 8, 1996.
- Rajeshwar, TV, 'Creation of a New State', *The Hindustan Times*, Patna, February, 9, 1996.
- Singh, Bhisma Narain, 'North-east; A Region in Unrest', *The Hindustan Times*, New Delhi, November, 1994.
- Singh, Gurumukh, 'Anti-Chakma stir may enter Violent Phase', *The Times of India*', December 31, 1995.
- Singh, Prakash, 'Changing a Mirage in Nagaland', *The Times of India*, New Delhi, August 7, 1997.
- Singh, Prakash, ' Manmohan, Beware of Becoming a Softie', *The Indian Express*, January 26, 2005.
- Supplement Review, 'Fear and Loathing in Meghalaya' *The Sunday Times*, New Delhi, January 21, 1996.
- Saha, BP, 'Infiltration in the East: A Threat to Nation's Security and Integrity', *The Hindu*, Madras, March 2, 1993.
- Sethi, Sunil, 'Aid to North-east is Shoring up Corrupt Governments', *The Times of India*, July 14, 1997.
- Saikia, Sabina Sehgal, 'Government Officers are paying taxes to Insurgents, Says Mohanta' *The Times of India*, New Delhi, October 1, 1997.

- Sood, VK, Lt Gen, 'Roots of Alienation' *The Hindustan Times*, New Delhi, October 1, 1992.
- Saturday Interview, "Check Infiltration and Educate Women" *The Times of India*, New Delhi, December 2, 1995.
- Saturday interview, ' Tata Tea has Resisted all Attempts at Taxation, *The Times of India*, September 13, 1997.
- Sinha, Abhijit, 'Money-Graph: North By North-east', *Sahara Times*, New Delhi, November 20, 2004.
- Shourie, Arun, 'Right on Course; The Silent Demographic Invasion', *The Indian Express*, New Delhi, October 9, 2004.
- Shourie, Arun, 'Further Warnings, Further Calumny: The Silent Demographic Invasion', *The Indian Express*, October 10, 2004.
- Shourie Arun, "How We Deal With Life and Death Matters: The Silent Demographic Invasion", *The Indian Express*, October 11, 2004.
- Shourie, Arun, "Another Conference, Another Warning: The Silent Demographic Invasion", *The Indian Express*, October 12, 2004.
- Shourie, Arun, "This is not Mr Advani Speaking", *The Indian Express*, July 21, 2004.
- Taksal, Vinod,' Only Division can end Assam's Violence', *The Times of India*, New Delhi, September 2, 1997.

Index

A

accession 131, 153
accord 217
administrative 170, 316
administrators 257
Advisory Committee 82
Ahoms 3, 199
Akbar Hydari Agreement 53
alienation 257
alcoholism 198
amnesty 113
ammunition 174, 280, 283, 289
Amra Bengali 140
animism 3, 199, 221
animists 223
Angami language 223
annexing 316
annexation 14, 72, 129, 155
anti-social 198
Apatanis 199
appellate authority 109
Aryans 2, 148
Assam Accord 189, 295, 315
Assam Assembly 84, 218
Assam Legislature 81
Assam Rifles 87, 262, 270, 293
Austic 2, 147
autonomous 4, 15, 82, 140, 185
Awami League 32

B

bandits 296
Bordoloi Committee 82
battalion 88, 261
Bodo insurgency 189
Bodo militants 202

Bodos 2, 151
Boer Campaign 265
brigade 272
Brahmaputra Valley 42, 150, 226
Brahmo Samaj 226
bureaucracy 166

C

cease-fire 17, 59, 63, 119, 122, 183, 230
Chakma militants 213
Chakma refugees 202
Christianity 195, 221
civilisation 24
colonial 1, 120, 252, 268
colonies 263
colonialism 116
colonialists 14, 221
communal rioting 257
communal riots 21, 30
communal tension 175
communications 9
communist 16
communists 111, 132
Communist Party 133
conflict 252
Constituent Assembly 82
Constitution of India 62, 82, 95
construction 9
copper-plates 3, 149
corruption 99
counter-insurgency 73, 134, 171, 258, 259
Cripps Mission 29

D

Dagger Brigade 88
deep valleys 81
demographic 27
dense forests 81
dialects 24
drugs 198
drug addicts 240
drug peddlers 240
drug trafficking 242

E

ecological 11
electoral rolls 162
East India Company 221
ethnic 13, 24, 121, 144, 301
ethnicity 245, 247
ethno-communal 136
extortion 166
extortionists 296

F

fervour 247
fratricidal feuds 105
fratricidal war 118, 121, 165
fugitives 169
fundamentalist 300
fundamentalists 319
fundamentalism 175, 189
futility 142

G

Garos 195
Government of India 63
Government of India Reform Act of 1919 81
guerrilla tactics 76, 281
guerrilla warfare 56, 63, 114, 252, 269
guerrillas 15, 93, 134, 211, 258
gunrunning 242

H

helipads 10
high ranges 81
hills 4
hilly 4
Hinduism 3, 4, 103, 129, 152, 195, 221, 226
hostiles 56, 259, 275
hostilities 93, 98, 104, 207
Human Rights 74, 265, 321

I

infiltration 158
Illegal migrants 173

immigration 161
immigrants 21
imperialism 204, 248
inaccessible 10
Independence 19, 52,116, 187, 226, 255
Indian Army 87, 253, 254, 259, 262
Indian Constitution 100
Indian Union 62
Infantry Brigade 272
infiltration 30, 306
influx 28
ingress 91, 111
Instrument of Accession 123, 196
Instrument of Merger 111
insurgencies 13, 67, 234, 252, 312
insurgency 64, 141, 216, 255
insurgents 299, 320
insurgent groups 235
insurrections 15
Islamic fundamentalism 307
Israeli Army 254

J

Jaintias 1, 24, 147, 195
jhoom cultivation 287

K

Kargil 253
Khasi Hills 155
Khasis 1, 24, 147, 195
kidnappings 166
killings 166

L

languages 24
Legislative Assembly 111
Liaison Committee 65
Lion Brigade 88
linguistic 170
livestock 259
Lushai Hills 82, 155
Lushais 80

M

massacre 258
megaliths 148
Meitei community 214
Meiteis 26, 103
Mlechha 148
migrants 33
migration 28
militancy 68, 119, 308
militant groups 307
Militants 143, 174, 198, 320
military 170, 252
military hardware 207
military operation 283
missionaries 13, 221, 228
Mizo guerillas 212
Mizo Hills 286
Mizo Union 82
Mongoloid 245
Mongolians 2, 148
Mountain Brigade 90
mountainous 80
mountainous terrain 4
Mughal territories 152
Mukti Parishad 133
Muslim League 29, 187
Mymensingh district 42

N

Naga Hills 73, 200, 261
Naga militants 122, 274
narco-terrorism 124, 309
narcotic trade 21
narcotics 123, 234
nationalism 157
Naxalites 208
Nehru-Liaquat 31
nepotism 99
Nine-Point Agreement 53

O

Operation Accomplishment 287
Operation Bajrang 295

Operation Blanket 287
Operation Bluestar 253, 261

P

paramilitary 215
partition of Bengal 27, 186
patriotic 172
passes 12
Pataskar Commission 86
Peace Mission 60, 281
plateaus 4
plebiscite 58, 275
political 170
population 13, 30, 128
Proto Austroloid 147
proletarian revolution 111
proselytise 246
proselytising 221, 222

R

range 6
Ramakrishna Mission 226
Rashtriya Rifles 261
rebellion 89, 107
rebellions 15
rebellious 319
refugees 33, 133, 158
religious 170
Religious nationalism 231
revenue collection 155
revolutionaries 308
riverine islands 4
rivers 4
robberies 166

S

Sakti 3
sanctuaries 260
secessionist 197
self-determination 83
self-styled 14, 59, 63
Shillong Accord 65, 241
Simon Commission 51
Sixth Schedule 84

solidarity 83, 247
sorties 10
sovereignty 66
strafing 260
subcontinent 27
supremacy 261
Supreme Court of India 306
Swadhikar 169
Swadhin Asom 169

T

tantricism 3
tea cultivation 41
terrain 151
territorial unity 83
territories 259
terrorism 236, 320, 298
traditions 24
traffickers 236, 242
Treaty of Yandeboo 72, 106, 195
tribal 247
tribal society 132
tribes 24, 221
tributaries 127
tripartite 185
tripartite agreement 142, 198
tripartite settlement 141
Tuensang Area 261
Tuensang Division 200

U

uprising 87

V

Vaishnavism 3, 105, 226
Vaishnavite 246
valleys 4

W

watershed 12
weapons 174
World War I 72
World War II 72, 252

CHINA (Tibe
NEPAL
Sikkim
BHUTAN
West Bengal
(Siliguri Corridor)
Assam
Bihar
Meghalaya
Jharkhand
BANGLADESH
Tripura
West Bengal
Bay of Bengal